THE PARADISE OF THE HOLY FATHERS

- *Volume II*

CONTAINING THE COUNSELS OF THE HOLY MEN AND THE

QUESTIONS & ANSWERS OF THE ASCETIC BRETHREN

GENERALLY KNOWN AS

THE SAYINGS OF THE FATHERS OF EGYPT

The Paradise of the Holy Fathers

– Volume II

§

Translated by

E. A. Wallis Budge

§

ST SHENOUDA COPTIC ORTHODOX MONASTERY
PUTTY, NSW, AUSTRALIA
2008

THE PARADISE OF THE HOLY FATHERS
- Volume II

COPYRIGHT © 2008
St. Shenouda Coptic Orthodox Monastery

Originally published by Chatto & Windus, London 1907.

All rights reserved. Except for brief quotations in critical publications or reviews, no part of this book may be reproduced in any manner without prior written permission from the publisher.

All scripture quotations, unless otherwise indicated, are taken from the New King James Version®. Copyright © 1982 by Thomas Nelson, Inc. Used by permission. All rights reserved.

ST SHENOUDA MONASTERY
8419 Putty Rd
Putty, NSW, 2330

email: pimonakhos@copticmail.com

ISBN 13: 978-0-9805171-2-5

Cover Illustration: Icon of St Anthony and St Paul from the wall painting in the St Anthony Monastery in Egypt.

Cover Design: Daniel Fanous

CONTENTS

§

The First Book

On Flight from Men and of Silent Contemplation— 9
On Fasting and Abstinence and on other similar Labors— 23
On the Reading of the Scripture, and Watching by Night— 33
On how it is Meet for Us to Weep for our Sins— 41
On Voluntary Poverty— 47
On Patient Endurance— 53
On Obedience towards God, Fathers and Brethren— 67
On Scrupulous Watchfulness in our Thoughts, Words— 71
On Love and Charity and the Welcoming of the Stranger— 103
On Humility— 119
On Fornication— 143
On the Acceptance of Repentance— 155
On the Father who wrought Wonderful Works— 161
On the Greatness the Sublime Rule of the Solitary life— 167

§

The Second Book

Questions & Answers on the Ascetic Rule— 173
Conversation between a Brother and an Old Man— 285
Questions & Answers on the Vision of the Mind— 295
Questions of the Brethren— 307

THE FIRST BOOK

CHAPTER ONE

On Flight from Men and of Silent Contemplation

WHEN ABBA ARSENIUS WAS IN THE PLACE he prayed to God and said, "O Lord direct me how to live," and a voice came to him saying, "Arsenius, flee from men and you shall live."

2. And when Arsenius was living the ascetic life in the monastery, he prayed to God the same prayer, and again he heard a voice saying to him, "Arsenius, flee, keep silence, and lead a life of silent contemplation, for these are the fundamental causes which prevent a man from committing sin."

3. A certain man said that there were once three men who loved labors, and they were monks. The first one chose to go about and see where there was strife, which he turned into peace; the second chose to go about and visit the sick but the third departed to the desert that he might dwell in quietness. Finally the first man, who had chosen to still the contentions of men, was unable to make every man to be at peace with his neighbor, and his spirit was sad and he went to the man who had chosen to visit the sick, and he found him in affliction because he was not able to fulfil the law which he had laid down for himself. Then the two of them went to the monk in the desert, and seeing each other they rejoiced, and the two men related to the third, the tribulations, which had confronted them in the world, and entreated him to tell them how he had lived in the desert. He was silent, but after a little he said to them, "Come, let each of us go and fill a vessel of water," and after they had filled the vessel, he said to them, "Pour out some of the water into a basin, and look down to the bottom through it," and they did so. He said to them, "What do you see?" and they said, "We see nothing." After the water in the basin ceased to move, he said to them a second time, "Look into the water" and they looked, and he said to them, "What do you see?" They said to him, "We see our own faces distinctly," and he said to them "Thus is it with the man who dwells with men, for by reason of the disturbance caused by this affair of the world, he cannot see his sins but if he live in the peace and quietness of the desert he is able to see God clearly."

4. On one occasion, Abba Ammon came during the season of winter to Abba Sisoes, and he saw that the old man was grieved because he had left the desert and Abba Ammon said to him, "Why are you distressed, O father? For what were you able to do in the desert in your old age?" The old man Sisoes looked at him fiercely, and said, "What did you say to me, Ammon? Are not the mere thoughts of the freedom which is in the desert better for us than living out of it?"

5. There were two brethren in the desert who were the equals of each other in the spiritual life, and they led a life of ascetic self-denial, and performed the exalted works, which belong to spiritual excellence. It happened that one of them was called to be the head of a habitation of the brethren, but the other remained in the desert, where he became a man perfect in self-denial. He was held by God to be worthy of the gift of healing those who were possessed of devils, and he knew beforehand the things, which were about to happen, and he made whole the sick. Now when he who had become the head of a habitation of brethren heard these things, he decided in his mind that his fellow monk must have acquired these powers suddenly, and he lived a life of silence and ceased from talking with men for three weeks, and he made supplication to God continually that He would show him how the monk in the desert wrought these mighty works, while he had not received even one of the gifts which he had. And an angel appeared and said to him, "He who dwelt in the desert makes supplication to God both by night and by day, and his pain and anxiety are for our Lord's sake but you have cared for many things, and you have conversed with many, and the consolation and encouragement of the children of men must be sufficient for you."

On Flight from Men and of Silent Contemplation

6. Abba Arsenius on one occasion went to the brethren in a certain place where there were some reeds growing, and the wind blew upon them, and they were shaken. And the old man said, "What is this rustling sound?" and they said to him, "It is that caused by the reeds which are being shaken by the wind." He said to them, "Truly I say to you, if the man who dwells in silence hears but the twittering of a sparrow, he shall not be able to acquire that repose in his heart which he seeks, how much less then can you do so with all this rustling of the reeds about you?"

7. A certain brother came to Abba Arsenius, and said to him, "My thoughts trouble me, and say, you can not fast and you are not able to labor, therefore visit the sick, which is a great commandment." Then Abba Arsenius, after the manner of one who was well acquainted with the war of devils, said to him, "Eat, drink, and sleep, and toil not but on no account go out of your cell," for the old man knew that dwelling constantly in the cell induces all the habits of the solitary life. And when the brother had done these things for three days he became weary of idleness, and finding a few palm leaves on the ground, he took them and began to split them up, and on the following day he dipped them in water and began to work (i.e. to weave baskets) and when he felt hungry he said, "I will finish one more small piece of work, and then I will eat. And when he was reading in the Book," he said, "I will sing a few Psalms and say a few prayers, and then I shall eat without any guilt. Thus little by little, by the help of God, he advanced in the ascetic life until he reached the first rank, and received the power to resist the thoughts and to vanquish them."

8. When Abba Sisoes was dwelling in the mountain of Abba Anthony, the man who used to minister to him departed and remained away for a period of ten months and did not come back to him, and he saw no man. And afterwards, as he was walking in the mountains, he saw a man hunting wild animals, and the old man said to him, "When did you come? And how long have you been here?" And the man said to him, "Father, I have been in this mountain eleven months, and I have seen no man except yourself." Then the old man having heard these things went into his cell, and hit his own face, and said, "Behold, O Sisoes, you may think that you have done nothing, for you have not made yourself even like this man who is in the world, and is not even a monk."

9. I once asked Abba Sarmata a question, and said to him, "What shall I do, O my father, for I do nothing which the monks do? On the contrary, I am negligent, and I eat, and drink, and sleep, and I think many filthy thoughts, and my mind is ever disturbed, and I depart from one work to another, and from one group of thoughts to another. What shall I do, then? For I am troubled, and my soul is little." Abba Sarmata said to him, "Sit you in your cell, and what ever you can do, that do, and do not trouble yourself. For I wish you to do now a little, even as did Abba Anthony in the mountain, and I believe that by sitting in your cell for the sake of the Name of God, you also will be found in the same place as Abba Anthony."

10. On one occasion the brethren went up from Scete to go to Abba Anthony, and having embarked in a boat to journey to him, they found there a certain old man, who was also going to visit him, and they were not acquainted with him. And as they were sitting in the boat, they spoke now and again a word of the fathers, or a word from the Book, or they talked about the work of their hands and the old man listened to all they said, but held his peace. Then, having crossed the ferry, the old man was found to be going also to Abba Anthony. When they had all arrived at the place where he was, he said to them, "You found excellent company in this old man" and to the old man himself he said, "You did find excellent brethren to travel with you, O father." The old man said, "They are excellent brethren, but they have no door to their house, and whoever wishes can go into the stable, and untie the donkey, and go where ever he pleases on him." Now this he said because they uttered every word, which came into their mouths.

11. A certain brother asked Abba Sisoes, saying, "Father, how was it that you did leave Scete where you were with Abba Macarius, and came here?" And the old man said to him, "When Scete began to be filled with monks, I heard that Abba Antonius had fallen asleep, and I came to the mountain here, and found that this place was quiet, and I lived here for a little time." The brother said to him, "How long have you been here?" The old man said, "Behold, I have been here seventy years this day."

12. They used to say concerning Abba Theodore and Abba Luke that they passed fifty years with disturbed minds, and were troubled the whole time about changing their place of dwelling and they said, "Behold, we will change in the winter." And when the winter arrived, they said, "We will change in the summer." Thus they did to the end of their lives.

13. A certain father came to Abba Arsenius, knocked at the door, and the old man opened to him thinking that it was his servant who had knocked. When he saw who it was, he cast himself upon his face. The father entreated him, saying, "Stand up, O father, that I may give you the greeting of peace."

But Arsenius disputed with him, saying, "I will not stand up until you have departed." And though he entreated him to do so often he would not stand up, and the father left him and departed.

14. Abba Battimion said, "When I went down to Scete they gave me some apples to take to the brethren, and when I had knocked at the door of Abba Abhila, he said to me when he saw me, 'If these apples had been of gold I would not have wished you to knock at my door and moreover, do not knock at the door of any other brother.' So I returned and placed the apples in the church and departed."

15. They said concerning Abba Sisoes that when the church began to fill he fled quickly to his cell, and, though the brethren said, "He has an devil," he was performing the work of God.

16. Abba Joseph said to Abba Nestir, "What shall I do with my tongue, for I cannot conquer it?" Abba Nestir said to him, "If you talk, will you have relief from this trouble?" And he said to him, "No." The old man said to him, "If then you have no relief when you talk, why do you talk?" Abba Joseph said to him, "What shall I do? For I cannot stand against it." The old man said to him, "Will you have relief then?" He said to him, "No." The old man said to him, "If you can not gain relief by talking, then hold your peace."

17. A certain brother went to Abba Poemen on the second Sunday in the Fast of Forty Days and repeated to him his thoughts, and sighing over what the old man had told him, he said to him, "I had almost kept myself from coming here today." The old man asked, "Why?" Then the brother said, "I said in my mind, perhaps during the fast the door will be closed against you?" Abba Poemen said to him, "We do not learn to shut a door made of wood, but to close the door of the tongue."

18. When a certain brother in Scete was going to the harvest, he went to Abba Moses, the Black, and said to him, "Father, tell me what I shall do shall I go to the harvest?" and Abba Moses said to him, "If I tell you, will you be persuaded to do as I say?" And the brother said to him, "Yes, I will listen to you." The old man said to him, "If you will be persuaded by me, rise up, go, and release yourself from going to the harvest, and come to me, and I will tell you what you shall do." The brother therefore departed and obtained his release from his companions, as the old man had told him, and then he came to him. The old man said to him, "Go into your cell and keep Pentecost, and you shall eat dry bread and salt once a day only, and after you have done this I will tell you something else to do later on." He went and did as the old man had told him, and then came to him again. When the old man saw that he was one who worked with his hands, he showed him the proper way to live in his cell and the brother went to his cell, and fell on his face upon the ground, and for three whole days and nights he wept before God. After these things, when his thoughts were saying to him, "You are now an exalted person, and you have become a great man," he used to contradict them, and set before his eyes his former shortcomings, and say, "Thus were all your offences." Again, when they used to say to him, "You have performed many things neglectfully," he would say, "Nevertheless I do small services for God, and He showed His mercy upon me." When by such means as these the spirits had been overcome, they appeared to him in the form of worldly creatures, and said to him, "We have been vanquished by you." He said to them, "Why?" And they said to him, "If we humble you, we are raised up by you to an exalted position, and if we exalt you we are accounted by you for humility."

19. There was a certain brother in the monastery who worked hard, and the brethren who were in Scete heard about him, and came to see him, and they entered into the place where he used to work and having received them, and saluted them, he turned round and began to work again. And when the brethren saw what he did, they said to him, "John gave you the garb of the monk, and made you a dweller in a monastery, but he did not teach you to receive a blessing from the brethren, or to give one, or to say to them, 'Pray, or, sit down.' And John said to them, "No, a sinner is not sufficient for these things."

20. Abba Anthony said, "As a fish when it is lifted up out of the water dies, even so does the monk who hangs around or stays outside his cell."

21. They tell the story of a certain brother who came to Scete to see Abba Arsenius, and who went into the church and entreated the clergy to take him to see him and the clergy said to him, "Refresh yourself a little, and you shall see him." The brother said to them, "I will eat nothing before I meet him and see him." When the clergy heard this they sent a brother with him to show him Abba Arsenius, because his cell was some distance away. When they had arrived there, they knocked at the door and went inside, and having saluted him, and prayed, they sat down and held their peace. The brother who was from the church answered, saying, "I will depart, pray for me." But when the other brother saw that he possessed not freedom of speech with the old man, he said

to the brother from the church, "I also, will go with you" and they departed together. Then he entreated him, saying, "Take me also to Abba Moses who was a thief." And when they went to him, the old man received them with joy, and having refreshed them greatly he dismissed them in peace. And the brother who had brought the visitor to Abba Moses said to him, "Behold, I brought you to a man from a foreign land, and to an Egyptian, which of the two pleases you?" He answered and said, "The Egyptian who has just received me, and refreshed me." When one of the old men heard what had happened, he prayed to God, and said, "O Lord, show me this matter, for one flees from the world for Your Name's sake, and another receives and is gracious for Your Name's sake." Behold, suddenly there appeared to him on the river two great boats, and Abba Arsenius and the Spirit of God were traveling in silence in the one, and Abba Moses and the angels of God were in the other, and they were feeding the monk with honey from the comb.

22. A certain brother asked Abba Poemen a question, saying, "If I see something done, do you wish me to tell it abroad?" The old man said to him, "It is written, 'Whoever shall declare a matter incorrectly, it is a disgrace to him and a subject for mockery.' And if you are asked, speak, and if you are not asked, hold you peace."

23. On one occasion there was an assembly in a great church, and all the old men were asked in a body, "What striving is the mightiest against the monks?" They all agreed that there was none stronger than that which would make a man leave his cell and depart, for when this striving is overcome, all the rest can quite easily be brought low.

24. They say concerning Abba Apos, who afterwards became Bishop of Oxyrhyncus, that when he was a monk he labored with great toil in the ascetic life, and that he was moved every hour by Divine Grace. After he became Bishop, he wished to perform the same labors, but he was not able to do so. He cast himself before God, and made supplication to Him, saying, "Perhaps, O my Lord, it is because of the Bishopric that You have removed Your grace from me?" And it was said to him, "It is not so, but formerly you were in the desert, and there were no men there, and God took care of you there, however, now you are in a portion of the world which is inhabited, and men care for you."

25. A certain brother from the cells soaked some palm leaves in water, and then sat down to weave ropes, and his mind said to him, "Go and visit such and such a brother," and he pondered on the matter, and said, "I will go after a few days." And again his mind said to him, "Supposing you should die, what will you do? For you would not see your brother." Once again he satisfied his mind by saying, "I will go after such and such a time." Now when the summer had come, he said within himself, "Today is not the right time for going" and again he said to his mind, "As soon as you have cut off the end of the palm leaves it will be time for you to go," and he said to himself, "I will finish these leaves, and then I will go." Once again his mind urged him and said, "The weather is beautiful today" and he rose up straightaway and left the palm leaves soaking in the water, and he picked up a cloak and ran off on his way. Now he had as a neighbor a certain old man who used to see visions, and as soon as this man saw the brother running, he cried out, and said to him, "Prisoner, prisoner, come here," and when he had gone in the old man said to him, "Go back to your cell." The brother went back, and related to him the whole story of his war. Having entered his own cell, he offered repentance to God, and the devils cried out with a loud voice, saying, "You have vanquished us, you have vanquished us, O monk." Now he had a palm-leaf mat under him, and it was charred as if it had been burned in the fire, and the devils vanished like smoke then straightaway the brother perceived their wiles, and he gave thanks to God.

26. Abba Poemen said, "A certain brother asked Abba Simon and said, 'If I go out from my cell, and I find a brother absorbed and immersed in matters unnecessary for salvation, shall I associate myself also with him?' And supposing also that I should find him laughing and that I also should laugh, when I have gone into my cell again shall I not be forgiven my relaxation?" The old man said to him, "What do you wish? Do you mean that having gone out of your cell and having found a man who was laughing, and you laughed with him, and having found a man who was talking, and you talked with him, you can go back to your cell and find yourself as you were before you went out?" The brother said to him, "If not, how then?" Then the old man answered, saying, "It is right for you to keep a careful watch both within and without."

27. An old man said, "One man is thought to be silent, and yet his heart judges and condemns others, and the man who acts thus speaks continually, another man speaks from morning till evening, and yet keeps silence, that is to say, he speaks nothing which is not helpful."

28. There were two excellent brethren in the cells, and they were considered to be worthy to see things of mystery. Each one of them saw the Might, which was sent down by God upon his brethren. It happened that one of them came on Friday to the coenobium, and while he was outside, he saw that some of the brethren were eating from the morning upwards, and he said to them, "Is it possible that you eat at this time on Friday? And do you usually hold a congregation at the turn of the day?" As his brother looked upon him, he saw that the might of God was going away from him, and he was grieved, for he was accustomed to see it upon him. When they had come to their own cell he said to him, "What have you done, O my brother? Or what thoughts have you had? For we do not see upon you as usual the might of God." The brother made answer and said, "I do not feel that I have any filthy thoughts in me, and I do not perceive in my soul that any evil act has been committed by me." His brother said to him, "Perhaps some vain and empty word has gone out from your mouth." Then that brother recalled the matter to his mind, and said, "Yes, yesterday I saw certain men outside the coenobium eating," and I said to them, 'Do you eat at this time on Friday? This is then my sin. But I entreat you to labor with me for two weeks, and you and I will beg God to forgive me." They did as he had said. After two weeks his brother saw that Might, which is of the goodness of God, comes upon him as usual.

29. The old men used to say about the blessed Abba Arsenius, and Abba Theodore of Parme, that they possessed in a far greater degree than many monks a hatred of the admiration of men. Abba Arsenius was never pleased at meeting and conversing with a man, and Abba Theodore, even though he was willing to meet a man, was in his conversation as sharp as a sword.

30. Abba Macarius said to the brethren when the service in the church was ended, "Flee O brethren." And one of the old men said, "Father, where can we flee further then this desert?" Then Macarius laid his hand upon his mouth, saying, "Flee in this manner." Immediately he went to his cell, shut the door, and sat down.

31. Abba Poemen said that Abba Moses asked Abba Zechariah a question when he was about to die, saying, "Father, is it good that we should hold our peace?" Zechariah said to him, "Yes, my son, hold your peace." And at the time of his death, while Abba Isidore was sitting with him, Abba Moses looked up to heaven, saying, "Rejoice and be glad, O my son Zechariah, for the gates of heaven have been opened."

32. A brother asked an old man, saying, "What is the virtue of humility?" The old man answered him, saying, "That you pay not back evil for evil." That brother said to him, "And supposing that a man cannot attain to this measure, what must we do?" The old man said to him, "Let us flee and follow after silence."

33. An old man said, "Lay hold upon silence. Look carefully and scrutinize the manner in which you train yourself, both when you are lying down, and when you are standing up. Meditate upon the fear of God, and be not afraid of the attack of sinners. Do not consent to everything. Be swift to hear and slow to believe."

34. An old man said, "The man, who has learned by experience the sweetness of the quietness which is in his cell, does not flee from meeting his neighbor because he is as one who despised him, but because of the fruits which he plucked from silence."

35. Abba Moses used to say, "The man who flees from the world is like ripe grapes, but he who dwells among the attractions of the children of men is like sour grapes."

36. An old man said, "Human care, worry and anxiety about the things of the body destroy the faculties of knowledge and expression in a man, and leave him like a piece of dry wood."

37. They used to say about Abba Nastir that the old man was like 'the serpent' which Moses made for the healing of the people, and that he was perfect in all spiritual excellences, and that, although he kept silence, he healed every man.

38. A certain brother posed a question to an old man, saying, "Father, what shall I do? For, although my body is in my cell, my thoughts wander about into every place, and because of this they trouble me greatly, saying, 'You have no benefit whatever, for your body is shut up in the cell, your thoughts wander and are scattered abroad. And these thoughts bring me to despair, and counsel me to go back to the world as one who does not have the ability to acquire the rule of life, which is proper for the ascetic monk." The old man said to him, "You must know, O my son, that this is an attack of Satan, but go and continue to abide in your cell, and do not go out of it at any time, and pray to God that He may give you the power to endure patiently, and then your mind shall pull itself together in you. For the matter is like that of a donkey, which has a sucking foal. If that donkey is tied up, however much the foal may gambol about or wander here and there, the foal will come back to her eventually, either because he is hungry, or for other reasons which drive him to her. But if his mother is roaming about loose, both animals will go to their destruction. And thus is the same with the monk. If the body remain continually in the cell, the mind will certainly come back to him after all its wanderings, for many reasons, which will come upon it. But if the body and the soul wander outside the cell, both will become a prey and a joy to the enemy."

39. A certain brother belonging to a habitation of brethren said to Abba Bessarion, "What shall I do?" The old man said to him, "Keep silence, and consider yourself to be nothing."

40. Abba Moses entreated Abba Zechariah, saying, "Speak a word of consolation to the brethren." Zechariah took his cloak and placed it under his feet, saying, "Except a man die thus, he cannot be a monk."

41. Abba Poemen said, "The rule of the monk is to bear at all times his own blame."

42. Abba Poemen said, "If you hold yourself in your own sight to be of no account, you may dwell where you please, and find rest."

43. The same old man used to say, "A man will be always tripped up by that thing which he will not cut off from himself."

44. Abba Alonis said, "If the man will only remember that which is written, 'You shall be justified by your words, and shall be condemned by your words (Matt. 12:37),' he would know that it is right to hold his peace."

45. Abba Poemen said, "If you wish to acquire the power to keep silence, then do not think or say within yourself that you are doing the works of spiritual excellence, but say, 'I am not even worthy to speak to You.'"

46. Abba Anthony said, "He who lives in the desert is free from three forms of spiritual attacks; namely those which arise through the ears, speech, and sight. He has only one form to fight, namely, that of the heart."

47. Abba Alonis said, "Unless a man says in his heart, 'Only God and I exist in this world,' he will not find rest."

48. Abba Sisoes used to say, "It is well for a man to dwell in his cell, and if he suffers with patient endurance he will find blessings of every kind."

49. A certain brother asked Abba Pambo, saying, "Is it a good thing for a man to praise his neighbor?" The old man said, "It is much better for a man to hold his peace."

50. Abba Poemen said, "In all the labor which comes upon a man, his victory is only assured when he holds his peace."

51. A certain brother said to an old man, "If a brother brings to me news from the outside world, do you wish me to tell him not to bring it to me?" The old man said to him, "No." Then, the brother said to him, "Why?" The old man said to him, "Because not even we are able to flee from this. For having told our neighbor that he must not do this, we ourselves afterwards may be found doing the very same thing." That brother said to him, "What then is the right course of action?" The old man said to him, "If we take upon ourselves to hold our peace, the example alone will be sufficient to make our neighbor do the same."

52. Once the blessed Theophilus, Archbishop of Alexandria went with a certain judge to Abba Arsenius, and begged the old man to let him hear some sayings from him. The old man held his peace for a while, and then, answered, saying, "If I speak a word to you, will you observe it?" They promised to keep it. The old man said to them, "In whatever place you hear that Arsenius is there, do not go near there."

53. Abba Macarius said to Abba Arsenius, "Why do you flee from us?" The old man said to him, "God knows that I love you, but I cannot be both with God and with men. The thousands and ten thousands of beings who are above have only one will, but men have many wills. I cannot, therefore, leave God and be with men." The old man was always uttering these words, "Arsenius, for this you did go forth." He used to say, "I have repented many times that I spoke, but I have never repented that I held my peace."

54. Abba Anthony said, "The cell of a monk is the furnace of Babylon where the Three Children found the Son of God, and it is also the pillar of cloud from where God spoke with Moses."

55. On one occasion the Fathers in Scete were gathered, and because certain folks were wishing to see Abba Moses, they treated him with revilement, saying, "Why does this Ethiopian come and go in our midst?" But Moses hearing this held his peace. When the congregation was dismissed, they asked him, "Abba Moses, were you not afraid?" He said to them, "Although I was afraid, I did not utter a word."

56. On one occasion certain brethren came to John the Less to tempt him, for they heard that he had never permitted his mind to think about any of the affairs of this world, and he had never spoken about them. They said to him, "Father, we thank God because He has brought down rain this year in abundance and the palms are thriving and are flourishing beautifully, and the works of hands of the brethren are abundant." John, the old man, said to them, "It is so with the Holy Spirit of God, for when He descends upon the hearts of holy men they blossom and bring forth the fruit of the fear of God."

57. A certain brother came to take some baskets from John the Less, and when he had knocked the door, the old man came out to him, and said, "What do you seek?" The brother said to him, "Father, I want baskets." John the Less went in to bring them out to him, but he forgot to do so, and sat down, and went on plaiting. The brother knocked the door again, and when Abba John went to answer him, he said to him, "Will you bring out the baskets to me, Father?" John went in again, sat down, and went on plaiting. When the brother knocked again, John went out and said to him, "Brother, what do you seek?" He said to John, "Baskets, father." John took his hand and led him inside, saying, "If you wish the baskets, then take them and get going, for I am not able to bring them to you."

58. Some time ago Abba Evagrius went to Scete to a certain father and said to him, "Speak some words whereby I may be able to save myself." The old man said to him, "If you wish to be saved, when you go to any man do not speak before he asks you a question." Now Evagrius was sorry about this sentence, and showed regret because he had asked the question, saying, "Truly I have read many books, and I cannot accept instruction of this kind." And having profited greatly he went away from him.

59. On one occasion there was a congregation in the cells concerning a certain matter, and Abba Evagrius spoke. A certain elder said to him, "We know, Abba, that had you been in your own country where you are a bishop and the governor of many, you would have been right in speaking, but in this place you ought to sit as a stranger." Now Evagrius was sorry, but he was not offended. He shook his head, bent his gaze downwards, and wrote with his finger and said to them, "Truly, it is even as you say, O my fathers, I have spoken once, but I will not do it a second time."

60. Abba John, who was in prison, said that there was a man sitting in his cell who always made mention of God, and in this was fulfilled that which is written, "I was sick, and you visited me: I was in prison, and you came to me." (Matt. 25: 36)

61. They used to say about Abba Agathon that for a period of three years he placed a stone in his mouth and kept it there, until he had learned thoroughly how to hold his peace.

62. A certain brother went to Abba Moses in Scete, and asked him to speak a word, and the old man said to him, "Go and sit in your cell, and your cell shall teach you everything."

CHAPTER TWO

On Fasting and Abstinence and on other similar Labors

They used to say about Abba Paphnutius that he would not readily drink wine, and that on one occasion he came by chance upon a band of thieves, and found them drinking. The captain of the thieves recognized him, and knew that he had never drunk wine. The captain looked closely at him and saw that he was a man of great ascetic works. The captain filled a cup with wine and, taking a sword in his hand, and said to the old man, "If you will not drink I will slay you," and the old man knew that the grace of God wished to work on the captain of the thieves through him. The old man sought to do good to him, and took the cup and drank the wine. Then the captain made excuse to him and said, "Forgive me, father, for having distressed you." The old man said to him, "I believe by God that through this cup God will forgive you your sins." And the captain of thieves said to him, "I believe, by God from this time forth I will never trouble any man." Thus, because for God's sake, Paphnutius gave up his own wish, he was able to do good to all that band of thieves.

64. A certain old man came to one of the holy men who was a companion of his, and who cooked a few lintel and one of the two said to his fellow, "Shall we sing a part of the service?" He sang the whole of the Psalms of David, and his companion repeated two books of the Great Prophets, and when it was morning the old man departed to his own place, and they forgot all about the food. The old man went another evening and found the food, which had been cooked. He was sorry and said, "Oh! How was it that we came to forget that little mess of lentils, and did not eat it?"

65. On one occasion a brother came to Abba Isaiah, who threw a handful of lentils into a saucepan to boil, but when the lentils began to boil he took them off the fire. The brother said to him, "They are not cooked yet, O father." The old man said to him, "Is not it sufficient for you to have seen the fire, for this alone is greatly refreshing."

66. A certain old man became very seriously ill, for he suffered from some disease of the stomach, and much blood came out from him. One of the brethren had some dried prunes, and because of the severe illness of the old man he cooked a little food, and put some of the prunes in it, and brought it to him. He entreated him, saying, "Father, do me an act of grace, and take a little of this stew, for perhaps it will do you good." The old man lifted up his eyes and looked at him, and said, "In which of the Scriptures have you found this thing? Truly I have wished that God would leave me in this illness for the last thirty years, for when I am weak then am I strong." The old man, although grievously sick, would not take even a little of the food, and when the brother saw this he took it and went back to his cell.

67. They used to say concerning Abba Macarius the Egyptian, that if it happened that he ate with the brethren, he would make an agreement with himself that if there was wine on the table and he drank one cup of it, he would drink no water for a whole day. The brethren, wishing him to be refreshed (or pleased), used to give him wine, and the old man took it joyfully so that he might torment his body. When his disciple saw this thing, he said to the brethren, "I entreat you, for our Lord's sake, do not to give him wine to drink, for if he drinks it he will go to his cell and afflict himself." And when the brethren knew this they did not give him anymore wine to drink.

68. There was a certain old man who made a vow not to drink any water during the Fast of Forty Days and when he became thirsty. He would wash a potter's vessel, and fill it with water, and hang it up in front of him. Then the brethren asked him why he acted thus, and he said, "That I may labor the more, and receive a reward from God." He said this that he might incite them to great labors.

69. A brother asked an old man questions about comforts or pleasures, and the old man said to him, "Eat grass, wear grass, sleep on grass, and then your heart will become like iron."

70. A certain brother was hungry one morning, and he fought against his inclination and determined not to eat until the third hour. When the third hour had passed, he dipped his bread in water, and sat down to eat, but he forced himself to wait until the sixth hour arrived, when he said within himself, "Let us wait till the ninth hour." When the ninth hour had come, he prayed, and saw the working of Satan rising up before him like smoke, and he suppressed his desire to eat, and his hunger passed away from him.

71. A certain brother from the cells brought some new bread, and he invited all the old men who were under vows at Scete to partake of a meal. When each of them had eaten two bread-cakes, they ceased eating. Then the brother, who knew their labors of abstinence, and that they did not usually eat, and never satisfied themselves, made excuses to them, saying, "Eat you this day, for our Lord's sake, until you are satisfied"; and hearing this, each ate ten more cakes. All this showed how much they afflicted themselves in not satisfying themselves with any kind of food.

72. On one occasion two old men were going up from Scete to Egypt, and because of the fatigue of the way they sat down on the bank of the river to eat some food. One of them took his bread-cake in his hand and dipped it in the water and said to his companion, "Will not you dip your cake in water, O father?" His companion answered him saying, "It is written, 'When a possession increases, do not set your heart upon it.'" (Psalm 62:10)

73. They used to say about Abba Isaac, the priest of the cells, that he ate the ashes of the censer, which was before the altar with his bread.

74. On one occasion there was an offering made in the mountain of Abba Anthony, and a skin of wine was there, and one of the monks took some of it in a small vessel, and with a cup in his hand he went and carried it to Abba Sisoes. He mixed him a cupful, and he drank it, and he mixed him a second cupful, and he took it and drank it, but when he mixed him a third cupful Abba Sisoes refused to drink it, saying, "Keep your hands, brother, do not you know that the third cup is of Satan?"

75. Abba John said, "If a king wishes to subdue a city belonging to enemies, he, first of all, keeps them without bread and water, and the enemy being in this way harassed by hunger becomes subject to him and thus it is in respect of the hostile passions, for if a man endures fasting and hunger regularly, his enemies become stricken with weakness in the soul."

76. They used to say about Abba Dioscurus that his bread was made of barley and lentils, and that at the beginning of each year he would set himself some new task of ascetic excellence, saying, "This year I will not converse or visit any man," or, "I will not speak at all," or, "I will not eat food which has been boiled," or, "I will not eat fruit," or, "I will not eat vegetables." He began each year with resolutions of this kind and carried them out, and each year he set himself some new tasks.

77. On one occasion when certain brethren went to the church during the Easter Festival, they gave a brother a cup of wine, and when they urged him to drink it, he said to them, "Forgive me, O my fathers, but you did the same thing to me last year, and I drank a cup of wine, and I was greatly troubled thereby for a long time."

78. The monks were celebrating a festival in Scete, and they gave a certain old man a cup of wine. He handed it back, saying, "Take this death away from me," and when the others who were eating with him saw him doing this they also would not take the wine.

79. On another occasion, certain first fruits of wine were sent that it might be given to the brethren a cup each. One of the brethren went up to a roof, that he might escape from drinking, and it parted asunder beneath him, and he fell through it and when the sound came to the brethren, they went and found him lying on the ground, and they began to think about him, and said, "O lover of vainglory, this has befallen you rightly." An old man laid him out, saying to them, "Forgive my son, for he has done a good work. And, as the Lord lives, this breach shall not be built up in my days, for all the world shall know that because of a cup of wine a schism has taken place in Scete."

80. It was reported to Abba Poemen about a certain brother that he would not drink wine, and the old man Poemen said, "The nature of wine is not such as to make it useful to the dwellers in monasteries."

81. They used to say about Abba Sisoes the Theban that he had never eaten bread. During the Easter Festival, the brethren came to him and having made excuses they entreated him to eat with them. He answered them saying, "I will do one of two things; I either eat bread and bread alone, or I eat of the meats which you have boiled." They said to him, "Then eat bread only."

82. A certain old man said, "Reduce you knowledge of the things of man, and your belly also, and you shall find all manner of delights."

83. Abba Poemen used to say, "The Spirit of God never enters into the house where there are delights and pleasures."

84. A brother asked Abba Sisoes, "What good do I do in going to church, for often the devils recognize me and seize me?" The old man said to him, "There is work in the matter."

85. Abraham his disciple thereupon said to him, "Father, if there happen to be a congregation on the Sabbath, or on Sunday, and a brother drinks three cups of wine, is that too much?" The old man said to him, "If Satan did not exist three cups would not be too much to drink, but since he does exist, three cups are too much."

86. On one occasion some early grapes were sent to Abba Macarius because he longed for them, and to give a proof of his abstinence, he sent them to another brother who was sick, and who craved for grapes. Having received them, he rejoiced over them greatly. Then he despised his desire, and sent them on to another brother, as one who had no wish for food of any kind, and who held his self-denial in contempt. When the brother had received the grapes, although he desired greatly to eat them, he did the same as the other brother had done, and no man wished to eat them. After the grapes had gone among many of the brethren, the last one who received them sent them to the blessed Macarius as a gift of great honor. When the blessed Macarius saw the grapes he marvelled at the extent of the self-denial of the brethren, gave thanks to God, and he did not eat them.

87. On one occasion, certain monks went down from Egypt to visit the Fathers, and when they saw that they were eating now it was after prolonged hunger and very much fasting, and continual abstinence, they were greatly offended. When the elder of the coenobium learned about this, he came to calm their minds. He proclaimed in the church of the congregation, saying, "You shall fast in your customary manner, and honor your ascetic rule of life, so that your voluntary abstinence may not be held in contempt." Now the

Egyptian strangers wished to depart, but the monks shut them in cells. And when they had fasted the whole of the first day they began to feel faint, but notwithstanding this the monks made them to fast two days at a time now the monks who were in Scete used to fast for a week at a time. And when the day of the Sabbath came, the Egyptians sat down to eat with the old men, and when one of the Egyptians began to eat hurriedly and voraciously, one of the old men caught hold of his hands, saying, "Eat moderately, like the monks." Then one of the others clutched at the old man's hand, saying, "Let me eat so that I may not die, for behold, I have not eaten a piece of boiled food for a whole week." And the old man said to him, "If now you have become very weak after having fasted but one night only, why were you offended by the brethren who live a life of self-denial for long periods of time, and who fulfil their seasons with voluntary abstinence? And straightaway those Egyptians made excuses to the old men, and they were edified by their patient endurance, and departed rejoicing."

88. Once Abba Agathon had two disciples, and they were separated from him, and each of them dwelt in a place by himself. One day he asked one of them, saying, "How do you live in your cell?" And the disciple answered, and said, "I fast until evening, and then I eat two bread-cakes," and Abba Agathon said to him, "It is a beautiful way of living, but it is very laborious." Then Abba Agathon said to the other disciple, "And how do you live?" And the disciple answered, saying, "I fast two days at a time, and after each fast I eat two bread-cakes." Then the old man said to him, "You toil greatly, and maintain a twofold strife. For one man eats every day and does not fill his belly, and another fasts two days at a time and takes whatever he needs. But you, though you do fast two days at a time, you do not fill your belly."

89. Abba Abraham went to Abba Areus. As they were sitting down, another brother came to the Abba, and asked him, saying, "Tell me what I shall do to live?" He said to him, "Go and pass the whole week in plaiting palm leaves and twisting ropes, and eat bread and salt once each day in the evening, and then come again to me, and I will tell you what else to do." And the brother went away and did as he was told to do. And when Abba Abraham heard this he wondered. Now when the week had ended, that brother came again to the old man Areus, with whom there happened to be also Abba Abraham. And the old man said to the brother, "Go back, and pass the whole week in fasting two days at a time." And when that brother had gone, Abba Abraham said to Abba Areus, "Why do you command all the other brethren to bear a light burden, but lays a heavy load upon the brother who was here?" Then the old man said to him, "The other brethren as they come, ask, and according as they ask they receive and depart but this brother comes for God's sake, that he may hear the word of profit, for he is a worker, and whatever I say to him he performs with care and diligence."

90. Abba Theodotus used to say, "Abstinence from bread quietens the body of the monk."

91. A certain old man used to say, "I knew Abba Patermuthis in the cells, and he did not drink wine, but when they took some wine and mixed it with water, and urged him to drink it, he said, 'Believe me, O my brethren, I consider it to be a most beautiful thing. And he blamed himself and condemned himself because of the mixing, and at the same time he gave thanks to God and accepted His gracious gift."

92. They used to say about Abba Paphnutius that he did not drink wine readily, even when he was sick.

93. Abba Poemen said, "The soul can not be humbled unless you weaken it by the eating of little bread."

94. They used to say about Abba Sarnios that he labored exceedingly hard, and that he only ate two bread-cakes each day, when he came to Abba Job. Abba Job was a perfect man in the laborious work of active excellence, and was also a man that practised strict self-denial and abstinence. He said to him, "As long as I live in my cell, I can observe my rule of life. But if I go outside my cell, I make openly submission because of the brethren." Then Abba Sarnaos said to him, "To be able to keep hold strong upon your rule of life only so long as you are in your cell is no great act of spiritual excellence, but it would be if you could do so when you did go forth outside your cell."

95. Abba Poemen used to say, "As smoke drives bees away, and men take the sweetness of their labor, even so also does the ease of the body drive away the fear of God from the heart, and it carries away all the good effect of its labor."

96. On one occasion Abba Sylvanus and Zechariah his disciple were going to a monastery, and they prepared a little food to eat before they set out on their journey. And when they had gone forth, his disciple found water on the way, and he wished to drink, but the old man said to him, "Zechariah, today is a fast day," but the disciple said, "No, O father, for behold we have eaten." Then

Abba Sylvanus said to him, "The food which we ate was obligatory, but let us keep the fast, O my son."

97. Abba Poemen said, "Every corporeal pleasure is contemptible before the Lord."

98. The disciple of Abba Sisoes had to say to him several times, "Rise up and let us eat." And he used to say to him, "My son, have not we eaten?" And the disciple would say to him, "No, O father" Then the old man would say to him, "If we have not eaten, bring the food and let us eat."

99. Abba Daniel used to say, "In proportion as the body grows, the soul becomes enfeebled and the more the body becomes emaciated, the more the soul grows."

100. Abba Benjamin, the priest of the cells, said, that on one occasion we went to a certain old man in Scete, and we wanted to give him some oil and he said to us, "Behold, that little vessel of oil which you brought to me three years ago is still lying in the place where you put it, and it has remained in the same state as that where you brought it." And when we heard this we marvelled at the old man's manner of life.

101. Abba Benjamin also said, "We went to another old man, and he took some food which we were going to eat, and threw into it little oil of radishes." And we said to him, "Father, throw into our food a little sweet oil." When he heard these words, he made the sign of the Cross over himself, and said, "If there be any other oil besides this, then I am not aware of it."

102. Abba Joseph asked Abba Poemen what was the proper way to fast, and Abba Poemen said to him, "I prefer the man who eats every day a very small quantity of food, and who does not satisfy his cravings for food." Abba Joseph said to him, "When you were a young man, did not you fast two days at a time, O father?" Then the old man said to him, "Yes, I did, and three days at a time, and four days at a time, and even a week at a time, and the old men, like men of might, have tried all these by experience, but they have found that it is beneficial for a man to eat an exceedingly small quantity of food each day, and because of this they have delivered to us an easy way to the kingdom."

103. One of the fathers said, "I knew a brother in the cells who used to fast the whole of the Great Sabbath, and when the brethren were assembled in the evening he used to flee to his cell in order that he might eat nothing in the church and he would eat a few plantains with salt, and without bread, that he might conceal his abstinence."

104. They used to tell about a certain monk who, having gone forth from the world, and lived in the coenobium for a number of years, was gracious to every man in his humility, and all the brethren marvelled at his abstinence from meats then he went to the barren desert, and lived there for many years, eating for food wild herbs. Afterwards he entreated God to inform him what reward He would give him, and it was said to him by an angel, "Go forth from this desert and get you along the road, and behold a certain shepherd shall meet you, and according to what he says so shall you receive." When he had made ready to depart, the shepherd of whom he had been told by the angel met him, and saluted him. Having sat down to hold converse with each other, the monk saw in the shepherd's bag some green herbs and he asked him, saying, "What is this?" The shepherd said to him, "It is my food." The monk said to him, "How long have you been feeding yourself on these green herbs?" The shepherd said to him, "Behold, for the last thirty years, more or less, and I have never tasted anything else except these herbs which I have eaten once a day, and I drink as much water as my food requires and the wages which are given to me by the owner of the sheep I give to the poor." Now when the monk heard these things he fell down at the feet of the shepherd, and said, "I imagined that I had laid hold upon abstinence, but you through your well-ordered life are worthy of a greater reward than I, because I have eaten every kind of green thing immediately as it came in my way." Then the shepherd said to him, "It is not right that rational men should make themselves like to the beasts, but they should eat whatever is prepared for them at the seasons which are duly ordered and appointed for them, and afterwards they should fast from everything until an appointed time." The monk profited by these words, and he added to his labor and became perfect, and he praised God, and marvelled how many were the saints in the world who were not known to the children of men.

CHAPTER THREE

On the Reading of the Scripture, and Watching by Night

They used to say about Abba Arsenius that no man was able to attain to the manner of life in his abode. They also said about him that on the night of the Sabbath which would end in the dawn of Sunday, he would leave the sun behind him, and would stretch out his hands towards heaven, and would pray in this position until the sun rose in his face, when he would satisfy his eyes with a little slumber.

106. A certain old man was complete in all perfection, and he could see what was happening from a very long way off and he said, "I once saw in a monastery a certain brother who was meditating on the study of God in his cell, and behold, a devil came and stood outside, and the devil wanted to go in, but could not do so, as long as the brother was meditating. Finally, however, when the monk ceased his contemplation the devil was able to enter his cell, for his power is notable to vanquish those whose converse is with God."

107. An old man said, "Whenever a man reads the Divine Books, the devils are afraid."

108. They used to say about Abba Pachomius that he spent much time in striving with devils like a true athlete, and after the manner of Saint Anthony.

Because many devils came against him in the night time, he asked God to keep away sleep from him both by day and by night, so that he might not sleep at all, and might be able to overcome the might of the enemy, even according to that which is written, 'I will not turn back until I have made an end of them for they are powerless against the faith which is in the Lord.' Now this gift was given to him, even as he had asked, for a certain time, and because he was pure, his heart used to see God, Who is invisible, as in a mirror.

109. They used to say about Abba Pachomius and Abba John that they lived together in the same religious house (now John was larger in stature than Pachomius), but both had adopted a life of poverty voluntarily, and they possessed nothing except for the fear of God. Whatever they gained by the work of their hands they gave to those who were in need, and they kept for themselves only what was sufficient for their bare necessities in respect of clothes. They were well near destitute, and they had few clothes that they were obliged to wash those, which they wore and put on again. Abba Pachomius always wore a garment made of hair, because of the toil of his body. Whenever they wished to refresh their bodies by a little sleep after their vigil and prayer, each of them would sit down in the middle of the cell, and, without leaning against a wall, would go to sleep. And they continued to do so for fifteen years, and many of the fathers heard of them, and saw them living in that manner, and they also strove in similar manner to humble their bodies for the redemption of their souls.

110. They used to say about Abba Joseph that when he was about to die, and the old men were sitting about him, he looked at the window and saw Satan sitting there and he cried out to his disciple and said, "Bring me a stick here, for this devil thinks that I have become old, and that I am no longer able to stand up against him." As soon as he grasped the stick in his hand, Satan, in the form of a dog, threw himself from the window, and the old man saw him taking to flight.

111. They used to relate concerning Abba Sisoes that if he did not bring down his hands swiftly when he was standing up in prayer, his mind would be carried off on high but whenever it happened that one of the brethren was with him, he would bring his hands down hurriedly lest perhaps his mind should be carried off, and he would be left alone.

112. Abba Isaiah, the elder of the church, rebuked the brethren when they were eating that which what had been prepared for them, because they began to talk with each other, and he said to them, "Hold your peace, O my brethren. I know a brother who eats with us and drinks with us full cups even as we do, and yet his prayer ascends up before God like fire."

113. One day Abba Arsenius called Abba Alexander and Abba Zolla, and said to them, "Because the devils are striving with me, and because I do not know but that they may carry me off during my sleep, toil here with me this night, and keep vigil, and watch me and see if I sleep during my vigil." So they sat down, one on his right hand, and the other on his left, from the evening even until the morning. They said, "We slept and we woke up, and we did not observe that he slept at all, but when it began to be light there came to us three times the sound of breathing in his nostrils, but whether he did this purposely so that we might think he slept or whether slumber had really fallen upon him we do not know. And he stood up and said to us, "Have I been asleep?" We answered and said to him, "We do not know, O father, for we ourselves went to sleep."

114. A brother asked Abba Poemen, saying, "How, and in what manner is it right for a man to walk in the path of righteousness?" Abba Poemen said to him, "We have seen Daniel, and also seen that his enemies were unable to bring any accusation whatever against him except in respect of his service of God."

115. On one occasion Abba Sisoes was sitting in his cell, and when his disciple knocked at the door asking to go in, the old man cried out, saying, "Flee, Abraham, and do not come in now, for this place is not empty."

116. They say concerning Abba Sisoes of Babylon that, wishing to vanquish sleep, he stood upright upon a mountain crag cliff, and that the angel of the Lord came and rescued him from that place, and commanded him never to do such a thing again, and not even to hand on this tradition to another.

117. An old man said, "I knew a brother who used to sit with the brethren at the meal which is made for the coming of the brethren, and although the brethren ate and drank, he never made himself to be remote from converse with God in his prayer, and he did not drink even a cup of wine. Now this man's manner of life was marvellous, and a certain man used to say about him, "I once wished to count the prayers which he made, and I saw that he did not cease to pray either by day or by night."

118. On one occasion a Bishop was sent secretly to Abba Epiphanius by the head of a certain monastery in Palestine, saying, "We have not treated lightly your services of prayer since your departure from us, but we perform most carefully the services for the third, and sixth, and ninth hours, and also vespers." Then Abba Epiphanius blamed those who sent him, and wrote a message, which he sent to them, saying, "You must know that you are indeed neglectful of the services and prayers which belong to the other eight hours which are in the day, for it is right for the monk who has made himself to be remote from the world to be occupied with prayers to God unceasingly, and he should pray either in his heart, or in a carefully defined service, or in that service which he performs with his will and with understanding. For the calumniator adds greatly to any small failing which he may find in a monk, and by being with him continually he enlarges greatly the breach which he has made, and by his habit of persistence he acquires his natural power, and more particularly is this so in the case of those who are careless and lazy."

119. Abba Epiphanius said, "Whatever food you wish to eat with gratification, that do not give to your body, especially when you are in good health, and that which you lust after, do not eat, and when you feed upon the things which are sent to you by God, give thanks to Him at all seasons, and receive His gracious gift, the delights and the pleasures which we have received through the name of monk, although we do not do the works of monks. And if you are a monk, will you not then make yourself strong, lest perhaps you are arrayed in apparel which is strange to you? Tell me, O brother, do you possess the seal of the service, that is to say, humility? For the holy man who sees another man sin, weeps bitterly, saying, 'It is this man who sins now, but some time subsequently it may be I.' However much then a man may sin before you, do not condemn him, but consider yourself a far greater sinner than him, even he may be a child of this world, and besides there is the fact that he may have sinned greatly against God."

120. He said also, "Know yourself, and you shall never fall. Give your soul some work, that is to say, constant prayer, and love of God, before another can give it evil thoughts and pray that the spirit of error may be remote from you."

121. He also said, "Whatever you successfully do, and what you boast of destroy, for it is not right for a monk to boast of his fair deeds, and if he boasts he will fall."

122. And he also said, "When you pray speak to God in a quiet voice and say, 'How can I possess You, O Lord? You know quite well that I am a beast, and that I know nothing. You have brought me to the prime of this life. Deliver me then for Your mercy's sake. I am your servant, and the son of Your handmaiden, O Lord, by Your will, vivify me.' The old man is falsehood, and the new man is truth. The truth is the root of good works, and falsehood is death. If the liar, and the thief, and the calumniator knew that they would finally be made known to all and their works revealed, they would never offend. And thus also was it with the adulterous sons of Eli, Hophni and Phinehas, for they were not priests of the Lord, and they did not fear God, and they perished, together with all their houses. And the man who takes hold of, and binds himself and shuts within himself the memory of evil things is like the man who hides fire in straw. If you speak to a man concerning life, and if you say a word to him, let it be with feeling, and penitence, and with tears and say your word to the man who will hearken and will do it, but if not, do not speak, lest you die, and you depart from this world without any profit from the words whereby you did wish to give life to others. For to the sinner God said, 'What have you to do with the Books of My Commandments? For you have taken My covenant in your mouth only' (Psalm 50:16)."

123. Abba Epiphanius said, "Whenever a thought comes and fills your bosom, that is to say, your heart, with vainglory or with pride, say to yourself, 'Old man, behold your fornication.'"

124. He also said, "If we do evil things God will be unmindful of His long suffering, but if we do good things, it will not help us greatly because we increase the advantage of freedom, and the merchandise is not plundered thereby, for the will rejoices in the striving."

125. Certain brethren entreated Abba Epiphanius on one occasion, saying, "Father, speak to us some word of life, even when you speak we may not grasp the seed of your word, because the soil is salt." Then the old man answered and said to them, "Whoever does not receive all the brethren, but makes distinctions between them, cannot become a perfect man. If a man reviles you, bless him, whether it is good for both of you, or whether it is not; it will be he who will receive a reward of blessing. This is the right way for a monk to live, and in this way lived Abba Arsenius, who took care each day to stand up before God without sin, and he drew near to Him with tears like the sinful woman. In this manner pray to the Lord God as if He were standing before you, for He is near to you and He looks upon you. It is right that the man who wishes to dwell in the desert should be as a teacher in his knowledge, and he must not be in need of instruction lest he be swept away by the devils and he must look into his mind most minutely, both in respect of the things which are above, and those which are below, lest he become a laughing-stock to them by some means or other. It is right that the manner of life of the man who loves God should be blameless."

126. A certain man made answer to the brethren against evil thoughts, saying, "I entreat you, O my brethren, let us cease from ascetic works, and let us give up also anxious thoughts. For what are we? A voice which comes out of the dust, or a cry which rises from the mud? 'And when Joseph of Ramah had taken the Body of Jesus, he took It, and wrapped It with a sheet of clean linen, and then laid It in his own new tomb.'" (Matt. 27: 59-60)

127. On one occasion a certain monk saw a devil who was calling to his fellow devil to come with him, so that the two together might wake up a monk for service, and might lead him into error thereby, and cause him to think that angels had appeared to him. And the monk heard the voice of the other devil who made answer to his fellow, saying, "I cannot do this. For once I woke him up, and he stood up and broke me with a terrible breaking, and all the time he was doing it he sang psalms and prayed."

128. A brother asked an old man and said, "Why is it that when I go forth to labor I feel wearied and disgusted in my soul, and my mind is wholly empty of spiritual thoughts?" And the old man said to him, "Because you do not desire to fulfil that which is written, 'I will bless the Lord always, and His praises shall be ever in my mouth' (Psalm 34:1). Therefore, whether you are inside or outside, and where ever you go, you must not cease from blessing God not only in actions, but with word and mind you shall bless your Maker. For God does not dwell in any place which has bounds and limits, but He is everywhere and by His Divine Power He sustains all things, and He is capable of all things."

129. A brother asked Abba Poemen concerning the thoughts, which invaded his mind, and he said to him, "This matter is like that of a man who has a fire on his left hand, and a tank of water on his right hand. If he wishes to extinguish the fire, he takes the water from the tank and does it. And it is right for a man to act thus every hour. Now the fire is the evil thought, which comes from enemies, and the water is the pouring out of the soul before the Lord, which every man should do."

130. There was a certain monk, who did not do any work with his hands, but he prayed without ceasing and at eventide he would go into his cell and find his bread laid there for him, and he would eat it. Now another monk came to him, who had upon him materials for the labor of his hands, and wherever he went, he worked, and made the old man, into whose cell he had entered, to work with him. When the evening had come, he wished according to his custom, to eat, but he found nothing, and he therefore lay down in sorrow and it was revealed to him, saying, "While you were occupied in converse with Me, I fed you, but now you have begun to work, you must demand your food from the labor of your hands."

131. They tell the story that on one occasion, while the blessed Anthony was dwelling in the desert, thoughts of dejection and despair rose up in his mind, and he was in deep gloom of thought, and said to God, "Lord, I wish to live, but my thoughts will not permit me to do so. What shall I do in my tribulations to be saved?" And he came a little nearer to the town from the place where he was, and he saw a man who was like to himself, and was in his own form, and he was sitting down and twisting palm leaves into ropes and this man rose up from his work, prayed, and afterwards he sat down again and continued his work, and then he stood up once more, and prayed. The man was an angel who had been sent from God to correct and to admonish the blessed Anthony, who afterwards heard him say to him, "O Anthony, do you also do this and live?" When Anthony heard this, the blessed man had great joy, and afterwards he did as the angel had done, and lived.

132. They said concerning Abba John the Less that, on one occasion, he steeped the palm leaves for two baskets in water, and sewed one basket to the other without perceiving it until he came to the side of it, for his mind was led captive by the sight of God.

133. And Abba Daniel used to say concerning Abba Arsenius that he would pass the whole night in vigil, and when, for the sake of nature, he wished for the approach of the morning so that he might have some relief, he would struggle against sleep, and say, "Go away, O wicked handmaiden," then he would snatch a very little slumber and stand up straight way.

134. Abba Arsenius used to say "One hour's sleep is sufficient for a monk, provided that he be strenuous."

135. They used to say about a certain monk who lived in a monastery of the brotherhood, that although he kept frequent vigil and prayed he was neglectful about praying with the congregation. And one night there appeared to him a glorious pillar of brilliant light from the place where the brethren were congregated, and it reached up into the heavens and he saw a small spark, which flew about the pillar, and sometimes it shone brightly, and sometimes it was extinguished. And while he was wondering at the vision, it was explained to him by God, Who said, "The pillar which you see is the prayers of the many brethren which are gathered together and go up to God and gratify Him and the spark is the prayers of those who dwell among the congregation, and who despise the appointed services of the brotherhood. And now, if you would live, perform that which it is customary to perform with the brethren, and then, if you wish to do so, and are able to pray separately, do so." And the monk related all these things before the brotherhood, and they glorified God.

CHAPTER FOUR

On how it is Meet for Us to Weep for our Sins

A BROTHER ASKED ABBA AMMON, SAYING, "Tell me some word whereby I may live," Abba Ammon replied, saying, "Go and make your mind like the minds of those evil-doers who are in the prison house, who ask those who go to them, saying, 'Where is the governor? When will he come here?' For their minds tremble in fearful expectation. Thus also is a monk bound to wait in expectation always, and he must admonish himself, saying, 'Woe is me! For how can I stand before the throne of Christ? And how shall I be able to make answer to Him?' If you are able to think in this manner always, you will be able to live."

137. Abba Poemen was once passing through Egypt, and he saw a woman sitting in the cemetery and weeping, and he said, "If every kind of instrument of sweet music in the world were to come here they would not be able to change the grief of this woman's soul into gladness even thus it is right for a monk to have grief within himself.

138. Three old men once came to Abba Sisoes because they had heard that he was a great man. The first one said to him, "Father, how can I escape from the river of fire?" Abba Sisoes never said a word. Then the second old man said to him, "Father, how can I escape from the gnashing of teeth, and from the worm

which never dies?" Abba Sisoes never said a word. Then the third old man said to him, "Father, what shall I do? For the remembrance of the outer darkness troubles me." Abba Sisoes answered them saying, "I never think on any of these things, but I believe that God is Merciful, and that He will show mercy to me." Then the old men went away grieved at the answer which Abba Sisoes had spoken to them. Because he did not wish to send them away sorrowful, he brought them back, and said to them, "Blessed are you, O my brethren, for I have been jealous of you." They said to him, "In what matter have you been jealous of us?" And he said, "The first one of you spoke about a river of fire and the second spoke about the gnashing of teeth and the worm which dies not and the third spoke about the outer darkness. If remembrances of this kind have dominion over your minds it is impossible for you to commit sin. What can I do who am stubborn of heart? For the hardness of my heart will not even allow me to perceive that a punishment for men exists, and because of this I sin every hour." When the old men had heard these words, they made excuses to him, and said, "In very truth according to what we have heard, even so have we seen."

139. A certain father said that on one occasion when the brethren were eating the food of grace, one of them laughed at table and Abba Sinu saw him, and burst into tears, and said, "What can there be in the heart of this brother who has laughed? It is meet that he should weep because he is eating the food of grace."

140. They say that when Abba Sisoes was sick the old men who were sitting with him saw that he was talking to some one, and they said to him, "What do you see you, O father?" And he said to them, "Some people came to take me away, and I entreated them to leave me here a little longer that I might repent." Then one of the old men said to him, "What power do you have now for repentance?" Abba Sisoes said to them, "If I can do nothing else I can sigh and lament a little over my soul, and this will be sufficient for me."

141. Certain brethren went to an old man and, making apologies to him, they said, "Father, what shall we do, for Satan is hunting after us?" And he said to them, "It is right for you to be watchful and to weep continually. My own thoughts are always fixed upon the place where our Lord was crucified, and I sigh and lament and weep about it always." And thus having received a good example of repentance the brethren departed and became chosen vessels.

142. A brother asked Abba Muthues, saying, "Speak a word to me and the old man replied, 'Cut off from you contention concerning every matter whatever, and weep, and mourn, for the time has come.'"

143. Abba Ammon said that he saw a young man who laughed, and he said to him, "Do not laugh, O brother, for if you do, you will drive the fear of God out of you soul."

144. Abba Paule used to say, "I had sunk in the mire up to my neck, and I wept and spoke before God, saying, 'Have mercy on me.'"

145. They used to say that Abba Theodore and Abba Or put on the skins of lambs for clothing and they said to each other, "If God were to visit us now what should we do?" And they left the skins, and departed to their cells weeping.

146. A blessed Archbishop, when he was about to depart from this world, said, "Blessed are you, O Arsenius, because you have remembered this hour."

147. An old man said, "God dwells in the man into whom nothing alien enters."

148. A brother asked a certain old man, and said to him, "My soul desires tears, even as I have heard that the old men desire them, but they will not come to me, and my soul is vexed." And the old man said to him, "The children of Israel entered into the land of promise after forty years. Now tears are the land of promise, and since you would enter there you must not henceforward be afraid of fighting. For God wishes to bring tribulation upon the soul in this manner in order that it may at all times be wishful to enter into that land of promise."

149. A brother asked Abba Poemen a question and said to him, "What shall I do? For my thoughts disturb me and they say to me, "Your sins have been forgiven you, and they make me to pry into the shortcomings of the brethren." Then Abba Poemen spoke to him about Abba Isidore, who dwelt in a cell and wept over his soul, and his disciple used to dwell in another cell and the disciple came to the old man, and finding him weeping, said to him, "My father, why do you weep?" And the old man said to him, "I am weeping for my sins." Then the disciple said to him, "And have you any sins, father?" And the old man said to him, "Indeed I have, my son, and if I were permitted to see my sins, not three or even four men would suffice to weep with me for them."

Then Abba Poemen said, "It is so with the man who knows himself."

150. I have heard that the old men who lived in Nitria sent to Macarius the Great, who was living in Scete, and entreated him, saying, "In order that all the people may not be vexed, we beseech you, O our father, to come to us so that we may see you before you depart to our Lord." And having gone to them they all gathered together to him, and the old men begged and entreated him to speak to the brethren one word of profit and the holy old man wept, and said to them, "Let us weep, O my brethren, and let us make our eyes to overflow with tears before we go to the place where the tears of our eyeballs will burn up our bodies. And they all wept, and they fell upon their faces, saying, Father, pray for us."

151. When the blessed Arsenius was about to deliver up his spirit the brethren saw him weeping, and they said to him, "Are you too afraid, O father?" And he said to them, "The dread of this hour has been with me in very truth from the time when I became a monk, and was afraid. And so he died."

152. And when Abba Poemen heard that he was dead, that is to say, that Abba Arsenius had gone to his rest, he said, "Blessed are you, O Abba Arsenius, for you did weep over yourself in this world. For he who does not weep not for himself in this world must weep forever in the next. He may weep here voluntarily or there because of the punishments which he will receive, but it is impossible for a man to escape weeping either here or there."

153. A brother asked Abba Poemen and said to him, "What shall I do in the matter of my sins?" And the old man said to him, "When Abraham went into the Land of Promise he bought himself a grave, and through the grave he inherited the land." And the brother said to him, "What is a grave?" Then the old man said to him, "Weeping and mourning are a grave and a place of burial."

154. One of the brethren asked Abba Poemen, saying, "Father, what shall I do in the matter of my sins?" The old man said to him, "Whoever wishes to blot out his offences can do so by weeping, and he who wishes to acquire good works can do so by means of weeping for weeping is the path which the Scriptures have taught us, and the fathers have also wept continually, and there is no other path except that of tears."

155. Abba Poemen also said, "There are two things to remember: we must fear our Lord, and do the good to our neighbor."

156. Abba Noah asked Abba Macarius, and said to him, "Speak to me a word" and the old man said, "Flee from the children of men." Noah said to him, "Father, what does it mean to flee from the children of men?" The old man said to him, "You shall sit in your cell and weep for your sins."

157. A brother asked an old man, and said to him, "What shall I do, father?" The old man said to him, "It is right that we should sigh and lament always." Now it happened that one of the old men fell asleep, and that after a long interval he came to himself again, and the brethren asked him, saying, "What did you see there, O father?" and he said to us with many tears, "I heard there the sound of the weeping of many, who were crying out and wailing incessantly, and saying, 'Woe is me! Woe is me!' And it is necessary that we should always be saying the same thing."

CHAPTER FIVE

On Voluntary Poverty

Abba Arsenius once fell sick at Scete, and he was in need of a bowl of porridge and since this was not to be found there, he took the remains of the Eucharist, and said, "I give thanks to You, O Christ, that, because of Your Name, I am able to receive the food of grace."

159. There was a certain holy man whose name was Philagrius, who lived in Jerusalem, and he worked with his hands and toiled to earn the food which he needed and the old man rose up to see the work of his hands, and he found a purse containing one thousand darics (gold coins) which had dropped from some one on the road, and he remained in the place where he was, saying, "The man who lost this will come back seeking for it." And behold the man did come back, and he was weeping, and the old man took him aside and gave him the darics and their owner laid hold upon him, and wished to give him some small sum of money, but the old man refused to accept anything. Then the owner of the darics began to cry out and say, "Come you and see what the man of God has done." But the old man fled secretly and departed from the city, lest what he had done should become known, and men should pay him honor because of it.

160. They say that Abba Serapion the Bishop went on one occasion to one of the brethren, and found in his cell a hollow in the wall which was filled with books and the brother said to him, "Speak to me one word whereby I may live." And the Bishop said to him, "What have I to say to you? For you have taken that which belongs to the orphans and widows and laid it up in a hole in the wall."

161. Abba Theodore of Parme possessed some beautiful books, and he went to Abba Macarius and said to him, "Father, I have three books, and I gain profit from them, and the brethren borrow them from me, and they also have profit from them tell me, now, what shall I do with them?" And the old man answered and said, "Ascetic labors are beautiful, but the greatest of them all is voluntary poverty." And when Abba Theodore heard these words he went and sold the books and gave the price of them to the poor.

162. They say about a certain monk that when his food came to him he was in the habit of taking so much of it as he needed, but that if it happened that another man was brought to him he would not accept any of it, saying, "It is sufficient for me behold my Lord has fed me."

163. A certain monk used to live in a cave in the desert, and a message was sent to him by his kinsfolk, saying, "Your father is grievously sick, and is near to die, therefore come, and inherit his possessions." And he made answer to them, saying, "I died to the world long before he will die, and a dead man cannot be the heir of a living one."

164. An old man was asked by a brother a question, saying, "How shall I live?" Then the old man took off his garment, girded up his loins therewith, lifted up his hands and said, "It is meet for a monk to be as naked in respect of this world's goods as I am of clothing. And in his striving against his thoughts he must stand as upright as a vigorous athlete. For when the athlete contends he also stands up naked, and when he is anointed with oil he is quite naked, having nothing upon him and he learns from him that trains him how to contend, and when the enemy comes against him he throws dust upon him (which is a matter of this world), that he may be able to grasp him easily. In yourself, then, O monk, you must see the athlete, and he who shows you how to contend is God, for it is He Who gives the victory, and Who conquers for us and those who contend are ourselves, and the striving is our opponent, and the dust is the affairs of the world. And since you have seen the cunning of the Adversary, stand you up and oppose him in your nakedness, being free from any care which belongs to this world, and you shal overcome him. For when the mind is weighed down with the care of the world it cannot receive the holy word of God."

165. They say concerning Abba Arsenius that as, when he lived in the world, his apparel was finer than that of anyone else, so, when he lived in Scete, he wore raiment which was inferior to that of every one else. And when, at long intervals, he came to church, he used to sit behind a pillar so that no one might see his face, and he might not see the faces of others. Now his face was like that of an angel, and his hair was as white as snow, and as abundant as that of Jacob. His body was dry by reason of his labors, and his beard descended to his belly. His eyelashes were destroyed through his weeping. He was tall in stature, but somewhat bowed by old age and he ended his days when he was ninety-five years old. He lived in the world, in the palace, for forty years, in the days of Theodosius, the great king, who became the father of the Emperors Honorius and Arcadius, and he lived in Scete for forty years, and for ten years in the Troja of Babylon which is opposite the Memphis which is in Egypt. He dwelt for three years in Canopus of Alexandria, and during the two remaining years he came to Troja again, where he died. And he finished his career in peace and in the fear of God.

166. On one occasion a certain Bishop came to the Fathers in Scete, and a brother went forth to meet him, and having met him, he took him and brought him into his cell and having set before him bread and salt, he said, "Forgive me, O my father, for I have nothing else to set before you." And the Bishop said to him, "I wish that when I come another year I may not find even bread and salt in your cell."

167. One of the old men said, "If you sit in a place and see people with abundant provisions, look not at them but if there be a man who is destitute, look at him as one who has no bread, and you shall find relief."

168. Abba Isaac, the priest of the Cells, used to say that Abba Pambo said, "The manner of the apparel which a monk ought to wear should be such that if it were cast outside the cell for three days no one would carry it away."

169. A certain brother asked one of the old men a question, and said to him, "Do you wish me to keep two darics as provision for the needs of the feebleness of the body?" And the old man, perceiving his mind and also that he wished to keep them, said to him, "Yes." Now when the brother had gone to his cell, he became troubled in his mind, and he debated in his thoughts, saying, "Did the old man speak truthfully or not?" Then he rose up, and went back to the old man, and made excuses to him, and said, "For our Lord's sake, tell me the truth, because my thoughts are troubling me about these two darics." The old man said to him, "I spoke to you as I did because I saw that your mind was to keep them, but it is not necessary for you to keep the two darics, except only for the need of your body. But why do you set your hope upon two darics? If by chance they were lost would not God take care of you? Let us then cast our care upon Him, for it belongs to Him to take care of us continually."

170. Some of the old men used to tell a story about a gardener who used to work and to give away whatever he gained thereby in alms, but subsequently his thoughts said to him, "Gather together a few silver coins, lest when you have grown old you fall into want so he gathered together some money, and filled a large vessel therewith." And it fell out that he became sick, and the disease seized upon his foot, and he spent the whole of the money in the vessel on the physicians, and was not in the least benefited thereby. At length another physician came to him and said, "If you do not cut off your foot all your body will putrefy," and he came to consider the cutting off of his foot. And in the night he came to himself, and he groaned, and wept, and said, "Remember, O Lord, my former deeds." Straightaway a man appeared behind him, and said to him, "Where are the silver coins?" and the gardener said immediately, "I have sinned, forgive me." And the man approached his leg, and it was made whole, and he rose up, and went to the garden to work. And in the morning the physician came to cut off his foot as he had said, and the servants told him, "He went to this work in the night." And straightaway the gardener glorified God.

171. Abba Agathon saw Abba Nastir wearing two shoulder wrappers, and he said to him, "If a poor man were to come, and ask you for a garment, which of them would you give him?" And Abba Nastir replied, I would give him the better of them and Abba Agathon said to him, "And if another poor man came, what would you give him?" Abba Nastir said to him, "I would give him the half of that which remained." And Abba Agathon said to him, "Supposing yet another beggar came, what would you give to him?" And Nastir said to him, "I would cut the half which remained into two pieces, and give one to him, and with the other I would cover my body." And Abba Agathon said to him, "And supposing yet another beggar were to come?" and Nastir said, "I would give him what was left. For I do not wish to receive anything from any man, yet I would go and sit down in some place until God sent me wherewith to cover myself."

172. The blessed woman Eugenia said, "It is right for us to beg, but only we must be with Christ. He who is with Christ becomes rich, but he who honors the things of the body more than the things of the spirit shall fall both from the things which are first and the things which are last."

173. One of the old men said, "How can a man teach to his neighbor that which he himself does not observe?"

174. They say that Abba Theodore excelled in the three following things more than any other man, and that he attained in their performance a degree which was greater than that of many, namely, voluntary poverty, self-abnegation, and flight from the children of men.

175. Abba Poemen used to say, "He who labors and keeps the result of his work for himself is a two fold grief."

176. Abba Isaac used to say to the brethren, "Our fathers and Abba Pambo used to wear old garments which were much mended and were patched with rags, but at this present you wear very costly apparel. Get you gone from this place, for you have laid the country waste, and I will not give you commandments, for you will not keep them."

177. On one occasion a brother came to the church of the Cells wearing a small head-cloth which came down to his shoulders, and when Abba Isaac saw him he followed him, and said, "Monks dwell here, but you are a man in the world, and you can not live here."

178. A certain man, having made himself remote from the world, and divided his possessions among those who were in need, left to himself the remainder of his riches. And when the blessed Anthony heard this he said to him, "Do you wish to become a monk? If you do, get you to such and such a village, and take some meat, and lay it upon your body, and come here alone." Having done this the dogs, and the hawks and other birds of prey rent and tore his body. And when he returned to the blessed man, Saint Anthony asked him whether he had done as he had commanded him, and when the man had shown him his body which was rent and torn, the blessed Anthony said to him, "Even thus are those who wish to go out from the world, and who nevertheless leave themselves certain possessions, from which arise for their owners war and strife."

179. A brother asked Abba Poemen the question, saying, "An inheritance has been bequeathed to me what shall I do with it?" Abba Poemen said to him, "Go, and after three days come to me, and I will give you counsel." And the brother came, and Abba Poemen said to him, "What counsel shall I give you, O brother? If I tell you to give it to the church, they will make feasts with it and again, if I tell you to give it to your kinsmen, you will have no reward. But if I tell you to give it to the poor, you will have no further care. Therefore go and do with your inheritance what you please, for I am not able to advise you rightly."

180. A certain man entreated an old man to accept from him a gift of grace for his wants, but he refused to do so because the labor of his hands was sufficient for him and when he who asked him to accept it persisted, saying, "If you will not accept it for your own needs, at least do so for the wants of others," the old man answered, saying, "It would be a twofold disgrace to me. First, because I should accept something which I do not want. Secondly, because I should be giving away with boasting the charity of another."

181. An old man used to say, "It is not right for a man to have any care whatsoever except the fear of God. For although I am forced to take care for the needs of the body, no thought whatsoever concerning anything rises in my mind before the time when I shall require to make use of it."

182. The same old man used to say, "When you rise up, in the morning, say, 'O body, work that you may be fed; O soul, rise up that you may inherit life.'"

CHAPTER SIX

On Patient Endurance

On one occasion certain brethren went to Abba Agathon, because they had heard that he took the greatest possible care that his mind should not be disturbed by anything. They sought to try him to see if his mind would rise to any matter. They said to him, "Are you indeed Agathon? We have heard that you are a whoremonger and a boastful man." Agathon said to them, "Yes, I am." They said to him, "Agathon, you are a garrulous and talkative old man," and he said to them, "Indeed I am." Again they said to him, "Agathon, you are a heretic," and he said to them, "I am not a heretic." Then they said to him, "Tell us now why in answer to all these things which we have said to you, you have replied, 'Yes,' and that you have endured them all with the exception of the accusation of being a heretic." Abba Agathon said to them, "The earlier things I accounted as profitable to my soul, but heresy means separation from God, and I do not wish to be separated from God." When the brethren heard these words they marvelled at his solicitude, and went away rejoicing.

184. A certain father used to tell the story of a father who had a book where were the New Testament and the Old Testament, and the price was more than eighteen darics, and he laid up the book in a hole in the wall. There came a certain stranger and stayed there, and he coveted the book greatly, stole it, and departed. The old man did not go after him, although he knew that he had taken it. The brother went to a neighboring village and wished to sell the book. He asked as its price sixteen darics, and the man who wanted to buy it said to him, "Give it to me that I may show it to a friend," and he took it and carried it to the old man who had lost it. Then the old man said to him, "How much does he ask for it?" When he heard how much he said to him, "It is a good price." Then the man went and said to the brother who wished to sell the book, "Behold, I have shown it to Father So-and-so, and he has told me that your price is dear." The brother answered and said to him, "I did not tell you anything to the contrary." The would-be buyer said, "No, you did not." The brother said, "I will not then sell you the book," and straightaway he repented, came to the old man, made excuses to him, and offered him the book. The old man refused to accept it. The brother entreated him, saying, "Allow me to restore it to you, O father, for if you do not accept it I cannot obtain life." So the old man was entreated, and he took it, and that brother remained with him until his death, and through the patient endurance of the old man he gained life.

185. On one occasion certain philosophers came to the desert to try the monks. There was a living man who led a life of fair works. They said to him, "Come here." His anger rose and he reviled them. Then, there passed by a certain great monk who was Libyan, and they said to him, "O you monk who have grown grey-headed in iniquity, come here." He went to them readily, and they hit him on one cheek, whereupon he turned the other to them. When they saw this they rose up straightaway, worshipped him, and said, "Truly this is a monk." Then they set him in their midst, and asked him, saying, "You fast, and we also fast, you lead pure lives, and we also lead pure lives, whatever you do we also do, what do you who live in the desert do more than us?" The Libyan said to them, "We keep watch over our minds." The philosophers said to him, "We are unable to keep watch over our minds."

186. They say that Abba Macarius the Egyptian once went up from Scete to the Nitrian mountain. As he drew near to a certain place, he said to his disciple, "Pass on a little in front of me." When he had done so there met him a certain heathen priest, who was running along and carrying some wood about the noon. That brother cried out to him, saying "O minister to devils, why are you running?" The priest turned round and hit him with many severe blows, and left him with but very little breath remaining in him. He took up his wood and went on his way. When he had gone a little further, the blessed Macarius met him on his journey, and said to him, "May you be helped, O man of labors?" The priest was astonished, came to him and said, "What fair thing have you seen in me that you should salute me in this gracious fashion?" The old man replied, "I see that you toil, and that you do not know that you are toiling for naught," then he said to the old man, "At your salutation I also was very sorry, and I learned that you did belong to the Great God. But a wicked monk met me just before you did, he cursed me, and I hit him even to death." The old man knew that it was his disciple of whom he spoke. The priest laid hold upon the feet of Macarius, saying, "I will not let you go until you make me a monk" They came to the place where the brother was lying, carried him and brought him to the church of the mountain. When the fathers saw the heathen priest with him, they marvelled that he had been converted from the error, which he had held. Abba Macarius took him and made him a monk, and through him many of the heathen became Christians. Abba Macarius said, "An evil word makes wicked even those who are good, and a good word makes good even those who are wicked, as it is written."

187. On one occasion thieves came to the cell of an old man, and said to him, "We have come to take away everything which you have in your cell" He said to them, "My sons, take whatever pleases you." They took everything, which they saw in his cell and departed. They forgot to take a wallet which was hanging there, and the old man took it, ran after them, and entreated them, saying, "My sons, take this wallet which you have left behind in my cell." When the thieves saw this they marvelled at the good disposition of the old man, and gave him back everything they had taken from his cell. They repented and said to each other, "Truly, this man is a man of God."

188. Abba Macarius the monk loved money so little that, on one occasion when thieves came to his cell by night, and took out whatever they could find. As soon as he perceived what they were doing, he helped them in their work and to carry their plunder out of the desert.

189. They say that once when Abba Macarius was absent a thief entered his cell. When he returned, he found a thief loading everything which he had in his cell upon a camel. He went in and took some of the things and laid them on the camel. When the thief had loaded the camel, he began to beat it to make it rise up, but it would not move. When Abba Macarius saw that the beast would not stand up, he took a basket which was remaining, and brought it out, laid it on the camel, and said, "The camel wishes to carry off this also, O brother, and because of this it would not stand up." The old man cried out to the camel, saying, "Stand up!" Immediately because of the old mans words, it stood up. When it had gone forward for a little it lay down again, and would not rise up until the thief had emptied the whole of its load.

190. Another father who was being plundered said to the thieves, "Make haste, and be quick, before the brethren come."

191. On one occasion, some men of iniquity, doers of wickedness, and thieves, rose up against him on the eve of the day of the congregation. An old man said to the brethren, "Let them do their work, and let us do ours."

192. When certain evildoers rose up against one of the brethren in his cell, he brought forth a basin and entreated them to wash their feet. The thieves were ashamed and repented.

193. Another brother who was traveling on a journey, did not know the road. He asked a man to show him the way and to direct him. The man whom he had asked was an evildoer, and led the brother out of his road into a waste place, and made him to arrive at the river Nile, which he commanded the brother to cross over. When he began to cross over, a crocodile was swiftly pursuing the man who was a thief, but the servant of God, being mindful of him, cried out to him, warning him about the fierce attack the animal was about to make. Then, the thief having been delivered from death, gave thanks to that brother, marvelled at his affection, and protected him.

194. The blessed Pior was on one occasion working for a man in the fields during the summer time. He was weary, and reminded the lord of his hire about his wages. When he delayed in paying him, Abba Pior returned to his monastery. On another occasion, at the time of harvest, Abba Pior went to the same man, and reaped his crops with a good will, and returned to his monastery, the man having given him nothing. Again in the third year, Abba Pior came and helped him to harvest his crops, and when he made an end to the work of harvest according to custom, and yet received nothing, he departed again to his monastery. Meanwhile the man, who was worthy of blessing, labored according to his custom in the life and works of spiritual excellence, and rejoiced that he had been defrauded of his reward. Christ worked upon the lord of his hire in his house, for he took the wages of the blessed man, and went about the monasteries searching for him. After the greatest difficulty, when he had found him, he fell at his feet and entreated him to receive his wage. The holy man refused the wage, saying, "Perhaps you need them, and as for me, God will give me my hire." The man increased his supplications to him, and finally the holy man permitted him to give the money to the church.

195. An old man used to say, "We do not advance because we do not know our capacity, do not have sufficient patience in the work which we begin, wish to possess spiritual excellences without working for them, go from one place to another, and expect to find some spot where Satan is not. When we see the temptation of Satan in that place where we have been called to, he who knows what the war is will remain in God. For the kingdom of heaven is within you."

196. An old man used to say, "If a sickness of the body overtakes you, let it not be grievous to you, for if your Lord wishes you to be sick in the body, who are you that you should be in despair? Does not He take care for you in everything? Could you live without Him? Be patient, and entreat Him to give you things that are helpful, and which are according to His will. Besides these, eat His food of grace with long suffering."

197. Abba Poemen used to say, "The certain sign that a monk is a monk is made known by trials."

198. A certain brother was estranged from a fellow monk, and he came to Abba Sisoes the Theban, and said to him, "I am estranged from a fellow monk, and I wish to take vengeance for myself." The old man said, "Let us pray." While he was praying, he said in his prayer, "O God, henceforward we have no need for You to take care of us, for we will take vengeance for ourselves." When the brother heard these words he fell down at the feet of the old man straightaway, and said, "Henceforward I will not enter into judgement with that brother. Forgive me, O Father." Thus Abba Sisoes healed that brother.

199. They say that Abba John the Less, the Theban and the disciple of Abba Ammon, ministered the Abba in his sickness for twelve years. He sat by him when the old man was in a state of exhaustion. He persevered and endured so patiently, while performing great labors, that the old man never said even once to him, "Rest, my son rest, my son!" And when the old man was about to die, and the other old men were sitting before him, Abba Ammon took his hand, and said, "Live, my son, live!" Then he committed him to the old men and said to them, "This is an angel, and not a man."

200. Abba Paul and Timath his brother dwelt in Scete, and there was contention between them frequently and Abba Paul said, "How long are we to remain thus?" Abba Timath said to him, "When I come upon you bear with me and when you come upon me I will bear with you." From that time they were at peace.

201. Certain brethren asked Abba Sisoes a question, saying, "If we are going along a road, and he who is leading us forgets the way, is it necessary for us to tell him?" Abba Sisoes said to them, "No." Then a brother asked, "Do we then let him lead us astray?" The old man said to him, "What then? You have a stick, can you not take it and smite him? Now I knew twelve brethren who were traveling along the road at night. He who was leading them lost the way, and all the brethren knew that he had done so. Every one of them struggled with his thoughts, and decided not to tell him. When the day had come he who had been leading them learned that he had wandered off the road. He made excuses and said to them, "Forgive me because I lost the way" and they all said, "We all knew it, brother, but we held our peace." When he heard this he marvelled, saying, "The brethren would endure even to death and would never utter a word." He glorified God. The distance, which they had wandered from the road, was twelve miles.

202. Certain brethren came to Abba Anthony, and said to him, "Speak to us a word whereby we may live." The old man said to them, "Behold, you have heard the Scriptures, and they are sufficient for you." The brethren said, "We wish to hear a word from you also, O father." Abba Anthony said to them, "It is said in the Gospel, 'If a man smite you on the one cheek, turn to him the other also (Luke 6:29).'" They said to him, "We cannot do this." Abba Anthony said to them, "If you cannot turn the other cheek, continue to be smitten on the one cheek" They said to him, "And this we cannot do." The old man said to them, "If you cannot do even this, do not pay back blows in return for the smiting which you have received." They added saying, "We cannot even do this." Then the old man said to his disciples, "Make then for the brethren a little boiled food, for they are ill." He said to them, "If you cannot do this, and you are unable to do the other things, prayers are necessary forthwith."

203. They used to say that Mother Sara, who dwelt above the river and was sixty years old, had never looked out from her abode and seen the river.

204. A certain old man dwelt in the desert at a distance of ten miles from the monastery, where he had always to draw water from. On one occasion the matter became very wearisome to him, and he said, "What is the necessity for me to labor so much? I will come and will take up my abode by the side of this stream." Having said this, he turned behind him and saw a man coming after him, who was counting his footsteps, and he asked him, saying, "Who are you?" He answered him, saying, "I am an angel of the Lord, and I have been sent to count your footsteps, and to give you your reward." Having heard this, the old man was consoled greatly, and went five miles further from the place where he was, and took up his abode there.

205. They say that three thieves went into the cell of Abba Theodore. Two of them laid hold upon him while the third carried off the things, which he had in his cell. Having taken out even the books which he had there, they were going to carry away his cloak, when he said to them, "Leave me this" As they refused to do so, he moved his arms and hands and hurled the two men who were holding him from him, and when they saw this they were afraid. Then the old man said to them, "Do not fear, but divide what you have taken into four parts, take three of them, and leave me one."

206. They used to say that the cave in Patara, which belonged to Abba Chaeremon who was in Scete, was forty miles distant from the church, and twelve miles further from a spring of water. He used to bring to the church, with the labor of his hands, two pitchers of water, one for each day, and when he was tired he would set one down by the roadside and go back afterwards and fetch it.

207. They used to say also that the cell of the blessed Arsenius was thirty-two miles from the church, but he never went anywhere and others brought him whatever he required.

208. The blessed Arsenius never changed the water where he soaked the leaves, which he twisted into ropes except once a year. Instead, he used to add frequently to it, for he twisted palm leaves and sewed them together until the sixth hour daily. The fathers entreated him, saying, "Tell us why you do not change the water of the leaves, for it is very foul." The old man answered, saying, "It is right that I should endure this foul smell in return for the odours of the sweet scents, and oils, and delightful odours, which I enjoyed when I was in the world."

209. It is related of a certain old man that if he heard a brother speak evilly to him he would labor very hard to make something which would please the brother who had spoken to him, and that if that brother did not live with him, the old man would send whatever he had made to the place where he was.

210. A certain old man used to say; "It is a disgrace for a monk to enter into judgement with the man who has done him an injury."

211. A brother asked a certain old man, saying, "Tell me one thing whereby I shall live if I keep it." The old man said to him, "If you can endure being reviled and cursed, this command is the greatest of all the commandments."

212. A brother asked Abba Poemen, saying, "What shall I do to my heart which wanes and is frightened if a little toil and tribulation overtake me, or if temptation comes upon me?" The old man said to him, "Therefore we should wonder and admire the righteous man Joseph who, being only a very young man that is to say, seventeen years of age was sold into slavery into the land of Egypt, the land of the worshippers of idols, and he endured temptations, and God made him glorious to the end."

213. And he said, "We may consider also the blessed Job, who never became sluggish, for he persevered in his trust in his God, and his enemies were not able to shake him from his hope."

214. On one occasion the brethren who were in Scete were cleaning and dressing palm leaves, and there was among them a man who had become ill through his excessive spiritual labors. He was coughing, and bringing up clots of phlegm and spittle and as he spat, involuntarily, some of the spittle fell upon a certain brother. Then the mind of that brother on whom the spittle had fallen said to him, "Tell that brother not to spit upon you." But immediately he licked up the spittle, and he turned and said to his mind, "You have not licked up the spittle, therefore do not tell him not to spit upon you."

215. Abba Poemen used to say that John Colobos, who made entreaty to God, eventually had his passions removed from him, and he was set free from anxious care, so he went and said to a famous old man, "I perceive that my soul is at rest, and that it has neither war nor strife to trouble it." Then the old man said to him, "Go and entreat God to let war and strife come to you again, for it is through war and strife that the soul advances in spiritual excellence." Afterwards, whenever war stood up before him, he did not pray, "O Lord, remove striving from me," but he made supplication to God, saying, "O Lord, give me patience to endure the strife."

216. There was a certain man, who had affection for the brotherhood within him. He had never had in his mind any evil thought. A certain brother stole some things, brought them and deposited them with him. The man did not perceive by what means the brother had obtained them. Some days later the matter was discovered, and it was pointed out to the owner of the things that they had been deposited with the old man, who made excuses to them, saying, "Forgive me, for I repent." After a few days the brother who had stolen the things came to him, and began to demand them from the old man, saying, "You did take the things." The old man made excuses to him, saying, "Forgive me." The old man brought out all the work of his hands, and gave it to him, and the brother took it and departed. Now the disposition of the old man was such that, if one of the brethren committed a fault, and denied it, he would make excuses for him, saying, "It was me who did this thing." The holy man was meek and humble, and he never aggrieved or blamed any man even by the least word.

217. A certain brother lived by himself, and he was disturbed in his mind. He went and revealed the matter to Abba Theodore of Parme. The old man said to him, "Go, humble your mind, and submit yourself to live with the brethren." So he went, did as the old man had told him, and took up his abode with other men. He then went back to the old man, and said, "Father, I am not content to dwell with other men." The old man said to him, "If you are not content to live either by yourself or with others, why did you come out to be a monk? Is not it necessary for you to endure trials? Tell me, how long have you lived this life?" The brother said to him, "Eight years." The old man said to him, "Truly I have led the life I lead now for seventy years, and not one pleasure has come in my way the whole time, and yet you wish to find rest in eight years!"

218. A certain brother, who had vanquished Satan in everything, subsequently had his eyes blinded by Satan so that he could not see, yet this blessed man did not pray for himself, and that he might be able to see, but he only prayed that he might be able to endure patiently his trial and through his constancy his eyes were opened.

219. A monk was smitten by a man on the leg and was severely injured. The holy monk was neither angry nor wroth with him who had smitten him. He nursed the wounded spot, and made excuses to the man who had struck him.

220. Abba Arsenius used to say, "When an unbaked or moist brick is laid in the foundations of a building by the river-side, it will not support it, but if it be burnt in the furnace it will support the building like a stone. It is thus with the man who possesses a carnal mind, and who does not become hot and burn with heat, even as did Joseph with the word of God, for when he comes to have dominion he will be found to be wanting. For very many of those upon whom trials have come have straightaway been swept away and have fallen. Therefore, it is a good thing for a man to know the gravity of dominion, and to be required to bear trials, which are like the onset of many mighty waters, so that he may remain firm and unmoved. And of this holy man Joseph if a man wishes to have the story told Arsenius used to say that He was not a being of earth at all so much was he tempted. And consider the country of Egypt where formerly there was not even a trace of the fear of God! But the God of his fathers was with him, and He delivered him out of all his tribulations, and Joseph is now with his fathers in the kingdom of heaven and let us also make supplication with all our might that we too may in the same manner be able to flee from and escape from the righteous judgement of God."

221. They say that there was with Abba Isidore, the priest of Scete, a certain brother who was infirm in his mind, and he was a man who used abusive language and possessed very little intelligence. Abba Isidore wished to turn him out from his abode. When that brother came to the door of the monastery, the old man said once again, "Bring him to me," and he rebuked him, saying, "Brother, be silent, lest through your little intelligence and impatience you provoke our Lord to anger." Thus by his long suffering Abba Isidore quieted that brother.

222. A lover of ascetic labors saw a man carrying a dead person on a bier, and he said to him, "Do you carry a dead man? Go and carry the living."

223. They say that there was a certain monk who, whenever he found a man reviling and cursing him, used to run towards him with all his power, saying, "These words are the causes of spiritual excellence in those who are strenuous, for those who ascribe blessing to a man disturb the soul, as it is written, 'Those who ascribe blessing to you lead astray your soul.'"

224. Certain old men came to an old man who dwelt in the desert that they might reveal to him their thoughts, and might profit by his knowledge. They found some young men outside his cell who were pasturing sheep, and they were saying to one another unseemly and inappropriate words. The old men said to the old man, "Father, how is it that you do not command these young men not to curse?" The old man said to them, "My brethren, believe me, I have many times wished to command them not to do so, but I have rebuked myself, saying, 'If you can not endure this little thing, how could you bear some severe trial if it were to come upon you?' I have therefore never said anything to them, so that the matter might be a cause of remembering that I have to endure the things, which are to come."

225. A certain brother ministered to one of the sick fathers. His disease was a decline of the body, and he used to bring up pus and the mind of the brother said to him, "Flee from him, for you can not endure this smell." Then the brother took an earthen vessel and put into it some of the water in which the old man had washed, and when he was thirsty he used to drink some of it and his mind began to say to him, "Flee not, but drink not of this filthy water." But that brother labored on greatly in respect of the water in which the sick man had washed, and all his soul shrank from that filthiness. He persevered in drinking it and God saw his labor and tribulation, and He changed the filthy washing water which was in the earthen vessel into clean water, and He healed that old man.

226. One of the monks wished to go out from his monastery and to wander about so that he might have a little relaxation and enjoyment. When they saw him, an old man said to him, "Do not seek gratification in this world, O my son, but work rather and persevere in the invincible power of the Holy Trinity."

227. Abba Moses used to say, "The secret withdrawal from work makes the mind dark, but for a man to endure and to persevere in his works makes the mind light in our Lord, and it strengthens and fortifies the soul."

228. And he used to say also, "Bear disgrace and affliction in the Name of Jesus with humility and a troubled heart, and show before Him your feebleness and He will become your might."

229. Certain people praised one of the brethren before the blessed Abba Anthony. When that brother came to the blessed man, the old man put him to the test, and he found that he could not bear contempt and disdain. The old man said to him, "You are like a palace the front of which is decorated and beautiful, but its back has been broken into by thieves and plundered."

230. A brother asked an old man a question, saying, "What shall I do?" And the old man said to him, "Go and learn to love putting restraint upon you in everything."

231. One of the old men said concerning Lazarus, the poor man, "We cannot find that Lazarus ever did one excellent thing except that he never murmured against the rich man as being one who had never shown him an act of mercy but he bore his infirmity with the giving of thanks, and because of this God took him to Himself."

232. Abba Macarius used to say, "If you account contempt as an honor, and blame as praise, and poverty as wealth, you will not die."

233. A certain brother asked Abba Poemen, saying, "What do these words mean: 'If a man be angry with his brother without a cause? (Matt. 5:22)'" The old man said to him, "If your brother makes use of oppression, wrong, and fraud to you, and you are angry with him because of these, you are angry with him without a cause. And if he tears out your right eye, or cuts off your right hand, and you are angry with him, you are angry with him without a cause. But if a man wishes to separate you or to put you away from God, then it is a good thing to be angry and wrathful with him."

234. There were two men in the desert, who were brothers, and a devil came to separate them from each other. One day the younger brother lit a lamp and set it upon a candlestick, but, by the agency of the devil, he overturned the candlestick and extinguished the lamp. Then the elder brother was angry and hit him. The younger brother made excuses to him, saying, "Have a little patience with me, and I will light the lamp again." When God saw his patient endurance, He punished that devil until the morning and the devil came and told the prince of devils what had happened. There was with the prince of devils a certain priest of idols. Straightaway this man left everything, and he went and became a monk. At the very beginning he laid hold upon humility, saying, "Humility is being able to bring to naught all the power of the adversary, as I have heard the devils saying, 'Whenever we stir the monks up, they turn to humility, and they make excuses one to the other, and thus they do away all our power.'"

235. Abba Poemen said that Abba Isidore, the priest of the church, on one occasion spoke to the people, saying, "My brethren, when you are working in a certain place it is not strength to depart from there because of the labor and as for myself, I wrap myself up in my cloak and I go to the place where labor is, and labor becomes a pleasure to me."

236. Paesius, the brother of Abba Poemen, had affection for the people who

On Patient Endurance 65

were outside his monastery. Abba Poemen did not wish this to be, and he rose up and fled to Abba Ammon, saying to him, "My brother Paesius has made a promise of love to certain folk, and I am not pleased at that." Abba Ammon said to him, "Poemen, you are still alive. Go, sit in you cell, and meditate in you mind, saying, 'Behold, there is a year for you in the grave.'"

237 There were two monks, living in one place, and an old man came to them, and wished to put them to the test. He took a stick, and began to beat to pieces the garden herbs of one of them. When one monk saw him doing this, he hid himself. When only one root was left, the other brother said to the old man, "Father, if it pleases you, leave me this root that I may boil it and we may eat together." Then the old man made excuses to that brother, and said to him, "The Spirit of God has rested upon you, O my brother."

CHAPTER SEVEN

On Obedience towards God, Fathers and Brethren

They say that Abba John, the disciple of Abba Paul, possessed great obedience. In the place where they used to live, there was a sepulchre where there dwelt a savage panther, and Abba Paul saw in it a few little heaps of goods, and he said to John, "Go to the sepulchre and bring me some of the things from there." John said to him, "My father, what shall I do with the panther?" The old man laughed and said to him, "If he comes against you, tie him up and bring him here." So John went there at eventide, and the panther came against him, and when he went to lay hold of him the animal fled from him. Then John pursued him, saying, "My father told me to fetter you," and he seized him, and bound him with cords. Meanwhile the old man was very much troubled about John, and he was sitting waiting for him anxiously and he came dragging along the panther which was tied with ropes. The old man saw and marvelled. Then the brother said to him, "Father, behold, I have taken prisoner the panther according as you commanded, and I have brought him here." The old man, wishing to remove from him the occasion for boasting, hit him, and said, "You have brought a wandering dog!" He untied the animal and let him depart.

239. Abba Joseph used to say, "There are three things which are held in honor before God: first, when a man is sick, and he adds to his toil, and receives it with thanks giving. Secondly, when a man makes all his works to be pure before God, and when he has in them no human consideration. Thirdly, when a man submits himself to authority, and obeys his father, and sets aside his own will. Such a man has one crown the more, but I personally would choose the sickness."

240. They used to say that Abba Sylvanus had in Scete a disciple whose name was Mark, and that he possessed to a great degree the faculty of obedience, he was a scribe, and the old man loved him greatly for his obedience. Sylvanus had eleven other disciples, and they were vexed because they saw that the old man loved Mark more than them. When the old men who were in Scete heard of this they were afflicted about it. One day when they came to him to reprove him about this, Sylvanus took them, went forth, and passed by the cells of the brethren. He knocked at the door of each cell, and said, "O brother, come forth, for I have need of you." He passed by all their cells, and not one of them obeyed him quickly. But when they went to the cell of Mark, he knocked at the door and said, "Brother Mark." As soon as Mark heard the voice of the old man, he jumped up straight way, and came out, and Sylvanus sent him off on some business. Then Sylvanus said to the old men, "My fathers, where are the other brethren?" They went into Mark's cell, looked at the quire of the book which he was writing, and they saw that he had begun to write one side of the Greek letter o (or *w*). As soon as he heard the voice of his master, he ran out and did not stay to complete the other side of the letter. When the old men perceived these things, they answered, and said to Sylvanus, "Truly, O' old man, we also love the brother whom you love, for God also loves him."

241. On another occasion the mother of Mark came to see him. She had with her an abundant company of members of her household. An old man went forth to her, and she said to him, "Abba, tell my son to come forth and see me." The old man went in, and said to him, "Go forth and see your mother." Mark wrapped himself up in rags, and blackened his face by standing up in the sooty chimney, and he went forth thus fulfilling the request of his master, and shutting his eyes, he said to those who were with his mother, "Live you! Live you!" but he did not look at them. His mother did not recognize him, and sent in again to the old man a message, saying, "Send me my son, O father, so that I may see him." Then the old man said to Mark, "Did I not tell you to go out and see your mother?" He said to him, "Father, I went forth according to word, but I beseech you do not tell me to go forth again, lest perhaps I feel myself compelled to disobey you." Then the old man spoke with her, calmed her, and sent her away in peace.

242. They used to tell about two brethren who lived in a monastery, that both had arrived at a high grade in the ascetic life. One devoted himself to an austere life of self denial and poverty, and the other was obedient and humble. Being angry with each other they wished to know which of the two kinds of service was the greater. They went down to the river where there were many crocodiles, and the brother who possessed the faculty of obedience went in, stood up among them, and they all worshipped him. Then he cried out to his fellow who was a mourner, and said to him, "Forgive me, O my brother, I have not yet attained to such a high degree of faith as you have." When they returned to the monastery, the head of the monastery heard a voice, saying, "The man who obeys is better than the man who leads a life of voluntary poverty."

243. Abba Daniel used to say, "On one occasion Abba Arsenius called me and said to me, 'Make your father to be gratified, so that when he goes to our Lord, he may make entreaties to Him on behalf of you, and good shall be to you.'"

244. A certain brother was engaged in a war against Satan, and he told the matter to Abba Herakles and wishing to strengthen and confirm him the old man told him the following story, "There was a certain old man who had a disciple, and he had been very obedient to him for many years, and when the war came upon him, he made a request to his master, saying, 'I beseech you to make me a monk.' The master said to him, 'Seek out a place for yourself, and we will build a cell for you, and you shall become a monk.' The disciple went and found a place, which was distant from his master about one hundred paces, and he made himself a cell. Then the old man said to that brother, 'Whatever I say to you, that do. When you are hungry, eat and when you are thirsty, drink and sleep, but you must not go out from your cell until the Sabbath Day, when you shall come to me.' Then the old man went back to his cell. The brother did according to what the old man told him for two days, but on the third day he became dejected, wearied, and he said, 'What has the old man done for me, seeing that he has not commanded me to make prayers?' Then he rose up and sang more Psalms than usual. After the sun had set he ate his food, he rose up, went, laid down upon his mat and he saw, as it were, an Ethiopian who stood up and gnashed his teeth at him. The monk, by reason of his great fear, ran quickly to his master, and he knocked hastily at his door, saying, 'Father, have mercy upon me, and open to me immediately.' Now because the old man knew that he had not kept his commandment he refused to open the door to him until the morning. When he opened the door in the morning, he found him there, and as the brother entreated him to be allowed to enter, the old man had compassion upon him and brought him in. Then he began to say to the old man, 'I beseech you, O father, to believe me. When I went to lie down to go to sleep, I saw a black Ethiopian on my bed.' The old man said to him, 'This happened because you did not keep my words.' Then he laid down a rule for him which was suitable to his strength and to the monastic life, and dismissed him, and little by little he became an excellent monk.

245. A man who wanted to be a monk came to Abba Sisoes the Theban, and the old man asked him if he had any possession whatever in the world. He said, "I have one son," and the old man, wishing to find out if he possessed the faculty of obedience, said to him, "Go, and throw him in the river, and then come, and you shall be a monk." Because the man was obedient he went straightaway to do that. When he had departed the old man sent another brother to prevent him from doing this thing. When the man had taken up his son to throw him into the river, the brother said to him, "You shall not cast him in." Then the man said to him, "My father told me that I was to cast him in." The brother replied, "He told me that you were not to cast him in," so the man left him, and came to the old man, and through his obedience he became a chosen monk.

246. The Abba who was in Iliu used to say, "Obedience comes into existence because of obedience for if a man obeys God, God also will obey him."

247. On one occasion four brethren came to Abba Pambo from Scete. They were wearing skins, and each one of them, whilst his neighbor was absent, recounted to him his works, saying, "The first one fasts very often, and the second leads a life of poverty, and the third possesses great love, and concerning the fourth the other three said, "He has been in subjection to the old men for twenty-two years." Then Abba Pambo said to them, "I say to you that the spiritual excellence of this man is great. Each of you has chosen the ascetic virtue which he possesses according to his own wish, but this man has cut off his own desire, and has performed the will of others and those who are thus will, if they keep these things to the end, become confessors."

CHAPTER EIGHT

On Scrupulous Watchfulness in our Thoughts, Words and Deeds

Abba Poemen used to say, "Satan has three kinds of power which precede all sin. The first is error, and the second is neglect (or laxity), and the third is lust." When error happens it produces neglect, and from neglect springs lust, and by lust man falls. If we watch against error, neglect will not happen, and if we are not negligent, lust will not appear. And if a man does not lust, he will, through the help of Christ, never fall.

249. They used to say that there was a certain father who was occupied in great works. On one occasion, while he was singing the Psalms and praying, one of the holy men came to him, and he heard him striving with his thoughts, and saying, "How long for the sake of one thought will you go through all this?" Then the man who had come thought that the father was striving with another man, and he knocked at the door before going in to make peace between them but when he had gone inside he saw no other man there. Because he possessed some authority over the father, he said to him, "Father, with whom were you striving?" And he said, "With my thoughts. For I can repeat fourteen Books, but if I hear one little word outside it will render my service useless to me, and the repetition of all these Books will be in vain. And this word only comes and stands before me at the season of prayer, and it is because of this that I strive." When the holy man heard these things, he marvelled at the spiritual excellence and purity of the old man, and how openly he had told him about his war.

250. One of the old men used to say, "The Prophets compiled the Scriptures, and the Fathers have copied them, and the men who came after them learned to repeat them by heart then has come this generation and its children have placed them in cupboards as useless things."

251. A disciple of Abba Ammon told the following story. On one occasion when we were singing the service, my mind became confused, and I forgot the verse in the Psalm. When we had ended the service Abba Ammon said to me, "Whilst I was standing up during the service it seemed that I was standing on fire and was being consumed, and my mind was unable to make me turn aside either to the right hand or to the left. As for you, where was your mind when we were singing the service? For you did omit a verse from the Psalm. Did not you know that you were standing in the presence of God, and that you were speaking to Him?"

252. A certain brother came to dwell in a cell with one of the fathers, and he told him of a thought whereby he was afflicted and the old man said to him, "You have left upon the earth the excellent service of the fear of God, and you have taken and have laid hold upon a staff made of a reed, that is to say, evil thoughts. Take to yourself the fear of God, which is the fire, and as soon as they come near to you they shall be burned like reeds. Now this man was, according to what his disciple related about him, a great old man, and for twenty years he never lay upon either of his sides, but slept upon the seat whereon he sat to work. Sometimes he ate once in two days, and at other times once in four days, and at others once in five days, and in this manner he passed twenty years. Now I said to him, "What is this which you do, O father?" He said to me, "Because I set the judgement of God before my eyes I cannot be negligent, for I keep in remembrance the fact that my sins are many."

253. Whilst Abba Arsenius was dwelling in Canopus of Alexandria a certain noble lady came to him. She was a virgin, exceedingly rich, and fearing the Lord. She was from Rome and had come to see Abba Arsenius. Theophilus, Archbishop of Alexandria, received her, and she begged him to entreat the old man to receive her. Theophilus went to Abba Arsenius and entreated him, saying, "Such and such noble lady has come from Rome, and she wishes to see you, and to be blessed by you." The old man refused to receive her. When Theophilus informed her that the old man refused to receive her, she commanded them to make ready the beasts for traveling, saying, "By God, I

On Scrupulous Watchfulness in our Thoughts, Words and Deeds

believe that I shall see him. I did not come to see men, for there are men in my own city, but I came to see a prophet." When she came outside the cell of the old man, he happened through the working of God, to be there. She saw him, and fell down at his feet. Then he lifted her up eagerly, looked at her, and said, "If you wish to look upon my face, behold, look." But she by reason of her bashfulness, was not able to look upon his face. Then the old man said to her, "Have not you heard about my works, and that I am a sinner? For it is these which are necessary for you to see. How did you dare to travel to here by a ship? Did not you know that you were a woman, and that it was incumbent upon you not to go forth anywhere? Would you go back to Rome and make a boast to the women there that you have seen Arsenius, and do you wish to make the sea into a road whereby women shall come to me?" The lady said to him, "Please God I will not let any woman come to you but pray for me that God may have me in remembrance always." Then Abba Arsenius said to her, "I will pray to God that He may blot out the memory of you from my heart." When she heard these words she went forth, being afraid. As soon as she had come to the city a fever began to come upon her because of her grief of mind, and the people told the Bishop, saying, "That noble lady is ill." He came to her, and entreated her to learn the cause of her sickness. Then she said to him, "If only I had never gone there! For I said to the old man Arsenius, 'Make mention of me in prayer,' and he said to me, 'I will pray to God that He may blot out the remembrance of you from my heart, and behold I shall die of grief.' The Archbishop said to her, "Do not you know that you are a woman, and that the enemy does battle with the holy men by means of women? It was for this reason that the old man spoke as he did for your soul, however, he will pray always." The noble lady remembered these things in her mind, rose up, and went to her country with gladness.

254. They say that Abba Hor of the cells dwelt for twenty years in the church, and that he never once lifted his eyes and saw the roof.

255. Abba Ammon asked Abba Poemen about the unclean thoughts which a man begets, and about vain lusts. Abba Poemen said, "Perhaps an axe shall boast itself without him that hews swings it? Do not from here on aid these thoughts and they will come to an end."

256. They say concerning Abba Paphnutius, the disciple of Abba Macarius, that when he was a youth he used to look after the oxen with others of his companions and they went to take some cucumbers to the animals. As they were going along one of the cucumbers fell, Abba Paphnutius took it up and ate it. Whenever he remembered this thing, he used to sit down and weep over it with great feeling.

257. One of the fathers went to Abba Akila and saw that he was throwing up blood from his mouth, and he asked him, saying, "What is this, O father?" and the old man said to him, "It is a word. I was vexed with a certain brother, and I was engaged in a strife of which I knew nothing, and I made supplication to God that it might be taken from me and straightaway that word became blood in my mouth, but when I spat it up I was relieved, and I forgot my vexation."

258. One of the old men used to say, "We were going on one occasion to the mountain of the blessed Anthony to visit Abba Sisoes. When he sat down to eat there came up to us a young man who begged for alms and when we were beginning to eat." The old man said, "Ask that young man if he wishes to come in and eat with us." When one had said this to him, the young man refused to do so, and the old man said, "Let whatsoever is left over by us be given to him to eat outside." Then the old man brought out a jar of wine which he kept for the Offering, and he mixed for each one of us a cup, but he gave to the young man two cups, whereat I smiled, and said to him, "I also will go outside, and you shall give me two cups of wine also." Abba Sisoes said, "If he had eaten with us he would have drunk the same quantity as ourselves, and he would have been convinced that we did not drink more than he did but now he will say in his mind, 'These monks enjoy themselves more than I do.' It is good therefore that our conscience should not hold us in contempt."

259. One of the old men came to another old man who was his companion, and as they were talking together one of them said, "I have died to the world." And his companion said, "Have no confidence in yourself that this is so until you go forth from the world, for although you say, I have died, Satan is not dead."

260. A brother asked Abba Sisoes, saying, "Tell me a word whereby I may live." The old man says to him, "Why do you urge me, O brother, to speak a useless word? Whatsoever you see me do, that do yourself."

261. A brother asked Abba Poemen, saying, "Is it possible for a man to keep hold upon all thoughts, and not to give any of them to the enemy?" The old man said to him, "There are some of them who give ten and keep one, and there are some who give one and keep ten." The brother told this saying to Abba Sisoes, who said, "There are some who do not give even one thought to the enemy."

262. Abba Joseph asked Abba Sisoes, saying, "How many times is it right for a man to cut off his passions?" The old said to him, "Do you wish to learn when you must cut them off?" and Joseph said to him, "Yes." Abba Sisoes said to him, "Whenever passion comes cut it off immediately."

263. Abba Nastir and a certain brother were walking together in the desert when they saw a serpent. They both took to flight and the brother said to Nastir, "Father, are you afraid too?" The old man said to him, "My son, I am not afraid, but it was a beneficial thing for me to flee, for otherwise, I should not have been able to escape from the thought of the love of approbation."

264. Certain men who lived in the world came to see Abba Sisoes, and although they spoke much, he held his peace and did not answer them a word. After a while, one of them said to his companions, "My brethren, why do you trouble the old man? He does not eat, and for this reason he is not able to talk." When the old man heard this, he answered straightaway, saying, "My sons, I eat whenever I feel the need of eating."

265. On one occasion a certain judge of the district wished to see Abba Poemen, but the old man refused to see him. Like a crafty man, the judge made an excuse, seized Abba's nephew, and threw him into prison, saying, "Unless Abba comes and makes entreaty on his behalf he shall not go out." Then the Abba's sister came and stood by the door of his cell and wept for her son. Although she relentlessly pursued him, he did not give her an answer. When the woman saw this she began to revile him, saying, "O you who possess mercy of brass, have mercy upon me, for my son is the only child I have." Abba Poemen sent her a message, saying, "Poemen has no sons," and thus she departed. When the judge heard these things he answered, saying, "If Abba will only give the order I will release him." After this the old man sent him a message, saying, "Examine and consider his case according to the Law, and if he deserves death, let him die and if he does not, do whatever you please with him."

266. They say that in the mountain of Abba Anthony seven brethren dwelt, each used to watch for the date season and drive away the birds. Among them was an old man who used to cry out, when it was his day for watching the dates, saying, "Depart, O you evil thoughts, from within, and depart, O you birds, from without."

267. On one occasion the Arabs came and plundered Abba Sisoes and the brother who was with him of everything they had. Being hungry, the brethren went out into the desert to find something to eat. When they were some distance from each other, Abba Sisoes found some camel dung, he broke it, and found inside two grains of barley. He ate one grain and placed the other in his hand. When the brother came, and found that he was eating, he said to him, "Is this love? You have found food, and you eat it by yourself and have not called me to share it with you." Abba Sisoes said to him, "I have not defrauded you, O brother, for behold, I have kept your share in my hands."

268. Mother Sarah used to say, "Whenever I put my foot on the ladder to go up, before I ascend it I set my death before mine eyes."

269. A certain brother came to Abba Theodore and entreated him to show him how he twisted palm leaves, and he sent him away, saying, "Go away, and come here tomorrow morning." The old man rose up straightaway, put some leaves to soak in water, and made it ready. When the brother came in the morning he showed him how to make one or two plaits, and said to him, "Work thus." The old man left him and went to his cell. At the proper season the old man took him food and made him eat, he rose up and went away. When he came back again in the morning, the old man said to him, "Why did not you take some palm leaves with you? Take some now, and get going, for you have made me fall into the temptation of caring about things," and he did not allow him to come inside his cell again.

270. On one occasion Abba Muthues and his brother Awsabh, went from Reith to Mount Gebel. Kantirsa, the Bishop, took the old man and made him a priest. When they were eating together the Bishop said to him, "Forgive me, Abba, for I know that you did not wish for this thing, but I ventured to do this thing that I might be blessed by you." The old man said to him with a meek spirit, and with a sorrowful mind, "I will labor in this work, though I must be separated from this my brother who is with me, for I cannot endure the making of all the prayers." The Bishop said to him, "If you know that he is worthy I will make him a priest also." Abba Muthues said to him, "Whether he is worthy or not I do not know, but one thing I know, and that is, that he is better than I am." So the Bishop laid his hands upon him and made him a priest also. They ended their lives together, but one of them never approached the altar for the purpose of offering up the Offering, for the old man used to say, "By God, I hope that ordination does not make it obligatory on me to do so, because I cannot offer up the Offering, for ordination belongs to those who are pure only."

271. A certain brother in Scete called one of his companions to come to him in his cell to wash his feet, and he did not go and twice and thrice he said, "Come to my cell, and wash your feet," and he did not go. After sometime, the brother went to him, and made excuses to him, and entreated him to go with him. He rose up, went and the brother said to him, "How is it that you did not come when I entreated you so often to do so?" He answered and said to him, "Whilst you were speaking my will would not consent to my coming, but when I saw that you were doing the work of monks, that is to say, repenting, then I rejoiced and came."

272. On one occasion when the old man Zeno was walking in Palestine. He became weary, sat down by the side of a cucumber bed to eat, and his thought said to him, "Take a cucumber and eat, for of what value is one cucumber?" He answered and said to his thought, "Those who steal go to torment, try your soul then, and see if it is able to endure the torment." He crucified himself in the heat for five days. Having tortured himself he said to his thought, "I cannot endure that torment how then can the man who cannot do this steal and eat?"

273. They say that on one occasion, when it was time for Abba Poemen to go to the congregation for the service, he sat down for about one hour examining and passing judgement upon his thoughts, and at the end of this time he went forth.

274. They say that a certain old man dwelt by himself in silence, and that a son of the world used to minister him continually. It happened that the son of that son of the world fell sick, and his father entreated the old man to go with him to his house and to pray over him. When he had entreated him to do so often, the old man went with him. The man went before him and entered the village, and he said to the people, "Come forth to meet the monk now." The old man saw the people from a distance, and perceived that they came to meet him carrying lanterns. He immediately stripped off his garments, dipped them in the river, and he began to wash them, being naked. When the man who ministered him saw this, he was ashamed, and entreated the people of the village, saying, "Get back, for the old man has certainly gone mad," then he approached the old man, and said to him, "Father, what have you done? For all the people are saying that the old man has a devil." The old man said, "This is what I wished to hear."

275. Paesius on one occasion had a strife with the brother who was with him whilst Abba Poemen was sitting by, and they fought with each other until the blood ran down from both their heads. Although the old man saw them, he uttered no word whatsoever. Then Abba Job came and found them fighting, and he said to Poemen, "Why have you let these brethren fight, and you have said nothing to them whilst they have been fighting?" Abba Poemen said to him, "They are brethren, and will become reconciled again." Abba Job said, "What have you said? You see that they continue to fight, and yet you say that they will be reconciled again." Abba Poemen said to him, "You must think in your heart that I am not here."

276. Mother Sarah sent a message to Abba Paphnutius, saying, "Do you think that you are doing God's work in allowing your brother to be reviled?" Abba Paphnutius said, "Paphnutius is here doing the work of God, and I have no concern whatsoever about man."

277. The old man Poemen used to say, "You shall have no dealings whatsoever with a child of the world, and you shall hold no converse with women." He also said, "You shall possess no knowledge of the judge or governor, lest, when you hear his words, you perform his work."

278. One of the old men used to say, "I have never taken one step forwards without first learning where I was about to set my foot, and I have neither crossed my boundary to walk on a height, nor have I descended into a deep place, and been troubled by so doing for my only care has been to beseech God until He brought me forth from the old man."

279. On one occasion the brethren were gathered together in Scete that they might enquire into the history of Melchizedek. They forgot to invite Abba Copres to be with them. Finally, they did call him, and enquired of him concerning the matter. He hit three times on his mouth, saying, "Woe be to you! Woe be to you, O Copres, for you have left what God commanded you to do undone, and you are enquired of concerning the things which God has not demanded of you," and they all left the place and fled to their cells.

280. An old man used to say, "Freedom of speech (or boldness) is a wind which parches, and it smites the fruit at the harvest."

281. An old man used to say, "The act of despising oneself is a strong fence for a man."

282. An old man said, "The withdrawal in secret from works makes dark the understanding, but the persisting in endurance with vigilance illuminated and strengthened the soul of a man."

283. An old man used to say, "Laughter and familiar talking are like the fire which kindles among the reeds."

284. Certain heretics came on one occasion to Abba Poemen, and began to calumniate the Archbishop of Alexandria, and to speak evil things concerning him. They sought to prove that as they had received consecration from the priests, they were consecrated like other priests and the old man held his peace. Then he called his brother, and said to him, "Make ready a table and make them eat," and he dismissed them that they might depart in peace.

285. Some of the old men asked Abba Poemen, saying, "If we see one of the brethren committing sin, would you wish us rebuke him?" The old man said to them, "If I had some business which made me pass by him, and in passing by him I saw him committing sin, I should pass by him and not see him."

286. The old man also said, "It is written, 'Whatever your eyes have seen, that declare. But I say to you, that unless you have not first touched with your hands, you shall not testify.' For on one occasion the devil led astray a brother in a matter of this kind. This brother saw a brother committing sin with a woman, and the war being strong against him, he went to them, thinking that what he saw was really a man and a woman, and he kicked them with his foot, and said, 'Enough, enough, how long will you act thus?' Suddenly he discovered that the things were sacks of wheat. For this reason I say to you that unless you have felt with your hands you should not offer rebuke."

287. One of the fathers related a story, saying: "On one occasion in Scete when the clergy were offering up the Offering, something which was like to an eagle descended upon the Offering, and no man saw the appearance except the clergy and one day a brother questioned the deacon about the matter." The deacon said to him, "I am not at leisure now to discuss it." Afterwards, when the time arrived for the Offering, and the clergy went in as usual, the form of the eagle did not appear as it did before and the priest said to the deacon, "What is this? The eagle has not come as usual, and the fault of this lies either upon me or you. But get you gone from me, and if the eagle then appears and descends, it will be evident that it did not come down now because of you, and if it does not descend you will know that the fault is mine." As soon as the deacon departed, the eagle appeared as usual, and after the Office had been said, and the service was ended, the priest said to the deacon, "Tell me what have you done." The deacon, wishing to show him everything, made excuses, saying, "I am not conscious in my soul of having committed any sin, except when a brother came to me, and asked me a question on the matter, and I made answer to him, saying, 'I am not at leisure to talk with you.' Then the priest said, "It was because of you that the eagle came not down, for the brother was offended at you." Immediately, the deacon went to the brother, expressed his contrition, and entreated him to forgive him his offence.

288. They used to speak about a certain father, who for seven years asked God to give him a certain gift. After long time, it was given to him. He went to a great old man and told him about the gift. When the old man heard, he was grieved, and said, "What great labor!" Then he said to the father, "Go and spend seven years more in entreating God that the gift may be taken away from you, for it will do you no good." The old man went, and did as he was told, until the gift was taken away from him.

289. A certain brother dwelt in a cell outside his village, and he had passed many years without going into the village and he said to the brethren who were with him, "Behold, how many years have I lived here without going into the village, while you are always going there." Now Abba Poemen was told about this man, and that he used to say words of this kind to the brethren, he said, "If I were that man I would go up and walk round about in the village during the night, so that my thoughts might not be able to boast themselves that I had not gone into it."

290. One of the fathers said, "God bears with the sins of those who live in the world, but He will not endure the sins of those who live in the desert."

291. Abba Job used to say, "Since the time when I was first called by the Name of Christ, falsehood has never gone out from my mouth."

292. Abba Poemen used to say, "If a man dwells with a youth, however much he may guard his thoughts he makes a means for sin."

293. A certain brother asked an old man, saying, "What shall I do because of my negligence?" The old man said, "If you do not root out this small plant, which is negligence, a great forest will come into being."

294. Abba Poemen used to say, "Do not dwell in a place where you see those who have envy against you, for if you do you will never advance."

295. Abba Chronius used to say, "The man who dwells with a youth will, unless he be mighty, go downwards, and if he is mighty, even though he does not go downwards temporarily, yet he will never advance in spiritual excellence."

296. Abba Anthony used to say, "There are some monks who trouble their bodies with the labors of abstinence and self-denial, and are remote from the path of God, because they have not found understanding."

297. Abba Poemen used to say, "Teach your heart to keep what your tongue teaches."

298. Abba Poemen used to say, "One man is thought to be silent, yet his heart condemns others, and he who is thus speaks everything and another speaks from morn until evening, and yet keeps silence, but such a man speaks not without profit."

299. I have heard that there were two old men who dwelt together for many years, and never quarrelled. One said to the other, "Let us also pick a quarrel with each other, even as other men do." Then his companion answered and said to him, "I do not know how a quarrel comes," and the other old man answered and said to him, "Behold, I will set a brick in the midst, and will say, 'This is mine,' and do you say, 'It is not yours, but mine' and from this a quarrel will ensue." They placed a brick in the midst, and one of them said, "This is mine," and his companion answered and said after him, "This is not so, for it is mine" and straightaway the other replied and said to him, "If it be so, and the brick be yours, take it and go." Thus they were not able to make a quarrel.

300. There was a certain brother who lived a life of extreme strict seclusion. The devils, wishing to lead him astray, used to appear to him, when he was sleeping at night, in the form of angels, wake him up to sing the Psalms and pray, and they would show him a light. He went to an old man, and said to him, "Father, the devils come to me with a light and wake me up to sing and pray," and the old man said to him, "Hearken not to them, O my son, for they are devils, but, if they come to wake you up, say to them, 'When I wish to rise up I will do so, but to you I will not hearken.'" When they came to wake him he said to them what the old man had told him, and they said to him forthwith, "That wicked old man is a liar, and he has led you astray. For a certain brother came to him and wished to borrow some silver coins on a pledge, and although he had money to lend, he lied and said, 'I have none,' and he gave him none, and learn from this thing that he is a liar." Then the brother rose up early in the morning and went to the old man and related to him everything which he had heard, and the old man said to him, "The matter is thus. I had some oboli (silver coins), and a brother came and asked me for some money, and I would not give him any because I saw that if I did so we should arrive at the loss of our souls. I made up my mind that I would treat with contempt one of the commandments, and not ten, and therefore we came to enmity with each other. But do not hearken to the devils who wish to lead you astray." When he had been greatly confirmed by the old man, that monk departed to his cell.

301. Abba Isaac, the priest of the cells, said, "I saw a certain brother reaping the harvest in the field, and he wanted to eat one ear of wheat." He said to the owner of the field, "Do you wish me to take one ear of wheat to eat?" The owner wondered (now he profited greatly there from), and said to him, "My son, the field is yours, and do you ask my permission to eat?" To this extent that brother showed conscientious care.

302. A brother asked an old man, saying, "What shall I do? For the thoughts which make war with me are many, and I know not how to contend against them." The old man said to him, "Do not strive against them all, but against one, for all devilish thoughts have only one head, and it is necessary for a man to understand and to make war upon this head only, for afterwards all the rest will perforce be brought low. Just as in war, if on one side a very mighty man appear, the men on the other side use every means in their power to set up in opposition to him a mighty man who is stronger than he is, because, if he be able to hurl down that chief, all the rest will take to flight and be vanquished. In this same manner there is one head to all the thoughts which come from devils, whether it be fornication, or riotous living, or love of money, or wandering about from place to place, for if you will first of all recognize it and will drive it out, it will not lead you astray in respect of other things. When that chief thought came, and stood up and fought against him, he recognized which it was, and contended against it only."

303. Abba Lot went to Abba Joseph, and said to him, "Father, according to my strength I sing a few Psalms, and I pray a little, my fasting is little, my prayers and silent meditations are few, and as far as my power permits, I cleanse my

On Scrupulous Watchfulness in our Thoughts, Words and Deeds

thoughts. What more can I do?" Then the old man stood up, spread out his hands towards heaven, with his fingers like ten lamps of fire, and said, "If you wish, let the whole of you be like to fire."

304. A certain brother entreated one of the old men to interpret to him some words which he had asked him, saying, "If I see a man doing something, and I tell others about it, I mean not by way of passing judgment upon him, but merely for the sake of conversation, would this be considered as evil talk of the thoughts?" The old man said to him, "If there is any motion of passion, the repetition is wicked. But if it is free from passion, the repetition is not wicked, but speak in such a way so that the evil does not increase." Another brother made answer to the old man, saying, "If I come to one of the old men and ask him, saying, 'I wish to dwell with such and such a man, may I do so? and I know at the same time that it will not be profitable for me, what answer must he give to me?' If he says, 'You shall not go, has he not condemned that man in his mind?' Then the old man answered him saying, "This refinement of thought is not given to many, and I do not regard it as a sure matter. If there be any passion in the motion of the soul I should say that he would injure himself but in words there is no power to do so. And as to 'What is he bound to say?' I say that I do not know, if his soul be not free from passion but if it be free from passions he will not condemn any man, and he will condemn himself, and say, I am a changeable person, now perhaps this will not help you, but if he be a man of understanding he will not go. Now the old man did not speak concerning wickedness, but how wickedness might not be multiplied."

305. Abba Arsenius said to Abba Alexander, "When you have finished the work of your hands, come to me and we will eat. But if strangers come, eat with them, and do not come to me." Alexander continued at his work late, and when the time for the meal arrived, and palm leaves were still standing before him, although he was anxious to keep the word of the old man, he also wanted to finish up the leaves, and then to go to him. When the old man saw that Abba Alexander delayed in coming to eat, he thought it was because strangers had come to him. When Abba Alexander finished his work he went to the old man, who said to him, "Did strangers come to you?" Alexander said to him, "No, father." Then the old man said to him, "Why have you delayed in coming?" Alexander answered and said, "Because you did say to me, 'When you have finished your leaves come to me and paying heed to your word, and having finished my work, behold, I have come.'" The old man marvelled at this scrupulous obedience, and said to him, "Make haste, perform your service of praise and prayer, when it ends drink some water, for if you dost not do it quickly your body will become sick."

306. Abba Poemen used to say, "We need nothing except a watchful and strenuous heart."

307. A brother asked Abba Poemen, saying, "How is it right for me to live in the place where I am?" The old man replied, "Acquire the thought of sojourning in the place where you live, and desire not to cast your word among the multitude, or to be the first to speak, and you will find rest."

308. Abba Agathon said concerning Abba Muam that, on one occasion, he made fifty bushels of wheat into bread for the needs of the community, and then laid it out in the sun, but before it became dry and hard he saw something in the place which was not helpful to him, and he said to the brethren who were with him, "Arise, let us go hence." They were greatly grieved. When he saw that they were grieved, he said to them, "Are you troubled about the bread? Truly I have seen men take to flight and forsake their cells, although they were well whitewashed and contained cupboards which were filled with books of the Holy Scriptures and service books, and they did not even shut the cupboard doors, but departed leaving them wide open."

309. Abba Copres used to say, "Blessed is the man who bears temptation with thanksgiving."

310. Abba Poemen used to say, "The mighty ones have been many, and those who never felt envy have been many, and they have neither been jealous in an evil way, nor have they stirred up their own passions."

311. Abba Sisoes used to say, "Seek the Lord, and search for Him, not only in the place where you dwell."

312. An old man used to say, "Do not eat before you are hungry, do not lie down to sleep before you are sleepy and do not speak before you are asked a question."

313. An old man used to say, "Do not prepare a table before the time when you are alone, and do not speak before you are asked a question, and if you are asked a question, speak that which is fair and helpful, not evil and destructive."

314. Abba Euprepius said, "If you are not certain in yourself that God is faithful and mighty, believe in Him, and associate yourself with those who are His, but if you are doubtful you can not believe. For we all believe and confess that God is mighty, and we are certain that all things are easy for Him to do. You will then show your belief in Him by your works, for in you also He works miracles, does wonders, and shows forth marvels."

315. Abba Theodore used to say, "If you are friends with a man, and it happens that he falls into temptation, stretch out your hands to him, and lift him up there from. But if he falls into heresy, and will not be persuaded by you to return, cut him off from you immediately, lest, if you tarry long with him, you be drawn to him, and you sink down into the uttermost depths."

316. One of the fathers used to tell the story of Abba John, the Persian, who by reason of the abundance of his spiritual excellence arrived at goodness now this man used to dwell in the Arabia of Egypt. On one occasion he borrowed one dinar from a brother, and bought some flax to weave, and a brother came and entreated him, saying, "Give me a little flax that I may make a tunic for myself" and he gave it to him with joy and then another brother entreated him, saying, "Give me a little flax that I may make myself a turban," and he gave to him also, and the man departed. Many other brethren borrowed from him, and he gave them the flax with rejoicing but finally the owner of the dinar came, and wanted to take it back. The old man said to him, "I will go and bring it to you," but as he had no place wherefrom he could give it to him, he rose up and went to Abba Jacob, so that he might persuade him to give him a dinar where with to repay the brother. As he was going he found a dinar lying on the ground, but he was not disposed to offer it to him, so he prayed and returned to his cell. The brother came again and pressed him to let him have what was his own, and the old man said to him, "Have patience with me this time only, and I will bring it to you." Again he rose up and went to that place where he had found the dinar, and, having made a prayer, he took it. He came to the old man Jacob, and said to him, "As I was coming to you, O father, I found this dinar on the road. Do now, O father, an act which is worthy of love, and make a proclamation throughout these borders, for perhaps someone has lost the dinar, and if its owner be found, give it to him." Then the old man went, made a proclamation for three days, and he could not find the man who had lost the dinar. The old man said to Abba Jacob, "If no man has lost the dinar give it to that brother to whom I owe one, for I was coming to obtain one from you for the Lord's sake, when I found it.' The old man Jacob marvelled at him, because, although he owed a dinar, and had found one, he did not immediately take it to pay his debt. Now this habit also was found with that old man who owed the dinar. If any man came and wanted to borrow something from him, he did not give it to him with his own hands, but he said to him, "Take for yourself whatever you wish" and when the man brought back that which he had taken, the old man would say to him, "Place it where you did take it from, and if he did not bring it back he would say to him nothing at all."

317. Abba Daniel used to say that on one occasion certain fathers came from Alexandria to see Abba Arsenius. One of them was the brother of Timothy, Patriarch of Alexandria, and they were taking his nephew also. The old man was ill at that season, and did not wish to spend much time with them, lest, perhaps, they should come to visit him another time and trouble him and he was then living in Patara of Estoris. The fathers went back sorrowfully. It happened on one occasion that the barbarians invaded the country, and Abba Arsenius came and dwelt in the lower countries and when those same fathers heard of his coming they went to see him, and he received them with gladness. The brother who belonged to them said to him, "Father, know you not that when these fathers came to you on the first occasion at Estoris you did not protract your conversation with us?" The old man said to him, "My son, you ate bread, and you drank water, in very truth, but I refused to eat bread and drink water, and I would not sit upon my legs through torturing myself, until the time when I knew from experience that you must have arrived at your homes, for I knew that for my sake you had given yourselves trouble." Thus they were pleased, gratified in their minds and they departed rejoicing.

318. Abba Daniel used to say, "Abba Alexander dwelt with Abba Agathon, and the old man loved Abba Alexander because he was a man of labor, and he was gentle and gracious. And it happened that all the brethren were washing their linen arm-cloths in the river, and Alexander was quietly washing his with them but the brethren said to Abba Agathon, "Brother Alexander does nothing," and the old man, wishing to quiet his disciples, said to him, "Wash well, O brother, for the arm-cloth is made of linen." Now when Alexander heard this he was grieved, and afterwards the old man entreated him, saying, "What then? Do I not know that you cannot wash well? But I spoke as I did to you before them so that I might rebuke their minds by your obedience."

319. They used to say that one day when Abba John came to the church which was in Scete he heard the brethren quarrelling with each other. He went back to his cell, went round it three times, and then entered it. Now the brethren saw him, and expressed their contrition to him, saying, "Tell us why you did go round your cell three times." And he said to them, "Because the sound of the quarrel was still in my ears," and I said, "I will first of all drive it out from them, and then I will go into the cell."

320. They used to say about Abba Or that whilst other monks would give a pledge for the palm leaves when they wished to buy, he would never give any pledge whatever, but whenever he required leaves he would send the price of them, and take them. His disciple went on one occasion to buy leaves, and the gardener said to him, "A man gave me a deposit, but he has not taken away his leaves, and therefore you may take them and having brought them he came to the old man and related to him the matter as it had happened." When the old man heard it, he wrung his hands, and said, "Or will not work this year." He did not cease to importune his disciple until he had returned the palm leaves to their proper place.

321. They used to tell the story of a certain brother who never ate bread, but only unleavened cakes soaked in water. Whenever he visited the monks when they sat down to eat, he would set before himself unleavened cakes and eat them. It happened that one day he went to a certain great Sage, and there also visited him at the same time other strangers. The old man boiled a few lentils for them. When they sat down to eat that brother also brought out his soaked cakes, set them before himself, and ate them. When the old man saw this, he held his peace and did not rebuke him before the brethren who happened to be there, but when they rose up from the table, he took him aside privately, and said to him, "O brother, if you go to visit a man do not reveal your rule of life, but eat with the brethren that you may not think within yourself that you are better than they, and so condemn them. But if you wish to keep hold upon your self-denial, sit in your cell and do not go out of it." The brother was persuaded by the old man, and ate with the brethren what they ate so as to deceive them, according to what the old man had said.

322. A certain father named Eulogius, who led a life of great austerity and labor in Constantinople, and obtained great fame and reputation. He came to Egypt in order that he might see something more excellent. When he heard about Abba Joseph he came to him, expecting to see a very much more laborious form of life than his own. The old man received him with gladness, and said to his disciple, "Make some distinction in the food which you have to prepare, and let it be suitable for strangers." Now when they had sat down to eat, those who were with Abba Eulogius said, "Bring a little salt, for the father will not eat this but Abba Joseph ate, and drank, and held his peace." Eulogius passed three days with him, but he never heard them singing the Psalms, and he never saw them praying, for every act of worship which they performed was in secret and he went forth from them having profited in no wise. By the Providence of God it happened that they lost their way. They returned the same day, came and stood at the door of the old man's cell. Before they could knock at the door, Eulogius heard them singing the Psalms inside. Having waited for a long time, they knocked, and immediately those of the company of Joseph who were singing inside stopped. When Eulogius and those who were with him had gone inside the old man received them again with gladness, and because of the heat which they had endured, Abba Joseph's monks gave Eulogius some water to drink and this water was a mixture, part being sea water and part being river water, and when Eulogius had tasted it he was unable to drink it. Then he repented within himself, and he went in to Abba Joseph and fell down at his feet, and entreated him to be allowed to learn his rule, for he wished so to do, and he said, "What does this mean? When we were with you, you sang no Psalms, but as soon as we have left you perform services overmuch. And when I want to drink water I find it to be salt." The old man said to him, "It was brother Sylvanus who did this," and he mixed the water without knowing and Eulogius entreated him to tell him about it, for he wished to learn the truth. Thereupon Abba Joseph said to him, "That mixture of wine which we drink we drink for the sake of the love of Christ, but the brethren always drink this water." Abba Joseph taught him the difference between their rules of life, and that he toiled in secret and not before the children of men and he ate a meal at the same table with them, and he partook of whatever was set thereupon and Eulogius learned that, even as the old man had said, "Abba Joseph performed his ascetic labors in secret, and having profited greatly he departed with gladness, giving thanks to God."

323. On one occasion there was a feast, and the brethren were eating in the church and there was among them a brother who said to him that ministered at the tables, I do not eat boiled food, but bread and salt, and the servant cried out to certain other brethren before the whole assembly, saying, "Such and such a brother does not eat boiled food, therefore bring him salt." Then one of the old men came to that brother, and said to him, "It would have been better for you this day to have eaten flesh in your cell than that this word should have been heard before the whole assembly."

324. On one occasion Ammon came to the brethren, and the brethren expressed contrition, saying, "Tell us a word whereby we may live." The old man said to them, "It is this: we must travel along the path of God with due order."

325. They used to say that the face of Abba Pambo never smiled or laughed. One day when the devils wished to make him laugh, they hung a feather on a piece of wood, and they carried it along and danced about it in great haste. They cried out, saying, "Hailaw, Hailaw." When Abba Pambo saw them, he laughed. The devils began to run and jump about, saying, "Wawa, Abba Pambo has laughed." Then Abba Pambo answered them, saying, "I did not laugh for myself, but I laughed at your weakness, and because it needs so many of you to carry a feather."

326. On one occasion a certain brother committed an offence in the coenobium and in the places which were there a certain old man had his abode. He had not gone out of his cell for many years. When the Abba of the coenobium came to the old man he told concerning the offence of that brother, and about his transgression. The old man answered and said, "Drive him out from you." When that brother was driven out, he departed and went into a reedy jungle. As some brethren happened to pass by to go to Abba Poemen they heard the voice of the brother weeping and they went in and found him in great labor. They entreated him to let them take him with them to Abba Poemen, but he would not be persuaded to go, and said, "I will die here." When they came to Abba Poemen they told him about him, and he entreated them, saying, "Go to that brother, and say to him, Abba Poemen calls you now." When the brother learned that Abba Poemen had sent the brethren to him, he rose up and went. When Abba Poemen saw that he was sorrow-stricken, he rose up, gave him the salutation of peace, smiled with him, and gave him food to eat. Then he sent his brother to the old man, saying, "For many years past I have greatly longed to see you, because I have heard about you, but through negligence both of us have been prevented from seeing each other. Now therefore that God wishes it, and the opportunity calls, I beg you to trouble yourself to come here, and we will welcome each other. Now, as I have already said, the old man had never gone out of his cell, up to that time." When the old man heard the message, he said, "If God had not worked in him he would not have sent for me and he rose up and came to him and having saluted each other, they sat down with gladness." Abba Poemen said to him, "There were two men living in one place, and both of them had dead, and one of them left weeping for his own dead and went and wept over that of his neighbor." When the old man heard these words he repented, remembered what he had done, and said, "Abba Poemen is above in heaven, but I am down, down, on the earth."

327. An old man used to say, "It is right for a man to keep his work in all diligence so that he may lose nothing there, for if a man works even a very little, and keeps it, his work remains and abides." The old man also used to narrate the following matter, "An inheritance was left to a certain brother, and whilst he was wishing to make there from a memorial to him that had died, a certain brother who was a stranger came to him, and he roused him up in the night saying, 'Arise, and help me to sing the service.' Then the stranger entreated him, saying, 'Leave me, O my brother, for I am away from labor, and I cannot get up.' And the brother who had welcomed him said, 'If you will not come, get up and depart from this place.' And the stranger rose up and departed. At the turn of the night he saw in his dream him who had driven him out giving wheat to the baker, and that the baker did not give him back even one loaf of bread and he rose up and went to an old man and related to him the whole matter even as it had taken place, and the old man said to him, 'You have performed a beautiful action, but the enemy has not allowed you to receive the reward.' After these things the old man said that this story was a proof according to which it is right for a man to be watchful and to guard his work with great care."

328. An old man said, "The Calumniator is the enemy. The enemy will never cease to cast into your house, if he possibly can, impurity of every kind. It is your duty neither to refuse nor to neglect to take that which is cast in and to throw it out for if you are negligent your house will become filled with impurity, and you will be unable to enter in there. Therefore whatever the enemy casts in little by little, throw it out little by little, and your house shall remain pure by the Grace of Christ."

329. On one occasion Abba Poemen entreated Abba Macarius with frequent supplication, saying, "Tell me a word whereby I may live." The old man answered and said, "The matter which you seek has this day passed from the monks."

330. Abba Nicetas used to tell about two brethren who had met together, who wished to dwell together. One of them thought, saying, "Whatever my brother wishes that will I do," and similarly the other meditated, saying, "Whatever will gratify my brother that will I do." When the enemy saw this, he went to them and wished to separate each from the other. As he was standing before the door, he appeared to one of them in the form of a dove, and to the other in the form of a raven. One of them said to his companion, "See you this dove?" and the other replied, "It is a raven." They began to quarrel with each other, neither of them yielding to his companion. They stood up and fought with each other, even to blood, and at length, to the joy of the calumniator, and they separated. After three days they came to themselves and were sorry for what had happened, they went back and lived together in peace as they did formerly. Each expressed his sorrow to the other. Each of them devoted himself to performing the will of his companion, and they lived together until the end.

331. One of the old men used to say, "If you see a man who has fallen into the water, and you can help him, stretch out your staff to him, and draw him out, lest, if you stretch out your hand to him, and you are not able to bring him up, he drags you down and both of you perish." Now he spoke this for those who thrust themselves forward to help other people who are being tempted, and who, through wishing to help others beyond their power, themselves fall. It is right for a man to help his brother according to his power, for God does not demand from a man what is beyond his strength.

332. A brother asked an old man, saying, "Supposing that I find sufficient for my daily wants in any place, do you wish me not to take care for the work of my hands?" The old man said to him, "Irrespective to what you may have, do not neglect the work of your hands work as much as you can, only do not work with an agitated mind."

333. An old man used to say, "When the soldier goes into battle he cares for himself only, and so also does the watchman. Let us then imitate these men, for riches, family, and wisdom, without a correct life and works, are dung."

334. An old man used to say, "I await death evening, and morning, and every day."

335. The same old man used to say also, "As he who is a stranger is not able to take another stranger into the house of one by whom he has not been entreated to enter, so also is it in the case of the enemy, for he will not enter in where he is not welcomed."

336. Abba Epiphanius said, "He who reveals and discovers his good work is like to the man who sows seed on the surface of the ground, and does not cover it up, and the fowl of the heavens comes and devours it but he who hides his good works is like to the man who sows his seed in the furrows of the earth, and he shall reap the same at harvest."

337. Abba Epiphanius used to say, "Whenever a thought comes and fills your heart with vainglory or pride, say to it, 'Old man, behold your fornication.'"

338. And he also said, "O monk, take you the greatest possible care that you sin not, lest you disgrace God Who dwells in you, and you drive Him out of your soul."

339. The old men said, "Let no monk do anything whatever without first of all trying his heart to see that what he is about to do will be done for God's sake."

340. One of the fathers asked a youthful brother, saying, "Tell us, O brother, is it good to hold one's peace or to speak?" Then the young brother spoke to him, saying, "If the words to be said be useless, leave them unsaid, but if they be good, give place to good things, and speak them. Yet, even though the words be good, prolong not your speech, but cut it short, for silence is best of all."

341. Abba Paul the Great, the Galatian, used to say, "The monk who living in his cell has small needs, and who goes out to provide therefore, is laughed at by the devils."

342. The blessed woman Eugenia said, "It is helpful to us to go about begging, only we must be with Jesus, for he who is with Jesus is rich, even though we be poor in the flesh. For he who holds the things of earth in greater honor than the things of the Spirit falls away both from the things which are first and the things which are last. For he who covets heavenly things must, of necessity, receive the good things which are on the earth. Therefore, it belongs to the wise to await not the things which now exist here, but the things which are about to be, and the happiness which is indescribable, and in this short and troublesome life they should prepare themselves for there."

343. On one occasion when Abba Arsenius was living in the lower lands, and was troubled, he determined to leave his cell without taking anything from it, and he departed to his disciples in the body, that is to say, to Alexander and Zoilus. Then he said to Alexander, "Arise, and go back to the place where I was living," Alexander did so and said to Zoilus, "Arise and come with me to the river, and seek out for me a ship which is going to Alexandria, and then come back, and go to your brother." Now Zoilus marvelled at this speech, but he held his peace and thus they parted from each other, and the old man

Arsenius then went down to the country of Alexandria, where he fell ill of a serious sickness. His disciples went back and came to the place where they had been formerly. They said to each other, "Perhaps one of us has offended the old man, and it is for this reason that he has separated from us but they could not find in themselves anything with which they had ever offended him." The old man became well again, and he said, "I will arise and go to the fathers," and he journeyed on and came to Patara where his disciples were. When the old man was near to the riverside a young Ethiopian woman saw him, and she came behind him, and drew near him, and plucked his raiment. The old man rebuked her. Then the maiden said to him, "If you are a monk, depart to the mountain." The old man being somewhat sad at this remark, said within himself, "Arsenius, if you are a monk, depart to the mountain." Afterwards his disciples Alexander and Zoilus met him, and they fell down at his feet, and the old man threw himself down on the ground also, and he wept himself, and his disciples wept before him. The old man said to them, "Did not you hear that I have been sick?" They said to him, "Yes." The old man said, "Why did not you seek to come and see me?" Abba Alexander said, "Because the way in which you did leave us was not right, and because of it many were offended," and they said, "If they had not wearied (or pressed) the old man in someway he would never have separated from them." The old man said to them, "I know that myself, but men will also say, 'The dove could not find rest for the sole of her foot, and she returned to Noah in the ark.'" Thus the disciples were healed, and they took up their abode with him again.

344. Abba Daniel used to tell concerning Arsenius that he never wished to speak about any investigation into the Scriptures, although he was well able to speak on the subject if he had been so disposed, but he could not write even a letter quickly.

345. A certain old man used to say, "Do not esteem yourself over your brother in your mind, saying, 'I possess a greater measure of self-denial than he does, and I can endure more than he can.' But be subject to the grace of Christ with a humble spirit, and love which is not hypocritical, lest through your haughty spirit you destroy your labors. For it is written, 'Let him that thinks he stands take heed lest he falls (1 Corinthians 10:12).' And, a man must be seasoned with Christ as with salt."

346. An old man used to say, "Do not be free to converse with the governor or with the judge, and do not be with either of them continually, for from such freedom of speech and boldness in speech, you will acquire the habit of thinking, and from merely thinking you will covet."

347. Abba Agathon used to say, "I have never laid down to sleep and kept anger in my heart, or even a thought of enmity against any man and I have never allowed any man to lie down to sleep keeping any anger against me."

348. The old man Hyparchus used to say, "Do not abuse your neighbor, and do not drive away a man who turns towards you, so that you may be able to say to our Lord, 'Forgive us our sins, even as we also forgive those who trespass against us.'"

349. One of the fathers used to say, "If a man asks you for anything, and you give it to him grudgingly, you will not receive a reward for what you have given, as it is written, 'If a man asks you to go with him a mile, go with him two,' and the meaning of this is, if a man asks anything of you give it to him with all your soul and spirit."

350. One of the fathers related that there were three things which were especially honored in monks; that is to say, with fear and trembling, and spiritual gladness they thought it meet to draw near, I mean to the participation in the Holy Sacraments, and the table of the brethren, and the washing of one another, according to the example which their true Christ showed to them, before the great day of His Resurrection was fulfilled. The old man himself produced an illustration of this, saying, "There was a certain great old man who was a seer of visions, and he happened to be sitting at meat with the brethren, and whilst they were eating, the old man saw in the Spirit as he was sitting at the table that some of the brethren were eating honey, whilst others were eating bread, and others dung and he wondered at these within himself. He made supplication and entreaty to God, saying, 'O Lord, reveal to me this mystery, and tell me why when the food is all the same,' and when the various things which are laid upon the table are only different forms, the brethren appear to be eating different kinds of food, for some seem to be eating honey, and others bread, and others dung. Then a voice came to him from above, saying, 'Those who are eating honey are those who eat with fear, and with trembling, and with spiritual love when they sit at the table, and who pray without ceasing, and whose praise goes up to God like sweet incense for this reason they eat honey. And those who eat bread are those who confess and receive the Grace of God, which is given to them by Him for these things. And those who eat dung are those who complain, and say, 'This is sweet and pleasant, and that is not seemly and prospers not.' Now it is not right to think about these at all,

On Scrupulous Watchfulness in our Thoughts, Words and Deeds

but we should glorify and praise God the more, and receive (or welcome) His abundant provisions which come to us without labor, so that there may be fulfilled in us that which was said by the blessed Apostle, 'Whether you eat, or whether you drink, or whether you do anything else, do all things to the glory of God.'" (1 Corinthians 10:31)

351. They say that Abba Or never told a lie, never swore, never cursed a man, and never spoke unless it was absolutely necessary.

352. One of the old men said, "A matter which you do not observe yourself, how can you teach to another?"

353. And it was he who said to his disciple, "Take heed that you never bring an alien word into this cell."

354. An old man used to say, "As far as I have been able to overtake my soul when it has transgressed, I have never committed an offence a second time."

355. An old man used to say, "Strive with all your might so that you may never in any way do evil to any man, and make your heart to be pure with every man."

356. Abba Agathon used to say to himself, whenever he saw any act or anything which his thought wished to judge or condemn, "Do not commit the thing yourself." Thus he calmed his mind, and held his peace.

357. The old men used to say, "For a man to be so bold as to condemn his neighbor resembles the sweeping of the lawgiver, or the judge, from off his seat, and the wishing to pass judgement in his place. And it is as if a man were to bring an accusation against the weakness of the judge and to condemn him, such an act will be found to be the rebellion of the slave against his Lord, and against the Judge of the living and the dead."

358. An old man used to say, "From the greatest to the least of the things which I perform, I carefully consider the fruit which will be produced from it, whether it be in thoughts, or in words, or in deeds."

359. They used to tell the story about Abba Pachomius and say that on many occasions he heard the devils repeating many evil things of various kinds, some of which were to come upon the brethren. First of all, he heard one of them saying, "I have conflicted with a man who constantly defies me, for when so ever I approach to sow thoughts in his mind, immediately he turns to prayer, and I depart from him being consumed with fire." And another devil said, "I have conflicted with a man who is easy to persuade, and he does whatever I counsel him to do, and I love him dearly." It is right then, O my brethren, that we should keep ourselves awake always, and that, making ourselves mighty men in the Name of the Lord, we should strive against the devils, and then they will never be able to overcome us."

360. One of the holy men used to say, "Through holding small wickedness in contempt we fall into great ones. Consider then attentively the following story which is told even as it took place. A certain man laughed in an empty manner, and his companion rebuked and condemned him. Another brother happened to be there, and he thought lightly of the matter, saying, This is nothing for what is it for a man to laugh? And the brother replied, From laughter pleasure is produced, and next empty words, and filthy actions, and iniquity, and so from the things which are thought to be small that wicked devil brings in great wickedness. And from great wickedness a man comes to despair, for this cruel and wicked evil has the Evil One discovered through the malignity of his craftiness, for a man to commit sin is not so destructive as for a man to cut off hope from his soul. For he who repents in a fitting manner, and according to what is right blots out his offences but he who cuts off hope from his soul perishes because he will not offer to it the binding up of repentance. Therefore let not a man hold in contempt small wickedness. For this is the seed which the Calumniator sows, for if he made war openly it would not be difficult to fight, and victory would be easy and even now, if we be watchful and strenuous, it will be easy for us to conquer, for it is God Who has armed us, and He teaches us and entreats us not to hold even the smallest wickedness in contempt. Listen to Him as He admonishes us, saying, 'Whoever shall say to his brother Raca, shall be guilty of the fire of Gehenna (Matthew 5:22)' and, 'He who looks upon a woman to desire her has already committed adultery with her in his heart (Matthew, 5:28).' And in another place He rebuked and admonished those who laugh. Concerning the idle word also He said, 'Its answer is given (in the bible), on account of this (idle words) the blessed Job, because of the thoughts which were in the hearts of his sons, offered up an offering. Now therefore, since we know all these things, let us take good heed to ourselves and avoid the beginning of the movement of our thoughts, and then we shall never fall.'"

361. A brother said to an old man, "Do not you see that I have not even one war in my heart?" The old man said to him, "You have an opening in you at each of the four points of the compass, and whatever wishes can go in and come out without your perceiving it. But if you will set up a door, and will shut it, and will not allow evil thoughts to enter, you will then see them standing outside for if our minds be watchful and strenuous in loving God, the Enemy who is the counsellor of wickedness will not approach us."

362. A certain Mother of noble rank said, "As the stamped silver coin which is current loses its weight and becomes less, so do the spiritual excellence which is apparent and is made manifest become destroyed and as wax melts before the fire, so also the soul becomes lax and confused, and strenuousness departs from it."

363. One of the old men used to say, "The man who does many good deeds does Satan cast down by means of small matters into pits, so that he may destroy the wages of all the good things which he has performed."

364. A brother asked Abba Poemen, saying, "For what purpose were spoken the words, 'Take no thought for tomorrow?'" The old man said to him, "For the man who is under temptation, and is in affliction. For it is not meet that such a man should take thought for the next day, or should say, 'How long shall I have to endure this temptation?' But he should think upon patient endurance, saying, 'It is today, and the temptation will not remain thus for a long time.'" And the old man said, "It is good that a man should be remote from temptation of the body, for he who is near to the temptation of the body is like to him that stands upon the mouth of a deep pit, and whom, whenever his enemy wishes, he can easily cast there. But if he be remote from the temptation of the body, he is like to a man who is far away from the pit, and even though his enemy may wish to cast him into it, he is not able to do so because the pit is far away from him, and whilst he is either urging him or dragging him thereto, God, the Merciful One, sends him a helper."

365. And a brother said to Abba Poemen, "My body is weak, and I am not able to perform ascetic labors speak to me a word whereby I may live" and the old man said to him, "Are you able to rule your thought and not to permit it to go to your neighbor in guile?"

366. And a brother also asked him, "What shall I do? For I am troubled when I am sitting in my cell." The old man said to him, "Think lightly of no man think no evil in your heart condemn no man and curse no man then shall God give you rest, and your habitation shall be without trouble."

367. And the same old man used to say, "The keeping of the commandments, and the taking heed to oneself in everything, and the acquisition of oblations, are the guides of the soul."

368. Abba Poemen said, "A brother asked Abba Moses, saying, 'In what manner is man to keep himself from his neighbor?' The old man said to him, 'Except a man lays it up in his heart that he has been already three years in the grave, he will not be sufficiently strong to keep this saying.'"

369. Abba Poemen said, "If you see visions or hear rumours, do not repeat them to your neighbor, for this is victory of the war."

370. The same old man also said, "The chief of all wickedness is the wandering of the thoughts."

371. Abba Poemen said, "If a man performs the desire and pleasure, and is accustomed of these, these will cast him down."

372. A brother asked Abba Poemen, saying, "If a brother owes me a few oboli, shall I remind him of it?" The old man said, "Remind him once." The brother said, "And if I have reminded him and he has given me nothing, what am I to do then?" The old man said to him, "Let the thought perish, only do not harass the man."

373. A brother asked Abba Joseph, saying, "What shall I do? For I cannot be disgraced, I cannot work, and I have nothing where from to give alms." The old man said to him, "If you can not do these things, keep your conscience from your neighbor, and guard yourself carefully against evil of every kind, and you shall live for God desires that the soul shall be without sin."

374. A brother asked Abba Sisoes of Shekipa about his life and works. The old man said to him as Daniel says, "The bread of desire I have not eaten, that is to say, a man should not fulfil the lust of his desire."

375. On one occasion Abraham said to Abba Sisoes, "Abba, you have grown old, let us draw near to the habitations of the children of men for a little." Abba Sisoes said to him, "Let us go where there are no women." His disciple said to him, "And what place is there without a woman except the desert? The

old man said to him, "Then let us go to the desert."

376. On one occasion certain brethren came to Abba Pambo. One of them asked him, saying, "Father, I fast two days at a time, and then I eat two bread-cakes. Shall I gain life, or am I making a mistake, O father?" Another asked him, saying, "I perform work with my hands each day to the value of two carats. I keep a few oboli by me for my food, and I spend the remainder upon the relief of the poor. Shall I be redeemed, or am I making a mistake, O father?" The other brethren asked him many things, but he did not answer a single word. After four days, they were wishing to depart, and the clergy entreated them, saying, "O brethren, do not trouble yourselves, for God will give you a reward. The custom of the old man is not to speak immediately, for he does not speak until God gives him permission to do so." Then the brethren went to the old man and said to him, "Father, pray for us." The old man said to them, "Do you wish to depart?" They said, "Yes." Then he took their actions into his consideration, put himself in the position of one who was writing on the ground, and said, "Pambo, one fasts two days at a time, and then eats two bread-cakes shall he become a monk by such things as these? No! Pambo, another works for two carats a day, and gives to those who are in need, shall he become a monk by such things as these? No!" And he said, "Your actions are good, and if you preserve your conscience with your good actions you shall live." Being consoled by these words, the brethren departed rejoicing.

377. A certain old man used to say, "If temptation comes to on you in the place where you dwell, do not forsake the place in the time of temptation, lest perhaps you find wherever you go the same temptation, from which you flee. Endure until the period of temptation be passed, then your departure can be effected without offence and without affliction. For you will have departed in a time of peace. If you depart during a period of temptation, many will be afflicted because of you, and will say that you did depart because of the temptation. This will be a source of grief to them."

378. On one occasion when Abba Sisoes was sitting down with a certain brother, he sighed unknowingly, and he did not perceive that the brother was with him, because his mind was carried away by the noonday prayer and he made apologies to that brother, and said to him, "Forgive me, O my brother, that I heaved a sigh before you proves that I have not yet become a monk."

379. An old man used to say, "Whenever I bring down the bar of the loom, and before I raise it up again, I always set my death before my eyes."

380. An old man said, "When I am plaiting a basket, with every stitch which I put into it I set my death before my eyes, before I take another stitch."

381. Abba Daniel used to say, "On one occasion we went to Abba Poemen. Having eaten together, he said to us subsequently, 'Go and rest yourselves a little, O my brethren.' When the brethren had gone to rest themselves I remained that I might be able to talk to the old man privately. I rose up and came to his cell. I saw that he was sitting outside on a mat, and seeing me he lay down. Now he did not know that I had seen him seated, and he pretended to be asleep. This was the custom of the old man, for everything which he did was done by him in secret."

382. One of the fathers asked Abba Sisoes, saying, "If I am living in the desert and the barbarians come against me to kill me, supposing that I have strength may I kill one of them?" The old man said to him, "No. Commit yourself to God, and leave it to Him. For with every trial which comes upon a man he should say, 'It has come because of my sins,' but if something good happens to him, let him say, 'It is of the Providence of God.'"

383. One of the old men used to say, "When the eyes of the ox are covered over then he is subjugated by the yoke bar. But if they do not cover his eyes he cannot be made to bow beneath the yoke. It is thus with Satan, for if he can cover the eyes of a man, he can bring him low with every kind of sin, but if his eyes be able to see, he is able to flee from him."

384. Abba Anthony said, "It is not seemly for us to remember the time which has passed. Let a man be each day as one who begins his toil, so that the excessive weariness which we shall feel may be to our advantage. Let him say, as Paul said, 'That which is behind me I forget, and I reach out to that which is before me (Philippians 3:13).' Let him also remember the word of Elijah, who said, 'As the Lord lives, before Whom I stand this day (1 Kings 17:1).'"

385. The same old man said also, "Let us not consider the time which is past, but let a man be even as he who begins. Let him take care in such wise that he shall make himself stand before God."

386. Abba Paphnutius said, "A monk is bound to keep not only his body pure, but his soul free from unclean thoughts. Now we find that the body is consoled by thoughts. Unless the thoughts withdraw themselves, they will sink the body. The manner in which the thoughts work is as following. The thoughts feed all lusts of the flesh, which is ruled by them. In welcoming the lusts they stir up the body in revolt, and they cast the body down. It is like a pilot who is caught in a storm, and they make the ship to sink. Is it fitting that we should know that if one man loves another he will say nothing evil about him? For if he does speak against him he is not his friend, similarly he who loves lust will not speak anything evil against it, and if he does so he is not its friend. But if a man speaks against that which he does not know, (or against that which cause him no affliction), or against that which causes him no pain, he may speak evil, but against that which he has suffered, and that wherewith he has been tried by the enemy, he will speak evil, and he will not talk about him as a friend, but as an enemy. Thus whoever speaks evil of and who despises lust is not a friend of lusts."

387. And he also said, "As judges (or governors) slay the wicked, even so do labors slay evil lusts and as wicked slaves fly from their lords even so do lusts fly from the exhaustion caused by ascetic labors. Good slaves hold their masters in honor as sons hold their fathers in honor. For the exhaustion caused by ascetic's labors produces good works, and from it the virtues spring up, even as the passions are produced from dainty meats. Exhaustion then begets good works, when a man has wearied himself with all his soul, and it brings out virtues and destroys vices, even as a righteous judge destroys the wicked."

388. A brother asked Abba Poemen, saying, "Since I suffer loss in spirit when I am with my Abba, do you wish me to continue to live with him any longer?" Now that old man knew that the brother was suffering loss through living with his Abba, and the old man marvelled how the brother could ask him the question, saying, "Do you wish me to dwell with him any longer." The old man said to him, "If you wish, dwell with him." The brother went and did so. But he came again to the old man, saying, "I am suffering loss in spirit." The old man said nothing. When, for the third time, the brother came to him, saying, "Indeed, I cannot henceforth dwell with him." Abba Poemen said to him, "Now you know how to live depart, and dwell with him no longer."

389. Therefore the old man said, "If there exists a man who knows how to suffer loss in his spirit, and who still feels the need to ask a question about his secret thoughts, it is a good thing that he should ask and it belongs to the old men to search into and investigate a matter of this kind, for concerning open sins a man does not feel it necessary to enquire, but he cuts them off immediately."

390. A brother asked one of the fathers, saying, "Tell me a word whereby I may live." The old man answered and said, "We must be careful to work a little, and we must be neither negligent nor contemptuous, and then we may be able to live." An old man told him the following story, saying, "There was a certain prosperous husband who was exceedingly rich, and wished to teach his sons husbandry. He said to them, 'My sons, behold, see how I have become rich, and if you will be persuaded by me, and will do as I have done, you will become rich also.' Then they said to him, 'Father, we will be persuaded by you, tell us how to become rich.' Now although the husband knew well that he who labors always becomes rich, yet because he thought that they might be negligent, and despise work, he made use of cunning in his words, and said to them, 'There is one day in the year, where on if a man works he will become rich. But because of my exceedingly great old age, I have forgotten which day it is. Therefore, you must work continually, and you must not be idle even one day. And you must go forwards, by every possible means in your power. But if you are neglectful and disinclined to work, even for one day, take good heed to yourselves lest the day whereon you do not work is that very day. And that lucky day passes you by, and your labor for all the rest of the year would be in vain. Thus also, O my sons, if we labor and work each day, and we do not make use of sloth, negligence or contempt, then we shall find the way of life."

391. Abba Agathon asked Abba Alonis, saying, "I wish to hold my tongue that it may not speak falsehood, what shall I do?" Abba Alonis said to him, "If you dost not lie, you are about to commit many sins." Agathon said, "How?" The old man said to him, "Behold, two brethren are going to commit a murder, and one of them will flee to you. And it will happen that the judge will come and search for him, and he will ask you, saying, 'Did this murder take place in your presence?' And if you do not wish to tell a lie you will deliver up to death the other man, whom it would be right for you to let go free, so that he might be reserved for the judgement hall of God, Who knows all things."

392. A certain brother was traveling on a road, with his aged mother. They came to a river which the old woman was not able to cross. Her son took his shoulder cloth and wrapped it around his hands, so that they might not touch his mother's body. In this manner he carried her across the river. Then his mother said to him, "My son, why did you first wrapped your hands with the cloth, and then took me across?" He said, "The body of a woman is fire, and through your body there would have come to me the memory of the body of another woman, and it was for this reason that I acted as I did."

CHAPTER NINE

On Love and Charity and the Welcoming of the Stranger

A CERTAIN OLD MAN USED TO DWELL WITH a brother in a cell in a friendly manner, and he was a man of compassionate disposition. Now a famine broke out, and the people began to be hungry. They came to him that they might receive charity, and he gave bread to them all. When the brother saw that he was giving away large quantities of bread, he said to the old man, "Give me my portion of the bread." The old man said to him, "Take it." He divided what there was and gave him his share. The brother took it from him for himself. The old man was compassionate, and gave away bread from his portion. Many people heard that he was doing this and came to him, and when God saw the generosity of the old man He blessed his bread. But the brother took his entire portion and ate it all. When the brother saw that his bread had finished, and the portion of the old man was still lasting, he made entreaty to him, saying, "My portion has come to an end, and this bread of yours is all that I have. Receive me as a partner there." The old man said to him, "Good." He associated him with himself again. When there was abundance again, the people came to take bread from him, and he gave it to them again. Now it came to pass that they lacked bread, and the brother went and found that more bread was needed. A poor man came for some bread, and the old man said to the brother, "Go in and give him some." The brother said, "There is none," for he was filled with bread. The old man said, "Go in and search for some." The

103

brother went to where the bread is normally kept, and he found that the place was filled with loaves to its top. He took some bread, gave the poor man, and he was afraid. The brother knew the excellence and the faith of the old man, and he gave thanks and glory to God.

394. Two brethren went to the market to sell their craft, and whilst one of them had gone to perform the service, he who was left by himself fell into fornication. The other brother came and said to him, "My brother, let us go to the cell," but he said to him, "I cannot go, for I have fallen into fornication." While he was seeking to do better, the brother began to swear to him, saying, "I also, when I was away from you, fell in the same manner, nevertheless, come, and let us repent together, and it may happen that God will pardon us." When they came to their cells they informed the old men about the temptation which had come to them. Whatever the old men told them to do the two brothers did. The one brother repented with the other, just as if he had sinned with him. God saw the labor of his love. In a few days God sent a revelation to one of the old men concerning the matter, saying, "For the sake of the love of that brother who did not sin, forgive him that did commit sin. This is what is meant by the words, 'A man should lay down his soul for his friend.'"

395. They also say that there was a certain self-denying ascetic brother who wished to go to the city to sell his handworks, and to buy the things which he needed. He called a brother, and said to him, "Come with me, and let us go and return together." When they had gone as far as the gate of the city, the man of abstinence said to his companion, "Sit down here, O my brother, and wait for me while I go in and perform my business and I will return speedily." Having gone into the city, and wandered around the streets, a certain rich woman tried her flattery on him. He stripped off his monk's garb and took her to wife. Then he sent a message to his companion, saying, "Arise, get you to your cell, for I can never see you again." Now the man who was sent to him with this message related the whole matter to him. He said to the messenger, "God forbids that such things should be spoken about my holy brethren, and God forbids that I should depart from this place until my brother comes, according to his word to me." Having tarried there along time, and not ceasing his weeping and praying, both by night and day, the report of him was heard throughout the city. The clergy, the monks, and the governors of the city entreated him to depart to his monastery, but he would not hearken to their supplication, saying, "I cannot transgress my brother's command, and I cannot leave this place until we go back together to the monastery." So he stayed there for seven years, during which he was burned by heat in the summer, dried up by the cold in the winter, with hunger, thirst, and weeping and watching. He made supplication on behalf of his brother. Then one day, his former companion came to him, dressed in costly garments, and said to him, "O So and so, I am he who was with you the monk so-and-so, arise, get you gone to your monastery." The brother looked at him and said, "You are not, for he was a monk, and you are a man in the world." Then God looked at the trouble of that brother, and at the end of the seven years the woman died. The brother who had married her repented, put on the garb of the monk, and went to his companion. When he saw him, he rose up, embraced him and kissed him. He took him with gladness, and went to the monastery. Then that brother renewed his former ascetic works. He was worthy of the highest grade of perfection. Thus by the patience of one man, another lived, and the saying, "A brother is helped by his brother, even as a city is helped by its fortress," was fulfilled.

396. On one occasion two old men came to an old man, whose custom was not to eat every day and when he saw them he rejoiced, saying, "Fasting has its reward, and he who eats for the sake of love fulfils two commandments, for he sets aside his own desire, firstly he fulfils the commandment, and secondly he refreshes the brethren."

397. They used to tell the story of a certain brother who fell into sin, and came to Abba Lot. He was perplexed, confused, going in and out, and was unable to rest. Abba Lot said to him, "What is the matter with you, O my brother?" He said, "I have committed a great sin, and I am unable to confess it before the fathers." The old man said to him, "Confess it to me, and I will bear it." The brother said to him, "I have fallen into fornication, and I thought you had discovered the matter." The old man said to him, "Be of good courage, for there remains repentance. Go and sit in your habitation, fast for two weeks, and I will bear with you one half of your sin." At the end of three weeks it was revealed to the old man that God had accepted the repentance of that brother, and he remained with the old man, and was subject to him until the day of his death.

398. One of the fathers came to Joseph to ask him a question about welcoming the strangers who came to them, that is to say, whether it was fitting for a man to forsake his work, and be with them in the ordinary way or not. Before they asked him, he said to his disciple, "Lay to heart that which I am about to do this day, and wait." Then the old man placed two pillows, one on his right hand, and the other on his left, and he said to the fathers, "Sit down." He went into his cell, and put on the apparel of beggars, and went out to them. He took this off, put on the beautiful apparel of the monks, he went out again, and passed among them. He went in again and took this off, and having put on his own clothes, he sat down in their midst. They marvelled at the deeds of the old man. Then he said to them, "Have you understood what I did?" and they said, "Yes." He said to them, "What is it?" They said to him, "You first put on the apparel of beggars." He said to them, "And have I been changed by that disgraceful apparel?" They said to him, "No." The old man said to them, "Since I have not myself been changed by all these changes of raiment, for the first change brought no loss upon me and the second did not change me, so are we in duty bound to welcome the brethren, according to the command of the Gospel, which said, 'Render therefore unto Caesar the things which are Caesar's; and unto God the things that are God's (Matt. 22: 21). Therefore, whenever strange brethren arrive we must welcome them gladly, for it is when we are alone that it is necessary for us to suffer." When the fathers heard these words they marvelled that he spoke to them as what was in their hearts before they had asked him. They glorified God, departed joyfully, and they received his word as if it had come from God, and did it.

399. They used to speak about an old Syrian man, who used to dwell on the road of the desert of Egypt, and whose work was as follows. At whatever time a monk came to him he would welcome him. It came to pass that on one occasion a man came from the desert and asked him to allow him to rest, but he would not permit him to do so, and said to him, "I am fasting." Then the blessed man was grieved and said to him, "Is this your labor, that you will not perform your brother's desire? I beseech you to come, and let us pray, and let us follow after him with whom this tree, which is here with us, shall bow." The man from the desert knelt down, and nothing happened. But when he who received strangers knelt down, that tree inclined its head at the same time. Seeing this he profited, and they glorified God.

400. On one occasion Abba Ammon came to a certain place to eat with the brethren. There was a brother concerning whom evil reports were abroad, for it had happened that a woman come and entered his cell. When all the people who were living in that place heard of this, they were troubled, and gathered together to expel that brother from his cell. As the blessed Bishop Ammon was there, they came and entreated him to go with them. Now when the brother knew this, he took the woman and hid her under an earthenware vessel. Many people having assembled, and Abba Ammon, understanding what that brother had done, for the sake of God hid the matter. He went in, sat upon the earthenware vessel, and commanded that the cell of the brother be searched. Although they examined the place, they found no one there. Then Abba Ammon answered and said, "What is this that you have done? May God forgive you." He prayed and said, "Let all the people go out." Finally he took the brother by the hand, and said to him, "Take heed to your soul, O my brother." Then he departed, and refused to make the matter of the brother public.

401. There were two brethren who lived in the wilderness. They were neighbors. One of them used to hide whatever he gained from his work, whether it was bread or oboli, and placed it with his companion's goods. Now the other brother did not know this, but wondered how it was that his goods increased so much. One day, he suddenly caught him doing this, strove with him, and said, "By means of your corporeal things you have robbed me of my spiritual goods." He demanded that he should make a covenant with him: not to act in this manner never again, and then he left him.

402. On one occasion Abba Macarius went to visit a certain monk, and he found him to be ill. He asked him if he wanted anything to eat, for he had nothing in his cell. The monk said to him, "I want some honey cakes." When the wonderful old man heard this he set out for Alexandria, without regarding this journey as a trouble, although the city was sixty miles away from them. There, he brought the honey cakes to give to the sick monk. This he did himself, and did not tell anyone else to bring them, and the old man thus made manifest the solicitude which he felt for the monks.

403. They used to tell the story of an old man who lived in Scete, who had fallen sick, and wished to eat a little of the fine bread. When a certain brother heard this, he took his cloak and placed in it some dry bread, and went to Egypt. There he changed it for fine bread and brought it back to the old man. The old man looked at him and wondered. But he refused to eat it, saying, "This is the bread of blood, O my brother." The old men entreated him to eat lest the offering of the brother be in vain. And having pressed him, the old man was persuaded and he ate the bread.

404. The blessed Anthony never deemed it right to do whatever was convenient for himself to the same extent as doing whatever was profitable for his neighbor.

405. An old man used to say, "I have never desired any work which does good to myself and harm to my neighbor. I have the hope that what is of benefit to my brother will be labor that is beneficial to me, and that it will be a thing that will invite a reward for me."

406. A certain brother from the Great Monastery was accused of fornication. He rose up and came to Abba Anthony. Some brethren came after him, from that monastery, to inform the Abba about the matter and to take the accused brother away. They began to accuse him, saying, "Thus and thus you have done." The brother made excuses, and said, "I never acted in this manner." Now Abba Paphnutius, who happened to be there, spoke a word to them, saying, "I saw a man in the river with the mud up to his knees. Some men came to give him help and to drag him out, and they made him to sink up to his neck." When Abba Anthony heard him say this, he spoke concerning Abba Paphnutius, saying, "Behold, indeed, he is a man who is able to make quiet and to redeem souls!" The eyes of those brethren were opened, by the word of the old men. They took that brother, and departed to their monastery.

407. They used to say about Abba Theodore that when he was young, he dwelt in the desert, and he went to make his bread in the same place as the monks made theirs. He found a certain brother who wished to make bread, but had no one to do the work for him, for he was unable to do it himself. Then Abba Theodore left his own bread and made bread for the brother. A second brother came and he made his also, and a third brother came, and he did likewise. Finally when he had satisfied them, he made bread for himself.

408. A brother asked an old man, saying, "There were two brethren, and one of them led a life of silent contemplation in his cell, and used to fast six days at a time, and to devote himself to great labor, and his companion used to minister to the sick; which of them will receive the greater reward for his service?" The old man said, "If he who fasted were to raise himself up upon the works which are profitable, he would not find himself equal before God with him that visited the sick."

409. There was a certain head of a monastery in a house of monks in the desert. It happened that the brother who ministered to him had a desire to leave the monastery. He departed and dwelt in another monastery. The old man was unwilling to let him go, and on this account he was always going to him to visit him. He entreated him to return to his monastery, but the brother refused to do so. For three whole years the old man used to go to the brother and entreat him to return. Finally he was constrained, and he departed with him. One day the old man told him to go out and bring in some fuel for the fire. While he was gathering the firewood, by the agency of Satan, a stick stuck in his eye and it was put out. When the old man heard of this he was greatly grieved. Being full of sorrow he began to speak to him words of good cheer. The brother answered, saying, "Do not be afflicted, O father, for I was the cause of this myself. This has happened to me through all the toil and labor which I brought upon you when you used to go and come to me." After a little time, when the brother had recovered from the sickness caused by his injured eye, the old man said to him, "Go out and bring in some palm leaves from the ground," for this was the work which the monks who dwelt there had to do. While the brother was cutting them, once again, as it were by the agency of Satan, a stick sprang up in the air, hit the man in the other eye, and it was put out. He came to the monastery in grief, and was then on idle and useless because he was unable to do any work. Thus the old man was deprived of a servant, and he had no one else with him, because each of the brethren dwelt in his own cell. After a short time, the day of his departure drew near, which he had known beforehand, he sent and called all the brethren. He said to them, "The day of my departure is near. Watch for yourselves. Take good heed to the service of your lives, and do not treat your ascetic labors lightly." Each one of them began to say to him sorrowfully, "Father, why are you leaving us?" The old man held his peace. Then he sent and brought the blind man, and revealed to him concerning his departure. The blind man wept and said, "Why leave you me, the blind man?" The old man said to him, "Pray that I may have openness of face with God, and that I may find mercy before Him, and have hope through His help, that on the first day of the week you will be able to perform the service with your companions." Immediately, the old man passed away. According to his word, a few days later, he appeared to that brother, his eyes were opened, he became an Abba and a head of monks. These things were related to us by those who were acquainted with the period where the old man lived.

410. A certain man of abstinence saw a man who had a devil, and was unable to fast. He was exceedingly sorry for him. By reason of the love for Christ which filled him, and because he took care for himself, and of his companion also, he prayed and entreated God that the devil might come to him, and that the man might be released from him. God looked upon his prayer and upon his good will. He saw that the holy man was carrying a great load on behalf of that demoniac. Since that brother began to prolong his fasting and prayer, and to practice continually self-denial, in a few days that evil spirit departed.

411. They used to say concerning Abba Poemen that when he was pressed by any man to go with him to eat at an unusual time, he would go, with the tears streaming from his eyes, so that he might not resist the wish of that brother and cause him annoyance for he would forgo his own will, and he would humble himself and go.

412. There was an old man in the cells named Apollo. Whenever a brethren came to call him to work, he would go joyfully, saying, "I go today with the King Christ to work on my own behalf, for this is the reward of this labor."

413. On one occasion Abraham, the disciple of Abba Sisoes, was tempted by Satan. The old man saw him falling down. Straightaway he spread out his hands towards heaven, and said to God, "My Lord, I will not let You go until You have healed him." Instantly, Abraham was healed.

414. A certain monk was sitting by the monastery, occupied in great labors. It happened that strangers came to the monastery. They forced him to eat with them contrary to his usual custom. Afterwards the brethren said to him, "Father, were not you afflicted by this?" He said to them, "My affliction is to break my will."

415. On one occasion three old men went to Abba Akila. On one of them rested some small suspicion of evil, one of them said to him, "Father, make me a net," he replied, "I will not make you a net." Another said to him, "Do us an act of grace, and make us a net, so that we may be able to keep you in remembrance in our monastery." Again, Akila said, "I am not at leisure to do so." The third brother, on whom rested the suspicion of evil, said to him, "Father, make me a net which I can possess direct from your hands." Akila answered straightaway, saying, "I will make one for you." Afterwards, the other two brethren said to him privately, "Consider how much we entreated you, and yet you would not be persuaded to make a net for us. And you did say to this man, I will make you one immediately!" The old man said to them, "I told you that I would not make one, and you were not grieved, because I did not have the leisure. But if I had not made one for this man, he would have said, 'It was because the old man had heard about my sins that he was unwilling to make a net for me.'"

416. On one occasion three brethren went to harvest, and the three of them undertook to reap the harvest in certain fields together for a certain sum of money but one of them fell sick on the first day, and was unable to work, and he went back and lay down in his cell. Then one of the two brethren who remained said to his companion, "Behold, O my brother, you see that our brother has fallen sick. Let us exert ourselves a little, you and I, and let us believe that by his prayers we shall be sufficiently strong to do his share of the work of harvest for him." When the harvest ended, they came to receive their hire. They called the sick brother, and said to him, "Come, brother, and take the hire of your harvesting," and he said, "What hire can there be for me since I have not been harvesting?" They said to him, "Through your prayers the harvest has been reaped, come and take your hire." Then the contention between them waxed strong, for the sick brother contended that he ought not to receive any wages, and they said, "We will not leave you until you do." So they went, that they might be heard by a certain great old man, and that brother answered and said, "O father, three of us went to harvest, but I fell sick on the first day, and went and lay down in my cell. Although I did not work even one day these brethren urge me, saying, "Come and take the hire for which you did not work." Then the two brethren said, "Three of us went to the harvest, and we took certain fields to reap together, and if we had been thirty we should have succeeded in reaping them with great labor but through the prayers of this our brother the two of us reaped them quickly, and we said to him, 'Come, take your you hire, because, through your prayers, God helped us, and we reaped quickly,' but he would not take it." The old man said to the brethren who were with him, "Beat the board, and let all the brethren be gathered together." When they were assembled, the old man addressed them, saying, "Come, O brethren, and hear this day a righteous judgement." He related before them the whole matter. They decided that the brother was to receive his hire, and he might do whatever he wished with it. The brother went away weeping and distressed.

417. On one occasion a certain demoniac came to Scete. Having passed a long time there without being healed, he complained about the matter to one of the old men. The old man made the sign of the Cross over him, and healed him. The devil was angry, and said to the old man, "Now that you have cast me out I will come upon you." The old man said to him, "Come gladly, and I shall rejoice." The old man passed twelve years with the devil inside him, vexing him. He used to eat twelve dates each day, after these years that devil leaped out of him, and departed from him. When the old man saw that he was taking to flight, he said to him, "To whom do you flee? Continue with me longer." The devil answered, saying, "By Jupiter, God has made you useless, O old man, God alone is equal to your strength."

418. The old man Theodore asked Abba Pambo, saying, "Tell me a word and with much labor," he said to him, "Theodore, go forward, and let your mercy be poured out on every man, for your loving-kindness has found freedom of speech before God."

419. A certain brother went to buy some linen from a widow. As she was selling it to him, she sighed. The brother said to her, "What is afflicting you?" The widow said to him, "God has sent you this day that my orphans may be fed." When that brother heard these words he was distressed. He took secretly from the linen he had, and threw it on to the widow's side of the scales until he fulfilled an act of charity towards her.

420. A certain brother came to Abba Or, and said to him, "Come with me to the village, and buy me a little wheat of which I am in need now." The old man was greatly troubled at this because he was not accustomed to go to the village. Nevertheless, being afraid of transgressing the commandment, he rose up and went with him. When they arrived to the village, the old man saw a man passing by. He called him and said, "Do an act of kindness, and take this brother and satisfy his need." In this way he was able to flee to the mountain.

421. On one occasion Adlep, Bishop of Neapolis, went to visit Abba Sisoes. When he wished to depart the old man made him and the brethren who were with him to eat in the morning. Now these were the first days of the fast. When they had prepared the table to eat, behold, certain men from the plough knocked at the door. The old man said to his disciple, "Open to them, and put some of the boiled food in a dish, and set it before them to eat, for they have just come from labor." The Bishop said, "Let it alone, or perhaps they will say that Abba Sisoes eats at this time." The old man looked at the youth and said to him, "Go, and give them the food." When the strangers saw the boiled food they said to him, "Do you have strangers with you? What if Abba is also eating with them?" The disciple said to them, "Yes." Then they cried out and spoke words of condemnation to the company, saying, "May God forgive you, for you have made the old man to eat at this time of the day. Perhaps you are unaware that you are causing him much vexation?" When the Bishop heard these things he expressed contrition, and said to him, "Forgive me, I have behaved after the manner of a man, but you have acted like God."

422. They used to say that, on one occasion when Abba Agathon came to the city to sell his handiwork, he found a stranger lying sick in the market. He had no man to care for him. The old man stayed with him, hired a room in the town and remained there working with his hands. Whatever he had received, he spent on the rent of the room and on the needs of the sick man, for a period of four months. When the sick man was healed, the old man departed to his own cell.

423. An old man used to say, "It is an imperfection if a man is reviled by his brother, or when any evil comes to him from him. He cannot strengthen his love before he meets him."

424. On one occasion, a brother was sent from Scete by his Abba on a camel to Egypt to fetch palm leaves for making baskets. And having gone down and brought the camel, another brother met him and said to him, "Had I known that you were coming up I should have begged you to bring a camel for me also." When the brother came and told his Abba what his companion had said to him, the Abba said, "Take the camel and lead it to that brother, and say to him, 'We have taken counsel, and we have given up the intention of bringing up palm leaves at present, but do you take the camel and bring some up for yourself.'" The brother did not want to accept the camel. His companion entreated him to do so, saying, "If you do not take him we shall waste what we have paid in hire for him." The brother took the camel and brought up his palm leaves. After he had gone up to Egypt that brother took the camel a second time, and came back that he himself might go up. The brother said to him, "Where take you the camel?" He said to him, "To Scete, so that we also may bring up our palm leaves." That brother repented, was exceedingly sorry, and expressed contrition, saying, "Forgive me, my brethren, for your great charity has taken away my hire."

425. One of the brethren said, "While we were sitting and talking about love, Abba Joseph asked, 'Do we know what love is?' He said that Abba Agathon had a little knife and that a certain brother came to him and said, 'Father, the little knife which you have is pretty. Abba Agathon did not let him depart until he had taken it.'"

426. Abba Agathon used to say, "If I could find an Arian to whom I could give my body and take his in its place, I would do so, because this would be perfect love."

427. A brother asked Abba Muthues, saying, "What shall I do if a brother comes to me, in a time of fast or in the morning, and I am in tribulation?" The old man said to him, "If you are afflicted, and eat with the brother you do well. But if you do not look at the man, and do eat, this is a matter of your will only."

428. Mother Sarah used to say, "It is a good thing for a man to give alms, even though he does so for the approbation of the children of men, for from this he will come to do it for God's sake."

429. A brother asked Abba Poemen, saying, "If I find a place where there is pleasure for the brethren, do you wish me to dwell there?" The old man said to him, "Where you will not do harm to your brother, there dwell."

430. Abba Poemen used to say that whenever Isidore, the priest of Scete, used to address the brethren in the church, he spoke the following words only, "My brethren, it is written, 'Forgive your brother that you also may be accounted worthy of forgiveness'" (Luke 6:37 & Matt. 6:14).

431. They used to say that at the beginning Abba Zeno refused to take anything from any man. Those who brought him things used to go away sorrowfully, because he would not be persuaded to accept anything from them. Other men used to come and ask him to give them gifts as of a great old man. They also went away sorrowfully, because he refused to do so. The old man said within himself, "Those who bring go away in sorrow, and those who beg also go away grieving because they have received nothing; I will, therefore, act as follows: If any man brings me anything I will take it, and if any man asks me for anything I will give it. And he did so, and pleased every one."

432. The disciple of Abba Theodore said, "A certain man on one occasion came to sell onions. He filled a basin with some of them and gave them to us. The old man said to me, 'Fill the basin with wheat and give it to him.' There were two baskets of wheat there, one full of clean wheat, and the other was full of wheat which was dirty. I filled the basin with the dirty wheat and gave it to him. The old man looked at me in wrath and anger, and in my fear I fell down, and broke the basin. The old man said to me, "Arise, you are not akin to me, but I know well what I said to you." The old man went in, filled his garment with clean wheat, and gave it to the man with the onions, together with his onions."

433. A certain monk used to dwell by the side of a coenobium. He was occupied in great ascetic labors, and led a life of hard work. Strangers came to the coenobium, and forced him to eat before his time. Afterwards the brethren said to him, "Are not you now afflicted, father?" He said to them, "Although I am afflicted I have cut off my desire."

434. A certain old man used to say, "It is right for a man to take up the burden for those who are near to him, to speak, and to put his own soul in the place of that of his neighbor. It is right too to become, if it were possible, a double man. He must suffer, weep, and mourn with him. And finally the matter must be accounted by him as if he himself had put on the actual body of his neighbor. And as if he had acquired his countenance and soul, and he must suffer for him as he would for himself. For thus is it written, 'We are all one body, and this passage also affords information concerning the holy and mysterious kiss.'"

435. An old man said that the father had a custom of going to the cells of the new brethren, who wished to live by themselves, to visit them, lest one of them might be tempted or be injured in his mind by the devils. If they found any man who had been harmed they would bring him to the church, and place a wash basin full of water in the midst. When prayers were made on behalf of him that had been brought there, all the brethren would also wash themselves and then pour some of the water upon him, and immediately that brother was cleansed.

436. A brother asked an old man, saying, "If I find a brother, about whom I have heard that he has committed an offence, I never rest until I have brought him into my cell. But if I see a man who leads a good life, I bring him to myself gladly." The old man said to him, "Do what is good twice over to the former, for he is sick, and needs help."

437. An old man used to say, "Defeat comes to a man if, when he is reviled and treated with contempt by his brother, he does not show him evenness of heart before he repents and asks him to forgive him."

438. There was a monk, and away on the mountain ten miles distant from him, was another monk. The first monk had some bread in his cell, meditated in his mind, determined to invite the other monk to come and to partake of his bread. Again he thought in his mind, saying, "Since the bread is with me I shall give my brother the labor of walking ten miles if I invite him to come here, but it will be more helpful to him if I take one half of the bread which I possess, and carry it to him"; so he took the bread, and carried it to the cell of the other brother. As he was journeying along, he tripped, fell, and injured one of his fingers. As the blood was running down, he began to cry because of the pain. There appeared to him suddenly an angel who said to him, "Why are you weeping?" The monk said to him, "I have hurt my finger, and it is painful"; the angel said to him, "Do you weep because of this? Do not weep, for the number of every step which you take for our Lord's sake is written down, and is estimated at a great reward before Him. The report of the labor of such things goes up to Him. That you may be certain that such is the case, behold, in your presence I will take some of this blood and carry it to our Lord"; and immediately the monk was healed. With rejoicing and thanksgiving to God, he set out again on his journey to go to his companion. Having come to him, he gave him the bread, related to him concerning the love for man which is found in the good Lord, the Creator of the universe, and then went back to his cell. After one day he took the other half of the bread and went to carry it to another monk. It happened that he also was found to be burning with anxiety to emulate works of this kind, and wanted to do even as the other monk had done. And having set out to go and carry the bread of the first monk, they happened to meet each other on the way. Then the first monk who had done good to the other monk began to say to him, "I possessed a certain treasure, and you wish to rob me of it"; and the other monk said to him, "Where is it written that the strait and narrow door is sufficient for yourself alone? Let us, even us, go in with you." Instantly, while they were talking, the angel of the Lord appeared, and said to them, "Your contending has ascended to the Lord even as a sweet smell."

439. On one occasion, a certain excellent man living in the world, who feared God in his life and his deeds, went to Abba Poemen. Some of the brethren who were also with the old man asked him questions wishing to hear a word from him. Then Abba Poemen said to the man who was in the world, "Speak a word to the brethren"; but he entreated him, saying, "Forgive me, O father, but I came to learn." The old man pressed him to speak, and, as the force of his urging increased, he said, "I am a man living in the world, and I sell vegetables, and because I do not know how to speak from a book, listen to a parable. There was a certain man who had three friends, and he said to the first, 'Since I desire to see the Emperor come with me'; and the friend said to him, 'I will come with you half the way.' The man said to the second friend, 'Come, go with me to the Emperor'; and the friend said to him, 'I will come with you as far as his palace, but I cannot go with you inside.' The man said the same to his third friend, who answered and said, 'I will come with you, and I will go inside the palace with you, and I will even stand up before the Emperor and speak on your behalf.' Then the brethren questioned him, wishing to learn from him the strength of the mystery saying. He answered them, saying, "The first friend is abstinence, which leads as far as one half of the way; and the second friend is purity and holiness, which lead to heaven; and the third friend is loving kindness, which establishes a man before God, and speaks on his behalf with great boldness."

440. A brother went to visit a certain monk. When he went before him, he said to him, "Forgive me, O father, for having made you to desist from your rule"; and the monk said to him, "My rule is to refresh you, and to send you away in peace."

441. On one occasion a command was given to the brethren who were in the Scete, saying, "Fast this week, and celebrate the Passover." It happened that some brethren came from Egypt to Abba Moses. While he was boiling a little food for them, his neighbors saw the smoke of his fire rising up. They said to the clergy, "Behold, Moses has broken the command, and has boiled some food in his cell." They said to them, "Hold your peace, and when he comes to us we will speak to him." When the Sabbath arrived, the clergy, having regard to his great ascetic labors, said to him before the whole assembly, "O Abba Moses, though you do break the command of men, you establish that of God."

442. They used to tell the story of a certain brother who, when he was throwing away the handles of his baskets, heard his neighbor saying, "What shall I do? For the festival draws near, and I have no handles to put on my baskets." The brother went immediately, picked up the handles of his baskets, and brought them to his companion, saying, "Behold I have these, of which I have no need, take them and put them on your baskets." And he left his own work and completed that of his companion.

443. Some old men went to Abba Poemen, and said to him, "Do you wish us if we see brethren sleeping in the congregation, to smite them so that they may wake up?" He said to them, "If I see my brother sleeping, I place his head upon my knees, and I give him a place to rest upon." Then an old man said to him, "And what do or would you say to God?" Abba Poemen said to him, "I say to Him thus, 'Your have said, 'First of all pluck the beam out of your own eye, and then you will be able to see to take the speck out of the eye of your brother'"(Matt. 7:3).

CHAPTER TEN

On Humility

Abba Isaac, the priest of the cells, used to say, "When I was a young man I used to dwell with Abba Chronius. He had never told me to do any work. When he became an old man and he trembled, he would stand up and give water with his hands to me, and to all of us alike. With Abba Theodore of Parme it was the same, for he never told me to do any work whatsoever, but he would make the table ready with his own hands, and would say, 'Brother, come and eat.' I said to him, 'Father, I came that I might assist you, and how is that you do not tell me to do something?' The old man in all this held his peace. I went up and informed the old men, and they came to him, saying, 'Father, this brother came to your holiness that he might be assisted by you, and why do you not tell him to do something?' The old man said to them, 'Am I the head of a monastery that I should give him a command? I shall say nothing to him except that I wish him to do what he sees me doing.' From that time I was always before him in doing that which the old man was going to do. Whatever he did, he did in silence, and in this manner he made me to know and taught me to work in silence also."

445. There was a certain Egyptian monk in Constantinople under the reign of Theodosius the Less. The monk, used to dwell in a little cell. On one occasion, the Emperor went out to take his pleasure. He came by himself to the monk. The Emperor took off his crown from his head, hid it, and knocked at the door of the monk. When the monk opened the door, he knew that it was the Emperor, but he feigned forgetfulness and would not recognize him. The monk welcomed him as one of his own rank in life, prayed and sat down. The Emperor began to question him, saying, "How are the fathers who are in Egypt?" The monk said to him, "They all pray for your health." The Emperor examined his cell, and saw that nothing was there except a small basket where there was bread, which the monk offered to him, saying, "Eat." The monk dipped the bread in water, poured oil and salt on it, and gave it to the Emperor. The Emperor ate it. The monk gave him some water, and the Emperor drank. The Emperor then said to him, "Do you know who I am?" The monk said to him, "God knows who you are." The Emperor said to him, "I am Theodosius, the Emperor," and immediately the monk paid respect to him. Then the Emperor said to him, "Blessed are you in that you have none of the cares of this world. Truly I was born to kingship and before this day I have never been satisfied with bread and water, and they have pleased me greatly." The Emperor began to pay honor to the monk. The monk immediately fled to Egypt hastily.

446. A certain brother came to Abba Macarius, the Egyptian, and said to him, "Father, speak to me a word whereby I may live." Abba Macarius said to him, "Get to the cemetery and revile the dead." The brother went and reviled them, stoned them with stones, came back and informed the old man what he had done. The old man said to him, "Did they say anything to you?" The brother said to him, "No." Again the old man said to him, "Go tomorrow, praise them, and call them, 'Apostles,' 'Saints,' and 'Righteous Men'" He came to the old man, and said, "I have praised them." The old man said to him, "Did they return any answer to you?" He said, "No." The old man said to him, "You see how you have praised them, and they said nothing to you, and that although you did revile them they returned no answer to you. Thus let it be with yourself. If you wish to live, become dead, so that you may care neither for the reviling of men nor for their praise, for the dead care for nothing; in this way you will be able to live."

447. One of the fathers used to relate that he had an old man in a cell who performed many ascetic labors, and clothed himself in a palm-leaf mat. This old man went to Abba Ammon. When Abba Ammon saw that the old man wore a palm-leaf mat only, he said to him, "This will profit you nothing." The old man asked him, saying, "Three thoughts vex me. Shall I go to the desert, or shall I go out into exile, or shall I shut myself up in a cell, receive no man, and eat once every two days?" Abba Ammon replied, "You are not able to do any one of these things, but go, sit in your cell, eat a very little food each day, and let there be in your heart always the words of the publican, God be merciful to me a sinner. Thus you shall be able to live (Luke 18:13)."

448. Abba Daniel used to relate a story, saying, "There was with us in Babylon of Egypt the daughter of a man who was the captain of a company of soldiers. She was possessed of a devil. Her father took her to many places, but found no healing. Her father had a friend who was a monk, and he said to him, 'No man is able to cure her except those monks of whom I spoke to you. But even if we entreat them to do this they will not agree to it, because they flee from the love of the praise of men.' Nevertheless, when they come to sell their baskets, pretend that you wish to buy some. And when they come to sell and to take the price of the baskets from your house, we will say to them, 'Put up a prayer, and this maiden shall be healed.' The man did so. They came as it were to buy baskets. They found the disciple of these holy men sitting down and selling them. They took him with the baskets, and carried him to their houses. Then they set another man in his place, and commanded him when the monks came to bring them to them. When their disciple entered the house, the maiden who was possessed of a devil went out and hit him on the cheek. But that brother fulfilled the commandment and turned to her the other cheek. Immediately the devil was unable to bear the blow of the commandment of Christ, which was fulfilled, cried out with a loud voice, and departed. When the monks came, the people in the house related the reason for what had happened, and glorified God, saying, "It is customary for the boasting of the evil One to fall before the humility of the commandments of Christ."

449. On one occasion Abba Ammon went to Abba Anthony. He lost the way, sat down for a little and fell asleep. He rose up from his slumber, and prayed to God, saying, "I beseech You, O Lord God, do not destroy what You have fashioned." Then he lifted up his eyes, and, behold, there was the form of a man's hand above him in the heavens, and it showed him the way until he came and stood above the cave of Abba Anthony. When he had gone into the cave of the old man, Abba Anthony prophesied to him, saying, "You shall increase in the fear of God." Then he took him outside the cave, showed him a stone, and said, "Curse this stone, and smite it," and he did so, and Abba Anthony said to him, "It is thus that you shall arrive at this state, for you shall bear heaviness, and great abuse." This actually had happened to Abba Ammon. Through his abundant goodness Abba Ammon did not know wickedness. After he had become a Bishop, through his spiritual excellence, they brought to him a virgin who had conceived, and they said to him, "So-and-so has done this deed. Let them receive correction"; but he made the sign of the Cross over her belly, ordered them to give her six pair of linen cloths, and said, "When when she brings forth either her or the child will die. If either dies, let them be buried." Then those who were with him said to him, "What is this that you have done? Give the command that they receive correction." He said to them, "See, O my brethren, she is near to death, and what can I do?" Then he dismissed her. The old man never ventured to judge anyone. He was full of loving kindness and endless goodness to all the children of men.

450. They used to say that on one occasion Abba Arsenius the Great fell ill in Scete. A priest went and brought him to the church. He spread a palm-leaf mat for him, and placed a small pillow under his head. One of the old men came to visit him, saw that he was lying upon a mat, had a pillow under his head, and he was offended and said, "And this is Arsenius lying upon such things!" Then the priest took the old man aside privately, and said to him, "What labor did you do in your village?" The old man said to him, "I was a shepherd." The priest said to him, "What manner of life did you lead in the world?" He said to him, "A life of toil, and sore want." When the old man had described all the tribulation, which he had endured in the world, the priest said to him, "And here what manner of life do you lead?" The old man said to him, "In my cell I have everything comfortable, and I have more than I want." The priest said to him, "Consider the position of Abba Arsenius when he was in the world! He was the father of kings, and a thousand slaves, wearing gold embroidered vests, and with chains and ornaments round their necks, and clothed in silk, stood before him; and he had the most costly couches and cushions to lie upon. But you were a shepherd, and the comforts which you did never enjoy in the world you have here; but this man Arsenius has not here the comforts which he enjoyed in the world, and now you are at your ease whilst he is troubled." Then the mind of the old man was opened, expressed contrition and said, "Father, forgive me; I have sinned. Truly this is the way of truth. He has come to a state of humility, while I have attained to ease." The old man profited and went his way.

451. They used to say that on one occasion Abba Macarius was passing along the road when Satan met him. The devil wished to cut him down with the axe which he held in his hand. But he was unable to do so, and he said to him, "Macarius, I am dragged along by you with great force, but I cannot overcome you. Now, behold, everything which you do I can do also. You fast, and I never eat at all. You watch, and I never go to sleep, and there is one thing only which you do conquer me." Then Macarius said to him, "And what is that?" Satan said, "It is your humility, for it is because of this that I cannot vanquish you." Then Macarius spread out his hands in prayer. The devil was no more seen.

452. On one occasion a devil took a knife and stood over Abba Macarius wishing to cut off his leg. When he was unable to do so on account of the humility of the old man, he answered and said to him, "Everything which you possess we possess also. It is only in humility that you are superior to us, and it is only by means of it that you conquer us."

453. Abba Anthony said, "I saw all the snares of the enemy laid out upon the ground, and I groaned and said, 'Who can escape from these?' And the devils said to me, 'Humility enables a man to escape from these, for we cannot attain it.'"

454. An old man said, "Whenever a man is praised it is meet for him to think about his sins, and he should consider, saying, 'I am unworthy of the things which are said about me.'"

455. The blessed Macarius behaved towards all the brethren without any wicked suspicion. Certain people said to him, "Why do you act in this manner?" He said, "Behold, for twelve years I have been supplicating my Lord to give me this gift, and would you advise me to relinquish it? If it happened that one of the brethren commits a sin before the eyes of one who possessed no wickedness, and he knows that it is an evil thing, is it not right that he should bear some of the pain of him who had fallen."

456. Abba Poemen used to say, "No monk should condemn any man in anything. No monk should reward a man with evil for evil. And no monk should be a man of anger."

457. An old man asked Abba Poemen, saying, "Some brethren dwell with me; do you wish me to give them commandments?" Abba Poemen replied, "No, but you yourself must first do work, and if they wish to live, they will observe you and do work." The old man said to him, "Ought I to govern them?" Abba Poemen said to him, "No, be to them an example, and not a lawgiver."

458. Abba Poemen said, "If a brother comes to you, and you are not going to benefit by his coming, ask your heart, and learn what thought you have in your mind before admitting that brother. Then you will learn what is the source of injury and where it comes from. If you do this with humility and knowledge, behold, you will live without blame with your brother. You will bear your own shortcomings. If a man makes his habitation with knowledge, it will not fall, for God is before it, and, as it appears to me, from this habitation a man may acquire the fear of God."

459. A brother asked an old man, saying, "By what means may a man go forward?" The old man said to him, "The greatness of a man consists of humility. Proportionally, as a man descends to humility, he becomes exalted to greatness."

460. Abba John used to say, "We relinquish a light burden when we condemn ourselves, but we take upon ourselves a heavy burden when we attempt to make ourselves righteous."

461. On one occasion Abba Theophilus went to the Nitrian Mountain to visit the fathers. The priest of the Mountain came to him. Abba Theophilus, the Bishop of Alexandria, said to him, "What thing of excellence have you found on this road?" The old man said to him, "I make accusations against myself, and I blame myself at all times" Abba Theophilus said to him, "Truly this is the way of truth." A variant reads: On one occasion the Archbishop Theophilus went to the mountain of Nitria. A certain Abba of the monks who was in the mountain came to him; Abba Theophilus said to him, "What more do the monks find in this way than in any other?" The old man said to him, "They condemn themselves continually, and they do not judge their neighbors"; and Abba Theophilus said, "There is no way but this."

462. On one occasion they brought a man possessed of a devil to one of the old men of Thebes, and they entreated him to cast the devil out. The old man was unwilling to do so. Since they urged him strongly he was persuaded. He had mercy on the man, and said to the devil, "Get out from him who God has created." The devil answered, saying, "I am going out, but I would ask you to tell me one thing. What is the meaning of what is written in the Gospel, 'Who are the goats and who are the sheep?' The old man answered, saying, "I myself am one of the goats, but God knows who the sheep are." When the devil heard this, he cried out loudly, saying, "Behold, I go forth because of your humility." Immediately he left the man and departed.

463. They used to say that on one occasion a few early, white figs came to Scete, but because they were nothing of importance they did not send any to

On Humility

Abba Arsenius, not wishing to insult him. When the old man heard of this he did not come to the congregation, saying, "You separated me from the blessed gift which God sent to the brethren because I was unworthy to partake of it." When the old men heard this they profited greatly by his humility. The priest went, carried some of the figs to him, and brought him to the congregation with great joy.

464. A certain Abba asked Abba Muthues, saying, "If I go to a place to dwell, how would you have me behave?" The old man said to him, "If you wish to dwell in a certain place, do so, but do not let go forth concerning yourself any fame for praiseworthy acts, or say, I do not eat, or, I do not drink, for such things only produce empty fame; and you will find at length that you will profit from many, for men will go where they can find qualities of this kind." Then the brother said to him, "What shall I do?" The old man said to him, "Wherever you dwell, conduct yourself in a simple manner like everyone else. And when you see what those who fear God do, I mean those in whom you have confidence, that you do also, and you shall be at ease, for to be like other men is the true humility. The men who see that you are like other men will regard you as they regard everyone else, and you will not be troubled."

465. A certain brother went on one occasion from Egypt to Syria to visit Abba Zeno. The Egyptians began to make accusations against his thoughts before the old man. When Abba Zeno heard this, he marvelled and said, "The Egyptians always hide the spiritual excellences which they possess, but they describe the shortcomings which they do not possess. On the other hand, the Syrians and the Greeks declare that they possess the virtues, which they do not have, and they hide the shortcomings which they do possess."

466. They used to talk about a certain old man who fasted for seventy weeks, and only ate each Saturday. He asked God that a word from the Book might be given to him, but it was not given. Then he said within himself, "Behold, I have labored in all these things, and I have omitted nothing; I will arise and go to my brother and question him about it." When he had shut the door to depart, the angel of the Lord appeared, and said to him, "The seventy weeks which you did fast have not come near to God, but, in as much as you have humbled yourself to go to your brother, I have been sent to make a word known to you, and to give you rest." Thereupon he made the word known to him, gave him rest, and departed.

467. A brother asked an old man, saying, "What shall I do? For the love of praise is killing me." The old man said to him, "You do well, for behold, you have made the heavens and the earth." Then the brother was sorry because of what the old man had said to him. He expressed contrition, and said, "Father, forgive me, but I have done nothing of the kind." The old man said, "If now He Who did make them came into this world in humility, why do you, who are mud, boast yourself?"

468. One of the old men said, "Do not be humble in your words only, but also in your deeds."

469. On one occasion a certain Governor came to see Abba Simon. When the old man heard of his coming from those who came to make it known to him beforehand, he immediately girded up his loins, and went up a palm tree to clean it. When those who came cried out to him, saying, "O, old man, tell us where the monk is," he said to them, "He is not here." They departed from that place.

470. One of the fathers from Parme told a story of how, on one occasion when he had returned to Abba Theodore, he found him wearing a ragged shirt, his breast was naked, and his outer garment was dragged round in front of him. Behold, a certain Count came to see him. When the Count's followers knocked at the door, calling the old man, he went out to meet him quite carelessly. I took a small piece of coarse cloth and threw it over his shoulders to cover his breast. The old man took it in his hand, waved it, and threw it away. When the Count left, I said to him, "Father, what was that you have done? For a nobleman came to you to be helped, and to gain profit. Behold, he had perhaps gone away offended." The old man said to me, "Do not worry, Abba. We are still subject to men. We have done the deed, and he is gone; but whether he wishes to be benefited, or whether he wishes to be offended is his affair. As for me, as far as I am able I shall always meet men of this kind in this way." He commanded his disciple, saying, "If any man comes wishing to see me, do not say to him anything after the manner of men, but if I am eating, tell him that I am eating, and if I am asleep, tell him that I am asleep."

471. A certain woman who was afflicted in her lungs with the disease called cancer, heard about Longinus, and wished to see him. He used to dwell in the monastery of Hanton in Alexandria. While the woman was seeking and wishing for him, it happened that the blessed man was gathering sticks on the seashore. When the woman found him, she said to him, "Father, where does the man of God, Abba Longinus, dwell?" She did not know that he himself was Longinus. He said to her, "What do you want with that lying hypocrite? Do not go to him, for he is a liar. What is it that causes you pain?" Then the woman showed him the place. The old man made the sign of the Cross over it, and he dismissed her, saying, "Go, may our Lord heal you, for Longinus is unable to do you any good whatever." The woman went away, believing in the word, and was healed immediately. Afterwards when she was telling some folks the story, she said, "I have learned by the marks which were on the old man that he himself was Abba Longinus."

472. On one occasion a certain governor arranged to see Abba Simon, and the clergy told him beforehand, saying, "Father, make yourself ready, for a certain Governor has heard of your life and works, and he wishes to come and be blessed by you"; and the old man said to them, "I am ready." Then the old man went in and took in his hand some bread and cheese, went out to the door, sat down there, and he changed about from place to place eating. When the Governor came with his companions, and saw him sitting and eating, they despised him, saying, "So this is the monk of whom I have heard!" They left him and departed.

473. An old man was asked, "How is it that there are men who say, 'We have seen a vision of angels?'" The old man said, "Blessed is he who sees his sins continually."

474. They used to say that when any man came to Abba Poemen he used to send him to Abba Job, his brother, saying to him, "He is older than I am"; and Job used to say to those who came, "Go to my brother Poemen, for he possesses the grace of these gifts." Now if Abba Joseph was sitting with him Abba Poemen would not speak before him.

475. When a certain brother went to the festival he asked Abba Poemen, "What would you have me to do?" The old man said to him, "Befriend him who leads you away by force, and sell your work graciously."

476. A brother asked an old man, "What is the work of exile?" The old man said to him, "I knew a brother who went forth into exile, and he went in to lodge in a church, and it happened that the brethren were about to eat some of the sacramental bread; and when they sat down this man sat down with them. Now when some of the other monks saw him, they said, 'Who has brought this man in to eat with us?' One of them said to him, 'Arise, and go outside,' and immediately he rose up and went out as the brother had told him. But the others being sorry about this matter went out and brought him in. After these things a certain man asked him, 'What was in your mind when you went out and came in again?' He said to them, 'I thought in my mind that I was like a dog which when is driven out goes out, and when he is called comes in.'"

477. They used to say that when Abba Moses was a clergy man, he wore a long outer garment, and that the Bishop said to him, "Behold, you are entirely white, O Abba Moses." The old man said to him, "Is the Papa within or without?" Again, wishing to try him, the Bishop said to the clergy, "When Abba Moses goes into the sanctuary, drive him out, go after him and hear what he says." When he went into the sanctuary, they rebuked him and drove him out, saying, "Go outside, O Ethiopian" Having gone out, he began to say to himself, "They have treated you rightly, O you, whose skin is dark and black; you shall not go back as if you were a white man."

478. An old man used to say, "Do not despise or think lightly of him who stands before you, for you do not know whether the Spirit of God is in you or in him, though you call him who stands before you him that ministers to you."

479. Abba John the Less used to say, "Humility and the fear of God are more excellent than all the other virtues."

480. They used to say that a certain old man, who had young men living with him, told them on one occasion to do something, and when they did not do it, he said nothing further to them about it, but rose up himself in their sight and did what he had told them to do without anger, and without labor.

481. Another old man used to say, "Humility is not without salt, but it is salted with salt."

482. An old man used to say, "I would rather learn than teach."

483. And he also used to say, "Do not learn before the time, so that you may not have little admonition all your time."

484. Abba Agathon said, "If a man of wrath were to raise the dead, he would not be accepted by any man." Or "Even if a man of wrath raises the dead, this man wound not be accepted by others."

On Humility

485. A brother asked Abba Timothy, saying, "I myself can see that my memorial is ever before God"; and the old man said to him, "It would not be any great thing for your mind to be with God, but it would be a great thing for a man to see his soul beneath all creation."

486. Abba Theodore used to say, "There is no spiritual excellence greater than that of a man who does not despise his companion."

487. An old man was asked, "By what means does the soul receive humility?" He said, "By searching into it, and by remembering the evil things, which have been done by it."

488. One of the old men said, I asked Abba Sisoes, saying, "'Tell me a word,' and he said, 'It is right for a monk to humble himself lower than the idols.' I went to my cell, took counsel with myself, and meditated for an hour, saying, 'What do the words lower than the idols mean?' Then I returned to the old man, and said to him, 'What do the words lower than the idols mean?' He said to me, 'It is written concerning the idols, 'They have a mouth but do not speak, have eyes but do not see, and have ears but do not hear. Thus it is right for a monk to be. Because idols are an abomination, a man must hold himself to be abominable in his own sight.'"

489. A brother asked Abba Sisoes of Thebaid, saying, "Speak a word to me" Sisoes said to him, "What have I to say to you? I read the New Testament, and I reflect on the Old Testament."

490. That same brother went to Abba Sisoes of Patara, and told him the word which Abba Sisoes of the Thebaid had spoken. Abba Sisoes said to him, "I lie down to sleep in my sins, and I rise up in my sins."

491. There was a certain monk who lost himself in the desert. He said to himself, "I have kept myself rightly, and I possess all the virtues," and he prayed to God and said, "If I am lacking in anything, show me how I may perform it." God, wishing to humble his mind, said to him, "Go to such and such a head of a monastery, and whatever he tells you to do, that do." God sent a revelation to the head of the monastery, and said to him, "Behold, such and such a monk will come to you, say to him, "Take a whip in your hands, and go forth and pasture swine." The monk went out immediately, even as the head of the monastery told him, and pastured swine. When those who had known him formerly, and those who had heard about him, saw him pasturing swine, they said, "You see the great monk, about whom we have heard, behold, his heart has gone mad, and a devil has seized him, and he is now pasturing swine." Then God, when He saw his humility, and that he was hearing and bearing the reproach of men, set him free so that he might go back where he had been formerly.

492. An old man used to say, "If a man has laid some work upon a brother to do, he must perform that command in the fear of God and in humility; for he who, for God's sake, lays some work upon a brother makes the brother to submit himself. The one brother must do what the other brother has laid upon him. But if a man wishes to give commands to a brother, not in the fear of God, but on his own authority, wishing to be his master and governor, God, Who sees the hidden things of his heart, will not allow him to be obedient to him and to do that work, for the work that is for God's sake is evident, and that which is of the man's own authority is well known. For that which is for God's sake comes with humility and entreaty, whilst the works which are of man's own authority are with wrath and trouble, and they come from the evil One."

493. A brother asked Abba Isidore, "Why is it that the devils fear you so greatly?" The old man said, "Because from the time that I became a monk I have not labored hard to allow anger to enter into my throat; that is why they fear me."

494. An old man used to say, "On one occasion I went to the fair to sell with other brethren a few things, and I saw anger drawing near to me, and I left the things and fled immediately."

495. Abba John the Less used to say, "On one occasion when I was going up on the Scete road with some palm leaves I heard a camel speaking words to me, and he was about to make me angry, but I immediately left the palm leaves and fled."

496. The same old man when he was in the harvest field heard a brother speaking to his companion in anger, saying, "Come here." Immediately he left the harvest and fled.

497. A brother asked an old man, "Why do I see, while performing my little services of prayer and praise, that I am lacking nothing in my heart, and that I do not wish to perform the services?" The old man said to him, "How then can a man appear to love God?"

498. Abba John the Less said to the brethren who were with him, "Although we are little folk in the eyes of men, let us consider how we may be held in honor before God."

499. They used to say that Abba Patra and Abba Ampikos were close and affectionate friends. When the old men were eating in the church, they urged them to come to the table of the fathers. It was only with hard work that Abba Patra would go by himself; and after he had eaten, Abba Ampikos said to him, "How did you dare to go to the table of the old men?" Abba Patra said to him, "If I had sat with you, the brethren would have honored me as an old man, they would have required it of me to say the blessing, and I might have thought in my mind that I was greater than you all. But since I went to the fathers I am the least of you all, and I am abased, and I think in my thoughts that I am nothing."

500. On one occasion a brother committed a sin in the church. The priest drove him out. There was a man of discretion whose name was Bessarion. He arose, went out of the church, and said, "If you have judged that this man who has committed only one offence is not fit to worship God, how very much less fit am I, who have committed many sins, to do so?" The old man said, "Woe to him who is without more than to him that is within, that is to say, woe to him who is within him that is without!" This is what I would say, "When a man in the world finds a cause of complaint against a man who lives a life of silent contemplation, or who have departed from the world, this is a cause of judgement and of a fall to him who gives him reason for complaint. Take the greatest possible care then, O monk, do not commit sin, lest you disgrace God, Who dwells in you, and lest you drive Him out from your soul."

501. Abba Pior worked hard to be able to overcome the disposition to say 'You' to any of the brethren.

502. The disciple of Abba Arsenius used to say, "When the old man was about to die, he commanded us, saying, 'Do not let it be a care of interest to you to make a commemoration for me, but offer up the Offering only; for, if during my life-time I have done anything which is worthy of commemoration, I shall most certainly find a memorial of it.'"

503. Abba Ammon said, "A man may pass one hundred years in his cell, and not know rightly how a monk should live in his cell, or even how to live secluded for one day." He used to say, "The proper way and manner for a monk to live is to condemn himself continually."

504. Abba Poemen used to say, "If a man only condemns himself, he will be able to endure and continue wherever he dwells."

505. Abba Poemen used to say, "We live in the troubles and trials which come upon us because we do not take to ourselves the humble names which the Scriptures have given us. And because we do not consider how our Lord Jesus relieved the Canaanite woman (Matt. 15:22) who took to herself abominable names. Also we do not consider how, when Abigail said to David, 'On me be the sin' (1 Sam. 25:24), he was entreated by her and loved her." Abigail must be taken as representing the person of the soul, and David as the Godhead. If then the soul will condemn itself before God, He will love it, and will give it the delight of rest."

506. An old man used to say, "In all your trials, do not blame any man; only blame yourself, saying, 'These things have happened to me because of my sins.'"

507. Once Abba John was called to the church. The brethren surrounded him and asked him questions about their thoughts. One of the old men said to him, John is like to a whore who adorns herself that she may multiply lovers for herself. Thus you are. Abba John sighed and said, "Father, you have spoken the truth." Afterwards a certain man told him that he loved him, and said, "Are not you disturbed within?" He said to him, "No. But as I am without, even so am I within."

508. One of the old men used to say about Abba John, that he lived in such a way that, through the humility which he possessed, he held all Scete suspended on his finger.

509. Abba John of the Thebaid used to say, "Before all else, it was right for a monk to acquire humility. Humility was the first commandment of our blessed Redeemer, Who said, 'Blessed are the poor in spirit, for theirs is the kingdom of God'" (Matt. 5:3).

510. John Kolob used to say, "Humility is the door which leads to the kingdom. Our fathers, through many reviling, have gone into the city of God rejoicing."

511. An old man used to say, "It is good for a man to say, 'Forgive me,' and then to make an offering of something. For this suits the garb of monkhood."

512. The same old man also said, "A dog is better than I am, for he has love, and he comes not to judgement."

513. Abba Eupraxius used to say, "The tree of life which rises in the heights, is humility. Make yourself like the publican. Do not be guilty as the Pharisee. Choose for yourself the meekness of Moses, so that your heart, which is as hard as steel, can be changed into a fountain of water."

514. One of the old men said, "I would rather have defeat with humility than conquest with boasting."

515. An old man said, "When the thought of pride goes within yourself, and you become arrogant, then examine your conscience and see if you have kept all the commandments. See if you love your enemies, if you love the approbation of your enemy, and if you are grieved when the enemy is afflicted. Also see if you consider yourself to be an unprofitable servant, and a sinner greater than any other man. Moreover see if you have performed rightly all the demands of ascetic excellence. When you examine all these, you shall not be proud, for you must know that the thought of pride abrogates and makes unprofitable all the virtues."

516. An old man used to say, "He who is held in greater honor or is more praised than he deserves, suffers a great loss. But the man who receives neither honor nor praise from men shall be praised above all."

517. A brother asked an old man, saying, "Is it a good thing for us to repent many times?" The old man said to him, "We see that when Joshua, the son of Nun, lay upon his face the Lord spoke with him" (Josh. 5:14).

518. An old man was asked, "Why do the devils fight against us in the way they do?" He replied, "Because we throw away from us our armour, that is to say, obedience, humility, and abstinence."

519. The old men used to say, "Whenever we have no war to wage then especially it is necessary that we should abase ourselves, because God Who knows our feebleness, gives His protection for nothing. But if a web casts ourselves, He removes His protection from us and we perish."

520. A brother asked an old man, saying, "What is the perfection of a monk?" The old man replied, "Humility, for when once the man arrives at humility, he can reach forward to the goal."

521. The old man said, "If a man can say to his brother, 'Forgive me, and can humble himself,' this belongs to the perfection of the monk."

522. An old man once said, "When a man said to his companion, 'Forgive me,' and at the same time humbles himself, the devils are perplexed."

523. A certain brother was offended at his brother. When the latter heard this he went to him to express his contrition. The other brother would not open the door. He who had offended his brother went to another old man and related the matter to him. The old man answered saying, "Observe lest in your mind you are justifying yourself, and are condemning your brother, as if he were the offender. It may be that because of this he would not be persuaded to open the door to you. Nevertheless, do what I am going to tell you. For although he has offended you, yet I say go, hold firmly to the belief that you have offended against him, and may God put into your brother's mind to be reconciled to you."

524. The old man related to him a story, which explained the matter, saying, "There were two men who were living in the world. They were fearers of God, and both were of the same mind. They went out to become monks. When they heard in a plain manner the word of the Gospel, which said, 'There are eunuchs who have made themselves eunuchs for the sake of the kingdom of heaven' (Matt. 19:12), they arrived at the peak point of their love. They made themselves eunuchs for the sake of the kingdom of heaven. When the Bishop heard of this he set them aside and excommunicated them. Those men, wishing to show that they had done what was good, said to one another, "We have made ourselves eunuchs for the sake of the kingdom of heaven, and this Bishop drives us out! Let us go and make a complaint against him to the head of our monasteries, the Bishop of Jerusalem" When they had gone to him they related to him the whole matter. Then the Bishop said to them, "And I also set you aside and excommunicate you." Being greatly grieved at this remark also they went to the Bishop of Antioch, and related the matter to him. He also drove them away with the same words. Then the two brethren said to each other, "Let us go to the Patriarch of Rome, and he will avenge us and will take vengeance on all these Bishops." Having gone to the great Patriarch and Bishop of Rome, they recited their matter, and what the Bishop and Patriarch of Antioch had said to them. The brothers said at length, "We have come to you because you are the head of them all." Then the Bishop of Rome said to them, "I also excommunicate you" Then, not knowing what to do, they said to each other, "All these men accept the persons each of the other, and each honors the other, because they are accustomed to assemble together at the Synods. Let us then go to the holy man of God, Epiphanius, Bishop of Cyprus, because he is indeed a Bishop, and he does not accept the person of any man." When they drew near to the city, it was revealed to Epiphanius concerning them. He sent a man to meet them, and to say to them, "You shall not come into the city." And when they came to themselves they repented, and said, "In very truth we have sinned. With what can we justify ourselves? For, even supposing that the Bishops and the Patriarchs have excommunicated us in an unseemly manner, it may be that this man is a prophet besides, for behold, God has revealed to him concerning us beforehand. Let us then condemn ourselves in respect of everything which we have done." Then when God, Who knows what in the hearts of men, saw that they had in very truth condemned themselves, He worked upon the mind of Epiphanius. Epiphanius sent, to bring them, and associated them in communion with him. He also wrote concerning them to the Bishop of Jerusalem, saying, "Receive your sons, for they have repented in truth." The old man said, "This is the healing of a man, and God desires that a man should lay the offence of his companion upon himself." When that brother heard this story he acted according to the words of the old man, went and knocked at the door of that brother. The brother immediately perceived and knew from inside that it was him, expressed his contrition to him while he was as still inside. Then straightaway he opened the door; and they became friends to each other, with all their souls. The two of them were in great peace.

525. Abba Poemen used to say, "As the earth does not fall, because it is fixed from below, even so is he who abases himself, shall never fall.

526. Abba Sisoes asked Abba Or, and said to him, "Tell me a word of excellence" He said to him, "Do you trust me, and believe my promise?" Abba Sisoes said to him, "Yes." Abba Or said to him, "Go, and whatever you have seen me doing, that also do yourself" Abba Sisoes said to him, "What do I see in you, O my father?" Abba Or answered saying, "My mind is more abased than that of the least of all the children of men."

527. On one occasion seven brethren came to Abba Arsenius and they entreated him, saying, "What is the work of monks?" The old man answered and said, "When I came to dwell in this place I went to two old men, and I asked them this same question. They answered and said to me, "Do you believe in us?" I said, "Yes.' Then they said to me, 'Go, and whatever you have seen us doing, that also do yourself.' The brethren asked him subsequently, saying, 'Tell us, Father, what was their work?' The old man said to them, 'One acquired great humility, and the other acquired obedience' They then said to him, 'Tell us what your work is?' The old man said to them, 'According to my will, and according to my mind; it is a great thing for a man not to bind himself with any matter.' Being profited they departed in gladness, and gave praise to God.

528. A brother asked Abba Poemen, saying, "What shall I do with the weight of weariness which holds me?" The old man said to him, "Both large and small boats are provided with thick ropes for towing. If there be a blowing wind which is unfavourable to the path of the ship, they throw them round their breasts, pull them along from dry land; and quietly little by little they let the ship go on its way until God sends a wind which is suitable for bearing it along wherever they want it to go. But if they learn that a storm has begun to rise, they make haste, drive a stake in the ground, and tie up the ship lest it drifts away. Now the stake is that a man should condemn himself."

529. A brother asked Abba Poemen, "How is it possible for a man to avoid speaking evil to his neighbor?" The old man answered saying to him, "We and our brethren possess two images. Whenever a man condemns himself, his brother appears to him as pleasing and excellent. But whenever a man appears pleasing to himself, his brother will be found to be, in his sight, hateful and abominable."

530. Another old man said also, "Humility is not insipidity, but it is seasoned, as it were, with salt."

531. He used to say, "For a man to despise himself is a strong wall."

532. He also used to say, "Him who has become despised for our Lord's sake, our Lord will make him wise."

533. An old man used to say, "Take heed, with all your might, that you do

On Humility

nothing which merits blame, and do not desire to adorn yourself."

534. An old man used to say, "If humility descended to Sheol it is exalted to the heavens. When pride goes up to the heavens it shall be brought down to Sheol."

535. There were two brethren in Scete, the one who was younger than his fellow was the older in the monastic garb. One of the fathers came to visit them. They brought out a vessel of water and wanted to wash him. The younger brother in number of monastic years drew near to wash the old man. The old man held his hands, and prevented him. Then the older brother in respect of number of monastic years drew near to wash him. The brethren who were standing near him said to the old man, "The younger brother, O father, is the older in respect of the monastic garb." The father said to them, "I take the priority in the monastic garb of the younger man and place it upon him who is the elder."

536. There was a certain brother in a monastery who used to take the whole weight of the brethren on himself. He used to make accusations against himself, even committing of fornication, and used to say, "I have committed it." He was seeking the contempt in the sight of everyman. The brethren did not understand his life and works, and used to murmur against him, saying, "How great is the wickedness of this man, and because of this wickedness he does not even work." Their Abba knew of his works, knew that he was taking the affairs of everyman upon himself, and knew that he did not have any wickedness. The Abba spoke to the brethren, saying, "I will undertake that he will make one mat in a week, in humility, which is more than all your work, which was done with boasting. If you wish to know whether the matter is so or not, bring here all your work, and bring here also the mat of that brother, light a fire and throw in all your work." When they had done so, behold, everything was consumed except the mat of that brother. When the brethren saw this, they feared, expressed their contrition, and from that time they held that brother to be an Abba.

537. They used to say that Abba Poemen never gave his mind to the Lord, and that his knowledge was superior to that of any one of the old men.

538. Abba Ammon asked Abba Poemen concerning the impure thoughts that were born of a man, and concerning vain lusts. Abba Poemen said to him, "Shall the axe boast itself against him who wields it?"

539. Abba Betimius asked Abba Poemen, saying, "If a man is angry with me, and I express my contrition, but he does not accept it, what shall I do?" The old man said to him, "Take two of your friends, and express your contrition in their presence." The old man Betimius said to him, "What if he is not persuaded to accept it then?" Abba Poemen answered and said, "Take five others." Abba Betimius answered and said, "And if he is not persuaded by these also?" Abba Poemen said, "Then take a priest." Abba Betimius said, "And if he is not persuaded then?" Abba Poemen said to him, "Without anger and without excitement, pray to God that He may put into his mind the desire for peace, and immedately you shall have no further worries about it."

540. An old man used to say, "Tell me, brother, if you have acquired the seal of work, which is humility. A holy man who saw another sinning wept bitterly, saying, this man may sin today, but how many times shall I sin tomorrow? In whatever way a man may sin before you, do not condemn him. But think in your mind that you are a greater sinner than him, even though he is a man in the world. Remember also that he is sinning greatly against God."

541. Certain brethren went to visit Abba Poemen. While they were sitting with him, they praised a certain brother, saying, "He hates evil things." Abba Poemen said to him who spoke to him, "What is the hatred of evil things?" The brother was astonished, and found nothing to say. He rose up and threw himself before the old man, saying, "Tell me what is the hatred of evil things." The old man said to him, "The hatred of evil things is for a man to hate his own sins, and to justify those of his neighbor."

542. A certain brother committed an offence in the camp of the monks in the Scete. When a congregation was assembled on this matter, they sent after Abba Moses, but he refused to come. They sent the priest of the church to him, saying, "Come, for all the people are expecting you." He rose up and came. He took a basket with a hole in it and filled it with sand, and carried it upon his shoulders. Those who went out to meet him said to him, "What does this mean, O father?" He said to them, "The sands are my sins which are running down behind me and I cannot see them, and I, even I, have come this day to judge shortcomings which are not mine." When they heard this, they set that brother free and said nothing further to him.

543. Abba Moses entreated Abba Zechariah, saying, "Speak a word of consolation to the brethren." Zechariah took his cloak, laid it beneath his feet, and said, "Except a man let himself be trampled upon thus he cannot be a monk."

544. A brother asked Abba Aloms, saying, "What is the meaning of a man despising himself?" The old man said to him; "It means that you must set yourself below all the beasts, for you must remember that they will not be judged."

545. The same old man said that if a man accustoms himself to be a teacher, this act belongs to labor.

546. A brother asked Abba Poemen, saying, "What is the right manner for me to live in my cell?" Abba Poemen said to him, "How a man should live in his cell is known to all men. He must work with his hands, and eat once daily. He must hold his peace always, and meditate on the Holy Scriptures. And for a man to gain profit inwardly, he must bear the condemnation of himself wherever he goes. He must not neglect the times of service and of secret labor. If it happens that you have made the time unprofitable, when you go into the congregation of service complete your service without troubling yourself; by the fulfilment of these things. Grasp to yourself an upright congregation, so that you may draw near to them. Keep yourself remote from the assemblies of evil things."

547. Once Abba Arsenius was in his cell. The devils rose up against him and vexed him. Those who used to minister to him came to him. As they stood outside his cell they heard him crying out to God, saying, "O God, do not forsake me. I have never done before You anything which is good. But grant, O Lord, according to Your grace, that I may begin in the way."

548. Now, when Abba Arsenius was about to die Alexander and Zoilus, his brethren and disciples, were greatly disturbed. He said to them, "Why are you troubled? The hour has not yet come." They said to him, "We are not troubled about you, Father." He said to them, "When the hour comes I will tell you, for it will be for me to rise up against you before the throne of Christ if you give my bones to any man." Then they said to him, "What shall we do then, for we do not know how to bury you?" The old man said to them, "Do not you know how to throw a cord round my legs and to carry me outside the mountain?"

549 His word at all times was this, "Arsenius, because you did go out." He used to repeat this saying, "That I have spoken I have many times repented; that I held my peace I have never repented."

550. On one occasion the governor of the country seized one of the inhabitants of his village. The people entreated the old man to go and bring out him who had been seized. The old man said to them, "Leave me for three days and afterwards I will go." Abba Poemen prayed to the Lord, and said, "Lord, if you do not grant me this act of grace, the people will not allow me to live in this place." The old man went to entreat the governor. The governor said, "Yes, father, you make entreaty for a thief." The old man rejoiced that he did not receive from Him this of grace.

551. Once certain old men went to visit Abba Anthony, and Abba Joseph was with them. The old man wishing to try them spoke a word from the Book, and began to question the youngest of them, saying, "What is the meaning of this word?" Each of them said, "I have never yet understood it." Last of all, Abba Anthony said to Abba Joseph, "And what do you say that this word means?" Abba Joseph said, "I do not know." Abba Anthony said to him, "In truth, Abba Joseph, you have found the way to say, I do not know."

552. Abba Muthues said, "In proportion as a man draws near to God, it is necessary that he should regard himself as a sinner, for the Prophet Isaiah (Isaiah 6:5), who saw the Lord, calls himself wretched and unclean."

553. The old man used to say, "Who sold Joseph?" They said to him, "His brethren." The old man said to them, "No. It was humility that sold him. For he never said, I am your brother, and he never answered them. But he held his peace. He sold himself by his humility, and this humility made him governor over the land of Egypt."

554. A brother came to Abba Muthues, and said to him, "How is it that those who are In Scete do more than that which is written in the Book, for they love their enemies more than themselves?" Muthues said to them, "I do not yet love even the man who loves me more than I love myself."

555. There was a certain old man in Egypt before those who belonged to the company of Abba Poemen came there, and he possessed knowledge and great honor. When those of the following of Abba Poemen went up from Scete, every man left that old man and came to Abba Poemen. Those who were with him, and the old man, were filled with envy, and he cursed the followers of Abba Poemen because of this. Abba Poemen heard of it, and was vexed about it. He said to the brethren who were with him, "What shall we do for this old man? For the men who have forsaken him have cast us into vexation, and they have left that holy old man and turned their looks upon us, who are nothing. How then can we satisfy this old man?" Then he said to the brethren who were with him, "Make you some bread and boil a little food, and we will go to him, and will take with us also a vessel of wine, and we will eat with him, and perhaps by these means we shall be able to pacify him." They took the food and went to him. When they had knocked at the door his disciple looked out and asked them, "Who are you?" They said to him, "Tell the Abba that it is Poemen, and he wishes to be blessed by him." When his disciple had told him this, the old man said, "Send them away." He said, "I have not leisure to receive them." Then the disciple told them these things, but they stayed there lovingly, saying, "We will not go away unless we are held to be worthy of the blessing of the old man." When the old man saw their humility and patient persistence, he repented, and opened the door to them. When they were eating together, he said to them, "Truly, the things which I have heard were in you are not in you, but indeed what I see in you is a hundredfold greater than what I expected." He became a friend to them from that day.

556. On a certain occasion when Abba John was sitting before the church, the brethren surrounded him, and asked him about their thoughts, and when one of the old men saw him, he said to him, "Your repentance is full of sorceries." Abba John said to him, "It is even so, and this you say having only seen what is without, but if you could see what is within what would you say?"

557. Muthues repeated the following, "When I was a young man I used to say to myself, 'Perhaps you will do something good'; but now that I am an old man I see that I have not done even one good work."

558. He used to say concerning Abba Macarius that, "If the brethren drew near to him in fear, as to a great and holy old man, he would not answer them a word, but if one of the brethren treated him with familiar contempt, saying, 'Father, if you were a camel would not you steal the natron and sell it, and would not the driver beat you?' He would answer him. If any man spoke to him in anger, or with words similar to these, he would answer any question which was put to him."

CHAPTER ELEVEN

On Fornication

A CERTAIN MONK WAS ENGAGED, ON ONE OCCASION, in a war against fornication, and he had in his heart, as it were, a burning fire by day and by night. He bore this agony, and did not bring low his mind. After a long time the war passed away from him. He was unable to vanquish it in any way except by patient endurance, and immediately light rose on his mind.

560. And another brother also was engaged in a war against fornication, and he rose up by night, and came to one of the old men and told him his mind, and the old man persuaded him to endure, and he was helped, and went back to his cell. And again he came to the old man, and again he helped him, and the brother went back to his cell; and the war came upon him the third time, and again he went back by night to the old man, and the old man did not cause him pain but spoke with him for his benefit, and said to him, "Give it no opportunity, but come here whenever the devil vexes you, and you will expose him, and when he has been exposed he will take flight. For nothing vexes the devil of fornication so much as that a man should hide his thoughts and not reveal them." Now that brother came to the old man eleven times and made accusations against his thoughts, for he wished to be helped; and when the old man spoke to him that devil took flight, but when he came back to his cell the war came upon him. At length the brother said to the old man, "Do an act of grace, father, and tell me a word so that I may live." The old man said to him, "Be of good courage, my son, and if God permits my thought it shall come to you, and you shall bear it no longer, but you shall depart being innocent." He said this, and God did away with the war of that brother.

561. Another brother was engaged in a war against fornication, and he bore it with very great self-restraint for fourteen years. He guarded his mind against being submissive to lust, and at length he came to the church, and made known the matter to all the people. When they heard it they were pained, and they prayed for a whole week to God on his behalf, and afterwards He did away with the war that was in him.

562. On one occasion Abba Moses of Patara was engaged in a war against fornication. He could not endure being in his cell, so he went and informed Abba Isidore of it. The old man entreated him to return to his cell, but he would not agree to this. Having said, "Father, I cannot bear it," the old man took him up to the roof of his cell, and said to him, "Look to the west." When he looked he saw multitudes of devils with troubled and terrified aspects, and they showed themselves in the forms of phantoms which were in fighting attitudes. Abba Isidore said to him, "Look to the east." When he looked he saw innumerable holy angels standing there, and they were in a state of great glory. Then Abba Isidore said to him, "Behold, those who are in the west are those who are fighting with the holy ones, and those whom you have seen in the east are they who are sent by God to the help of the saints, for those who are with us are many." Having seen these, Abba Moses took courage and returned to his cell without fear.

563. One of the old men said concerning the lustful thoughts which come into the heart of a man, and which are not carried into effect, that they are like a man who sees a vineyard, and who desires to eat the grapes, but is afraid to go in lest he be caught and suffer death. If he be caught outside the hedge he will not die, because he has neither gone into the vineyard nor has eaten the grapes, but has only desired; now he shall be beaten with few stripes, because he has coveted, but he shall not die.

564. There was a certain old man, who lived in a cell, and his thoughts said to him, "Go, and take a woman to yourself." He rose up immediately and kneaded together some mud, made the figure of a woman, and he said to himself, "Behold your wife! It is necessary for you to labor with all your might that you may be able to feed her." He labored with his hands and twisted many

On Fornication

ropes. After a few days, he rose up, made a figure of a woman, and said to his thoughts, "Behold, your wife has brought away, it is necessary for you to work harder to keep your wife and to clothe your daughter." By doing thus, he vexed his body sorely. He said to his thought, "I cannot bear all this work, and since I am unable to bear the work, a wife is unnecessary for me." God saw his labor, removed away his thoughts of fornication, and he had peace.

565. Abba Poemen used to say, "As the sword-bearer stands before the king, being always ready to smite, so is it necessary for the soul which is prepared to stand ready to resist the devil of fornication."

566. They used to say that Mother Sarah contended against the devil of fornication for seven years on the roof of her house, before she vanquished him.

567. One of the old men said, "It is written concerning Solomon that he loved women, but every male loves the females, and we must restrain and draw onwards our nature by main force to purity."

568. A brother asked Abba Daniel, and said to him, "Deliver to me a commandment." He said to him, "Never place your hand in a dish and eat with a woman, and you will be able to flee from the devil of fornication."

569. They used to say that the great old man Abraham arrived at a monastery. There he saw a youth, and then he refused to pass the night there. The brethren who were with him said to him, "Are you also afraid, O Father?" The old man said to them, "Indeed, my sons, I am not afraid, but of what use is a vain war to me?"

570. A brother asked an old man, saying, "What shall I do? For my thoughts are fixed always upon fornication. My thoughts do not give me peace even for a moment; and thus is my soul vexed." The old man answered and said to him, "When these thoughts spring up in you speak not with them, for it belongs to them to rise up with continual anxiety, and not to be sluggish, but they have no power to force you, for it belongs to you either to accept them or not. Have you not seen what the Midianites did, how they adorned their women and set them up, but they forced no man to take them? Those who wished to do so fell into them, and those who did not became wroth, and made a slaughter in their wrath. Even so is it with the thoughts." Then that brother said to him, "What then shall I do? For I am weak, and passion overcomes me." The old man said to him, "Consider your thoughts well, and when they begin to speak to you, never answer them with a word, but rise up, pray, and meditate on holy words." The brother said to him, "Behold, father, I do meditate on holy words, and the passion does not rise in my heart, but I do not know the power of the words." The old man answered and said to him, "You can only continue to meditate, but I have heard Abba Poemen and many fathers say this word, 'The enchanter does not know the power of the words which he utters.' But when the animal hears them, it knows their power, and he becomes submissive, and submits itself to him. Even so it is with us, for although we do not know the power of the words where on we meditate, the devils know their power as soon as they hear them."

571. The old men in Scete were asked concerning fornication, "When does a man see a face in the passion stirred up in him?" They said, "This matter is likened to a table which is loaded with meats of all kinds, and a man who seeks and desires to eat of them; but if a man does not put out his hand and does not take of the meats he becomes a stranger to them."

572. They used to say that Abba Isaac went out and found the footprint of a woman on the road. He thought about it in his mind and destroyed it, saying, "If a brother sees it he may fall."

573. A brother asked Abba Agathon concerning fornication, and he said to him, "Go, cast your feebleness before God, and you shall find relief."

574. A brother asked a father, and said to him, "There is a war of fornication against me." The old man said to him, "If it is a good thing, why do you go away from it. But if it is a bad thing why do you not command it to depart?"

575. A certain brother, being vexed by the spirit of fornication, went to a great old man, and entreated him, saying, "Do an act of grace, and pray for me, for I am disturbed by fornication." The old man made supplication to God and entreated Him. The brother came to him a second time, and said the same words as before. The old man also was not neglectful in beseeching God on his behalf. When the brother had come to the old man, and troubled him in this way many times, because he was disturbed by fornication, the old man afterwards entreated God, and said, "O Lord, reveal to me the manner in which this brother lives, and where does it come from, as this is the reason why I have entreated You so often on his behalf, and he has not found relief." Then God revealed to him the affair of that brother. He saw him dwelling with the spirit of fornication by him. The brother was lusting for it. An angel was standing by ready to help him. The old man was angry with that brother because he did not cast himself on God, but was involving his mind with the thought. Immediately the old man knew that the cause rests with the brother himself. He made him understand this, he roused him up, and afterwards he took heed to himself.

576. A brother asked Abba Poemen, saying, "The body is feeble, but my passions are not weak." The old man said to him, "The passions make thorns to grow and burst into flower."

577. A brother asked Abba Poemen concerning the passions of the body. The old man said to him, "They are like those who sang praises to the image of Nebuchadnezzar, for if those who sang had not burned men, people would have never worshipped the image. In this wise the enemy also sings to the soul by means of the passions, so that he may perchance be able to make it commits sin through the passion of the body."

578. An old man used to say, "Salt is produced by water. But if it falls into water it becomes dissolved and is lost. Similarly monks are born of women, but if they fall into women they are dissolved and perish from God."

579. A certain father was a virgin when he went out to become a monk. He did not even know that a whore existed among the children of men. When he was dwelling in his cell the devils began to stir the passion of fornication in him. When he lifted up his eyes, he saw the devils going around him in the forms of Ethiopians. They incited him to yield to that passion. Then he immediately rose up and prayed, saying, "O Lord, help me." After he finished praying, immediately a stone fell from the roof, and he heard a sweet voice. He seemed to enjoy a short respite from the thoughts of fornication. He rose up, came to one of the old men and related the matter to him. The old man answered saying, "I do not know not what this means." The old man sent him on to Abba Poemen. The brother related the matter to Abba Poemen as well. The old man said to him, "The stone which you saw falling is the calumniator. And that voice which you heard is lust. Take heed to your soul, and make supplication to God. Behold, you then shall be freed from this war." Abba Poemen taught him how to contend against devils, and having prayed, he dismissed him. The brother returned to his cell, made entreaty and supplication to God. God granted him to attain to such a gift of excellence. So when that brother died, God was pleased for this excellence to be revealed to him, whether it was well with his soul or not. According to another manuscript, "He rose up and prayed. It is thus written, He saw the devils surrounding him in the forms of Ethiopians. They were inciting him to yield to the passion. He said, "This natural member, that establishes man, is like a spout in a tank which lets out water. It is also like a conduit, which carries the water off a roof. Similarly this member carries off water from a man." Having said these words, immediately the stone fell.

580. Once a certain man went out to Scete to become a monk, and he took with him his son as soon as he had been weaned; and when the boy was grown up and had become a young man, the war of fornication attacked him, and he said to his father, "I will go into the world, father, for I cannot endure this striving against fornication." Then his father entreated him to persevere, but at length the boy said to his father, "Father, I cannot bear it any longer, let me go." His father said to him, "My son, listen to me for this time only. Take seven pairs of cakes of bread, and a few palm leaves, sufficient for forty days, and go into the desert. May God's will be done." The son listened to him, took the bread and palm leaves and departed. He remained in the desert working, twisting dry palm leaves into ropes, plaiting mats, and eating dry bread. He lived a life of seclusion for twenty days. He looked, and behold, the work of fornication came and drew near to him. It stood up before him in the form of an Ethiopian dark woman whose smell was exceedingly foul. But he was unable to endure her smell, and he drove her away from his presence. Then she said to him, "In the hearts of men I am a sweet and a pleasant smell. But because of your obedience and labor, God has not permitted me to lead you astray. I have, nevertheless, made you acquainted with my smell." The young man rose up, came to his father, and said to him, "I no longer wish to go into the world, for I have seen the matter of fornication, and I have smelled its foul odour." Now the father knew of a certainty that the young man had been satisfied in his mind on the subject, and he said to his son, "Had you remained in the desert forty days and kept my commandment, you would most certainly have seen a vision which was far more excellent."

581. Once a brother came to Abba Poemen, and said to him, "What shall I do, father, for I am vexed by fornication? Behold, I came to Nebation [Anicetus], and he said to me, "It is not right that those thoughts should stay with you so long." Abba Poemen said to him, "The labor of Abba Anicetus is high and exalted, and his thoughts are above with the angels, and he has forgotten that I and you are whore mongers. But if you wish, listen to me, and I also will speak to you. If a monk can hold fast his belly, his tongue, and his love for going around as a stranger, you may be assured that he is able to become a monk in very truth, and that he will not die."

582. A brother asked an old man, and said to him, "What shall I do? For fornication is killing me." The old man said to him, "When a mother is about to wean her son she smears aloes over her breasts. When the child comes to suck as usual, he shrinks away and rejects sucking. You too then put bitter aloes in your heart, and immediately the wicked devils will fly from there." The brother said to him, "What kind of bitter aloes is it right for me to place there." The old man said to him, "The remembrance of the death and punishment which are laid up in the world which is to come."

583. A brother asked an old man, "Where do the temptations of fornication which attack me come from?" The old man said, "They come because you eat and drink plenty, and because you sleep until you are satisfied."

584. Abba John used to say, "Whoever talks as much as he can with a woman, has already committed adultery with her in his mind."

585. Once a certain brother came to Abba Muthues and asked him, saying, "Is slander worse than fornication?" The old man said, "Fornication is worse." The brother said to him, "How can this be?" The old man said to him, "Calumny is a wicked thing, but it receives healing quickly, and the calumniator repents, saying, 'I have spoken evil many times. Fornication in the body is death in its nature.'"

586. There was in Scete a certain monk who strove hard against a particular sin, where the enemy sowed in him the remembrance of a certain woman with a beautiful face. The enemy troubled him greatly through her. By the Providence of God, a certain brother who came down from Egypt went to visit him. It happened that while they were conversing together the brother who had gone to visit him said, "Such and such a woman is dead." She was the same woman whom remembrance was being stirred up in the monk. When the other brother heard this, he rose up, took his head cloth, and went up by night to Egypt. There, he opened her grave, and smeared himself with the filthy and putrefying matter of the dead body of the woman. Then he went back to his cell. He set that thing of filth before his mind at all times, and battled with his thought, saying, "Behold your lust, and that which you did require! Behold, I have brought it to you; take your fill." He used to torture himself with the remembrance of that filthy thing until the war, which within him was quietened.

587. One of the brethren asked Abba Zeno, now he had great freedom of speech with him, saying, "Behold, you have grown old. What about the matter of fornication?" The old man said to him, "It knocks, but it passes on." Then one of the brethren asked him, "What is the meaning of 'it knocks, but it passes on'?" The old man said to him, "Imagine now that one brought to your mind the remembrance of a certain woman, and that you did say, 'Oh, but that you did not allow it to go up in your mind. That is what 'it knocks, but passes on' means." The young men were excited by this speech.

588. A brother asked Abba Theodore of Scete, saying, "The thought of fornication comes, troubles and disturbs the mind. It is not able to commit the deed. And it certainly cannot help, but it can hinder the course towards spiritual excellence." The old man said to him, "The man who is wakeful and struggles and casts it from him and stands up to prayer."

589. A certain old man from Parmis spoke against this thought, saying, "If we do not possess thoughts we become the prey of the enemy. For this enemy, like an ordinary enemy, demands what is his. Therefore let us, in the same manner, do what we have to do. Let us stand up in prayer, and immediately he will flee. Be constant in the service of God, and you shall conquer. Strive, and you shall be crowned."

590. Against this thought of fornication a brother asked an old man, saying, "What shall I do about the mind of fornication which vexes me?" Abba Copres the Alexandrian answered and said, "If you have no thoughts, you will have no hope, so then their work is with you; for he who performs their work has no thoughts. Perhaps you have the custom of talking with a woman?" The brother said to him, "No, I have not, but they are thoughts of former times and of recent times which trouble me." The old man said to him, "You shall not be afraid of the dead, but fear the things which are living, and cast yourself down in prayer before God. For if we have no thoughts we are mere animals. As the enemy works for that which is his, even so let us do for that which is ours. Let us stand up in prayer, and let us have a care for doctrine, and let us endure, for patient endurance is victory. Unless a man strives he will never be crowned. For there are in the world athletes who though wounded conquer nevertheless, and however many times one man may be wounded by two others, if he can endure the blows he will be able to conquer those who hit him. Observe then what a degree of endurance is possessed by such men for the sake of the merchandise of this world! Do you then endure, and God shall strive with your enemies on your behalf while you may remain quiet."

591. Against the thought of fornication, another old man who dwelt in the desert used to say, "You wish to live while you are asleep! Go and labor. Go and work. Go, seek, and you shall find. Awake and stand up. Knock and it shall be opened to you. There are athletes in the world who are called boxers. They smite each other. They deserve the victory because they endure and fight persistently. These men do not withdraw defeated when they are wounded, although one of them may be smitten many times by two others, and irrespective to the number of the blows which he might receive from them, yet, he continues to fight, and he conquers and is crowned."

592. Against the thought of fornication another old man said, "Such things will happen to you through negligence. For if it is certain to us that God dwells in us. We can never become a habitation for others. We can never give our souls over to become vessels for the service of aliens. For our Lord Who dwells in us, and is found in us, is able to watch over our lives. It is not right for us to neglect or to hold lightly Him for Whose sake we have put Him on, and Whom we see. But let us make ourselves pure even as He is pure. Stand up then upon a rock, and if the river be violently disturbed you shall not fear. Behold, your building shall not shake. Sing with might, saying, 'Those who trust in the LORD are like Mount Zion, which cannot be moved, but abides forever.' He who dwells in Jerusalem shall never be moved. The Enemy said to our Redeemer, 'I will send these who belong to me against those who belong to you that they may drive them back; and if they do evil to Your chosen ones I cannot help it, and I will trip them up, even though I can only do so in dreams of the night.' Then our Redeemer said to him, 'If an abortion can inherit his father's possessions this also shall be accounted as sin to My chosen ones.'"

593. Against the thought of fornication another old man spoke, saying, "Be like a man who passes through a street of tavern-keepers. He smells the odour of boiling meats, or the whiff of something, which is being roasted; he who wishes enters into one of them and eats, and he who does not wish to do so smells the meats as he passes by and then goes on. Drive away then from you the fetid smell of evil thoughts, and stand up and pray, saying, 'O Son of God, help me.' The same thing is also to be said about other thoughts, for we are not the roots of the thoughts, but are those who strive against them."

594. "Now on your account, O son of man, Christ was born, and the Son of

God came that He might make you to live. He became a Child. He became a man, being also God. He Who was the Lawgiver became a reader of the Law, and He took the Book in the congregation, and He read, saying, 'The Spirit of God is upon me, and for this reason He has anointed me, and has sent me to preach the Gospel to the poor.' Like a servant He made a whip of rope, and He drove all those who sold oxen, cattle, doves, and other things out from the temple. Like a servant, He girded a napkin about His loins, and washed the feet of His disciples. He commanded them to wash the feet of their brethren. Like an elder He sat among the elders, and taught the people. Like a Bishop He took bread, blessed it, broke it, and gave to His disciples. He was beaten for your sake, that is to say, for your sake He was crucified, and for your sake He died. Yet you for His sake will not even endure an insult! He rose as God. He was exalted as God. All these things for our sake, all these things by Divine Providence, all these things properly and in due order did He do that He might redeem us. Let us then be watchful, strenuous, and constant in prayer. Let us do everything which will please Him, and will gratify His friends, so that we may be redeemed and live. Was not Joseph sold into Egypt, and did not he live in an alien land? The three simple young men in Babylon, were not there men who opposed them? Yet, because they feared God, He helped them, and made them glorious."

595. An old man who had delivered himself to God used to say, "The monk must have no will of his own, but he whose will is of God continues to minister to Him unwearyingly; for if you do your own will, you become weary, and you labor, and God does not listen to you." The old man also said, "He who lives in God lives with Him, for He said, I will dwell in them, and I will walk in them, and they shall be to Me a people, and I will be to them a God'" (Exodus 6: 7).

596. The old man also said, "God said to you thus, 'If you love Me, O monk, do what I ask, and do not do what I do not desire. For monks should lead lives where they do not act in iniquity. A man should not look upon evil things with his eyes, nor hear with his ears things which are alien to the fear of God, nor utter calumnies with his mouth, nor plunder with his hands; but he should give especially to the poor, and he should not be unduly exalted in his mind, and he should not think evil thoughts, neither should he fill his belly. Let him do then all these things with discretion, for by them is a monk known.'" The old man also said, "These things form the life of a monk: good works, obedience, and training. A man should not lay blame on his neighbor, should not utter calumnies, and should not complain, for it is written, 'The lovers of the Lord hate wickedness.'"

597. A brother on several occasions troubled an old man, and said to him, "What shall I do with the impure and wicked thoughts of diverse kinds which force their way into me by various means?" The old man answered and said to him, "You are like a cistern which has been dug out, and which is sometimes full, but which, when a man comes to draw water from, he found it dry. Why do you not make yourself more like a fountain of water, which is never without water? Persistence is victory, and victory is constancy, and constancy is life, and life is kingdom, and kingdom is God."

Here ends the questions concerning the thoughts of fornication and the answerers to them, and the counsels of the holy old men.

CHAPTER TWELVE

On the Acceptance of Repentance

Two brethren were in restraint to the lust of fornication. They went and took wives to themselves. At length, however, they repented, and said to each other, "What have we gained by leaving the labor of angels, and coming to this state of impurity, since after the present life we shall be delivered over to fire and everlasting torture? Let us return to the desert and repent." They went immediately, and came to the desert to the fathers. They entreated them to offer up supplications on their behalf. The outward appearance of both was the same. They shut themselves up for one year, and they made supplications to God, and entreated Him to pardon them. To each of the two brethren a similar quantity of bread and water was given. After their period of repentance was fulfilled, they went out of their seclusion. The old men saw that the countenance of one was changed, and that it was exceedingly sad, whilst that of the other brother was cheerful and glad. The fathers marvelled why, seeing that the two men had been partaking of the same amount of food, and had endured the same restraint, the face of one was so different from that of the other. They asked him of the sad face, saying, "What were you thinking about while in your cell?" He said, "On the evil things which I have committed, and I think about the torture which is to come, and by reason of my fear my flesh cleave to my bones." They asked him whose appearance was cheerful, saying, "Tell us, what you thought about while you were in your cell."

He said, "I gave thanks to God, Who has delivered me from the impurity of this world, and from everlasting punishment, and Who has brought me to this labor of angels, and with such things I remembered God and rejoiced." Then the old men said, "The repentance of each is equal before God."

599. An old man was asked by one who toiled, "Is the repentance of sinners accepted by God?" The old man, after he had taught him with many words, said to him, "Tell me, O my beloved one, if your cloak were to be torn in rags, would you throw it away? He said to him, "No, but I would sew up the rents, and then I could use it again." The old man said to him, "If you would show pity upon your garment which has no feeling, shall not God show pity on that which He has created, and which is His work?"

600. A certain brother fell into temptation. Through tribulation he relinquished the garb of monkhood; and wished to begin a new ascetic life. He saw a great difficulty of the matter, drew back, and said, "When shall I ever find myself in the same condition as I was formerly?" Through fear he did not begin his work, went and made the matter known to an old man. The old man said, "The matter is thus; 'There was a certain man who possessed an estate. He held it to be of no account and did not cultivate it. It became full of tangled undergrowth and thorns. One day he remembered it, sent his son, and said to him, "Go and clean the estate." When he had gone and seen the abundance of the undergrowth, the son was afraid, and said to himself, "When shall I be able to clean away all this undergrowth?" He threw himself upon a bed, laid down, and went to sleep. He did so everyday. His father went out, and found that he was asleep, and that he had done nothing. The father said to him, "How come, my son, you have not done any work whatsoever?" The son said to his father, "When I came to work and saw the abundance of the undergrowth, I was afraid and said, 'When shall I be able to clean all this away?' His father said to him, "My son, work according to the measure of your sleep each day, and it shall be sufficient for you" When the young man heard this, he plucked up courage, and did the work, and in a short time cleansed the estate. Thus also you shall not be afraid, but begin the work of your rules, and God, by His Grace, will establish you among those in the first rank." Now when the brother had done thus he was helped.

601. A brother asked one of the old men, and said, "If a monk stumbles and falls into sin, are many labors necessary for him, and if he does them will he be able to stand in the grade where he was formerly? He who goes out from the world, and begins the cultivation of spiritual excellence, will find it easy to advance, for he who is occupied in labors, if it be that he is reduced from the grade where he stood by his stumbling, will be afflicted and grieved in his mind." Then the old man answered and said to him, "A monk is like a house which has fallen down. If he is awake in his mind, and if he is zealous and anxious to build that which was fallen down, he will find ample material which will be of use in his building among the remains of that which fell down before he begins to build. For he will find the foundation stones, and the old stones from the walls, and other things, which were employed in the old building, and out of these, if he is so disposed, he will be able to make his building to rear itself up better than the man who has not yet dug the places for the foundations and laid the foundation stones, and who does not possess the materials which are to be employed in the building, and who only begins to build with the hope that he will be able to finish. Thus is it with him that falls from the practice of rules and works of the monastic life into temptation, for if he turn back, and repent, he will possess ample material from his former works of the ascetic life which he possesses to begin his building afresh, I mean to say, the training and the service of the work of the hands, which is the foundation of this. Whoever then has gone from the world, and begins the cultivation of ascetic excellence, when he has done these things he will still be found standing in the front rank of the solitary life."

602. One of the old men told the following story, saying: There was a certain monk who dwelt in the desert, and he lived a life of strict and severe rule, and he was famous among men, and he could even cast out devils and heal the sick. It came to pass that, through the agency of Satan, the passion of fornication was stirred up against him. Because he was not sufficiently humble to reveal his war to the old men who were before him, in a few days time he fell into fornication with a woman who used to come to him continually for assistance. Having fallen, he despaired about himself, and rose up to go to the world. He was sad, grieved about his fall, and meditated, saying, "I will go into the desert which is further away, and I shall not see any man, and I shall not be seen of any, and there I will die like the wild animals." When he had gone, and was wandering about in the desert and mountains, there he used to cry out by night and by day, saying, "Woe to me! Woe to me!" He did not cease to weep and groan. There was in that desert a certain solitary old man who dwelt in a cleft in the rock. When the old man heard the sound of the weeping and lamentation, his mercy for him revealed itself. He went out to meet him, and they saluted each other. The old man said to him, "Why do you weep in this fashion?" The young man said, "Because I have angered God, and because I have fallen into fornication." Then was the old man astonished, and said, "O how greatly did I fear and tremble at your lugubrious voice. For I thought that you had been entrusted with the governorship of the brethren, and that you had governed unjustly, or that you had squandered in an unseemly manner the work of the community. For the harlot repented, and for the unbeliever there is a foundation, and the thief is a son of the kingdom, but Ananias and Sapphira were slain because they stole the money of the community of the brethren, and thus is slain the soul of every one who with fraud or carelessness squanders the possessions of the religious houses. But be of good courage, O brother, and go back again to your cell, and make your entreaty to God as you repent, and He will establish you in your former grade." Then the monk went back to his place, and he shut himself in, and never again undertook to talk with any man, except him that handed in to him his food through the little window of his cell. There he remained until the end of his life, and he attained to a most exalted state of perfection.

603. Abba Ammon of Ritheaon asked Abba Poemen about the impure thoughts which are produced in a man, and the vain lusts. Abba Poemen said to him, "It belongs to Satan to sow them, but it is our affair not to welcome them."

604. A brother asked Abba Ammon, saying, "Behold, there were two men, one was a monk, and the other was a son of the world. The monk used to determine in the evening to cast away from him in the morning the garb of the monk. While the son of the world used to make up his mind that on the next day where he would take the garb of monkhood. It happened that both men died on the same night. How will they be regarded, and which determination will be reckoned to them?" The old man said to him, "He who was a monk died as a monk. He who was a child of the world died as such, for as they were found to be so were they taken."

605. A brother asked Abba Sisoes, saying, "What shall I do, father? For I have fallen." The old man said to him, "Rise up." The brother said to him, "I did rise up, but I fell again." The old man said to him, "Rise up again." The brother said to him, "I did rise up again, many times, and I fell again." The old man said to him, "Rise up again." The brother said to him, "Until when?" The old man said to him, "Until you advance, either in good deeds or in falling, for in the road where a man advances he goes, either it be to death or to life."

606. It happened on one occasion that a brother in the monastery of Abba Hatil (or Helit) was tempted, and fell. Having been expelled from that place he went to the mountain, to Abba Anthony. He remained with him for a

On the Acceptance of Repentance

long time. Abba Anthony sent him back to the monastery from which he had gone from. When the brethren at the monastery saw him, they cast him out. He returned to Abba Anthony, and said to him, "Father, they have refused to receive me." Abba Anthony sent a message to them, saying, "A storm rose up against a ship on the sea, and destroyed the freight which it carried, but with the greatest difficulty it was saved and brought to land. Now what do you wish to do? Do you wish to drown him who has been saved?" When the brethren heard the words of Abba Anthony, they sent to the brother, and welcomed him with gladness.

607. Abba Anthony used to say, "There are many who fall and who rise up to an attitude of rectitude. But there are some who fall from good deeds to polluted things. It is better where a man falls and rises up than a man who stands and then falls."

608. Abba Poemen said, "If a man sins, and says, 'I have not sinned,' and you reproach him, you cut off his will. But if you say to him, 'Do not be sorry about this, but guard yourself from sinning again,' by this means you wake his soul to repentance."

609. He also said, "I prefer a man who has sinned, done wickedly, and repented, to a man who has not sinned, has not manifested repentance; for the former possesses a humble mind, while the latter esteems himself in his thoughts as a just man."

610. Abba Sarmata used to say, "I prefer a man who has sinned, and knows how to acknowledge his sins, to a man who does righteousness, and says, I do what is fair."

611. Abba Theodore of Parme used to say, "The man who is in a state of repentance is not bound by the Law."

612. They used to say that the thoughts of a certain old man used to say to him, "Let today go by, and repent tomorrow." And he would say, "No, not so, for I will repent today, and tomorrow shall be as God desires."

613. There was at one time among the brethren a certain man who at the beginning of his ascetic life took good heed to his soul. After a short time, he began to treat the salvation of his life with contempt. His Abba ordered him to strip off the garb of the monks, to put on the apparel of men who are in the world, and to depart from among the brethren. The man fell down at his feet, and entreated him, saying, "If you will forgive me this once only, you will gain me henceforward, for I repent of these things which I have done through negligence." He multiplied and prolonged his entreaties. He made many promises that he would in the future mend his ways. He was held worthy of forgiveness. He struggled with all the power of his soul to such purpose as to become a pattern to great and small.

CHAPTER THIRTEEN

On the Father who wrought Wonderful Works

Abba Sisoes said, "When we were in Scete, with Abba Macarius, seven of us went up to reap with him. A certain widow followed after us gleaning, and did not cease weeping. The old man cried to the lord of the estate, and said to him, "What is the matter with the old woman who weeps continually? He said to him, "Her husband took a deposit of money from a man and he died suddenly without saying with whom he had placed it, and the owner of the deposit wishes to take her and her children as slaves." The old man said to him, "Tell her to come to us at the place where we rest at the season of noon." It was told to her. At the season of noon the woman came to them, and the old man said to her, "Woman, why do you weep continually?" She said, "My husband is dead. He had taken a deposit from a certain man, and he died suddenly without telling us where he had laid it up." The old man said to her, "Come and show me where you have laid him." He took the brethren with him, and went with her. Having arrived at the place where the man was laid, the old man said to her, "Go to your house." After she departed, he made an end of his prayer. The old man cried out to the dead man and said, "O such a one, where have you laid up the deposit which belongs to the stranger?" The dead man answered immediately, and said, "It is hidden in my house beneath the leg of the bed." The old man said to him, "Sleep now until the Resurrection." When the brethren saw what had been done, they all fell down at his feet in fear. The old man said to them, "This has not happened because of me, O my brethren.

Nor is the matter a great one, but God has wrought this thing for the sake of the widow and the orphans. But what is great is that God desires a soul which is pure and sinless." When they had come they told the widow that the deposit was laid up in such and such a place. The old woman brought it up, and gave it to its owner, and set her children free from slavery. Everyone who heard of this gave thanks to God.

615. When Abba Miles (or Manilius) was passing through a certain place he saw a man holding a monk by force as if he had committed murder. The old man drew near and questioned the brother. When he learned that he was being wrongfully accused, he said to those who had seized him, "Tell me, where is the man who was murdered." They showed him. Then the old man drew near to the murdered man, and said to all who were standing there, "Let us pray." When he spread out his hands in prayer before God, the dead man rose up. The old man said to him before every man, "Tell us who slew you." He answered, saying, "I went into the church and gave some money to the elder. It was him who rose up, killed me, carried me out and threw me in the habitation of this monk. I entreat you that the goods which I have given to him may be taken back and given to my children."

616. On one occasion a certain man in the world went to Abba Sisoes in the mountain of Abba Anthony. He had his son with him. As they were going along the road his son died. The man was badly disturbed, but he took him up in faith and brought him to the old man. He came with his son, fell down before him with his son upon his knees as if he was entreating him to bless them. The father of the boy went out and left his son lying dead at the feet of the old man. The old man did not know that the boy was dead, but he thought that he was making supplication and entreaty to him. He answered and said to him, "Arise, and go out." Immediately without any delay, the youth rose up and went out to his father. When the father saw him, he marvelled. The father took him and went in and did homage to the old man, and informed him about the matter. When the old man heard this he was troubled, for he did not wish this thing to happen because of the praise of men. His disciple commanded them not to tell the story before any man until the day of his departure.

617. One of the fathers used to relate that Abba Paul, who dwelt in Thebes, would take snakes, scorpions, and horned snakes in his hands, and kill them. The brethren made apologies to him, and said, "Father, tell us through what labor you have received this gift." He said to them, "Forgive me, O my fathers, if you possess purity of heart, every living thing will be subject to you as it was subject to Adam before he transgressed the commandment of God."

618. On one occasion one of the old men of Thebes came to Mount Sinai. And having departed from there, one of the brethren met him on the way, and with a groan he said to the old man, "We are distressed, O father, through the need for rain." The old man said to him, "Why do you not pray and ask God for some?" The brother said to him, "We have prayed, made the earnest supplication, and the rain has not come." The old man said to them, "Then you did not pray with all your hearts; do you wish to know that the matter is?" After this, the old man stood up in prayer, spread out his hands to heaven, and immediately, without any delay, the rain came. The brother saw, feared, fell down and did homage to him. The old man took to flight, but the brother made everything happened known. When the brethren heard what happened, they all glorified God.

619. They used to say that, when on one occasion, Abba Moses of Scete was going into Patara, he grew weary through the length of the road. He was afraid and said, "How can I bring water for myself into this place?" He heard a voice saying, "Go on, and do not fear." One day a large number of the fathers came to him, and he had there only one vessel of water. Having boiled some lentil the water finished. At this, the old man was troubled, went out and in, and prayed to God. Afterwards a great cloud came and poured down upon them much rain. The rain filled all the vessels, which he had with water. Then afterwards the fathers said to him, "Abba Moses, tell us why did you come in and out." He said to them, "I entered into judgement with God, who brought me here because there was a need for water, and because I had no water for His servants to drink; therefore I came in and out."

620. The old man Joseph used to say, "I went on one occasion to Abba Poemen and found many old men with him. Behold, a certain man had brought a youth who was a kinsman of Abba Poemen, and whose face had been turned backwards through the operation of the devil. When his father saw the multitude of the old men who were coming to Abba Poemen, he brought his son outside the door of the monastery, sat down and wept. When one of the old men had ended his business, and was going out from the building, he saw him, and said to him, "Why are you weeping, O ,an?" The father of the youth said to him, "I am of the family of Abba Poemen. A trial has come upon this youth, but we are afraid to take him to Abba Poemen, for he refuses to see us. Now, if he learns that I am here, he will drive me away. But when I knew that you were coming here, I ventured to come also." He cast the youth down on the ground at his feet, wept, saying, "If you will, have mercy on me, and take this youth inside, and pray over him." The old man took him, carried him in to Abba Poemen. The old man acted wisely in the matter. He did not take the youth at once to Abba Poemen, but beginning with the last of the brethren who was there, he brought the youth to each and every one of them, saying, "Make the sign of the Cross upon this youth." Having brought him alike to all the brethren and to all the old men who were there, finally he brought him to Abba Poemen. The blessed man refused to touch him. Thereupon a contention arose, and they all entreated him, saying, "Father, please do as we all have done." Abba Poemen sighed, rose up and prayed, saying, "O God, heal that which You have created, so that it may not be destroyed by the enemy." He finished his prayer, and made the sign of the Cross over him. Immediately the face of the youth was made straight, and was healed. Abba Poemen gave him to his father made whole, so he took him and departed rejoicing.

621. They used to say that the face of Abba Pambo was shining like a lightening, as Moses when he received the glory of the likeness of Adam. And when his face shone, and was like a king who sits upon his throne; thus it was also with Abba Silvanus and with Abba Sisoes.

622. They used to say about one of the old men that he was lightened during the day, as well as during the night in his cell. He used to work with his hands and read in the night, just as he did during the day.

623. One of the old men sent his disciple to draw water. The well was very far from their cell. And that brother forgot to take the rope with him. Being distressed there, he bowed himself in prayer, and cried out, saying, "O well, my father said, 'Fill this vessel for me with water, and without delay' and the water came up, and the brother filled the vessel, and as soon as he had done so the water descended to its place."

624. On one occasion Abba Moses came to the well in order to draw water. There he saw Abba Zechariah praying to the stream, and the Spirit of God was resting upon him like a dove.

625. On one occasion one of the brethren went to the cell of Abba Arsenius in Scete. He looked through the window, and saw the old man standing up, and all his body was like fire. That brother was worthy to see this sight. Having knocked at the door, the old man came out to him. Seeing that the brother was marvelling at the sight which he had seen, he said to him, "Have you been knocking a long time? Perhaps you have seen something?" He said to him, "No, I have not." Abba Arsenius spoke with him and dismissed him.

626. They used to say that a certain old man said, "Truly, as he who works gold, and as he who makes beautiful work, cleanly and at peace, so you also by your beautiful thoughts must inherit the kingdom of God; but I who have passed the whole period of my life in the desert have not been able to overtake you."

627. They used to say about a certain great old man, who lived in Purpirine, that when he lifted up his eyes to heaven he could see whatever was there, and that if he gazed into the earth, he could see into the depths, and whatever was in them.

628. Abba John, who was cast out by the Marcionites, used to say, "On one occasion we went from Syria to Abba Poemen, and when we wished him to speak to us about hardness of heart we found that the old man did not know Greek, and there was no interpreter with leisure to interpret there. The old man saw that we were troubled at this, and he began to talk to us in the Greek tongue, and at the beginning of his speech he said, 'Water is by nature soft, and stone is hard, nevertheless if you suspend a vessel full of water above a stone, and will pour it out upon it drop by drop, it will wear away the stone. In the same way the Word of God is soft, and our heart is hard, but if it hears continually the Word of God, the heart will be opened, and will turn to the fear of God.'"

629. A certain monk lived in the desert, and there was another brother who lived in a cell by his side. When he visited him from time to time he used to see him praying and entreating our Lord that the wild animals might be at peace with him. After the prayer he found the panther, which was suckling her youngster. That brother went down upon his knees and sucked with them. On another occasion the blessed man saw that brother praying and beseeching God to make fire to be at peace with him; and he lit a fire, and knelt down in the middle of it, and prayed. That old man used to say, "If you wish to become a monk, bring yourself into subjection that you may be in the congregation of the community, and may enter the monastery; but if you can not cast away from your care concerning all kinds of occupations and affairs, you can never dwell in the congregation. All the power you have is over a bottle of water."

630. There are wonderful things, which the blessed Bessarion performed. He made the waters of the sea sweet, and Saul his disciple drank of this water. He crossed over the water of the river. He prevented the sun from setting in the heavens. The rooting up of the temples of the idols was revealed to him. As they were going to John the Theban his disciple became thirsty, and Bessarion prayed, and water bubbled up. He gave him to drink. He healed the young man who was a paralytic, so that he ran to his father. He cast out a devil from a young man who was always asleep, and whom his parents besought him to wake up. I have, however, written down all these things in the history of the holy man Bessarion, where it is written that he was sitting at the door of the monastery and weeping bitterly.

CHAPTER FOURTEEN

On the Greatness the Sublime Rule of the Solitary life

There was a certain old man amongst the fathers who used to see visions. This man testified, and said, "That power which I have seen existing in baptism, I have also seen in the apparel of the monks when they take the garb of the monk."

632. An old man from Thebaid used to say, "I was the son of a priest of idols. When I was young I lived in the temple. I have on many occasions seen my father go into the temple to perform the sacrifices to the idols. Once I went in secretly after him, and I saw Satan sitting there, with his whole army before him, and, behold, one of his devils came and did homage to him. Satan answered and said to him, "When did you come?" The devil answered saying, "I was in such and such country, and I stirred up many wars and revolts, and I caused the shedding of blood, and I have come to tell you these things." Satan said to him, "How long did it take you to do this?" The devil said "Thirty days." Then Satan commanded him to be beaten, saying to him, "Is this all that you have done in so long a time?" Behold, another devil came and worshipped him, and he said to him, "When did you come? The devil answered and said, "I was in the sea, where I stirred up storms, and sank ships, and drowned many men, and I have come that I may inform you of these things." Satan answered and said to him, "In how much time have you done this?" The devil answered and said to him, "In twenty days." Satan commanded that he also should be beaten, saying to him, "Why is it that in all these days you have only done what you said?" When he had said this, behold, a third devil came and worshipped Satan, who answered and said to him, "And where do you come from?" The devil answered and said to him, "I have been in such and such a city where there was a marriage feast, and I stirred up a war there, and caused the shedding of much blood, and the death of the bridegroom and the bride; and as soon as I had done this I came to inform you." Satan said to him, "In how many days have you done this?" The devil said, "In ten days" Satan commanded that he should be beaten, saying, "In all these days you have only done this." Afterwards, behold, a fourth devil came and worshipped him, and Satan said to him, "And when did you come also?" And he who was asked answered and said to him, "I have been in the desert for forty years striving with a monk, and tonight I have hurled him into fornication"; and when Satan heard this, he rose up immediately, embraced and kissed that devil. Satan took the crown off his head, and placed it upon him. He made him to sit by his side upon his throne, saying, "And so you have been able to do so great a work as this in so short a time! For there is nothing which I prize so highly as the fall of a monk." The old man went on to say, "When I saw these things I said within myself, Yes, so great then is the army of the monks! And by the operation of God, Who desired my redemption, I came forth, and became a monk."

633. In the time when Julian, the rebellious Emperor, was going down to the territory of the Persians, he sent a certain devil to go speedily to the country of the West, and to bring him from there an account of what he had sent him to do. When that devil arrived at a certain place where a monk was dwelling, he stopped and tarried there for fifteen days without being able to move anywhere. He was unable to travel onwards, because the monk did not cease from praying, day or night. He returned to the heathen who had sent him without having done anything. The wicked Julian said to him, "Why have you tarried so long?" The devil answered and said to him, "I delayed incoming, and I have done nothing; for a monk, who continued in prayer, came in my way and I tarried with him fifteen days, expecting that he would some time cease to pray and that I should be able to go on my way; but he never ceased from his prayer, and I was prevented from going on, and so I delayed in coming, and I have done nothing." Then the angry wicked Julian, said, "When I come back I will take vengeance upon him." Before a few days were over, he was slain by Divine Providence. Immediately one of the eparchs who were with him went and sold everything he possessed and gave the money to the poor. He came to that monk, and himself became a chosen monk. He died with a good ending, and with works, which were pleasing to God.

634. On one occasion Abba Pambo was traveling with some monks in the districts of Egypt; and seeing some worldly folk sitting down he said to them, "Rise up, and salute the monks so that you may be blessed, for they are always holding converse with God, and their mouths are holy."

635. Abba John used to say, "The whole company of the holy men is like a garden which is full of fruit-bearing trees of various kinds, and where the trees are planted in one earth, and all of them drink from one fountain; and thus it is with all the holy men, for they do not have one rule only, but several varieties, and one man labors in one way, and another man in another way, but it is one Spirit which operates and works in them."

THE SECOND BOOK

CHAPTER ONE TO FIFTEEN

Questions & Answers on the Ascetic Rule

Two of the fathers entreated God to inform them as to the measure of spiritual excellence to which they had arrived. A voice came to them which said, "In such and such a village of Egypt there is a certain man in the world who is called Eucharistos, and his wife is Mary. You have not yet arrived at the same measure as they." When the fathers heard this they marvelled, they rose up and came to that village, and they enquired for and found the house and the wife of Eucharistos. They asked her, saying, "Where is your husband?" She answered and said to them, "He is a shepherd, and he is in the field pasturing sheep." She brought them into her house. When the evening had come her husband came from the field. He rejoiced greatly at seeing the fathers, and prepared a table for them. He brought water that he might wash their feet. The fathers answered and said to him, "We will eat nothing, but tell us about your work." Eucharistos said to them with great humility, "I am a shepherd, and this is my wife." The fathers entreated him to inform them concerning his life and works, but he concealed the matter, and refused to speak. Finally they said to him, "God told us to come to you." When Eucharistos heard this he was afraid, and said to them, "Behold, we inherited these sheep from our parents. Whatever God provides as our income from them we divide into three portions; one portion we devote to charity, one portion to the love of strangers, and the remaining part serves for our own use. Since the time when

I took this woman to wife, we have not defiled ourselves. She is a virgin. Each of us sleeps alone. At night time we wear sackcloth, and in the daytime we take it off and array ourselves in our ordinary attire. No man has known this thing until the present moment." When the fathers heard this they glorified God.

2. They say concerning Abba Anthony that on one occasion, when he was praying in his cell he heard a voice which said to him, "Anthony, you have not yet arrived at the state of excellence of a certain man who is a tailor and who dwells in Alexandria." Then Anthony rose up in the morning, and took a palm stick and departed to him. When the man saw him, he was disturbed; and the old man said to him, "Tell me what you do, and how you live." The tailor said to him, "I do not myself know that I do any good, and I know only that when I rise up in the morning, before I sit down to the labor of my hands, I give thanks to God, and praise Him, and that I set my evil deeds before my eyes, saying, 'All the men who are in this city will go into the kingdom of God, because of their alms and good deeds, except myself, and I shall inherit punishment for my sins' and again in the evening, before I sleep, I do the same things." When Abba Anthony heard these things, he said, "Truly, as the man who works in gold, and who does beautiful work, cleanly, and in peace, even so are you; through your beautiful thoughts you will inherit the kingdom of God, while I, who have passed the whole of my life in the desert, separated from men, have never overtaken you."

3. Abba Anthony received a revelation in the desert, saying, "In such and such a city there is a man who resembles you. He is a physician, works and gives whatever he earns to the poor and needy. Each day he, with the angels, ascribes holiness to God three times a day."

4. When Abba Macarius was praying in his cell on one occasion, he heard a voice which said, "Macarius, you have not yet arrived at the state of excellence of two women who are in such and such a city." The old man rose up in the morning, took in his hand a palm stick, and began to set out on the road to that city. When he arrived at the city, and learned the place of the abode of the women, he knocked at the door. One of the women went out and brought him into the house. When he had been sitting down for a little, the other woman came in. He called them to him, and they came near and sat down before him. The old man said to them, "On your account I have made this long journey, and have performed all this labor, and with great difficulty have come from the desert; tell me, then, what works do you do." They said to him, "Believe us, O father; neither of us has ever been absent from, or kept herself back from her husband's couch up to this day. What work, then, would you see in us?" The old man made apologies to them, and entreated them to reveal to him their labor. They said to him, "According to worldly considerations we are strangers one to the other, for we are not kinsfolk. But it happened that the two of us are married to two men who were brethren in the flesh. Behold, up to this present we have lived in this house for twelve years, and we have never wanted to quarrel with each other, and neither of us has spoken one abominable word of abuse to her companion. We made up our minds together to leave our husbands and join the army of virgins. Although we entreated our husbands earnestly to allow us to do so, they would not undertake to send us away. As we were unable to do what we wished, we made a promise between ourselves and God that, until death, no worldly word should go out from our mouths." When Macarius heard this he said, "Truly, virginity by itself is nothing, nor marriage, nor life as a monk, nor life in the world; for God seeks the desire of a man, and gives the Spirit to every man."

5. They used to tell a story about certain brethren who were members of the household of Abba Poemen. While these men were dwelling in Egypt their mother wished to see them, but was unable to do so. She watched for them as they were going to the church, and went out to meet them. As soon as they saw her they went back to their cell and shut the door on themselves. Their mother took up her stand by the door, spoke to them, wept and sighed heavily. When Abba Job heard her, he went in to Abba Poemen and said to him, "What shall we do in respect of this old woman who is weeping by the door?" Then Abba Poemen rose up and drew near to the door and pressed himself against it. He heard her speaking in the deepest sorrow. He said to her, "Why do you cry in this fashion?" As soon as she heard his voice she wept the more. She cried out, saying, "I want to see my sons. For what is this that I see in you? Did I not rear you? Am I not your mother? Did you not suck at my breasts? Did you not go out from my womb? I am prevented by my old age, but now when I have heard your voice my bowels have been moved." The old man said to her, "Do you wish to see us here, or would you see us in that country beyond the grave?" She said to him, "My sons, if I do not see you here I shall see you there." The old man said to her, "If you will compel yourself not to see us here, you shall, in very truth, see us there." The old woman departed, saying, "Yes, my son, if I shall see you there I shall not seek to see you here."

6. There was a certain old man who lived a life of such strict self-denial that he never drank wine. When I arrived at his cell we sat down to eat, and one brought dates and he ate, and he took water and drank. I said to him laughingly,

"So are you angry with abstinence, O father? Since you have eaten dates and have drunk water, why do you not drink wine?" He answered and said to me, "If you take a handful of dust and throw it on a man will it hurt him?" I said to him, "No." He said to me, "If you take a handful of water and throw it over a man, will he feel pain?" I said to him, "No." He said to me, "And again, if you take a handful of chopped straw and throw it over a man, will it cause him pain?" I said to him, "No." Then he said to me, "But if you bring them all, mix them together, knead them well, dry them, you may throw and hurl the mass on the skull of a man and will you not break it?" I said to him, "Yes, true." He said to me, "The monks do not abstain from certain things without good reason. You must not listen to the men who are in the world who say, 'Why do they not eat this, and why do they not drink that?' Is not there a sin in them? Such people do not know. Now we abstain from certain things not because the things themselves are bad, but because the passions are mighty, and when they have waxed strong they kill us."

7. On one occasion the priest of Scete went to the Archbishop of Alexandria. When he had returned to Scete he wanted to send the brethren to Alexandria. He said to them, "I have heard you saying that there is a large assembly of people in Alexandria. Truly, I say to you that I, who went there, did not see the face of any man except the Archbishop." When they heard this they were disturbed, and said, "Have they sunk into the ground, then?" He said, "No, not so, but my thoughts did not compel me to look at a man." When they heard this they marvelled, and were greatly confirmed by these words in their desire to keep themselves from looking upon the vain things of the world.

8. One of the old men used to say, "On one occasion the fathers were sitting and conversing together on the subject of ascetic excellence. There was in their midst one of the old men who was a seer of visions. He saw angels flying about over the fathers. When they came to another subject of discourse, the angels departed. He saw pigs rolling about among them and wallowing in the mire. Afterwards when the fathers renewed their conversation on spiritual excellence the angels came back and he glorified God."

9. One of the fathers used to say that there were two brethren who were neighbors of his in the desert, one was a stranger and the other was a native of the country. The stranger was a man of little faith, but the native performed many works in the service of God. It happened that the stranger died, and the old man, who saw divine visions, saw multitudes of angels bearing away in triumph his soul until it arrived in heaven. An inquiry arose concerning this, and the old man heard a voice from heaven which said, "He was certainly a negligent man, but because of his being a stranger they opened to him." Afterwards the man who was a native of the country died, and his kinsfolk came to him and buried him. The old man saw that there were no angels with him, and he marvelled. He fell on his face and entreated God to inform him how it was that the stranger who was a negligent man was worthy of glory, while the man who had all those labors to his credit was not granted the same thing. He heard a voice which said, "When the native with all his works came to die, he opened his eyes and saw his kinsfolk weeping, and his soul was refreshed; but the stranger, although he was negligent, saw none of his kinsfolk, and he sighed and wept."

10. One of the fathers told a story, saying, "There was a certain monk in the desert of Linopolis, and a man who was in the world ministered to him. There was in the city a certain rich and wicked man who died, and was accompanied to his burial by the whole city, by the Bishop, with lights and great honor. The man who ministered to the monk went forth to give him some bread. He found him dead and eaten by the panthers. He fell upon his face before the Lord and said, "My Lord, I will not rise up from this place until You make me know why this wicked man is buried with such great honor, and why this monk who served You by night and by day has come to such an end." An angel came and said to him, "That wicked man did one good work, and he was rewarded here so that he might not find even one pleasure in the world to come. But this holy man, because he was a man who was adorned with divine virtues, although inasmuch as he was a man he possessed certain shortcomings, will receive these things in the world to come, so that there he may be found perfect." Having heard this he returned, and glorified God for His judgements because they are good.

11. A brother asked an old man, saying, "Is it the name or the work which makes one to live?" The old man said to him, "I knew a certain brother who was praying on one occasion. He thought within himself, saying, 'I wish to see the soul of a righteous man, and the soul of a sinner when they are leaving the body' and because God wished neither to make him grieve, nor to deprive him of his desire, while he was sitting in his cell a wolf went in to him, and laid hold of him by his clothes and dragged him outside. Then having pulled him along he carried him to the outside of a certain city, then he left him there and departed. While he was sitting outside the city there was a man who lived in a monastery, and who had gained renown, and concerning whom report had gone forth that he was a monk of spiritual excellence; and this man was grievously sick, and was waiting for the hour of his departure from this world. That brother looked on and saw the preparations which they were making, and the things, which they were putting ready for the event, namely, the wax candles, and the lamps which they were trimming and preparing, and he saw that all the city was weeping for him, and that his people were in grief, and saying, 'By his hand God has given us meat and drink, and by his hands he has delivered us, and has kept us and the whole city alive. If anything happens to him we shall die." When the time for this man to end his life had come that brother looked, and saw, and behold, the keeper of Sheol went in having in his hand a fork of fire with three prongs, and he heard a voice which spoke to the keeper, saying, 'You shall not give his soul any rest, even for a moment, and you shall not show any compassion to him when you take away his soul.' Then he who had appeared to that brother went in, and he drove that fiery, three-pronged fork which he had in his hand into the heart of the dying man, and he tortured him for a long time, and then he carried away his soul. After these things, when that brother was going into the city, he saw a certain brother who was a stranger, and who was lying sick in the marketplace. There was none to care for him. He remained with him for one day, and at the time when his soul was departing the brother saw Gabriel and Michael come for his soul, sat down, one on his right hand, and the other on his left, they stayed there entreating his soul and wishing to carry it away. Since his soul refused to leave its body, Gabriel said to Michael, 'Lift up his soul and take it, so that we may depart.' Michael said to him, 'We were commanded by our Lord to bring it out without pain and without suffering, and therefore we cannot constrain it and do it violence.' Michael cried out with a loud voice, saying, 'What do You command concerning this soul which will not be entreated to come forth, O Lord?' There came to him a voice which said, 'Behold, I will send David and his harp, and all those who sing with him, so that when the soul hears the sweetness of their voices it shall come forth; and they came down and surrounded the soul.' As they were singing psalms and hymns the soul leaped forth, rejoicing in the hands of Michael, and was taken up on high with gladness."

12. They used to say that a certain old man went to a city to sell his handiwork. It happened that he sat down by the door of a house of a rich man who was dying, and whose death was very near at hand. As he was sitting there he looked and saw black horses, with their black riders, who were exceedingly terrible. They held in their hands staves of fire. When they had come to the door of the house, they set their horses outside, and they went in together. As soon as the sick man saw them, he cried out with a mighty voice, saying, "O

Lord, help me." Those who had been sent to him said, "Now that the sun has set upon you, you call God to remembrance? Why did you not seek Him while it was yet day? You have neither an option of hope nor consolation left. Then they took away his soul and departed."

13. There were two brethren who lived in cells, and one of them was an old man who had persuaded the younger man, saying, "My brother, let us dwell together," but he said to him, "I am a sinner, and I cannot let you be with me, O father." The old man entreated him, saying, "Yes, we can live together." That old man was pure in his thoughts, and he was not content to hear that there was in the young man the thought of fornication. The brother said to him, "Father, leave me for one week, and we will speak on the subject again." When the week ended, the old man came, and wishing to try him, the brother said to him, "During the past week, O Father, I fell into great temptation, for I went to a certain village on business, and I met a woman." The old man said to him, "There is repentance." The brother said to him, "Yes, there is." The old man said to him, "I will bear the half of this sin with you." The brother said to him, "We shall now be able to dwell together." So they dwelt together until the end of their lives.

14. Certain brethren from the great monastery went forth and departed to the desert. They came to one of the monks who received them with gladness. When he saw that, as was usual with monks, they had come from labor, he prepared for them a table before the appointed season, and whatever he had in his cell he set before them, and refreshed them. When the evening came they sang twelve Psalms, and they did the same thing during the night. The old man left them to rest, and departed that he might sing and pray by himself. While he was keeping vigil, he heard the brethren conversing together and saying; "The monks who live in the desert live more comfortably than do we who are in the monasteries." When they were making ready in the morning to go to an old man who was his neighbor, he said to them, "Salute him for me," and they said to him, "You shall not water the green herb." When he heard this, he understood the matter. He kept them until the evening working and fasting, and when the evening had come they sang the great service through, and the brother said to them, "Today, because you have come from toil, we have shortened the service somewhat." He also said to them, "We are not in the habit of eating every day, but because of you we will eat a little." He prepared for them dry bread and salt, and he said to them, "It is fitting that on your account we should this day make a feast," and he sprinkled a little vinegar in the salt, and they rose up to sing and pray until the morning, and he said to them, "We are, on account of you, unable to perform the whole of the service as we want to do, for you must rest a little, and you are strangers." When the morning had come they wished to escape, but he entreated them saying, "Spend a few days with us, especially that you may live according to the custom of the desert, for we cannot let you go." When they saw that he did not want to send them away, they rose up and fled secretly.

15. On one occasion a certain brother came to Mount Sinai to visit Abba Sylvanus. He saw the brethren working with their hands to supply their wants, and he said to Abba Sylvanus, "With boasting, you toil for the food which perishes. Mary chose a good portion for herself." Abba Sylvanus said to Zechariah, his disciple, "Give him a book and take him to a cell where there is nothing." When the time of the ninth hour had come, the brother looked this way and that way to see if they were going to send for him to command him to eat, but no man came to seek him. Then he rose up and came to the old man and said to him, "Father, have not the brethren eaten today?" He said to him, "Yes." The brother said to him, "Why have not you called me?" The old man said to him, "You are a spiritual man and have no need of the meat which is for the body. But we are corporeal beings and we need to eat. It is for this reason that we work. You have chosen the good part; read all day, and do not seek after the food of the body." When that brother heard this he expressed his contrition, and said, "Father, forgive me." The old man said, "Even Mary had need of Martha, for through the labor of Martha, Mary triumphed."

16. It happened that a certain heathen priest came to Scete, and visited the cell of one of the brethren. He passed the night there, and saw the labors of his rule. He marvelled and said to him, "Do you labor so greatly and yet do not see visions from your God?" The brother said to him, "We do not see visions." The priest of idols said to him, "When we perform the part of priests to our god he hides nothing from us, and he revealed to us his mysteries, while you who perform the labors of vigil, and abstinence, and silent contemplation, as you say, see nothing. There must be in your hearts evil thoughts which separate you from your God, and it is for this reason that He does not reveal to you His mysteries." The brother went and informed the old men of the words of that priest of idols. They marvelled and said, "It is thus, for the thoughts which are not clean alienate a man from God."

17. One of the brethren said to one of the great old men, "If I could find one of the fathers according to my desire, I would choose to die with him," and the old man said to him with a laugh, "Good, my lord," and the brother said,

"Such is my desire." Now he did not understand the thought of the old man. When the old man saw that the brother was in truth speaking concerning him who he thoroughly believed, he said to him, "If you did find an old man according to your desire, would you be able to dwell with him?" He said to him, "Yes." The old man said to him, "Well have you said, if I could find an old man according to my desire." Afterwards he said to him, "You do not wish to be subject to the will of the old man, but the old man must be subject to you!" Then the brother rose up, and made apologies to him, saying, "Forgive me, father; I have boasted greatly. I thought that I was saying that which was good, but I find that I possess that which is of no value."

18. Abba Daniel used to say about Abba Arsenius that immediately when he heard that the fruits were ripe on the trees, he would tell him in his desire to bring him some, and that he used to eat once a year of every kind of fruit, so that he might give thanks to God.

19. Abba Abraham asked Abba Theodore, saying, "Father, which is the better thing for me to do, to give praise or to blame?" The old man said to him, "I myself prefer to perform the works of praise, and not of blame." Abba Abraham said to him, "How is this?" The old man said to him, "If I perform good works, and I be praised for them, I find that I can bring an accusation against my mind whilst I flee from the love of approbation, and I can say that I do not deserve this praise. But blame belonged to evil works, and how shall I be able to comfort my heart, because men are offended at me? It is necessary for us to do good works, and to be praised, without receiving upon ourselves the love of approbation, and not evil deeds, lest we be blamed." Abba Abraham said, "You have said well, O father; even so is it."

20. They used to say about one of the fathers who had lived in the world, that when he was in the desert he was occupied in fighting his desire to return to his wife whom he had married before he became a monk, and when he related the matter to the fathers, they appointed him certain works, so that he might be kept back from the fight within him. Now because he was an obedient man and one who labored, he performed these works in excess, and at length his body became so emaciated that he was unable to rise up from his place. By the operation of God, a certain father who was a stranger came to the place of Scete, and he passed by the cell of that monk and found it to be empty. As he passed by he said in his mind, "How is it that no man has come out to meet me from this cell?" He went back there, and knocked, saying, "Perhaps he is sick." When he knocked the brother who was grievously sick went forth, and the father said to him, "What is your sickness, O father?" The brother told him of all his suffering, saying, "I belonged to the world, and the enemy made war upon me through my wife, and I told the fathers the story, and they imposed upon me severe labors; and having performed these, my body has become ill, and the war has become stronger against me." When the old man heard these things, he was grieved, and he said to him, "The fathers have imposed upon you great labors as if you had been a mighty man. But if you will listen to my feeble voice you will relinquish those labors, and partake of a little food, at the appointed time, and will sing and pray a little, and will cast your business upon God. For by Your pains and sickness you will not be able to conquer this matter, because our body is like a garment; if you take care of it, it will last, but if you neglect it, it will come to an end." The brother having heard these things acted thus, and in a few days the war passed away from him.

21. One of the fathers asked Abba Nastir, the friend of the blessed Anthony, saying, "What is the best work for me to do?" He said to him, "Not all kinds of labor are the same. For The Book says that Abraham was a lover of strangers, and that God was with him; and Elijah was a lover of a life of silent contemplation, and God was with him; and David was a humble man, and God was with him; therefore whatever work your soul wishes to do, provided that it be of God, that do, and keep your heart from evil things." The brother asked him again, saying, "Father, tell me other things." The old man said, "Abba Anbastion asked Abba Athri, saying, 'What shall I do?' He said to him, 'Go, make your belly little, and the work of your hands great, and be not troubled in your cell.'" Again the brother asked him, saying, "If there be a persecution, is it better to flee to the desert or to the habitation of men?" The old man said to him, "Go wherever you hear that true believers are, and have no friendship with a youth, and do not dwell with one. If you are able so to do, dwell in your cell, for this is good, and cleanse your garden herbs. This is far better than going to a man and asking him questions." Again the brother asked him, "I wish to dwell in close friendship with a brother, and I want to live a life of silent contemplation by myself in my cell, and he must give me what I want, and I will give him the work of my hands." The old man said to him, "The fathers have never sought after a thing of this kind; and if you do not give bread to the poor Satan will not permit you to live so."

22. Abba Daniel Parndyd, the disciple of Abba Arsenius, used to tell about a man of Scete, and said that he was a man of great labors but simple in the faith, and in his ignorance he considered and declared that the bread which we receive is not in very truth the Body of Christ, but a similitude of His Body.

Two of the fathers heard this word which he spoke, but because they knew of his sublime works and labors, they imagined that he had spoken it in his innocence and simple mindedness; and they came to him and said, "Father, we have heard a thing from a man which we do not believe, for he says that this bread which we receive is not in very truth the Body of Christ, but a mere similitude." He said to them, "It is I who have said this thing." They entreated him, saying, "You must not say thus, father, but according to what the Holy Catholic Church has handed down to us, even so do we believe, that is to say, this bread is the Body of Christ in truth, and is not a mere similitude. As, in truth, God immediately took dust from the earth, and fashioned man in His image, and no man is able to say that he is not the image of God, so also was it the case of the bread of which He said, 'This is My Body,' for it is not to be regarded as a merely commemorative thing, and we believe that it is indeed the Body of Christ." The old man said, "Unless I be convinced by the thing itself I will not listen to this." The fathers said to him, "Let us pray to God for the whole week on this mystery, and we believe that He will reveal it to us." The old man agreed to this with great joy, and each man went to his cell. Then the old man prayed to God, saying, "O Lord, You know that it is not from wickedness that I do not believe, but in order that I may not go astray through ignorance, reveal therefore to me, O Lord Jesus Christ, this mystery." The two other old men prayed to God and said, "O Lord Jesus Christ, make this old man to have knowledge concerning this mystery, and we believe that he will not destroy his labors." God heard the entreaty of the two fathers. When the week ended they came to the church, and the three of them sat down by themselves on one seat. The old man was between the other two. The eyes of their understandings were opened, and when the time of the Mysteries had arrived, and the bread was laid upon the holy table, there appeared to the three of them as it were a child on the table. When the priest stretched out his hand to break the bread, behold the angel of the Lord came down from heaven with a knife in his hand, and he slew the child and pressed out his blood into the cup. When the priest broke off from the bread small members, the old man drew near that he might partake of the Holy Offering. A piece of living flesh smeared and dripping with blood was given to him. When he saw this he was afraid, and he cried out with a loud voice, saying, "I believe, O Lord, that the bread is Your Body, and that the cup is Your Blood." immediately the flesh which was in his hand became bread like to that of the Mystery, and he took it and gave thanks to God. The old men said to him, "God knows the nature of men, and that it is unable to eat living flesh, and for this reason He turns His Body into bread, and His Blood into wine, for those who receive Him in faith." Then they gave thanks to God for that old man, and for he had not permitted Satan to destroy him from his labors. The three of them went to their cells in gladness.

23. Abba Daniel used to say that Abba Arsenius told him a story, as if he were speaking of some other man, saying, "A certain old man was sitting in his cell. A voice came to him saying, 'Come here, and I will show you the works of the children of men.' He rose up and went out. The voice led him out and showed him an Ethiopian (a black) cutting wood, and he made up a large bundle and wished to carry it away. But he was unable to do so. Then instead of making the bundle smaller, he went and cut down some more wood, and added to it, and he did this many times. When he had gone on a little further, the voice showed him a man who was standing by a pit drawing up water, which he cast in a certain hollowed out place, and when he had thrown the water there it ran down again into the pit. Again the voice said to him, 'Come, and I will show you other things.' Then he looked, and, behold, there was a temple, and two men, who were riding horses, were carrying a piece of wood as wide as the temple was. They wanted to go in through the door, but the width of the wood did not permit them to do so, for they would not humble themselves to go in one after the other, and to bring it in endwise. Therefore they remained outside the door. These are the men, who bear the yoke of righteousness with boasting, and they will not humble themselves to make themselves straight and go in the humble way of Christ, and therefore they remain outside the kingdom of God. The man who was cutting wood is the man who labors in many sins, and who, instead of repenting and diminishing from his sins, adds other wickednesses to it. Now he who was drawing water is the man who does good works, and who, because other things are mingled in his good works, destroys his works. It is necessary that a man should be watchful in his labor, lest he toil in vain."

24. Once Abba Macarius was going from the wood to his cell, and was carrying with him some palm leaves, and Satan met him on the road holding a hack in his hand. When Macarius sought to wound him, Satan was afraid, fell down and did homage to the blessed man. Then the old man fled from that place. He related to the brethren everything which had happened, and when they heard it they glorified God.

25. An old man used to say, "Be like a camel when you bear your sins, and be tied closely to him who knows the way."

26. An old man used to say, "Do not become a lawgiver to yourself. Judge no man, for you are not under the Law, but under grace. Give everything to Him Who is able to do everything, for you are unable to do anything. Judge then in this way, and do not sin at any time."

27. He also said, "He who wishes to dwell in the desert should become a learner. He should not practise doctrine lest he suffers loss. His occupation should be with a man who loves God."

28. Satan appeared to one of the old men in the form of an angel of light, and said, "I, even I, am Gabriel who have been sent to you." He said to him, "Have you not been sent to another? For I am a sinner." When Satan heard this he did not again appear. The old man said, "If in truth an angel appears to you, say, 'As to whom you have come to me? I am not worthy.'"

29. When Abba Gregory was dying he said these words, "God demands three things from the man who has been baptized; true faith from the soul, truth from the tongue, and chastity from the body."

30. The old man said, "God seeks nothing from Christians except true faith, the belief that the things which are spoken shall come to pass in deed, and that we should be persuaded by the orthodox fathers."

31. An old man was asked, "How can a man find God? By fasting? By works? By watching? By mercy?" He said, "By means of these certainly when they are mingled with discretion, but I say that there are many who have afflicted their bodies without discretion, and they have departed vainly, having gained nothing. Our mouth becomes foul through thirst, and we repeat the Scriptures with our mouth, and we go through all the Psalms of David in our service, but that which God requires, and which is necessary we have not, that is to say, a good word for each other. For as a man cannot see his face in troubled waters, so is the soul, unless it is cleansed from alien thoughts, is not able to appear before God in prayer."

32. A certain monk was going along the road and he met some nuns. He turned aside out of the path. The nun who was leading them said to him, "Had you been a perfect monk you would have never regarded us as women."

33. Abba Anthony used to say, "A man's life or death comes from his neighbor. If we benefit our brother we benefit ourselves. If we offend him we sin against God."

34. A certain brother came to Abba Theodore, and he began to talk and to speak about the things which he had not done. The old man said to him, "So far you have not found a ship, and you have not let down in it your possessions, and before you have embarked you have gone to the city where you wishe to go. First of all do the work, and then you shall arrive at that concerning which you are now talking."

35. A brother asked Abba Anthony, saying, "What commandment shall I keep so that I may please God?" He answered and said to him, "That which I command you observe. Set you God before your eyes continually, wherever you go; whatever you do, make to it a witness from the Scriptures. In whatever place you dwell do not be easily moved there from, but abide there persistently. Observe these three things, and you shall be saved."

36. They used to say about a certain old man that whenever he sat in his cell toiling in the contest, he saw the devils face to face. He treated them with contempt and despised them through his contest. When Satan saw that he was being overcome by the old man, he appeared to him in human form, and said to him, "I am Christ." When the old man saw him, he winked his eyes and made a mock of him. Satan said to him, "Why do you wink your eyes? I, even I, am Christ." The old man answered and said to him, "I do not desire to see Christ here." When Satan heard these things he departed from him and was no longer seen.

37. Abba John used to say that he saw in a vision one of the old men in a state of bewilderment. Three monks were standing on the shore of a lake, and a voice came to them from the other shore of the lake, saying, "Take your wings of fire and come to me." Two of them took wings of fire and flew over to the other side, even as it was told them. The third remained behind, wept abundantly, and cried out. At length wings were given to him also, but they were not of fire like those of his companions. They were weak and feeble wings, flying only with the greatest difficulty. After dropping down into the water, and with most painful exertions that he reached the opposite shore. This is the case with this generation. Although it takes to itself wings, these wings are not the powerful wings of fire, but it forces itself to take weak and feeble wings.

38. An old man used to say, "Every wickedness which is not perfect is not wickedness. And every righteousness which is not perfect is not righteousness. For the man who does not have good and evil thoughts is like the land of

Sodom, which is salted, and brings forth neither green herb nor fruit. Good ground produces wheat and expels tares from itself."

39. Certain brethren came and asked Abba Anthony a question about the Book of Leviticus. The old man went out to the desert. Abba Ammon, who knew his habit, followed him secretly. When the old man had gone some distance, he cried out with a loud voice, saying, "O God, send Moses to me, and let him teach me the meaning of this verse." Immediately a voice was heard holding converse with him. Abba Ammon heard this voice, and said, "I heard the voice which spoke with him, but the force of the verse I never learned."

40. When Abba Poemen was a youth, he went to an old man to ask him concerning three matters. Having gone into his presence he forgot one of them, and returned to go to his cell. As he put the key in the door to open it, he remembered the matter which he had forgotten. Immediately he left the key in the door and returned to the old man. The old man said to him, "You have returned quickly, brother." Abba Poemen told him the story thus, "When I put the key in the door to open it, I remembered the matter which I wanted to know. I did not open the door because I came back here speedily." The rocky ground which he had traversed in the interval was of not inconsiderable length. The old man said to him, "Your name shall be spoken about throughout all Egypt."

41. A brother said to an old Abba, "Behold, I have entreated the old men, and they talk to me about the redemption of my soul. But I can lay hold upon nothing in their words. What is the use, then, of making them toil when I can do nothing with what they say, for I am wholly in a state of uncleanness?" There were two basins. The old man said to him, "Go, bring me one of these basins, pour some oil into it, rinse the basin round with it, and then empty it out." And he did so twice. Then the old man said to him, "Bring now the two basins together." The brother did as he was told. The old man said, "Look and see which basin is the cleaner." The brother said to him, "The one which the oil has been poured is cleaner." The old man said to him, "And thus also is it with the soul, for even if it lays hold of nothing through what it asks, it is cleaner than if it had never asked a question at all."

42. A brother asked Abba John, and said to him, "How is it that the soul which has blemishes in itself is not ashamed to speak about its neighbor, and to defame it?" The old man spoke to him a word concerning defamation, saying, "There was a certain man who was poor, and had a wife. He saw another woman who listened to him. He took her to wife also. The two women were naked. When there was a fair in a certain place the two women persuaded him to take them to it. He took his two wives, and put them in a boat. When he had gone up out of the boat he arrived at a certain place. When the day had become hot, and every man was resting, one of the women looked out, saw that there was no man outside, leaped up, went out to a heap of waste rubbish. She chose from there some old rags and made a girdle for herself. She then walked about boldly. Meanwhile her companion was sitting down naked, and she said to her husband, "Look at that harlot going about naked and without shame." Then her husband, with sadness, said to her, 'The thing to be wondered at is that, while she has, at least, covered her shame, you are entirely naked, and do speak these words without being ashamed.' Now a defamation uttered against a neighbor is like to this."

43. They used to say that one of the old men asked God that he might see the fathers. He saw them all, with the exception of Abba Anthony. And he said to him who showed him the fathers, "Where is Abba Anthony?" He said to him, "Wherever God is there is Anthony."

44. Abba Poemen used to say, "This is what is written, 'As the hart cries out for the water brooks, even so cries out my soul to You, O Lord' (Psalm 42:1). For the harts in the desert swallow many serpents, and when the poison of these makes them hot within, they cry out to come to the water-brooks. But as soon as they have drunk, the burning which comes from the serpents inside them is cooled. Thus is it with the monks who are in the desert, for they are burnt up by the envy of the devils. They wait for the Saturday and Sunday that they may come to the fountain of water, that is to say to the Body of Christ, and they sweeten and purify themselves from the gall of the evil one."

45. When the brethren were sitting with Abba Moses, he said to them, "Behold, this day have the barbarians come to Scete; rise up and flee." They said to him, "Will you not flee, father?" He said to them, "I have been expecting this day to come for many years past, so that might be fulfilled the command of our Redeemer, Who said, 'Those who take the sword shall perish by the sword'" (Matt. 26:52). They said to him, "We then will not flee, but will die with you." He said to them, "This is not my affair, but your own desire. Let everyman look after himself in the place where he dwells." The brethren were seven in number. After a while, he said to them, "Behold, the barbarians have drawn near the door." The barbarians entered and slew them. One of them had been afraid, and fled behind the palm leaves. He saw seven crowns come down and placed themselves on the heads of those who had been slain.

46. The brethren asked an old man, saying "How is God's promises in the Scriptures good things to the soul, that the soul does not desire them, but turns aside to impurity?" He answered and said to them, "It is my opinion that it is because it has not yet tasted the good things which are above, and therefore the good things which are here are dear to it."

47. Abba Arsenius used to say, "The monk is a stranger in a foreign land. Let him not occupy himself with anything there, and he will find rest."

48. They used to say that on one occasion when Abba Macarius the Great went up from Scete, carrying palm leaves, he became weary. He sat down and prayed to God, saying, "God, you know that I have no strength." Immediately he found that he was by the side of the sea.

49. There was a certain old man in the mountain of Athribis, and thieves came to attack him. He cried out. When his neighbors heard his cry they hunted down the thieves, and sent them to the governor. The governor shut them up in prison. The brethren were sorry, and said, "They were delivered into our hands." They rose up, went to Abba Poemen, and informed him about the matter. Abba Poemen wrote to that old man, and said to him, "You must understand when has come the first betrayal, and then you will perceive how the second betrayal arose. For if you have not been betrayed first of all by things within, you would have never effected the second betrayal." The old man heard the letter of Abba Poemen, who was famous throughout all that country, for keeping himself strictly secluded in his cell, and for never leaving his cell. Immediately the old man rose up, went into the city, and took the thieves out of prison. Thus the assembly set them free.

50. On one occasion Abba Macarius, wishing to rebuke the brethren, said to them, "There came here a young man with his mother, and he was under the power of a devil. He said to his mother, 'Rise up, let us depart from here.' She said to him, 'I cannot walk.' The young man said to her, 'I will carry you.'" Abba Macarius marvelled at the wickedness of that devil, and sought to drive them away.

51. On one occasion five brethren came to visit a great old man. He asked the first one, saying, "What kind of work do you do?" He said to him, "I twist palm leaves into ropes, father." The old man said to him, "God shall plait a crown for you, O my son." Then he said to the second brother, "What do you do?" He said to him, "I make mats, father." The old man said to him, "God shall give you strength, O my son." He said to the third brother, "And what do you do?" He said to him, "I make sieves, father." The old man said to him, "God shall preserve you, O my son." He asked the fourth brother, saying, "What do you do?" He said to him, "I can write well." The old man said to him, "You know." He said to the fifth brother, "And what do you do?" He said to him, "I weave linen." Then the old man said, "I am not concerned." He said also, "If the twister of palm-leaf ropes be watchful with God He will plait him a crown for him; mat-making requires strength because there is labor in it; and God must protect him of the sieves because he has to sell them in the villages; as to the scribe, he must be humble in heart, for there is in his business exaltation of spirit, as regards the linen weaver, I am not concerned to speak, for he is a merchant and he trades. But if a man sees a brother afar off carrying palm branches, or palm-leaf mats, or sieves, he says, 'This man is a monk, for grass is the work of our hands, and he is avoiding the burning of the fire; and if he sees a man selling linen, he says immediately, 'Behold, the merchants have come, for the selling of linen is the work of this world, and it does not benefit many.'"

52. Abba Jacob used to say, "It is not only words that are required, for in this life of time many have abundance of words. It is work which is required. It is necessary to have it, and not words where there is no work."

53. One of the old men used to say, "What is hated by you, is so by your companion; if it be hateful to you for him to defame you, do not defame any man; if it be hateful to you to be accused, do not accuse any man; if it be hateful to you for a man to revile you, or to treat you with contempt, or to pluck you away, or to do any such thing to you, do not do to any man anything of that kind. He who is able to perform this commandment is able to redeem his own soul."

54. I went to Abba Muthues, and when I was about to return, I said to him, "I wish to go to the cells." He said to me, "Salute Abba John for me." When I came to Abba John, I said to him, "Abba Muthues salutes you." The old man said to me, "Behold, Abba Muthues is indeed a man of Israel in whom there is no guile." After one year I went to Abba Muthues, and told him the greeting of Abba John. The old man said to me, "I am unworthy of the old man's words. But I know, if ever you hear an old man praising his companion more than himself, that he has attained a great measure of perfection. It is indeed obedience for a man to praise his companion more than himself."

55. A brother asked an old man, and said to him, "My brother abuses me, and I cannot bear him any longer; what shall I do? Shall I rebuke him, or shall I speak evil words to him?" The old man said to him, "Both things are bad, whether a man rebukes him, or whether a man speaks to him evil words." The brother said to him, "And what shall I do? For I cannot endure either." The old man said to him, "If you cannot bear both things, speak to him, but do not rebuke him. If you speak to him with words of evil, and he listens, you will be able to quiet him, saying, 'I did not say such and such a thing,' and it will be possible for the matter which is between you to be healed. But if you rebuke him to his face, you will make a sore which will be incurable."

56. Certain brethren came to Abba Anthony that he might tell them about the visions which they used to see, whether they indeed came from devils or not. Now they had with the man an ass. The ass died on the road as they were coming. When they had gone into the presence of the old man, he said to them imediately, "How was it that your ass died on the road?" They said to him, "How does the Abba know that our ass is dead?" Abba Anthony said to them, "The devils showed me the matter." Then they said to him, "We have come to ask you questions because we have seen phantoms. On several occasions these phantoms have actually become real things. We want to learn whether we have erred or not." The old man showed them that such phantoms which arise through certain devils cannot be inquired into.

57. They were saying that Abba Sylvanus used to sit in secret in a cell with a few chick peas. He made of them one hundred bundles. Behold, a man came from Egypt leading an ass loaded with bread. Having knocked at the door of his cell, he went in, and set down the bread. The old man took these bundles, loaded them upon the ass, and sent him away.

58. They used to say that when Abba Zeno dwelt in a cell in Scete he went out one night from his cell as if for a purpose, and wandered about. When he had passed three days and three nights in traveling, he became exhausted by toil and hunger, and ready to die. He fell upon the ground. Behold, a youth stood before him carrying some bread and a pitcher of water. He said to Abba Zeno, "Arise, and eat bread." The old man rose up and prayed, thinking that the youth was a phantom. Then the youth said to him, "You have done well." Again Abba Zeno prayed twice and three times. The youth said to him, "You have done well." The old man took the bread and ate. Then afterwards the youth said to him, "How is it that you have gone so far from your cell? But arise and follow me." Immediately he found himself in his cell. The old man said to him, "Come, enter into the cell with me, and make your prayer." As he was going on in front he was swallowed up from his sight.

59. They used to say that a certain brother had such an attack of blasphemy that he was ashamed to speak, and wherever he heard that there were great old men he used to go to them wishing to tell them about it. Whenever he had come to one of them he was ashamed to speak to him. Having gone to the fathers several times, on one occasion Abba Poemen saw him, he perceived that he was full of thoughts, and he was sorry for him. When the brother would not reveal the matter to him, and he made as if he would pass him by, as soon as the brother had gone a little way from him, the old man said to him, "How often have you come here to tell me the thoughts which you have in your mind! Yet, when you come here, you find it hard to tell me. How long will you go on in this manner and be vexed by such thoughts in your mind? Tell me, my son, what is it that ails you?" Then that brother answered, and said to him, "I am fighting against the devil of blasphemy of God, and though I have often sought to tell you I have been ashamed to do so." When he had told him the matter, the face of Abba Poemen broke into a smile, and he said to him, "Do not be vexed, O my son, for when this thought comes to you, speak to it, saying 'I have nothing to do with this thought, and my soul does not desire it; let this blasphemy be upon you, Satan, for nothing in my soul desires it, for the time is short." When that brother heard these things he departed rejoicing.

60. A brother asked an old man, saying, "Why is the soul obstinate, and does not wish to fear God?" The old man said to him, "The soul wishes, O my son, to fear God. There is no time, for the fear of God belongs to perfection."

61. One of the old men used to say, "Do not ask for one thing after another. But ask concerning the matter of the war where you are at the time engaged, and when you have eradicated the war, then ask concerning something else. If when there is in you one passion, you set it aside and ask about another. The former passion will never be eradicated from you."

62. A brother asked one of the old men, saying, "What shall I do? For my thoughts wish to wander and go around by reason of the sight of the fathers." The old man answered and said to him, "If you see that your thoughts wish to go around by reason of the strictness of its strain, or through need, make yourself a division in your cell, and you will henceforward seek not to go out. But if you see that they wish to go out for the benefit of the soul, go out."

63. There was a certain brother in the cells, who, when the service in the church was ended, used to remain until the last and to wait for someone to lead him home. One day, when the church was being dismissed, he went out before anyone else and ran to his cell, and the priest saw him and marvelled. When the brother came on the following day, the priest said to him, "Tell me truly why do you, who had been in the habit of going out last, go out first of all?" He said, "Up to the present I made a distinction by not boiling any food on the first day of the week, and I waited that someone might take me to his cell; on that day, however, before I came to the church I boiled a few lentils, and therefore I departed quickly." When the priest heard this he gave a commandment to the brethren in the church that before each man came to the service in the church, he should on the first day of the week boil some food, by way of making a distinction.

64. The brethren used to tell about a certain old man who had a disciple who, when he sat down to eat, used to put his feet on the table. Although the old man had suffered this war for many years he did not rebuke him. However, he went to another old man, and told him about the brother. The old man said to him, "Complete your love, and send him to me." When the brother came to that old man, at the appointed time for the meal, the old man rose up and made the table ready. As soon as they had seated themselves the brother immediately put his two feet on the table. The old man said to him, "Father, it is not good for you to set your feet on the table." The brother said to him, "Forgive me, O my son. You have well said, for it is a sin." The brother returned to his master, and told him about it. When the old man learned about his, he perceived that this matter had been corrected in his disciple. From that time the brother did not put his feet on the table.

65. A brother asked Abba Muthues, saying, "Speak to me a word whereby I may live." He said to him, "Go, entreat God to give you mourning and meekness of heart. Consider at all times your sins. Do not judge other people. Make yourself lower than every other man. Have no love for a boy. Do not have any acquaintance with a woman. Have no friendship with heretics. Put aside from you all freedom of speech and boldness. Restrain both your tongue and your belly. Guard yourself somewhat against wine. If a man speaks with you concerning any matter whatsoever, do not quarrel with him. If he says that a thing is good, say 'Yes,' and if he say that it is bad, say, 'You know.' This is a meek spirit."

66. A brother came to Abba Poemen and said to him, "I have very many thoughts, O father, whereby I am vexed." The old man took him out into the air, and said to him, "Spread out your skirt, and catch the winds." The brother said to him, "I cannot do this." The old man said to him, "You can not do this, neither can you prevent your thoughts from coming, but it is your duty to stand up against them."

67. The brethren were once gathered with Abba Joseph. As they were sitting and asking him questions about their thoughts he said to them, "By way of affording them consolation, this day I am a king, for I have controlled my passions."

68. A brother asked Abba Ammon, saying, "Why is it that a man labors in prayer and makes petitions, and what he asks is not given to him?" The old man said to him, "Have you never heard how Jacob wearied himself for her whom he took to wife, and that he did not obtain her whom he sought, but her whom he did not seek, and how afterwards he worked and toiled more, and finally received her whom he loved? Thus is it with the monk also, for he shall fast and keep vigil, and yet shall not receive what he asks; and again, he shall labor with fasting and vigil, and shall receive the gift of grace which he asks."

69. An old man asked Abba Sisoes, saying, "Did Satan persecute the men of old time as he does today?" Sisoes said to them, "He persecutes the men of this age especially, because his time has come."

70. Abba John the Less, who was a young man, and had an elder brother, used to say, "I wanted to be without any care, and to be like the angels of God, who do nothing except sing and pray to Him." Immediately he cast from him the garments which he had on, and went out to the wilderness. When he had passed one week there, he returned to his brother. When he knocked at the door his brother did not answer it, but asked him, "Who are you?" John said to him, "I am John." His brother answered and said to him, "John has become an angel and is no longer among men." John entreated him, saying, "I indeed am John", but his brother left him outside in affliction, and did not open the door until the morning. When he came to open the door he said to John, "If you are indeed a man, it is necessary for you to work so that you may live."

71. Abba Purt said, "If God wishes me to live, He knows how to lead me, to strengthen me, and to provide for me. If He does not wish it, to whom shall I go to live?" And he would accept nothing from any man, not even when he was lying upon his bed for, he used to say, "If a man makes an offering of any kind to me, and not for the sake of God, I myself have nothing to give him, and he will receive nothing from God, for I am not in the place of God, so therefore he who offers will suffer loss."

72. Abba Poemen used to say, "Everything which arises through passion is a sin." He used to say also, "Every exercise of power which is for God's sake, is thanksgiving."

73. An old man used to say, "Acquire silence, and take no care for any earthly thing. Examine closely your meditations. When you sleep and when you rise up, be with God, and do not fear the attack of the wicked."

74. On one occasion a brother came to a father, and said to him, "Abba, I sow a field, and I reap the harvest from there, and I give alms also from it." The old man said to him, "Be strong, my son, for you are doing well." The brother went away rejoicing in this desire. Abba Job said to Abba Poemen, "Since you have spoken to that brother in this fashion, I know that you do not fear God." Then, after two days, Abba Poemen sent, calling that brother, and said to him "While Abba Joseph was listening, what did you say to me when you came to me, for my mind was occupied in another place?" The brother said to him, "I sow a field, and I reap the harvest from there, and I also give alms from it." Abba Poemen said to him, "I thought in my mind that it was your brother, who is in the world, of whom you were speaking when you did tell me that he did these things. But if it is you yourself who does them I must say that it is not the work for monks." When the brother heard these words he was grieved, and said, "I cannot do without sowing, for I do not know how to do any other work but this." When that brother had departed, Abba Job expressed his contrition to Abba Poemen, and said to him, "Forgive me." Abba Poemen said to him, "I also knew that this work was not the works of monks, but, according to the measure of his desire, I gave him for I knew he would be edified, and I knew that he would thus abound in love; but now he has departed in sorrow."

75. Mother Sarah said, "If I were to pray to God that all men might be built up through me I should be found expressing contrition at the door of each one of them; but I pray to God especially that my heart may be pure with Him and with every man."

76. Certain brethren, whilst talking to an old man about the thoughts, said to him, "Our hearts are hard, and we are not afraid of God; what shall we do that we may fear God?" The old man said to them, "I think that if a man has knowledge in his heart about Him that will rebuke him, it will bring him to the fear of God." Then the brethren said to him, "What is the rebuke?" The old man said, "In every matter a man should rebuke himself, saying, 'Remember that you are about to go out to meet God.' He should also say, 'What do I require from man?' And I think that if a man remains in these things the fear which is in God will come to him."

77. Abba Poemen used to say, "An evil will is a wall of brass between a man and God. If a man would set it aside he must also say, 'By the help of my God I will leap over a wall' (Ps. 18:29). God Whose way is without blemish, but if that which is seemly lends help to the thought, a man is not easily turned aside."

78. They used to say that on one occasion, when Abba Alonis was singing the service, and the old men were sitting close by, these old men watched him performing the service, and that they praised him. When he heard them he did not answer them at all. Then a certain man spoke to him privately, saying, "Why do not you make answer to the old men who have praised you?" Abba Alonis said to them, "Because if I made answer to them I should be as one who had accepted the praise."

79. An old man used to say, "If a word of The Book goes up in the heart of a brother when he is sitting in his cell, and if he pursues that word before it has arrived at its maturity, not being driven by God, the devils will demonstrate the word before it become complete according to their desire."

80. Abba Saranis used to say, "I have worked during the whole period of my life in reaping, and in twisting ropes, and in sewing mats, and notwithstanding these things, if the hand of the Lord had not fed me I should not have had enough to eat."

81. An old man used to say, "Spread abroad the Name of Jesus in humility, and with a meek heart. Show your feebleness before Him, and He will become strength to you."

82. Abba Macarius said to Abba Zechariah, "Tell me, what is the work of monks?" He said to him, "Do you ask me, father?" The old man said to him, "I beseech you, my son, Zechariah. For there is something which is right I should ask you." Abba Zechariah said to him, "Father, I give it as my opinion that the work of monks consists in a man restraining himself in everything."

83. An old man also said, "He who constrains himself in everything, for God's sake, is a confessor." Again he said, "He who constrains himself for the sake of the Son of God will not be forgotten by the Son of God." He also said, "Him who has made himself a fool for the sake of God, God will make him to be wise."

84. An old man used to say, "If when you are sitting down, or standing up, or when you are doing anything else, God sits before your eyes continually, no act of the Enemy can terrify you; if this thought abides with a man, the power of God will abide with him also."

85. An old man also said, "The man who has his death before his eyes continually will overcome littleness of soul."

86. Abba Poemen used to say, "Hunger and slumber have not allowed me to notice these small matters."

87. Abba Theodore said, "Many men in this age are desirous of life before God gives it to them."

88. He used to say also, "Be a free man, so that you may not be crafty in your words."

89. Abba Poemen used to say, "Keep yourself away from every man who is contentious in speech."

90. An old man said, "In all your trials blame no man except yourself, and say, these have happened to me for my sins."

91. An old man said, "In the sluggard and the useless man God has no pleasure."

92. A brother asked Abba Timothy, saying, "I wish to guard my soul from things that will hurt it." The old man said to him, "How can we guard our soul when the doors of our tongue and belly are open?"

93. They used to say that a certain man asked Abba Sisoes about Abba Pambo, saying, "Tell us about his life and conduct." The old man answered him, saying, "Abba Pambo is great in his works."

94. Abba Joseph related that Abba Poemen said, "The meaning of the words which are written in the Gospel, 'Whoever has a garment, let him sell it, and buy a sword' (Luke 22:36), means, let him that have a life of ease relinquish it, and lay hold upon a life of toil."

95. They used to say that on one occasion when certain of the old men were sitting with Abba Poemen they were discussing some of the fathers, and were asking each other if they remembered Abba Sisoes. Abba Poemen said, "Quit talking about Abba Sisoes, for he has surpassed the measure of all histories."

96. On one occasion a father came to Abba Theodore of Perdme, and said to him, "Behold, O father, such and such a brother has gone back to the world." The old man said, "Do you wonder about that? Do not marvel at this, but you may marvel when you hear that a man has been able to flee completely from the world."

97. An old man related of Moses that when he slew the Egyptian he looked on this side and on that, and saw no man, and explained the meaning of the passage as being that Moses did not see his thoughts. When he saw himself, and that he was doing no evil thing, and that, that which he was about to do was for God's sake, he then slew the Egyptian.

98. An old man also said concerning the verse of the Psalms where it is written, 'I will place his hand in the sea, and his right hand in the rivers' (Ps. 89:25), "That it was spoken concerning our Redeemer, Whose left hand is on the sea, that is to say the world, and Whose right hand is in the rivers, that is to say, the Apostles, who water the whole world with faith."

99. A brother asked one of the old men, saying, "What shall I do? For I am troubled about the works of my hands: I love making mats, but I am unable to make them here." The old man said to him, "Abba Sisoes used to say, 'It is not the work which is easy for us that we ought to do, but that which befits the place, and a brother should labor according to what it will cost to keep him.'"

100. Abba Joseph used to say, "When we were sitting with Abba Poemen he made mention of Abba Agathon, and we said to him, 'He was a young man, why do you call him Abba.' Abba Poemen said, 'His mouth made him to be called Abba.'"

101. One of the old men used to say, "Wherever the bee goes it makes honey; and thus also it is with the monk, for wherever he goes he does the work of God."

102. An old man used to say, concerning the thoughts, "Satan is a twister of cords, and as long as you give him threads he will plait them."

103. Abba Sisoes showed us the cave of Abba Anthony, and said, "Thus in the cave of a lion a fox dwells."

104. They used to say of those who were in Scete that no pride was found among them, because they surpassed each other in spiritual excellences. They fasted so much that one would only eat once every two days, and another once every four days, and another once every seven days; another would eat no bread, and another would drink no water, and to speak briefly, they were adorned with every spiritual excellence.

105. They used to relate that a certain old man entreated God and made supplication to Him that the devils might appear to him, and it was revealed to him that "It is not necessary for you to see them." But the old man made entreaty, saying, "Lord, You are able to hide me in Your grace." Then God opened his eyes, and he saw them like bees surrounding a man, and they were gnashing their teeth upon him, and the angels of God were rebuking them and driving them away from men.

106. A man asked a certain old man from Thebes, and said to him, "Tell me how I may be redeemed." The old man said to him, "Three things you must do. Sit in your cell and keep silence, and consider attentively your sins, and keep yourself wholly from judging any man, and accept no gift from any man, and let your hands be sufficient to find your food. If you are unable to give alms of your work at least supply all your needs by your own hands."

107. They used to say that one day when Abba Sisoes was sitting down he cried out with a loud voice, and said, "O my feebleness." His disciple said to him, "What ails you, O father?" The old man said to him, "I wish to speak to a certain man, and I am unable to do so."

108. They used to say that when the barbarians came the brethren took to flight, and that Abba Daniel, who was in Scete, said, "Unless God takes care of me, why should I live?" He passed through all the barbarians, and they did not see him. Then afterwards he said in himself, "Behold God has cared for me, and I am not dead, I also will do as a man does, and I will flee as the other fathers have fled."

109. When Abba Sisoes was about to die, and the fathers were sitting around him they saw that his face was shining like the sun and he said to them immediately, "Behold, Abba Anthony has come." After a little while he said also, "Behold, the company of the prophets has come." His face shone again, and he said, "Behold the company of apostles has come." Again his face shone with twofold brightness, and he became suddenly like one who was speaking with someone. Then the old men who was sitting there entreated him, and said, "Show us with whom you are talking, father." Immediately he said to them, "Behold, the angels came to take me away, and I besought them to leave me so that I might tarry here a little longer, and repent." The old men said to him, "You have no need to repent, father." The old man said to them, "I do not know in my soul if I have the right to beg to repent." They all learned that the old man was perfect. Then again suddenly his face beamed like the sun, and all who sat there were afraid. He said to them immediately, "Look you, Look you. Behold our Lord has come, and He says, 'Bring you to me the chosen vessel which is in the desert.'" Immediately he delivered up his spirit, he became like lightning, and the whole place was filled with a sweet odour.

110. Abba Paphnutius, the disciple of Abba Macarius, used to say, "I entreated him, saying, "Father, tell me a word." He said to me, "Do no harm to any man, and condemn no man. Observe these words, and you shall be redeemed."

111. A brother asked a certain old man, saying, "In what form does the fear of God dwell in the soul?" The old man said to him, "If a man possesses humility, practises abstinence, and judges no man, in this manner does the fear of God dwell in the soul."

112. Abba Hilarion of Syria came to the mountain to Abba Anthony. Abba Anthony said to him, "Have you come, O star of light, who shines with the morning?" Abba Hilarion said to him, "Peace be to you, O pillar of light, who sustains creation!"

113. Certain of the fathers used to say, "God does not bring young men to monasteries, but Satan, so that he may turn back the mighty men."

114. A brother said to Abba Anthony, "Pray for me, father." The old man said to him, "I cannot help you, and God will not, if you will not abolish yourself and ask Him yourself to do so."

115. They used to tell of a certain old man who had passed fifty years of his life without eating bread or drinking water, and he used to say, "I have slain fornication, the love of gold, and the love of glory." Abba Abraham heard of him, came to him, and said, "Did you say these things?" He said, "Yes." Abba Abraham said to him, "If you were to go into your cell, and find a woman on your mat, would you be able to keep from thinking that she was a woman?" The old man said to him, "No, but I should struggle against my thoughts so as not to touch her." Abba Abraham said to him, "Behold, then, you have not slain the lust for fornication, but the passion is still alive, though fettered. Behold, also, if you were traveling along a road and you did see lying there some potsherds and among them a talent of gold, would your mind be able to look upon the money in the same way as the potsherds?" The old man said to him, "No, but I should contend against my thoughts in such a way as not to take it." Then Abba Abraham said to him, "Behold, the passion of love of money is still alive, though fettered. Behold now, if you did hear of two brethren, one of whom was esteeming you highly and praising you, and the other was hating you and reviling you, if these men came to you would you be able to regard each of them with equal friendliness?" The old man said to them, "No, but I would strive against my thoughts in such a way that I would treat him that cursed me as well as I did him that loved me." Then Abba Abraham said to him, "Behold, then, the passions are still alive, but they are fettered in the saints."

116. There was a certain old man who was a monk dwelling in a far desert. He had a kinswoman who with difficulty discovered after very many years where he was living. By the operation of Satan, she rose up and came to the road to the desert, found camels which were going to travel on that road, and she entered the desert with them. She was driven to do this by the devil. As soon as she had come to the cell of the old man, she began to give him proofs about herself, saying, "I am indeed your kinswoman." She remained with him. There was another monk who lived in the neighborhood of men. This monk filled a vessel of water, and set it down. At the season when he ate, being urged by the operation of God, he meditated within himself, and said, "I will arise and will go into the desert, and will learn from that old man what this is." As he was traveling along the way, the night overtook him, he went into a house of idols which was on the road, and passed the night there. He heard the devils saying to each other, "This night we have cast down such a monk by fornication." When he heard this he marvelled, came to the old man, and found him sad. He said to him, "Father, what shall I do? For I filled a vessel with water, but when I came to eat my meal I found that it had been spilled." The old man said to him, "Have you come to ask me about a vessel of water which have been spilled? What am I to do? For this night I have fallen into fornication." The monk said to him, "I know it also; hold your peace." The old man said to him, "How did you know?" The monk said to him, "Last night when I was sleeping in a house of idols on the road, I heard the devils say so to each other, and I was distressed at that." The old man said to him, "Hence, I will go to the world." The monk persuaded him, saying, "No, father, but stay in your place, and send the woman away, for this is a temptation of the enemy." The old man listened to him, sent her away, and he himself continued in his ascetic works. He mourned, and made supplication to God with abundant tears, until at length he arrived at his former state of ascetic excellence.

117. A brother asked one of the fathers, saying, "What shall I do, for I am disturbed in mind when I go up to perform the office of the deacon?" The old man said to him, "It is not good for you to be disturbed when you go up to minister. But if you are disturbed in your cell, you must labor, give thanks, and receive the hire of which you are worthy." Then that brother said to him, "If I can find a man who will minister to me for a gift, and I do not cheat on him, may I let him do so?" The old man said to him, "If you can find a man who is in the world who can perform your ministry, and will take his hire, yes, but if he be a monk, no."

118. A brother said to Abba Poemen, "Can a man rely upon anyone's work of spiritual excellence for salvation?" The old man said to him, "John the Less said, 'I should wish that a man should take to himself a little of each kind of spiritual excellence.'"

119. These are the words which Abba Moses said to Abba Poemen, and the first word which was spoken by the old man was:

120. "It is better for a man to put himself to death rather than his neighbor, and he should not condemn him in anything."

121. "It is good for a man to die to every work which is evil, and he should not vex a man before his departure from the body."

122. "If a man does not put himself in the attitude of a sinner, his prayer will not be heard before God." A brother said to him, "What is a sinful soul?" The old man said, "Everyone who bears his own sins, and does not consider those of his companion."

123. The old man also said to him, "If works do not correspond to prayer he who prays labors in vain." A brother asked him, "What is the equality of works with prayer?" The old man said to him, "He who prays that he may receive the remission of sins must not henceforth be negligent, for if a man relinquishes his own will, he will be accepted by God rightly."

124. A brother asked an old man, saying, "Fasting and praying which spring from men, what do they effect?" The old man said to him, "They make the soul to be humble before God, for it is written, 'Look upon my subjugation, and my labor, and forgive me all my sin' (Ps. 25:18). For if the soul be afflicted it will receive mercy from God."

125. A brother said to an old man, "What shall a man do in every temptation which comes upon him, and during every thought of the enemy?" The old man said to him, "It is right for a man to weep before the grace of God so that He may help him, and he shall speedily find relief if he makes his supplication with knowledge, for it is written, 'The Lord is my Helper, I will not be afraid what man shall do to me.'" (Ps. 118:6); (Heb. 13: 6)

126. The perfection of all spiritual excellences is for a man not to judge his neighbor. For when the hand of the Lord slew the firstborn of Egypt, there was no house where there was not a dead person. Then a brother said to the old man, "What is the meaning of these words?" The old man said to him, "If we allow ourselves to view closely our own sins we shall not see those of our neighbor. It is folly for a man to forsake his own dead and to lament over that of his neighbor."

127. And in respect of the words, "a man should put his own soul to death rather than that of his neighbor," they mean that a man should bear his own sins, and should be remote from the anxiety of all men. He should not say, "This is good, and this is bad." He should not do harm to any man. The wickedness of your neighbor should not be remembered in your heart. You must not hold in contempt the man who has done wickedness to your friend. You must not deliver your will over to him who does evil does to your neighbor. You must not rejoice in that which causes evil to your neighbor. This is the meaning of the words that a man should die rather than his neighbor. You shall not speak evilly of a man, but say, "God knows every man." You shall not take pleasure in evil converse. You shall not deliver your will over to him that reviles your neighbor. This is the meaning of the words, "Do not judge so you will not be judged." You shall not make enmity against any man. You shall not make any enmity in your heart. You shall not hate him who works enmity against his neighbor. You shall not judge his enmity. You shall not keep wrath against a brother who keeps wrath against his neighbor. For this is peace.

128. Now the conclusion of all these things is that whatever you hear, you must speak. This is not the opinion to which I incline. I am a sinner; for because of these things God will give you rest. When you rise up in the morning each day, lay hold upon a governor who will suit every kind of spiritual excellence, and every command of God with abundant longsuffering, in humility of soul and of body, with patience and tribulations, with thoughts and prayers, supplications, with groaning, and the cleansing of the tongue, with watching of the eyes, in suffering abuse without being angry and maintaining peace in not rewarding evil for evil without discretion. You must not regard the lapses of others. You must not measure your own excellence, but you must be the lowest thing in creation through alienation from the things of the body and multitudinous affairs, through the agony of the cross, poverty of spirit, good desire, spiritual self-abnegation, fasting, repentance, and tears, through the strife of war, through discretion, through purity of soul, through noble patience, through vigil by nights, through hunger, and thirst, through nakedness, and cold, and through labors. You must keep hold upon your grave as if you were already dead, and as if death were your neighbor every day, in mountains, in caves, and in the holes of the earth. Take heed that you do not become merely a hearer of the word and not a doer of it. For those who do these things are indeed whose who are clothed in the wedding garments, and those who have worked with the talents.

129. A brother asked an old man, saying, "Father, what answer shall I return to those who abuse us and say that we do not return to the world because of our laziness, and that by the work of our hands and the labor of our souls we do not relieve strangers?" The old man said to him, "Although we have from the Law and from the commandments of our Lord many things wherewith we could make answer concerning the crown of perfection, yet we must make answer, with humility, in this wise. Beloved, when the Ninevites were in need of repentance, which of them did these things for the necessity of the world and its rights? Did not the king himself refrain from this thing and take the same course as the men of olden time, and those of the later time, and those who were before them? He kept silence and was quiet, even according to all the characteristics of the world, and up to the present no men have described the punishment which befitted them. Thus also it is with us, and because we have sinned against and transgressed the natural and written law we bring to naught all the characteristics of the world until we shall perceive that reconciliation has come, and the penalty of the rights of olden time and of the commandments has been dissolved. Did not Paul also teach us this, when he said, 'He who wages a strife keeps his mind free from everything else?' (1 Cor. 9:24-25) A man must not rest until the Lord blots out seed from Babylon."

130. A brother asked an old man, saying, "What shall I do with my mind which fights against me? For it is a greater thing for me to go into the world, to teach and convert many, and to become like the Apostles." The old man said to him, "If there is in your mind no fear that you have fallen short in the matter of any of the commandments, if you have also felt that you have arrived at the haven of rest, and if you have no feeling about anything in your mind, then go. But if you do not have all these things together in you, the desire is due to the operation of wickedness which urges you on, so that it may cast you down from your integrity."

131. Once the brethren were eating together in Scete, and John Kolob was with them. A great priest rose up to give them a pitcher of water, but no man would accept it from him except John Kolob. They all marvelled and said to him, "How is it that you who are the least among all of us have been so bold as to take the pitcher from him, and drink, whilst none of us dared to do so?" Then Abba John said to them, "When I stand up I rejoice that everyman should take the pitcher from me and drink, so that I may have a reward, and I considered on this occasion also, and I took the pitcher and drank so that there might be a reward to him, and that he might not be grieved because no man accepted water from him, and that his good will might not be wronged." When he said this, the fathers marvelled at his intelligence, and obtained benefit by his words.

132. A brother asked Poemen, saying, "I observe my soul, so that wherever I go I may find help." The old man said to him, "Even those who bear swords have a God, Who has mercy upon them in this life. If then we were to find ourselves in islands of terror God would deal with us according to His mercy."

134. Abba Poemen used to say that Abba Ammon said, "One man spends the whole period of his life holding an axe in his hand ready to cut down a tree, and never finds the opportunity of wielding it. While another man, who knows well how to fell trees, hews with three axes, and wields them against trees. Now, he said, the axe in this case is discretion or discernment."

135. Abba Poemen also said that Abba Anthony said concerning Abba Pambo, "This man feared God so greatly that he made the Spirit of God to dwell in him."

136. Abba Poemen used to say, "The fear of God teaches a man all spiritual excellences."

137. A brother asked Abba Poemen, saying, "Why do my thoughts persuade me to esteem myself and compare myself with one whose rule of conduct is more excellent than mine, and to despise that man as much as if he had been my inferior?" The old man answered and said, "The blessed Apostle spoke concerning this, saying, 'In a large house there are not only vessels of gold and vessels of silver, but also vessels of wood and of earthenware. If now a man will cleanse his soul from all these things, he shall become a vessel which is suitable and convenient for the honor of his Lord, and he will be ready for every good work.'" (2 Tim. 2:20-21) That brother said to him, "How are these matters to be explained?" The old man said to him, "They are to be explained thus. The house is the world and the vessels are the children of men. The vessels of gold must be taken as representing the perfect and those of silver are the men who are inferior to them in the measure of ascetic deeds, and the other vessels of wood and earthenware are those who possess a little ascetic excellence. If now a man will cleanse his soul from all the things which are outside what is right, he will become a pure vessel of honor suitable for the use of his Lord, and be ready for every good work."

138. A brother also asked Abba Poemen, "Why is it that I am not allowed to be free in my thoughts like the other old men?" The old man said to him, "John Kolob used to say, 'the enemy does not rejoice in anything so much as in those who do not reveal and lay bare their thoughts to their fathers."

139. Abba Poemen used to say, "Men tend to speak great and perfect things, but in their deeds they draw near to the things which are little and inferior."

140. An old man used to say, "Neither shame nor fear confirms sin."

141. An old man used to say, "As the company of the monks is more excellent than and superior to the children of the world, so it is necessary that the monk who is a stranger should be a mirror to those who are found in a monastery which is devoted to the ascetic life."

142. A brother asked an old man, saying, "What shall I do?" The old man said to him, "Go and love the constraining of you in everything."

143. The same old man said to him, "Reveal and show your gift." The brother said to him, "My thoughts will not permit me to do so." The old man said, "It is written, 'Call upon Me in the day of affliction, and I will deliver you, and you shall praise me (Ps. 50:15).' Call then Him, and He shall deliver you."

144. An old man used to say, "Teach your heart to keep and to take heed to the things which your tongue speaks."

145. An old man used to say, "If a man teaches and does not perform, he is like the large basin which receives the water for the assembly, which waters and cleanses many, but cannot itself be cleaned, and is full of dirt and impurity."

146. Abba Jacob used to say, "As a lamp illuminates a dark chamber, so does the fear of God, if it abides in the heart of a man, illumines him, and teaches him all the excellences of the commandments of God."

147. Abba Muthues used to say, "I would rather have the man with a little work, who abides and is constant, than him who at the beginning labors severely, and soon ceases altogether."

148. On one occasion Abba Theodore went to Abba John, who was a eunuch from his mother's womb. As they were talking together about spiritual excellences, he said, "When we were in Scete the cultivation of the soul was our labor. We worked with our hands only in the ordinary way. We only worked of this kind when it came in the way. Today, however, the cultivation of the soul has become our ordinary work, which is performed whenever it happens to come in the way. The work of our hands, which was always regarded as a common matter, has become to us a serious matter and an object of earnest solitude."

149. A brother asked an old man, saying, "What is the cultivation of the soul like? What is the labor of the hands like?" The old man said to him, "Whatever happens for God's sake is the cultivation (or labor) of the soul; but whatever a man does for himself, or whatever he gathers for himself, is the labor of the hands." The brother said to him, "Father, teach me a proof of this matter for I do not understand." The old man said, "It is as if a man were to say, 'Behold, you hear that I am sick,' and you say in yourself, 'Now I have a piece of work to do, shall I leave it, and go and visit him, or shall I finish it first and then go?' However many times you are prevented from going for some reason or cause, and however many times the brother says to you, 'Come, take me, and help me,' you say within yourself, 'Shall I leave my work and go and help him?' If you do not go, behold, you have abrogated the commandments of God, which are for the cultivation of the soul, because of the work of the hands. If then a man asks you, go with him, since this is a work of God, for He said, 'If a man compel you to go a mile with him, go two (Matt. 5:41).'"

150. A brother asked Abba Marcianus, saying, "What shall I do so that I may live?" The old man answered and said, "He who looks above does not see what is below; he who is occupied closely with the things which are below has no knowledge of what is above. He who understands the things which are above is not concerned with what is below, for it is written, 'Turn, and know that I am God (Ps. 46:10).'"

151. Abba Poemen said that Abba John cultivated all spiritual excellences.

152. A brother asked one of the old men, saying, "If I am being tempted, and a temptation comes upon me, and I have no one to tell about it in confidence, what shall I do?" The old man said to him, "I believe in God, He will send His Grace, will comfort you, and give you strength if you will ask Him in truth and will make supplication to Him. For I have heard that a matter like this took place in Scete. There was a man whose rule and conduct were excellent. He fell into temptation, and he became oppressed in his mind. Because he had no man in whom he had confidence to reveal the matter to, and none to bid him of good courage. He made himself ready to depart. Behold, the grace of God appeared to him by night in the form of a virgin, and comforted him, saying, 'Do not depart, but dwell here with me, for none of the things which I have heard shall be performed.' Straightaway his mind was healed, consoled and strengthened."

153. A certain brother used to say, "I knew an old man who dwelt in the mountain who would never agree to accept anything from any man. Now he possessed a little water, and used to care for it and water a few garden herbs which he had. He lived this life for fifty years, and never went outside the fence of his cell. He was exceedingly famous because of the numerous cures which he wrought daily upon those who came to him. He died in peace, leaving in his place five brethren."

154. There was a certain old man in Scete who toiled in the works of the body, fasting and standing up. In his thoughts he was a simple man, and was neither keen in intellect nor learned. He went to Abba John Kolob to ask him about his thoughts. When the old man had spoken to him he returned to his cell, and forgot what the old man had said to him. He came a second time to the old man, who told him what he had already said to him. When he had departed, he forgot it again. He did so for several times, forgetting what had been said to him. After these things, he went to the blessed man once more, and said to him, "You know, O father, that I forgot your words again; but I did not come to you because I did not wish to weary you." Abba John said to him, "Go, and light a lamp." He went and did as he commanded him. Abba John again said to him, "Bring several lamps, and light them all from it" He lit them as he had told him. Abba John said to the old man, "Is the lamp wherefrom you have kindled the many lamps in anyway the worse?" He said to him, "No." The old man John said to him, "If all Scete were to come to him John would not be the worse for it, neither would the gift of the grace of Christ be impeded thereby. Whenever then you wish, and are in doubt, come to me" By the patient endurance of both of them he removed away the error from that brother. This was the work of those who were dwelling in Scete. They devoted themselves, and delivered over their wills to compel those who were engaged in spiritual war to inherit the good things (or virtues) each from each.

155. There was a certain old man who was sick. He possessed nothing which he required for his needs. The Abba of the coenobium received him there, and said to the brethren, "Exert yourselves a little to relieve this sick man." The man who was sick had a pot full of gold, and he dug a hole below where he was lying and buried it. It happened that he died without confessing and revealing the matter. After he was buried, the Abba who had taken him in said to the brethren, "Remove this bench from here." While they were rooting it out they found the gold. The Abba said, "Since he did not confess about this when he was alive, he cannot reveal the matter now when he is dead. He knew that the sick man's hope had been in it but go and bury the gold with him." A fire came down from heaven, and it continued above his grave for many days in the sight of every man, and all those who saw it marvelled.

156. A certain brother came on one occasion to the cell of Abba John at the time of evening, and he was in a great hurry to depart; and they talked about spiritual excellences for a long time without realising it, and he went out to set him on his way. They tarried talking together until it was the sixth hour of the night. Then Abba John made him go back to his cell, they ate together, then he sent him away, and he departed.

157. Abba Ammon said, "Once I and Abba Betimius went to visit Abba Akhila, for we heard that he was meditating upon the passage, 'Fear you not, O Jacob, to go down to Egypt.' (Gen. 46:3) He was repeating these words several times. When we knocked he opened to us, and he asked us, saying, 'Where are you from?' Being afraid to say, 'We come from the cells,' we answered that we were from the Mountain of Nitria, and he let us in. We found that he was working by night at plaiting palm leaves. We asked him, saying, 'Speak a word to us.' He answered saying, 'Between the evening and the morning I have twisted twenty branches. But in very truth I have no need for all this, only I am afraid lest God be angry with me, and He reproaches me, saying, "Though you were able to work you have not done so." Therefore I toil and I work with all my might.'"

158. A certain father used to tell a story about a holy man who was indeed a great man. When people asked him a question, he would reply with wisdom, saying, "Behold, take upon myself the face (or Person) of God, and I sit upon the throne of judgement. What do you now wish me to do for you? If you say, 'Have mercy upon me,' God says to you, 'If you wish Me to have mercy upon you, you also must have mercy upon your brother, and then I will have mercy upon you. If you wish Me to forgive you, you also must forgive your brother, and then I will forgive you.' Can any put the blame upon God? God forbids! But the cause rests with us, and if we wish we are able to live."

159. Once a certain brother departed into exile from the countries and places where dwelt Abba Poemen, and he went to a monk who used to live in that country whereto he was going. This man was one who possessed love, and many folk thronged to him. The brother related to that monk stories concerning Abba Poemen, and when he heard about his spiritual excellences he longed to see him. The brother came back again to Egypt. After some time the monk to whom he had gone, who lived in that country, came to Egypt to him, for the brother had already told him where he lived, and when the monk saw the brother he rejoiced greatly. The monk said to the brother, "Do me an act of love, and take me so that I may go to Abba Poemen." He took him to Abba Poemen. The brother told him the story of the monk who was with him, saying, "He is a great man, much beloved, and does not have the least honor in his own country. I related to him stories concerning your holiness, and he greatly desired to come and see you." Abba Poemen received him with gladness. Having saluted each other they sat down. Then the stranger began to converse with Abba Poemen from the Scriptures concerning spiritual and heavenly things. Abba Poemen turned his face away and did not answer. When he saw that Abba Poemen would not speak to him, he was grieved, went outside, and said to the brother who had brought him, "In my opinion I have toiled in vain in coming all this long journey to see the old man, for behold, he refuses to speak to me." When the brother went in to the old man Poemen, he said to him, "Father, this great man, who is so greatly praised in his own country, came on your account. Why did not you speak with him?" Poemen said, "He spoke about the things which are above and concerning heavenly matters, but I can only talk about things which are below and about the things of earth; had he spoken to me about the passions of the soul I would have given him an answer; but since he talked about spiritual things, I know nothing about them." Then that brother went out to the monk and said to him, "The old man is not one of those who wish a man to talk to them from the Scriptures, but if you converse with him about the passions of the soul he will answer." Straightaway the monk repented, and came to the old man, saying, "Father, what shall I do so that I may bring into subjection the passions of the body?" The old man looked upon him gladly, and said to him, "Now you are welcome! Open now your mouth on such matters as these, and I will fill it with good things." The monk, having been greatly helped, and gained benefit, said, "In very truth this is the way of truth." He went back to his country, giving thanks to God that he had been held worthy of such converse with the holy man.

160. Abba Poemen said concerning Abba John that he cultivated spiritual excellences of every kind.

161. Abba Muthues used to say that there were three brethren, two were in the habit of coming to Abba Anthony, and asking him questions about the thoughts, life, redemption, and the discretion of the soul, whilst the third one held his peace continually. After a long time Abba Anthony said to him, "Brother, you come here each year, and ask nothing!" The brother answered, saying, "It is sufficient for me to see you."

162. Abba Sisoes asked Abba Poemen about filthy thoughts, and the old man said to him, "The matter is like a box of clothes. If a man leaves the clothes inside it for a long time without being turned, they will become eaten up in process of time and destroyed. Thus also is it with the thoughts, and if a man does not drive them out from his body they will be destroyed and perish."

163. Abba Joseph asked Abba Poemen about the wicked and vain thoughts which a man produces. The old man said to him, "It is as if a man were to take a snake and a scorpion, and throw them in a vessel (or cloth), and close (or wrap) them up tightly for a long time, when they would die owing to the period which they have been shut up; even so do the evil thoughts, which spring up in the mind through the workings of devils, decay and become destroyed through patient endurance."

164. Abba Elijah used to say, "What is the sin able to do where repentance is found? What will love profit where there is pride?"

165. One of the fathers said, "The early fathers did not depart from their places except for the following three reasons, firstly, if one of them was vexed with his neighbor, and it was impossible for him to clean his heart in respect of him. Secondly, if the abundant approval of the children of men was gathered to him. Thirdly, if the temptation of fornication clung to him. Whenever they saw these three reasons they departed."

166. On one occasion when he saw him pouring some water over his feet, Abba Isaac said to Abba Poemen, as one who possessed freedom of speech before him, "How is it that, whilst the fathers exercised themselves in such stern labors and mighty deeds of asceticism that they oppressed their bodies, behold, are you washing (their feet)?" Abba Poemen said to him, "We have not learned to be slayers of the body, but slayers of the passions."

167. This same Abba Isaac heard the voice of a cock, and said to Abba Poemen, "Are there such things as fowls here, father?" He answered and said to him, "Isaac, why do you force me to speak to you? It is only people who are like yourself that hear such sounds as these. He who is strenuous does not concern himself with matters of this kind."

168. An old man used to say, "Wisdom and simplicity form the perfect order of the Apostles and of those who examine closely their rules of life and their conduct, and to this Christ urged them, saying, 'Be harmless as doves and subtle like serpents.' (Matt. 10:16) Paul the Apostle also admonished the Corinthians to the same effect, saying, 'My brethren, do not be childish in your minds, but be as babes in respect of things which are evil, and be perfect in your minds.' (1 Cor. 14:20) Now wisdom without simplicity is wicked cunning. It is the subtlety of the philosophers among the pagans of which it is said, 'He catches the wise men in their own cunning.' (Job 5:13); (1 Cor. 3:19) Again, 'The Lord knows the thoughts of the wise, that they are vain.' (Ps. 94:11); (1 Cor. 3:20) Simplicity without wisdom is the foolishness which is prone to error. Concerning this also the Apostle spoke, and wrote to those who possessed it, saying, 'I fear lest, even as the serpent led Eve into error by his craftiness, so your minds also may be destroyed in respect of your simplicity which is towards Christ.' (2 Cor. 11:3) For they accepted every word without testing it, even as it is said in the Book of Proverbs, 'The simple man believes every word.'" (Prov. 14:15)

169. They used to say that one of the old men in Scete had been a slave. He came each year to Alexandria, and brought with him a gift for his owners from the results of labor, they received him, and paid him homage. The old man formerly poured water into a basin, and brought it so that he might wash the feet of his owners, but they said to him, "No, father, you shall not honor us thus." He said to them, "My lords, I acknowledge that I am your slave, and that I have received from you an act of grace in that you have let me become a free man to serve our Lord, and if I may not wash your feet accept at least my gift." They objected to this, and would not accept it. He said to them, "Since you refuse to accept it I shall dwell here, and be subject to you." They allowed him to do what he wished. They sent him away with great gifts of various kinds, so that he might do acts of kindness on their behalf to the brethren who were in need. Because of this he became famous in Scete. He conducted himself with great humility towards every man.

170. There was a certain man who was a slave and became a monk. He persisted in a life of self-abnegation for forty five years. Bread, water, and salt, were sufficient for his food. After some time the man who had been his master repented, and also made himself remote from the world. When the time came for him to depart from this world, he said to his slave, who was now his Rabba, "I see the hosts of wickedness surrounding me, but through your prayer they are going back from me." When the call came for that slave one stood on his right hand, and the other on his left. He heard them saying to him, "Do you wish to come, O father, or shall we go and leave you?" He said, "I do not desire to remain. Take my soul." Thus he ended his life.

171. A certain man made himself remote from the world. He had a wife and a daughter. The daughter died before she had been baptized by the disciples. Her father distributed the portion which came to her, and also that of his wife among the poor. He never ceased to make entreaty to God on behalf of his daughter who had departed from the world without being baptized. He heard a voice while he was praying, saying, "I have baptized your daughter, have no sorrow." He did not believe. That hidden voice spoke again to him, saying, "Uncover her grave, and look in. You will not find her." He went to her grave, dug it up, and he did not find her, for she had departed, and had been laid with the believers.

172. The old man Macarius used to say, "These are the three principal things, and it is right that a man should set them before him at every season. The remembrance of his death should be before him at every hour, and he should die to every man. He should be constant always in his mind towards our Lord. For, if a man does not have the remembrance of his death before him at all seasons, he will not be able to die to every man. If he does not die to every man he will be unable to be constantly before God."

173. The old man Macarius used to say, "Strive for every kind of death, for the death of the body. If you do not have the death which is in the spirit; strive for the death of the body, and then the death which is in the spirit shall be added to you. Death of this kind will make you die to everyman. Hence forward you will acquire the faculty of being constantly with God in silence."

174. The same old man also said, "If you do not have the prayer of the spirit, strive for the prayer of the body, and then the prayer in the spirit shall be added to you. If you do not have humility in the spirit, strive for the humility which is in the body, and then the humility which is in the spirit shall be added to you. For it is written, 'Ask, and it shall be given you (Matt. 7:7)'; and 'And all things, whatever you shall ask in prayer, believing, you shall receive.'" (Matt. 21:22)

175. A brother asked an old man, saying, "Why do I keep my sins in remembrance without being pained about them?" The old man said to him, "This happens to us through contempt and negligence. When a man wishes to boil some food for his need, and he finds some small sparks of fire in his fireplace, he desires to take care of them, preserves them, and to kindle there from a large flame. If he neglects them they become black and die out. Thus also is it with ourselves, for if, according as God has bestowed upon us, we remember our sins, we desire and come to the life of silence. If we possess persistence in remembering our sins, we shall acquire great grief in our hearts; but, if we hold them in contempt and do not even remember them, we shall be rejected."

176. A brother asked Abba Poemen, saying, "Who is a hypocrite?" The old man said to him, "The hypocrite is he who teaches his neighbor to do a certain thing which he himself has not performed, and to the doing of which he has not attained; for it is written, 'Hypocrite! Why do you look at the speck which is in the eye of your brother, and behold there is a beam in your own eye? And how can you say to your brother, Let me take out the speck from your eye, seeing that you have not first taken the beam out of your own eye?'" (Matt. 7:5)

177. A brother asked Abba Chronius, saying, "What shall I do in respect of the error which leads captive my mind? For I do not perceive it until it brings me to the committal of sin." The old man said to him, "When the Philistines (those of Ashdod) arose early on the morrow, behold, Dagon [was] fallen upon his face to the earth before the ark of the LORD. And they took Dagon, and set him in his place again." (1 Sam. 5:3) The brother said to him, "What does it mean this word?" The old man said to him, "If the unclean devils take captive the mind of a man by their own means, they lead it on until they bring it to invisible and unknown passion; but if, on the spot, the mind turns and seeks God, and remembers fervently the judgement of the world which is to come, straightaway the passion departs, and is destroyed. For it is written, when you repent and groan, you shall be redeemed, and you shall know in what condition you are."

178. Again a brother asked Abba Chronius, saying, "In what manner does a man come to humility?" The old man said to him, "In my opinion a man does this by restraining and withdrawing himself from everything, and by devoting himself to the labor of the body, and as far as he has the power so to do he should remember his departure from the body, and the awful judgement of God."

179. Abba Anthony used to say, "Behold a time shall come to the children of men when they shall become silly, and they shall turn aside and depart from the fear of God, and if they see a man who is neither as mad nor as silly as they are, they shall rise up against him, saying, 'You are both mad and silly, because he is not like to them.'"

180. Abba Ammon of Nitria went to Abba Anthony, and said to him, "I see that the labors which I perform are greater than yours. How then is it that your name is more renowned among men than mine?" Abba Anthony said to him, "Because I also love the Lord more than you do."

181. When Abba Poemen heard that Abba Nastir was dwelling in the coenobium he desired greatly to see him. He told his Abba that he ought to send him to go and visit him. He refused to send him by himself, and he would not let him go. A few days afterwards the steward of the coenobium, who had certain thoughts, persuaded Abba to send him to Abba Nastir. He dismissed him, saying, "Take this brother with you, and send me an old man because of him; and because I could not trust myself to send him alone I did not send him at all." When the steward had come to the old man Nastir, he told him his thoughts and Abba Nastir healed him. Afterwards the old man asked Abba Poemen, saying, "Where have you got such humility that whenever it happens that there be trouble in the coenobium you do not speak, and do not interfere to put an end to contention?" The old man having pressed the brother, Abba Poemen answered and said to him, "Forgive me, father! When I first entered the coenobium I said to my mind, 'I and the ass are one.' As the ass is beaten and does not speak, and is cursed and makes no answer, so also I act, according to what the blessed David said, I was a beast before You' (Psalm 73:22)."

182. On one occasion Saint Theophilus, Archbishop of Alexandria, came to Scete. When the brethren were gathered together they said to Abba Pambo, "Speak a word to the Bishop, so that we may be built in this place." The old man said to them, "If by my silence we are not helped, we shall not be built by my word."

183. One of the brethren entreated Abba Sisoes, saying, "Do an act of love, father, and speak a word to me." He answered and said, "He who holds with knowledge the belief that a man should not esteem himself fulfils the whole Book."

184. An old man used to say, "This is what is written, 'Thus says the LORD; For three transgressions of Tyrus, and for four, I will not turn away [the punishment]; because they delivered up the whole captivity to Edom, and remembered not the brotherly covenant.' (Amos 1:9) That is to say, to be content with wickedness, to fulfil a thought, to utter it; and the fourth is to carry a thought into effect. For at such a thing as this last the wrath of the Lord does not turn back."

185. They used to say concerning a great old man who dwelt in Scete. Whenever the brethren were building cells in Scete, he would go out and lay the foundation. He would not depart until the building was completed. Once, when he went out to build, he was exceedingly sad, and very sorry. The brethren said to him, "Why are you thus grieved and sorry?" He said to them, "My sons, this place shall be laid waste. For I have seen a fire kindled in Scete, and have seen that the brethren took palm leaves and beat upon it until they extinguished it. The fire broke out again, and the brethren took palm leaves and extinguished it. It broke out a third time, and it filled all Scete, and the brethren were never again able to extinguish it. It is for this reason that I am grieved, and sad, and sorry."

186. An old man used to say, "It is written, 'The righteous man shall blossom like the palm tree.' (Psalm 92:12) These words make known that the soul acquires height, straightness of stature, and sweetness from beautiful deeds. There is another quality which is found in the palm, that is, a single, white heart, which is wholly suitable and useful for work. This must be found in the righteous man, for his heart must be single and simple. It must be accustomed to look towards God only. The heart of the palm tree is also white by reason of that fire which it possesses naturally, and all the service of the righteous man is in his heart; and the hollowness and the evenness of the tops of the leaves typify the setting up of sharpness of the soul of the righteous man against the calumniator."

187. A father used to say, "The eyes of the pig are so arranged by nature that they look always on the ground. The animal can never look upwards to heaven. Thus is it with the soul which has once been swallowed up in the gratification of the lusts, for it is caught hence forward in the filthy mire of the gratification of the passions. It is only with difficulty that it is able to look towards God, or to meditate upon any of the things which are worthy of praise."

188. The fathers prophesied concerning the later generation, saying, "What manner of work will they do?" One of them, Isokhoron, whose conduct was exalted, said, "We perform the commandments of God." The others answered him saying, "And those who will come after us, what manner of work will they do?" He said, "They will attain to the half of our service." Again they answered and said, "What manner of work will those who come after these do?" He said, "Those who are in that generation will possess no work of any kind, for many trials are about to come upon them. Those among them who are found to be chosen men will be found to be greater than ourselves and our fathers."

189. An old man was once asked, "How is it that you are never dejected?" He said, "Because each day I hope to die."

190. A brother asked an old man, "Why do I get attacked by fear when I go out by myself at night?" The old man said, "Because the life of this world is still dear to you."

191. An old man was asked, "What is the work of monks?" He said, "To cultivate all the virtues, to make themselves strangers to all wickedness, and to be watchful against judging and condemning others. Prayer, obedience, and the cultivation of the virtues are the mirror of the monk. The monk's soul is a fountain. If it casts out the things which are abominable it, shall be made pure. If he digs a pit, God is not wicked that He should lead us out from one house of bondage and carry us into another."

192. An old man used to say, "Do nothing without prayer, and afterwards you will never be sorry."

193. Abba Poemen used to say, "The work of the monastic life is poverty, trouble, and separation. It is written, 'Though these three men, Noah, Daniel, and Job, were in it, they should deliver [but] their own souls by their righteousness, says the Lord.' (Ezekiel 14:14) Noah represents the personification of self-abrogation, Job represents labors, and Daniel represents separation. If then a man possessed these three rules of conduct, the Lord dwells in him."

194. A brother asked Abba Poemen, "Which is the better, to speak or to keep silence?" The old man said to him, "He who speaks for God's sake is a good man, and he does well, and he who holds his peace for God's sake does well."

195. A brother asked Abba Poemen about pollutions and impurities of all sorts and kinds, and he said to him, "If we establish in ourselves a portion only of the work of our souls, a man may seek for impurity or uncleanness and it shall not be found."

196. An old man used to say, "We saw in Abba Pambo three virtues which appertained to the body, namely, fasting from one evening to the other, and silence, and abundant work of the hands."

197. Abba Pambo asked Abba Anthony, saying, "What shall I do?" The old man said to him, "Put no confidence in your own righteousness. Do not regret or cogitate upon a matter which is past. Be persistent in restraining your tongue and your belly."

198. An old man was asked, "What is it right for a man to do that he may live?" The old man himself used to plait palm leaves into mats, and he never lifted up his head from the work of his hands, but he occupied himself at all times. The old man answered and said to him that asked him, "Behold, what you see."

199. The old men used to say, "There is nothing worse than a man passing judgement upon his neighbor."

200. And the old men used to say, "From those who are beginners in the monastic life God demands nothing except work, and the vexing of the body, and that a man should be obedient."

201. An old man used to say that separation was the most excellent of all spiritual virtues.

202. Abba Arsenius used to say, "You shall not depart from a place without great labor, and you shall do none of the things which, evilly, you desires, and you shall do nothing without the testimony of the Scriptures."

203. Abba Arsenius used to say, "If we seek God He will be revealed to us, and if we lay hold upon Him, He will remain with us."

204. Abba Poemen used to say to Abba Job, "Turn away your eyes from beholding what is vain, the lust for which destroys souls."

205. The old man used to say also, "It is impossible for him who believes rightly, and who works in the fear of God, to fall into the impurity of the passions, and into the error of devils."

206. Abba Macarius used to say, "If we remember the wickedness of men we destroy the power of the memory. But if we remember how the devils act wickedly we shall remain uninjured."

207. Once, Abba Macarius went up from Scete to Therenuthum. At eventide he came upon a certain place where he went that he might refresh himself and rest. There were some old bones and bodies of the dead. He took some of them and placed them under his head that he might lie down and rest a little from the labor of the road. When the devils which dwelt there saw his confidence and courage, they were smitten with envy. Wishing to disturb him they cried out and shouted from one to another the name of a woman, saying, "O So-and-so, O So-and-so, come with us, and let us go to the bath." Another answered from out of the bones which were under the head of the blessed man, and said to him that called him, "There is a stranger who is lying upon me, and I am unable to come." But the blessed man was not moved, neither was he astonished, but with confidence and great courage he knocked upon the bones, saying, "Rise up, and get into darkness backwards." When the devils heard this, they cried out with a loud voice, saying, "You have conquered us." They fled away ashamed.

208. Abba Anthony used to say, "Let us put God before our eyes continually. Remember death and Christ our Redeemer. Hate the world and everything which is there. Hate the world and all bodily pleasure. Die to this life, so that you may live to God, for God will require it of you in the day of judgement. Be hungry, thirsty, and naked. Weep and mourn. Watch and groan in your heart. Examine yourself and see if you are worthy of God. Love labor and tribulation, so that you may find God. Treat with contempt and despise the body, so that your soul may live."

209. An old man was asked, "What is the straight and narrow way?" He answered and said, "The straight and narrow way is for a man to constrain his thoughts, and to restrain his desires for God's sake, and this is intended to be understood when it is said, 'Behold, we have left everything and followed you.'"

210. Abba Poemen asked Abba Joseph, saying, "What am I to do when passions rise up against me, wishing to make me quake? Shall I stand up against them, and drive them away, or shall I allow them to enter?" The old man said to him, "Let them shake you, and strive with them." But another brother who had come from Thebes, gone down to Scete, asked the same old man the same question and the old man spoke differently. When he returned from Scete to

Thebes, he said before all the brethren, "I went to Abba Joseph, and I asked him, saying, 'If passions draw near to me, shall I drive them away so that they may not make me shake, or shall I permit them to enter into me?' He said to me, 'You shall not let them draw near to you in any way, but cut them off quickly.'" When Abba Poemen, who happened to be there, heard that Abba Joseph had spoken differently to that Theban, he rose up, went again to Abba Joseph, and said to him, "Abba, I have believed in you as in God, and I have revealed to you my thoughts, and behold, you have spoken to that Theban in one way, and to me you have declared the opposite." The old man said to him, "Do not you know that I love you?" He answered and said to him, "Yes, I do." The old man said to him, "Did not you say to me, tell me as if you were telling yourself? If, then, thoughts enter into you, and you are mingled with them, and you give and take, and are not injured, they prove you to be one who is tried and chosen especially. Now I spoke to you as I would to myself. But there are others whom the passions cannot even approach or touch, nevertheless it helps them to cut them off quickly."

211. Abba John Kolob used to say, "I am like a man who is sitting under a great tree, and sees multitudes of wild beasts and creeping things coming towards him. Because he is unable to stand up against them, he runs, goes up the tree, and is delivered. In this manner I sit in my cell, I see evil thoughts coming against me, and because I cannot stand against them I flee and take refuge in God by prayer. I am delivered from the enemies, and I live forever."

212. Abba Hilarion was asked, "How can it be right for a strenuous brother not to be offended when he sees other monks returning to the world?" The old man said, "It is necessary that he should consider the hunting dogs which follow after hares, for as one of these dogs gives chase to the hare so soon as he sees it (now the other dogs which are his companions look at that dog as he runs, and although they run with him for a certain time, they at length become exhausted and turn back, whilst he continues his running by himself, and is not impeded in his headlong course, and he strives to advance, and neither rests nor ceases from running because of those who have remained behind, but he runs until he has overtaken what he sees, even as I have already said, and he does not fear neither the stones which come in his way, nor the thorny brambles and briars, and passes on among the thorns, and though often torn and lacerated thereby he neither rests nor ceases from his course). So also for the brother, who wishes to follow after the love of Christ, is it right to fasten his gaze upon the Cross until he overtakes Him that was crucified, even though he sees others who have begun to turn back."

213. A brother asked an old man, saying, "What work ought the soul to do in order to produce fruits of excellence?" The old man said to him, "In my opinion the work of the soul is as following. To live in silence, persistent endurance, self-denial, labor, humility of body, and constant prayer. A man should not consider the shortcomings of other men, but his own lapses. If a man will persist in these things the soul will after no great time make manifest the fruits of spiritual excellence."

214. An old man used to say, "Strife delivers a man over to anger, anger delivers him over to blindness of the mind, and the blindness of the mind makes him to do everything which is bad."

215. Abba Elijah used to say, "I am afraid of three things, when my soul shall be about to go out from the body, when I am about to go out to meet Christ; and when the sentence of doom shall be about to be sent onward on me."

216. Abba John used to say, concerning the soul that wishes to repent, "There was a certain harlot in the city who had many lovers, and a certain judge came and said to her, 'Consent to lead a good life, and I will marry you.' She agreed, he took her and brought her up to his house. When her lovers wanted her, they said, 'A judge has taken her up to his house, and if we go to his door, and he learns about it he will punish us. But let us come behind the door and whistle to her, then she will recognize the whistle, will come down to us, and we shall be blameless.' When the harlot heard the sound of the whistling, she sealed the hearing of her ears, she jumped up, went into the inner bedchamber, and shut herself in. The harlot is the sinful soul, the lovers are the passions, the judge is Christ, and the house is the wakeful mind. Those who whistle to the soul are the wicked devils but the soul always flees to God."

217. They used to tell a story of a certain great old man, saying, "When he was traveling along a road two angels cleaved to him and journeyed with him one on his right hand and the other on his left. As they were going along, they found lying on the road a dead body which stank. The old man closed his nostrils because of the evil smell, and the angels did the same. After they had gone on a little further, the old man said to them, "Do you also smell as we do?" They said to him, "No, but because of you we closed our nostrils. For it is not for us to smell the rottenness of this world, but we do smell the souls which stink of sin, because the breath of such is near to us."

218. Abba Anthony besought God to inform him why young children died while so many old men lived, why upright men were poor while the wicked were rich, why some were blind and others had their sight, and why the righteous suffered from illness while the wicked were healthy. A voice came, saying, "Anthony, take care of your own self, for these matters are the judgments of God."

219. While Abba Sylvanus was sitting down and the brethren with him, he dropped into a stupor from God. He fell upon his face. And after a long time, he stood up and wept. The brethren entreated him, saying, "What ails you, O father?" He held his peace. They continued to press him to tell them. He answered, saying, "I have just been snatched away to the place of the judgment of God, and I have seen many who belonged to our order, that is to say, Christians, going to punishment, and many men who have lived in the world going into the kingdom." And the old man mourned and refused to come out of his cell." He covered his face with his cloak, saying, "Why should I seek to see the light of time where there is no profit?"

220. On another occasion his (Abba Sylvanus') disciple Zechariah came to him. The disciple found him in the stupor of prayer, with his hands raised to heaven. He went out and closed the door and he came [again] at the ninth hour. He found him in the same state. When he came again about the tenth hour, he found him still in the same state. He knocked the door, went in and found him in a state of silence. He said to him, "What has happened to you today, O father?" The old man said to him, "My son, I felt weak and ill," but the disciple fell on his feet, saying, "I will not leave you until you tell me what you have seen." The old man said to him, "Swear to me that you will not reveal the matter to any man until I go out from the body, and then I will tell you." The disciple entreated him. The old man said, "I was snatched up into the heavens, and I saw the glory of God, and I remained there until now, when I was dismissed."

221. On one occasion Abba Macarius went to Abba Anthony in the mountain, and he knocked at his door. He went out to him, and said, "Who are you?" Macarius said to him, "I am Macarius." Abba Anthony closed the door, and left him outside. When he saw the patient endurance of Macarius he opened the door to him, and said with a smile, "O Macarius, I have been wishing to see you for a long time, for I have heard about you." Having welcomed him he made him rest and refresh himself, through his love for strangers, for Abba Macarius had [come] from great toil. When the evening had come,

Abba Anthony soaked a few palm leaves in water for himself. Abba Macarius said to him, "Give the command, and I will soak some for myself." Abba Anthony said, "Soak [some]," and he made up a large bundle for himself, and soaked it in water. They sat down from the evening [until the morning]. They talked together about the redemption of souls as they plaited the palm leaves. They threw their work into the cave through the window. When the blessed Anthony went into the cave in the morning, and saw the heap of palm-leaf work of Abba Macarius, he marveled, he seized his hands and kissed them, saying, "Great strength has gone forth from these hands."

222. Abba Poemen said, "If a man throws himself before God, does not esteem himself, and casts his pleasures behind his back, he will find that such things are the instruments of the work of the soul."

223. The same old man also said, "If a man observes his grade he will not be troubled."

224. The same old man also said, "Make your desire that lust does not affect you through the remembrance of God, and you shall find rest."

225. He also said, "A certain brother went to Abba Simon to ask him for a word, and although he remained with him for seven days the old man returned him no answer but as he was making himself ready to go away he said to him, 'Go, and take good heed to yourself, for at present my sins have become a dense wall between myself and God.'"

226. Abba Alonis said, "If I had not hidden (or suppressed) myself wholly I should not have been able to build myself."

227. The same old man said, "A man is not able to know outside himself the thoughts which are in him, but when they resist him from within, if he is a warrior, he will cast them out from him."

228. The same old man also said, "Wherever a man cleaves, is built up, do not look upon your mind."

229. The old man often said, "Do not esteem yourself, but cleave yourself to he who leads a good life."

230. He also said, "[In] this [life] we do not discern matters, and it does not permit us to profit by the things which are good."

231. The old man said, "If a thought about some bodily need comes to you and you cast it away once, and if it comes to you a second time, and you drive it away, and if it comes to you a third time, do not look upon it, because it is war."

232. A father who was about to die said to his sons, "Do not dwell with heretics, have no converse with a brother who has a sister, have no business with the Government, and do not let your hands be spread out to gather in, but rather to give to the poor who are in need."

233. On one occasion Abba Evagrius said to Abba Arsenius, "Since we are without learning according to the world, and we have no wisdom whatever, [how is it that] these Egyptian villagers possess such spiritual excellences?" Abba Arsenius said to him, "We possess nothing whatever of the learning of the world, but these Egyptian villagers have acquired spiritual excellences through their labors."

234. On one occasion Abba Arsenius asked an Egyptian old man about the thoughts. Afterwards another brother said to Abba Arsenius, "How is it that while you have so much learning, both Greek and Latin, you ask questions about the thoughts of this villager?" Abba Arsenius said to him, "I am well acquainted with Greek and Latin learning, but I have not yet learned the alphabet of this villager."

235. Once the Archbishop wished to go to visit Abba Arsenius. He sent a message to this effect to him, and the old man sent his [back] word, saying, "If you come I will open to you. If I open to you I must open to every man. If I open to every man I cannot remain here." When the Archbishop heard these things, he said, "If I would drive him away I must go to the old man, therefore I will not go."

236. A brother entreated him to let him hear a word from him. The old man said, "As far as it lies in your power, lead an ascetic life. Work that secret work which is within. If it is for God's sake, [for] it shall vanquish [your] passions which are external."

237. Abba Poemen said, "If there are three [brethren] together, and one leads a fair life of silent contemplation, the other being a weak man gives thanks, and the other sings and prays with a lowly mind, all three are performing work [of equal merit]."

238. A brother asked Abba Poemen, saying, "Tell me: what does it mean that you do not reward an evil for an evil?" Abba Poemen said to him, "In this perception there are four divisions. The first is of the heart, the second is of the sight, the third is of the tongue, and the fourth is in actions a man returns evil for evil. If you are able to overcome the heart, you will not come to the sight, but if you come to the sight, take heed that you do not speak with the tongue. If you speak, cut it off immediately, so that you may not actually reward evil for evil. This is the first of the four which a man may cut off, the tongue is the second, the third is the sight, and the fourth is the heart."

239. The old man Anthony used to say also, "If the baker did not put a covering over the eyes of [his] animal, it would turn round and eats up its hire. In this manner we also have received a covering by the operation of God, so that we may first of all be working good deeds without seeing them, so that we may not ascribe happiness to ourselves and destroy the hire of our labor. Therefore we are left from time to time in unclean thoughts. We see these only so that we may condemn ourselves, and those filthy thoughts may become a covering of the few good things which we perform. For when a man blames himself he will not destroy his hire."

240. Abba Moses asked Abba Sylvanus, saying, "Is it possible for a man to make a beginning each day?" He replied, "If he is a man who is a worker, then it is possible for him to make a beginning every day."

241. A brother asked Abba Sisoes, "Why don't my thoughts depart me?" He said to him, "Because your thoughts are from within yourself. Give them their pledge and they will depart."

242. A brother asked Abba Theodore, saying, "If an earthquake were to take place suddenly, would not you be afraid, O father?" The old man said, "Even if the heavens were to cleave to the earth, Theodore would not be afraid." He besought God formerly that trembling might be removed from him, and it was because of this that he who puts the question to him asked him.

243. They used to say that when Abba Theodore was a deacon in Scete he refused to perform the ministrations of deacon. He fled to several places to avoid doing so, but the old men would bring him back again, saying, "You shall not forsake your place." Abba Theodore said to them, "Permit me to make a request to God, and if He permits me I will stand up in my place." When he made his petition to God, he said, "If it is Your will, O my Lord, for me to remain, permit me [so to do]." Then there appeared to him a pillar of fire [which reached] from earth to heaven, and a voice said to him, "If you like to be like this pillar, go and perform your ministrations." Although he heard these things he would not consent to minister. When he came to the church the brethren fell down before him and entreated him, saying, "If you refuse to minister, at least hold the cup." He refused and said, "If you will not allow me [to be] here [as I am], I will depart from these places." So they left him [there].

244. They used to tell a story about Abba Macarius the Great, who became, as it is written, an earthly God, for as God overshadows the world so also did Abba Macarius cover over the shortcomings which he saw as if he did not see them, and the things which he heard as if he did not hear them.

245. Once, a maiden came to Abba Macarius to be healed of a devil. A certain brother arrived from a monastery in Egypt. The old man went out by night and saw that the brother was committing sin with that woman. He did not rebuke him, but said, "If God Who created him sees [him], and his long suffering, for if He so desired He could consume him, who am I that I should rebuke him?"

246. I heard that the blessed man Anthony used to say, "God does not permit wars to wax as fierce in this generation as He did in the generations of old, for He knows that men are [more] feeble [now], and that they could not bear [them]."

247. Abba Macarius used to say to the brethren concerning the desert of Scete, "Whenever you see cells which are turned towards the wood, know that the fall is near. And whenever you see trees planted near the doors, [know] that it is near the door. And whenever you see young men dwelling there, take up your possessions and depart."

248. Abba Muthues used to say, "Satan does not know how the passion of the soul may be conquered, but he sows, not knowing whether he will reap but with the thoughts of fornication, of calumny, and of all the passions towards which he sees the soul inclines, he fights against it, and fetters it."

249. Once I was sitting with a certain old man at Oxyrhyncus. This old man used to make great alms and oblations. A widow came to him and demanded a little wheat, and he said to her, "Go and bring a measure, and I will measure out [some] for you." When she had brought it, he took the measure in his hand and said to her, "This is too large." He put the widow to the blush. When she had gone, I said to the Abba and priest, "Were you selling the wheat to the widow?" He said, "No I gave it to her in charity." I said to him, "If you gave her all this wheat in charity, why did you act harshly with her, measure it, and [so] put her to shame?"

250. Three fathers came to an old man at Scete. One of them spoke to him, saying, "I repeat the Old and the New Testaments by heart." The old man answered and said, "You have filled the air with words." The other father said to him, "I have copied the Old and New Testaments." The old man replied to him, "You have filled the cupboards with quires of paper." The third father said to him, "In my fireplace the grass grows." The old man answered, saying, "You also have driven away the love of strangers from you."

251. Abba Poemen used to say about Abba Isidore that he used to twist the ropes into a great bundle of palm leaves each night. One of the brethren entreated him, saying, "Rest yourself a little, for you have worked too much." He said to them, "If we were to burn Isidore and to scatter his ashes to the winds, he would win happiness, for the Son of God came to the Passion because of us."

252. A brother said to Abba Poemen, "If I stumble and commit a few minor sins, my mind afflicts me, blames me, and makes accusations against me, saying, why did I fall?" The old man said to him, "Every time a man falls into any shortcoming or folly, if he says, I have sinned, immediately God will receive him."

253. Abba Poemen used to say, "It is not right for a man to be inclined towards the thought of fornication, or to utter calumny against his neighbor. He should not in any way be inclined towards these two thoughts, should not utter them, and should not meditate upon such things in his heart. If he desires to think about them and to turn them over in his heart, he will not benefit by such. But rather he will harm himself. If he fights against such with ferocity, he will subsequently find rest."

254. One of the brethren asked Abba Poemen, saying, "Father, what shall I do when the thoughts of fornication are stirred inside me, or any other evil passions that are injurious to the soul?" Abba Poemen said, "The first time they come to you, flee. The second time they come to you, flee. Also the third time they come, set yourself against them like a sharp sword."

255. The same old man used to say, "Unless Moses had been gathering together sheep in the field he would never have seen Him that was in the bush."

256. The brethren saw that Abba Joseph was sad and greatly distressed. They asked him to tell them about his sorrow and its cause. But he was unable to speak to them. They began to say to each other, "What are the suffering and grief which possess the old man, for behold, we have dwelt with him for many years, and we never saw him before in such grief and suffering? Perhaps we have in some way offended him." They threw themselves on their faces before the feet of the old man, saying, "Perhaps we have offended you in some matter, O father, [and if we have] forgive us for Jesus' sake." The old man answered them in grief, saying, "Forgive me, O my brethren, for I am not offended by you. I am grieved by myself, because I see that I am going backwards rather than forwards. I am the cause of offence and loss, not only to myself but also to all the others. For I see that at this present we are trafficking, and are losing in respect of our souls very much more than we ever gained at any time of the profit of the fear of our Lord, because shamelessness and fearlessness have gained dominion over us. For in the past times when the fathers were gathered together to each other they were wont to form bands and ascend into the heavens, but we are lax folk, and are dead in our sins. Whenever we draw near to each other we come to speak what is hateful about one another, and one by one we are raised up that we may descend to the bottom of the deepest abyss. We do not only make ourselves and others sink, but also the fathers who come to us, the strangers who gather with us, and also the people who are in the world who visit us as solitary monks. If we were holy men, these become a cause of stumbling and loss. For thus Abba Sylvanus and Abba Lot said to me, 'Let us not abide here any longer.' When I asked them, 'Why do you depart from us?' They spoke to me as follows, 'Up to this day we have benefited by our abiding with the fathers, but from the time of Abba Pambo, Abba Agathon, Abba Petra, and Abba John, the commandments of the fathers have been held lightly, and we do not observe the ordinances and the laws which our fathers laid down for us. By assemblies together we suffer loss over and over again through the useless things which are spoken among us. When we sit down at table, instead of doing so in the fear of God, with gratitude, and eating what God has prepared for us with praise and thanksgiving, we occupy ourselves by conversing together and telling insipid stories. As we sit at table in this fashion we become so much changed that we do not even hear what is being read to us on account of the noise of the profitless talk which we hold with each other. Besides this, after we have risen up from eating, we converse together with empty talk. What benefit is it to us to live in the desert, seeing that we profit nothing thereby?' Abba Lot said, 'Many times I have heard from brethren who are strangers, from the people who live in the world, and who come to visit us, that we hold the commandments of the fathers lightly, and they have said of us, "We should never have thought that they were monks!" One of the brethren who were strangers said, 'I have come to the fathers on several occasions, and [I see that] year by year they certainly observe less and less the early rules and conduct of the fathers.' What do you wish now? Will you correct your lax behavior, and observe carefully the commandments of our fathers, or must I also depart from you?" It came to pass that when the brethren heard these things, they beat the board for assembling the monks. The whole brotherhood gathered. Abba Joseph spoke to them all the words which are [written] above. When all the brethren heard the words of Abba Joseph, learned the reason of his pain and grief, and that he wished to depart from them, they cast themselves down upon their faces weeping. They expressed their contrition to him, saying, "Forgive us, O father, for the sake of Jesus. We have made God angry by our deeds, and we have caused grief to your holiness." Then each of the fathers said, "Would that you had rebuked us on the very first day where you did hear [about us] from the fathers, and that they had not departed from us! Also, would that we had roused ourselves up from our slumber and sluggishness! But what are we to do? For the old men and the holy men do not teach us, and they do not even take their proper places in our congregations, or when we sit at meals. Very many of us wish to hear the histories and commandments of the fathers read while we are either sitting at table or sitting together. But we are never able to hear a word of their talk." Abba Elijah said, "Abba Abraham and Abba John spoke much at table, at the time of reading, and at the time of the service. They began to become excited against each other, and the one said, 'Father, such and such a man is excited,' and the other said, 'Such and such a man makes us excited.'" When Abba Joseph saw that the whole brotherhood was stirred up, he made supplication to them, and besought them, saying, "I beseech you, O my brethren, to cease from your commotion, for God has called us to peace. I therefore beg you to come, pray, and make supplication to God that He may make us to pass by the legions and the host of the enemy. For, I see them standing up in wrath and anger, with their swords drawn. They wish to destroy us all if God does not stand up to help our wretchedness." When he had said these things he was able, with some difficulty, to quiet them. Abba Joseph himself began tossing the words of the harpist David, said, "'The

LORD looks from heaven; He sees all the sons of men' (Ps. 33:13), 'Their sword shall enter their own heart, And their bows shall be broken' (Ps.37:15), 'O my God, make them like the whirling dust, Like the chaff before the wind!' (Ps. 83:13), 'Let God arise, Let His enemies be scattered; Let those also who hate Him flee before Him' (Ps. 68:1), and, 'O God, when You went out before Your people, When You marched through the wilderness.' (Ps. 68:7)" When they had recited the Psalms of the spirit altogether, and made an end of the service, they said, "O holy God, O holy mighty One, O immortal holy One, have mercy on us." They all knelt down in prayer. As they were praying they heard the voices of the devils in the air, the sounds of armor and horses, and of many horsemen. They also heard the voices of the devils who were saying to one another, "You shall not have mercy on them." Again they said, "O unfortunate monks, why do you stand up against us? If we were to do [what we could do] to you not one of you would be found on the face of the earth! We will never be absent from you, and we will never cease from you." After the filthy legion had been driven away by the secret power, the wicked devils rested from their wickedness. All the fathers rose up from the earth and had been poured out in prayer. The earth has been adorned by their tears. They all offered repentance to Abba Joseph, saying, "Forgive us, and pray for us that the Lord may forgive us, for we have sinned and have provoked Him to wrath." Abba Joseph said to them, "Revive yourselves, O my brethren, and take good heed to your souls, for, behold, you have heard with your ears the sound of the chariots of the Adversary, who threatens us and seeks to destroy us. Let every man be reconciled to his neighbor, and forgive every man from his heart the offence [which he has committed]. Bind yourselves with the love of our Lord, with an urgent mind, and a pure heart, to the Lord and to each other. Draw near to God that He may draw near to you. Stand up against the Adversary, who is Satan. If you will observe the commandments of the fathers, I assure you that Satan shall not be able to injure you, and that the Barbarians shall not come here. But if you do not observe them, believe me, O my beloved, this place shall be laid waste." They offered repentance to each other and reconciled to each other, lived in love and in great peace and laid down ordinances among themselves on that day to the effect that no man should conduct himself with negligence, without absence of fear and that they should neither do nor say anything at the table which was alien [to their mode of life]. If any man is found here after despising and holding lightly the commandments of the fathers in such a way that he become an occasion of offence and a cause of loss to himself, to those who dwell with him, and to the strangers who come to us, he shall know that he is bringing a punishment upon himself. He shall become an alien to all the brotherhood. Abba Joseph sent a brother to bring back Abba

Sylvanus and Abba Lot. When these fathers knew what had happened among the brethren, that the ordinances had laid down to keep the commandments of the fathers, they praised God, rose up, and came. [When] they saw Abba Joseph they saluted him and wept. Abba Joseph told them everything that happened. They glorified God, Who had not rejected those who feared Him. As regards to the canons and the ordinances laid down among themselves, the brethren observed and performed them all the days of their life. They died at a good old age, [after] living well pleasing lives before God.

257. Abba Ammon used to say, "I have spent fourteen years in Scete in making supplication to God by day and by night that He would grant me to overcome anger."

258. An old man used to say, "Be like a camel when you are loaded with your sins, and be tied to and cleaved to him who knows the way."

259. One of the old men used to say, "Formerly, whenever we met each other we used to speak words of profit about each other. We formed gatherings, and were lifted up into the heavens. But now when we are gathered together, we come to hateful conversation concerning each other, and we drag each other down to the bottom of the deepest abyss."

260. Abba Achilles came to the cell of Abba Isaiah, and found him eating. There were in the basin [from which he ate] water and salt. The old man saw him hide the basin behind a mat. Abba Achilles said to him, "Tell me what had you been eating?" Abba Isaiah said to him, "Forgive me, I was cutting some palm leaves, I went up in the heat, placed in my mouth a morsel of bread and salt. My throat was dry by reason of the heat, the food did not go down, and I was in pain. I threw a little salt and water in my mouth, so that I might be able to eat. Forgive me." The old man said to him, "Come and see Abba Isaiah who eats food which stinks in Scete. If you seek to eat stinking food, get to Egypt."

261. There was a certain monk who had a brother living in the world. This brother was poor, and whatever the monk earned by the labor of his hands, he used to give to his brother. In spite of this the brother became poorer. The monk went to one of the old men and told him the matter. The old man said to him, "If you will hearken to me, do not give him any more, but say to him, 'My brother, when I have anything to give I give it to you. But you must bring me some of what you earn by your labor,' and whatever he brings to you, take from him. If you know a stranger, or a poor old man, give it to him." He entreated them to offer a prayer on his behalf. The monk went and did thus. When his brother who lived in the world came to him, he spoke to him even as the old man had told him to do. The brother went to his house with a sad mind. On the first day he brought [to the monk] the result of his labor a few garden herbs. The monk gave them to the old men, and entreated them to pray for him. He was blessed and departed. The old man who was in the world returned on another occasion and brought the monk some bread and garden herbs. His brother took them, and did [with them] as he did the first time. He came for the third time and brought many costly gifts, wine, and fish. His brother saw [this] and wondered. He called the poor and gave them these gifts. The monk said to his brother who was in the world, "Perhaps are you in need of some bread, O my brother?" He said to him, "No, my lord, while I took from you that which used to enter into my house, I spent everything I had. Since I ceased to take anything from you, God has blessed me and has done mercy to me." The monk went and informed the old man everything that happened. The old man said, "Do not you know that the labor of a monk is fire, and that wherever it enters it consumes? But it is beneficial for him to show mercy from his own toil. The prayer of the holy men shall be with him, and thus he shall be blessed."

262. While Abba Macarius was passing through Egypt with certain brethren, he heard a child saying to his mother, "My mother, a rich man loves me, but I hate him. A poor man hates me, and I love him." When Abba Macarius heard [this] he marveled. The brethren said to him, "What is the [meaning of] these words, father?" The old man said to him, "Truly our Lord is rich, and He loves us, and we do not desire to hear Him. Our enemy, Satan, is poor, and he hates us, and we love his hateful things."

263. While Abba Zechariah was dwelling in Scete, a vision from God appeared to him. He rose up and came to his father, Abba Kirion, the perfect old man. He did not take pain to boast of these things. He rose up hit him, and said to him, "They are of devils." When he had thought about the matter a long time, he rose up and went by night to Abba Poemen. He informed him about the matter, and how his thoughts were burning in his heart. The old man knew that the matter was of God, and said to him, "Go to such and such an old man, and whatever he says to you, do." Having departed to that old man, before he could tell him anything, the old man said to him, "The vision is of God but do go and be subject to your father."

264. An old man from Scete was dwelling in the mountain of Pilision. A man from the palace who had a devil came to him, and was healed. The man who had the devil offered him a bag full of gold. The old man refused to accept it. When he saw that he was offended, the old man took the bag, which was empty, and said to him, "Go, distribute the gold among the poor and the wretched." He made the bag into a colubium, wore it (it was made of hair), and it was very stiff. He wore it for a long time so that he might vex his body.

265. Abba Longinus asked Abba Lucius three things, saying, "I wish to become a stranger." The old man said to him, "If you do not hold your tongue, where will you go? Will not you become a stranger? Hold your tongue here, and behold you are a stranger." Abba Longinus said to him also, "I wish to lead a twofold life." The old man said to him, "If you do not bend your neck like a hook you are nothing. Purify your wicked thoughts." Abba Longinus said to him, "I wish to flee from men." The old man said, "If you cannot first of all set yourself straight with men, you will never be able [to live] by yourself."

266. A brother asked Abba Joseph, saying, "I want to go out from the monastery, and live a solitary life." The old man said, "Where you see that you will find rest for your soul, there dwell." The brother said to him, "I am content to live in the monastery, and I am content to live alone what shall I do then?" The old man said to him, "If you are content to live in the monastery, and are [equally] content to lead a solitary life, do this: weigh your thoughts as it were in a balance, and the thought which outbalances the other, that fulfill."

267. An old man used to say, "What beast as mighty as the lion, for the sake of his belly falls into the snare, and all his strength is made weakness? In this wise also we shall fall if we be overcome by our bellies."

268. An old man also said, "When the fathers of Scete were eating bread and salt, they said, 'We must not afflict ourselves much with bread and salt. Living with this thought makes them valiant in the works of God.'"

269. While Abba Sylvanus was living on Mount Sinai, brother Zechariah went to the work of the service [i.e., singing and prayer]. When he had gone the old man said to him, "Open out the water [courses] and water the garden." He went out straightaway, and covered his face with his cloak. He could see only his feet. During the time when he was watering [the garden], a brother came to him, and perceived what he was doing. He went in to him, made an apology, and entreated him, saying, "Tell me, O father, why did you cover your face with your cloak and did water the garden in this manner?" The old man said to him, "My son, [I did] so my eyes might not look upon the trees, and that my mind might does not be distracted in its work, and become buried in the trees."

270. They used to say that, "Once, when a certain old man was sitting in his cell, a brother happened to come by night and went to him. When he arrived at the door, he heard his voice loud in a dispute, saying, "It is sufficient, for how long? Go away." Then he said, "Come, come to me, my friends." When the brother had gone in to him, he said to him, "With whom were you speaking, O father?" He said to him, "I was driving away my evil thoughts, and calling my good thoughts to me."

271. There was a certain old man who had a disciple who dwelt in the desert. The old man took a piece of dry wood, planted it, and said to his disciple, "Pour a basin of water over it every day until this piece of wood bears fruit." The fountain of water was so far away from them that a man would set out for it in the evening and return the next morning. The disciple did as he had been told. After two or three years that wood became alive, and bore fruit. The old man took the fruit of it, and brought it to the church, and said to the brethren, "Take, and eat the fruit of obedience."

272. A certain brother on one occasion found on the road a piece of wood which had dropped from camels. He came to the cell of Abba bringing it with him. The Abba said, "Where have you got this piece of wood from?" The brother said to him, "From the road." The old man said to him, "If it is of the things which are taken from the road bring it inside, but if not, go and put it in the place wherefrom you took it."

273. They used to say that Zechariah, the disciple of Abba Sylvanus, took certain brethren without [the knowledge of] Abba Sylvanus. They broke through the fence of the garden, enlarged the garden, and then built up the fence again. When the old man learned this, he took [his cloak], wrapped himself up there, went out, and said to the brethren, "Pray for me." When they saw him, they fell down at his feet, saying, "Tell us, father, what has happened to you." He said to them, "I will neither go inside [my cell], nor unwrap myself from my cloak until you bring the fence back to its former position." [When they had done so] straightaway the old man went into his cell.

274. They used to say that when the old man Abba Magatis went out from his cell. The thought rose up in his mind that he would depart from the place. He did not return to his cell. He possessed nothing whatever of the things of this world. He took pleasure in the work of splitting up the palm leaves and twisting it into ropes. He performed sufficient labor each day to provide him with the very small amount of food which he needed.

275. A brother asked an old man, saying, "If a certain brother comes to me, and says, 'Perform an act of love, and come with me here, or go [with me] to a certain place,' and I am inconvenienced by the command, what am I to do?" The old man replied, "If you know that without offence you cannot fulfill the commandment, go, and it shall be accounted to you as an acceptable sacrifice. But if you know that there will be some offence, you shall not go. If you do go, take good heed to your soul."

276. A brother asked an old man, saying, "Explain why there are, at this present, men who labor, but do not receive grace as the early fathers did?" The old man said to him, "In the beginning love existed, and one brother was raised up by the other. But now love has grown cold, and we drag each other down, and in consequence we do not receive grace."

277. They used to say that when Abba Theodore dwelt in Scete, a devil came and wanted to go into him. The old man perceived that he wanted to go into [his cell], but he kept him fettered outside. Another devil came to go in, and the old man fettered him also. A third devil also came, and finding the other two fettered by the door, he said to them, "Why do you stand outside here?" They said to him, "He who dwells within will not permit us to go in." The third devil stirred up strife, and, holding Abba Theodore in contempt, made (his wish) so boldly to go in. When the old man saw the devil, he fettered him also. Being afraid of the prayers of the old man, the devils entreated him, saying, "Set us free." The old man accepted their petition, released them, saying, "Get away," and then they departed ashamed.

278. They used to say that a certain old man had a young man living with him. One day he saw him doing something which was not beneficial for him and he said to him once, "You shall not do this thing." The young man did not hearken to him. When the old man saw that he would not hearken to him, he left him alone, and did not trouble him anymore. The young man shut the door of the place where the bread was kept, and departed from the cell. He left the old man without bread for three days. When he went back, the old man did not say to him, "Where have you been?" or, "What have you been doing outside?" The young man treated the old man (in this fashion) like a beast. Afterwards, when one of the old man's neighbors perceived the delay of the young man, he boiled a little food, and let it down to the old man from the wall. He made him eat it. When, by chance, his neighbor said to him, "The young man tarries a long time," the old man said to him, "He has not tarried, but when he is disengaged he will come."

279. A certain brother made a second key, opened the cell of one of the old men and took his money out of the cupboard. The old man wrote on a piece of paper, saying, "Do me an act of love and leave me one half of my money, for I have need of it for my necessities." He divided the money (or oboli) into two parts, and laid the paper on them. The brother who stole the money came as usual, tore up the paper and took all the money. Two years later that brother was about to die. His soul was not permitted to go out from him. He called the old man, and made entreaty to him, saying, "Father, pray on my behalf it was I who he who took your money." The old man said to him, "Why did not you confess this before the light became black to you?" The old man prayed, set free the spirit of that brother, and sold his Book of the Gospel and made a memorial for him.

280. A certain man used to relate that an old man from Scete went up to the Thebaid to dwell there. According to the custom with those who are from Scete he made bread sufficient for his needs for several days. The men of the Thebaid came to him, saying, "Why do not you keep the word of the Gospel which commanded men not to care for the morrow?" The old man said to them, "What is your custom?" They said to him, "We work day by day with our hands, sell [what we make], and buy food for ourselves in the market." The old man said to them, "My market is my cell, and when I have need I lay down the work of my hands, and take up food for myself."

281. An old man used to say, "Discretion is the most excellent thing of all."

282. They used to say that certain men came to plead a case for judgment before Abba Ammonius. The old man paid no attention to them, but behaved as if he did not hear them. Behold, a woman said to her companion, "This old man has no stability." The old man heard her speaking thus to her companion. He called her, and said, "How many labors have I performed in the desert so that I might acquire this instability! Yet, through you, I have destroyed this day."

283. An old man used to say, "Do not eat before you are hungry. Do not lie down before you are sleepy. Do not speak before you are questioned."

284. A brother asked an old man, saying, "Do I eat too many garden herbs?" The old man said to him, "It will not benefit you [to do so], but eat bread and a few vegetables, and you shall not go to your kinsfolk for the sake of things [to eat]."

285. An old man used to say, "It is necessary that a monk should be like the Cherub: all eyes."

286. An old man used to say, "For a man to attempt to teach his neighbor, when he has not been required [so to do], is the same as offering him a rebuke."

287. Abba Poemen used to say, "Why does a man distress himself to build the house of others, and to overthrow his own?"

288. He also used to say, "Why is it necessary for a man to enter by cunning, and not to learn [how to do so] properly?"

289. He also used to say, "Everything which is immoderate is from the devils."

290. The old men used to say, "God demands nothing from Christians except that they shall hearken to the Divine Scriptures, and shall carry into effect the things which are said in them, and shall be obedient to their governors and the orthodox fathers."

291. An old man used to say, "Whenever I have been able to overtake my soul when I have transgressed, I never stumbled a second time."

292. An old man used to say, "The man who sets death before his eyes at all times easily overcomes dejection and littleness of soul."

293. An old man used to say, "Take heed, with all your might, not to do anything which deserves blame, and do not take pleasure in making yourself acceptable."

294. Abba Theodore used to say, "There is no spiritual excellence so sublime [as that which consists in] not despising a man and treating him with contempt."

295. An old man was asked, "How, and by what means can the soul acquire humility?" He answered saying, "By examining and enquiring into its own wickedness only."

296. Abba Poemen used to say, "All the spiritual excellences have entered into this monastery, with the exception of the one without which in labor [no] man stands." And they asked him, saying, "Which spiritual excellence is that?" He said, "It is that which makes a man blame and despise himself."

297. The disciple of a certain old man and Abba was attacked by the lust for fornication. He went into the world, and betrothed to himself a wife. The old man, being greatly grieved, prayed to God, and said, "O Lord Jesus Christ, do not permit Your servant to be denied." It came to pass that when he was shut up with the bride in the bed chamber he yielded up his spirit. He was not polluted with the union of marriage.

298. An old man used to say, "If temptation comes upon a man, and attacks him on all sides to such a degree that his mind falls into despair, and he murmurs, all his friends will turn away their faces from him as if by reason of the temptation. He related the following story in illustration of this statement and said, 'There was a monk in a cell, and temptation came upon him. All his friends and beloved ones who met him refused to even salute him. None of them would allow him to enter into his cell. If he lacked provisions, and wanted a man to lend him some, none would lend him. He was compelled by reason of his tribulation to go and work in the harvest field and when he came back he did not find any bread in his cell. It was the custom among the holy men that every man who went to work in the harvest field should on his return eat in the church. When that brother came on the Sabbath, no man took him or gave him refreshment in the usual way. He went to his cell, and gave thanks to God without complaining. When God saw his patient endurance, He abated the temptation in him. Straightaway a man came and knocked at his door and he had with him a camel carrying bread which had been sent to him from Egypt. Then he began to smite himself and weep, saying, "I am not worthy [of this]." The temptation having departed. All the fathers took him, gave him refreshment, persuaded him to let them take him to their cells, and through his patient endurance he found great benefit.'"

299. Certain Greeks came to give gifts of grace in the city of Estarkina. They took with them the stewards of the city that they might show them what it was necessary for them to give them. They went to a certain brother who had elephantiasis, but he refused to accept anything, saying, "Behold, I have these few palm leaves, I will work at them, weave ropes, and will eat bread." They carried them to a certain widow and knocked at the door. Her daughter answered from inside, for she was naked. Her mother had gone out to work, for she was washing clothes and lived by her labor. When they saw that the maiden was naked, they gave her clothes and money. She refused to accept them, saying, "My mother will come, and say to me, 'My daughter, God has willed [it], and I have found some work today, and again we have sufficient food for this day.'" When the mother came, she refused [to accept the apparel and money], and said to them, "O you men, I have One Who provides for me, that is, God, and you seek to take away from me this day Him Who has provided for me all my days." When they saw her faith they glorified God.

300. A certain man offered gold to one of the aged fathers, saying, "Take [it], and let it be for your expenses, because you have grown old now." The old man was an Arian, and he answered and said to him that had given [the gold] to him, "Have you come to take away from me Him Who has reared me for sixty years? For it is sixty years since I have been in this sickness, and I have wanted nothing because God fed me and provided for me and he would not consent to accept anything."

301. One of the fathers told the following story, saying, "I was in the room for receiving strangers. Some poor folks came to receive charity at eventide on the Sabbath. There was among them only one man who had a mat to lie upon when they lay down. He threw it down under him, and reclined upon it. It was exceedingly cold. He took a half of the mat from under him and covered himself over with it, and reclined on the other half. I went out during the night and heard him complaining about the cold. The man turned to himself and said, 'I give thanks to You, O Lord, because how many are the rich men, and the owners of possessions who are at this present moment lying in irons, in afflictions, and in prisons. There are, others whose feet have been put in the stocks, who are unable to turn round to any side, while I, like a king, can spread out my feet, lie down, and besides this, I can go wherever I desire.' When he had said these things, I was standing up and listening to him. I went in and told these to the brethren, and they benefited by the words of that poor man.

302. An old man used to say, "Let me think first, pray next, and then let us begin the work. Afterwards let us boast ourselves in God."

303. A certain brother asked an old man, saying, "Why do I feel disgusted when sitting in my cell, and sluggish in respect of works of spiritual excellence?" The old man answered, saying, "Because you do not keep in mind the rest which those who labor expect, and the torments which are laid up for the lazy. For if, in very truth, you were seeing these things, you would be watchful and strenuous in your labor."

304. An old man used to say, "The man who makes a boast of the Name of God, and who does not do the works which are suitable to His Name, is like a poor man who, when a feast comes, borrows some clothes, puts them on, and who, when the feast has passed, strips them off himself because they are not his own, and gives them to their owners."

305. Abba Ammon used to say concerning Abba Paphnutius the Simple, who was from Scete, "When I went down there I was a young man, and he would not allow me to dwell there, saying, 'In my days I will not permit the faces of young men, which resemble those of women, to dwell in Scete, because of the war of the Enemy against the holy men.'"

306. Abba Poemen (or Ammon) used to say, "If Nuzardan (Nebuzaradan), the chief of the warriors, had never come to the land of Judea, he would never have burnt down the temple of God which was in Jerusalem with fire. [Now the meaning] of these words is that if the pleasures of the lust of the belly had never entered in on the soul the mind would never have been vanquished in the war of the Adversary."

307. A certain man asked Abba Sisoes, saying, "Have not you even yet arrived at the measure of Abba Anthony, our father?" The old man answered and said, "If I had even one thought like to Abba Anthony, the whole of me would become like to fire but I know one man who, even with great labor, is able to bear his thoughts."

308. Abba Abraham asked Abba Agathon, saying, "How is it that the devils make war upon me?" Abba Agathon said to him, "Do the devils make war upon you? They do not make war against us so fiercely as we ourselves do with our own wishes, though they do make war against us in proportion as our wishes do. Our desires become devils, and they force us to fulfill them. Now if you wish to see against whom they have made war, [it is] against Moses and those who resemble him."

309. A brother asked an old man, saying, "In what condition is it necessary for a monk to be?" He said, "Even as I myself am, if one may [compare] one man with another."

310. An old man was also asked, "Why am I afraid when I go about in the desert?" The old man said to him, "Because you are still alive."

311. A brother asked an old man, saying, "Why does my spirit go round and round violently?" He said to him, "Because you have not yet seen the storehouse of life."

312. He was also asked, "What is necessary for a monk to do?" He said, "Let him perform all kinds of good works in very deed, and let him acquire remoteness from every evil thing."

313. He was also asked, "What is a monk's work?" He said, 'He must possess discretion."

314. An old man said, "To every thought that rises upon you say, 'Are you of us, or of our enemies?' The thought will always make confession to you."

315. Abba Agathon used to say, "The crown of the monk is humility."

316. Abba Isidore said, "When I was a youth and was living in a cell, I did not possess the capacity for the service [of prayer and praise], for by day and night there was service to me."

317. He also said, "For forty years, I neither leaned upon anything nor lay down."

318. He also said, "I was standing forty nights, and did not lie down."

319. He also said, "For twenty years I continued to fight against one thought that I might see all men of one mind."

320. An old man was asked, "Why is it that while I am sitting in my cell my heart wanders about?" The old man answered, "Because your external lusts to feel the motions which are in hearing, in breathing, and in taste, for from these, if it be possible for a man, there is pure labor, and he should make them to be healthy and satisfied within."

321. An old man was asked, "How is it possible for a man to live so that he may be seemly in God's sight? He said to him, "It is possible if a man has an unvarying mind."

322. An old man said, "Our labor is wood which burns away."

323. Abba Benjamin said to his disciples, "Do these things and you shall be able to live. Rejoice at all times, pray without ceasing, and give thanks for everything."

324. He said, "Abstinence in respect of the soul consists of making straight its ways, habits, courses of action, and in cutting off the passions of the soul."

325. He said, "Travel in the path of the kingdom, and count the miles. Your spirit shall not be sad in you."

326. An old man said, "You must be in the same state of fear as a man who is going to endure tortures."

327. An old man used to say, "A man shall not cause trouble, but let him live a life of silent contemplation, and hide himself, for these meditations are the begetters of purity."

328. An old man used to say, "You shall desire to become a eunuch, for this will help you."

329. He said, "The giving of thanks makes entreaty on behalf of the feeble before God."

330. An old man used to say, "I do not as yet carry all my body so that I may fulfill all my desire."

331. Abba Sisoes said, "Exile consists in a man living a silent and solitary life."

332. One of the fathers said, "I once asked Abba Sisoes and besought him to speak a word of life to me. The old man answered and said, 'He who takes care to guard himself against esteeming himself, and against comparing himself [with other men] in every work of understanding, is he who fulfills the Book."

333. And I asked him, "What is the power of exile?" He said to me, "Wherever you dwell hold your peace about whatever you see, whether it is good or evil, say nothing. If you hear anything from a man which does not befit the upright conduct of the ascetic life, say, 'This does not concern me. I have to do it myself, and myself only.' This is [the power of] exile."

334. One of the old men said, "The love of the work of the hands is the ruin of the soul but the establishment of it is rest and peace in God."

335. Abba Theodore said, "If I did not cut off my soul from the friends of this world they would not let me be a monk."

336. He also said, "If we seek God He will reveal Himself to us, and if we lay hold upon Him He will protect us."

337 On one occasion some old men were sitting and talking about the thoughts, and one of them said, "They would not appear to be a great matter if a man were to see his thoughts from a distance."

338. Another [old man] said, "I have never allowed an error to have dominion over me even for an hour."

339. Abba Poemen said, "As long as the food which is being boiled is on the fire the flies will not approach it. As soon as it is taken off they cluster round it. The meaning of this is that as long as our hearts are fervent in the spirit impure thoughts will not approach us, but that if we are negligent and make ourselves to be remote from the converse of the spirit they will then gain dominion over us."

340. An old man used to say, "It is necessary to make enquiries concerning spiritual works, for through them we advance in excellence. For it is great labor for us to go out of the body in such wise that we do not perform the works of the body."

341. An old man used to say, "Affliction and poverty are the instruments with which a monk cultivates his craft."

342. Certain of the old men used to say, "Whoever does not have the instruments of the craft of labor cannot remain long in his cell, whether they are the instruments of the craft of the labor of spiritual beings, wherewith he finds comfort from God in his inner man in the spirit, or the instruments of the craft of human labor. He who possesses not the one or the other class of instruments cannot remain very long in his cell."

343. The spirit of God rested upon Abba John because of the fear in which he held God, for it is the fear of God which teaches a man all good works.

344. Abba Poemen used to say that Abba Paphnutius was exceedingly great and mighty, and that he ran at all times to minister to shortcoming.

345. An old man was asked by a brother, "How should a monk dwell in his cell?" The old man said, "Let him dwell by himself, so that his thoughts may be with God."

346. A brother asked him, saying, "What shall I do, for when I am by myself I am greatly afflicted by the multitude of evil thoughts of all kinds which crowd upon me, and by the weight of the disgust which troubles me?" The old man answered, "Give your soul work, that is to say, have a care to pray and have love towards God, and straightaway the spirit of Satan will flee from you."

347. An old man used to say, "If you do something which is good, and you are praised for it, destroy it. Guard yourself against the thoughts which praise you, and hold your neighbor in contempt."

348. Abba Isidore's thoughts praised him, saying, "There is none like to you among the fathers." He said to them, "Am I like Abba Anthony or Abba Agathon?" The devils said to him, "After all the labors which you have performed you will go to torment." And he said to them, "You also will be below me. For a thief through one word inherited the kingdom. Judas also, who wrought mighty deeds with the Apostles, in one night lost all his labor, and he went down from heaven to Sheol. Therefore do not let him who conducts himself uprightly boast in himself, for all those who have been over confident about themselves have fallen among the devils of greed. Slow down [your desire], saying, 'You have had enough, so wait a little.' Eat moderately and slowly. For he who eats is like him who seeks to eat much."

349. An old man saw a brother who pretended not to be of them sitting among the brethren. The old man said to him, "How can you walk in a country which is not yours?"

350. They used to say that Abba Poemen never wished to magnify his word over that of any old man. In everything he praised the other and belittled his own.

351. There was a certain monk who led a life which was full of severe ascetic labors. The devil laid many plans and schemes to make him abate them, and to make him to desist there from. The monk would not give him a hearing in any way, but, on the contrary, the man worked more strenuously than ever, and resisted his wiles and crafts. When the devil had spent much time in this strife against him, another devil came to help him. Having enquired of his companion what manner of war and battle he should set in array against him, and how it was that the holy man was abating and making an end of all the things which he was making [against him]. The accursed devil who had come last said by the counsel of the first devil, "Do not lift up yourself below him, but raise up yourself above him, and in this way you shall be able to be stronger than him."

352. An old man asked Abba Poemen, saying, "What shall I do, father, with my son Isaac, who hearkens to me with pleasure?" Abba Poemen said to him, "If you wish to be of benefit to him, show him [an example] by deeds and not by words, lest through observing words only he is found useless. If you show him by deeds, the deeds themselves will abide with him, and he will profit."

353. Some fathers said to Abba Macarius the Egyptian, "Whether you eat or whether you fast, your body has already dried up." The old man said to them, "A piece of wood which has been burned and consumed by the fire burns wholly, and thus is the heart of a man, if he is purified by the fear of God, consumes the lusts from his flesh, and dries up his bones."

354. Abba Theodore used to say, "If God imputes to us carelessness in prayer, and the snare in [His] service where we have been captured, we shall not be able to stand."

355. They used to say of one of the old men that he had passed twenty years in the church, and had never lifted his eyes to see the roof.

356. There was a certain monk whose name was Paul. His rule of life and conduct was neither to approach the excessive labor of the work of the hands, nor any trafficking, except such as was sufficient to provide for his small amount of daily food. He performed one sort of work of excellence; praying continually without cease. He laid down the rule for himself that he should pray three hundred prayers each day. He placed sand in his bosom, and at every prayer which he prayed, he would lay one grain of sand in his hand. This man asked Saint Macarius, saying, "Father, I am greatly afflicted." The old man pressed him to tell him the cause of his affliction. He answered and said, "I have heard about a certain virgin who has led an ascetic life for thirty years, and Father Pior related concerning her that every week she went forth and recited five hundred prayers in the day." When I heard these things I despised myself greatly, for I am not able to recite more than three hundred prayers. Then the holy man Macarius answered and said to him, "I have led an ascetic life for sixty years, made fifty prayers a day, worked sufficiently to provide myself with food, received the brethren who came to me, said to them what it was seemly to say, paid my debts, and my mind did not condemn me as one who has treated [God] lightly. But you who make three hundred prayers in the day, are you condemned by your thoughts? Perchance you do not offer them with purity [of heart], or you are able to do more, and dost not do it!"

357. I used to know a certain holy man whose name was Aurelius. He labored so hard that he might have been thought to be a shadow because of his disposition to work during the Forty Days Fast he used to pass whole weeks [without eating], and in respect of the other days he would eat only once every two or three days.

358. An old man was asked [by a brother], "If I see the sin of my brother, should I despise him?" The old man said, "If we hide [the fault] of our brother God will also hide our [faults]. If we expose our brother's [faults], God will also expose ours."

359. An old man used to say, "There was a brother named Timothy, and he used to lead a life of silent contemplation in a religious house. A temptation came upon one of the brethren of that house. The head of the house asked Timothy, saying, 'What shall I do to this brother?' Timothy said to him, 'Expel him.' When he had expelled him, the temptation of that brother was sent upon Timothy. Timothy cried out to God, saying, 'I have sinned, O my Lord, have mercy upon me.' He passed the whole night in a grave of dead men, crying out, saying, 'I have sinned, O my Lord, forgive me.' The temptation was upon him until he was greatly exhausted. A voice came to him, saying, 'Timothy, do not imagine that these things have happened to you for any other reason but because you offended your neighbor in the time of his trial.'"

360. A brother asked an old man, saying, "How shall I be able to avoid despising my brother?" The old man said to him, "We and our neighbor are two faces. If we provide the mirror of prayer we shall see the beam in our own eye, and we shall also see in the mirror the face of our brother polished and pure."

361. A brother asked an old man, "What shall I do? For there is no feeling in my soul, and I have no fear of God." The old man replied, "Seek out a man who fears God, and then cling closely to him. From him you shall learn to fear God."

362. Abba Poemen said that Abba Athanasius used to say, "Unless a man possesses good works before God gives him a gift because of himself, it is well known that no one can be made perfect through the weariness which comes to him through himself. But if he reveals [it] to his neighbor, he will then receive the gift because of his neighbor, and be gratified."

363. A brother asked an old man, saying, "Show me a word whereby I may live." The old man said, "Work with your hands with all your power, and give alms."

364. They used to say that Abba Copres attained a measure [of perfection] that even when he was sick and wanted something, he would cut off his desire from what his soul asked him [to give it]. He would give thanks to God and endure his sickness with joy and without complaint.

365. A brother asked Abba Poemen, "What is the meaning of these words which the Prophet spoke, 'My heart shall rejoice in those that fear Your name?'" (Psalm 33:21) The old man answered saying, "The Holy Spirit spoke this word to man even to death, and [to] today also."

366. An old man said, "If a man were to make new heavens and new earth he would not be able to be free from care, because the wickedness of the devil is hidden behind them. But for a man to have no care either for his raiment or his food is possible."

367. A [brother] asked an old man, "What shall I do in respect of that which

I love, but which is not profitable to me?" The old man said to him, "Do not approach it, and do not touch it. It will of its own accord become an alien thing to you. For David the Prophet wrote to Joab the captain of the host, and said to him, 'Make your battle more strong against the city, and overthrow it.' (2 Sam. 11:25) In this case the city is enmity."

368. Anthony said, "The greatest might of a man is to bring upon his soul his transgression at all times before God, and he must expect temptation until the end."

369. An old man used to say, "This is the rule of conduct which God gave to Israel, that he should remove himself from that which is outside nature, that is to say, anger, and wrath, and envy, and hatred, and evil-speaking, and a man must not judge his neighbor, together with all the other commandments of the olden time."

370. Certain brethren came to Abba Sisoes in order that they might hear some profitable words. When they had spoken much with him, he said nothing to them other than, "Forgive me." Then they saw that he was plaiting palm leaves, and they said to Abraham his disciple, "What are you doing with these palm-leaf ropes and mats?" He said to them, "We send them out here and there." When the old man heard this he said, "Sisoes eats here and there." When they had heard [these things] they were greatly profited, and they departed in great joy because they had seen his humility.

371. Abba Copres said, "Whoever loves the gratifying of his own will more than the gratification of the will of God has no fear of God."

372. A brother asked Abba Amonis, saying, "How ought a man to act when he wishes to begin some [kind of] work, or when he wishes to go or to come, or to go from one place to another, so that action may be according to the will of God, and may be free from the error of devils?" The old man said to him, "He must first consider in his mind and see the motive for doing what he wishes to do. When it comes, and if it be from God or Satan, or from the man himself, let him do the work [which he contemplates]. Let him flee from going and coming, and from going from one place to another. If he does not [act] [thus], he will finally become a laughing-stock for the devils. Let him pray and beseech God that the work of His he may do. Let him begin the work, and afterwards he may boast in God."

373. He said, "Bear with every man in such a way that God may also bear with you."

374. The disciple of Abba Ammon told the following story. One night the old man came out and found me lying down in the courtyard of the cell. He stood up above me, and with lamentation and tears he said, "Where is the mind of this brother who can thus lie down without care?"

375. There was a certain priest in Thebes whose name was Dioscurus. He was the spiritual father of many monks. At the time when they were about to receive the Holy Sacraments, he used to say to the brethren, "Think and see, lest any man among you have been snared by the phantom of a woman during the night, and be so bold as to receive the Holy Sacraments. Now the emissions which occur as the result of a phantom are not caused by the desire of a man, but take place independently, for they happen naturally, and are due to the excess of matter [in the body]. They do not, therefore, lead [a man] into subjection to sin. The phantoms which arise from the desire are the sign of an evil wish. For it is necessary that the monk should be superior to the law of nature. He should not be found with the smallest impurity of body. He should waste the body and humble it. He should not permit any superfluity of matter to be found in his body. Work out plans, then, that you may cut off [the superfluity of] matter by means of a long period of fasting. If we do not do thus, it will incite the other lusts to come upon us. It is necessary that a monk be occupied with the lusts which rise up in him daily. If we do not thus, how are we different from those who live in the world? We have observed that men of this kind often make themselves remote from the desires of their lust, either for purposes of bodily health, or for other reasons which are not worth mentioning. How very much more, should it thus be especially a care to the monk for the sake of the health of his spirit, his soul, and of his body!"

376. They used to say that Abba Macarius the Alexandrian at one time dwelt in a cave in the desert. Beyond his cave was another cave where a panther dwelt. One day when he opened the door of his cave the panther came in and did homage to the blessed man. The panther drew near, took hold of the corner of his garment, dragged him along gently and went outside. The old man answered and said, "What can this animal want?" He went with the panther until it arrived to her cave. It left him outside, went in and brought out her young, which were blind. It dropped them at his feet. When he saw them, he prayed, and spat in their eyes, which were opened straightaway. The panther gave them suck, took them and went inside. On the day following the panther came bringing a sheepskin, approached the old man and placed it before him. The old man smiled to himself at the discernment and knowledge which the animal had shown. He took the skin and slept upon it, until it was quite worn out.

377. On another occasion, when the door of Abba Macarius the Alexandrian's cell was shut, he was sitting in his courtyard, that panther leaped down into the courtyard from the wall and came to him carrying one of its young in her mouth. When the old man saw that the little panther was blind, he spat in its eyes, and its eyes were opened. Its mother took it and departed. One day later the panther brought to the blessed man a sheepskin. The blessed woman Melania told me, saying, "I received this very skin from the hands of the old man as a gift."

378. A brother asked an old man, saying, "What shall I do if when I have given to my brother a little bread or money, the devils pollute it, as if [it were given to gain] the approbation of men?" The old man said to him, "Even though the adulation of men may come, we must give to our neighbor what is necessary." The old man adduced a proof of this statement, saying, "Two men dwelt in a certain city, and one sowed [a field] and produced a crop of somewhat dirty grain, but the other sowed [no field] at all, and produced no crop of any kind, neither clean nor dirty in the time of tribulation which of these two men would live [and not die] of hunger?" The brother said to him, "He who produced the crop of dirty grain." The old man said to him, "Let us then produce few [good actions], even though they be defiled, so that we may not die in the time of famine."

379. An old man used to say, "Dainty meats remove [a man] from heavenly honors. For satiety, luxurious living in this world, and the multitudes of lustful habits shut the door in our face and prevent us from entering into the happiness of God. Consider the history of the rich man and Lazarus. What was it that carried Lazarus into the bosom of Abraham? Was not it the immeasurable troubles among which he had been brought up? What brought the rich man to Gehenna? Was not it the pleasures and lusts which were burning within his body? Each one of us, according to his measure, by the nod of the fire of his person which is found with him, shall receive his deserts in the world which is to come and each one of us, unless he be watchful, shall be shaken up with the wood, the straw, and the stubble. Since it is necessary for us to extinguish carefully the lusts which bestir themselves in us, we have need [to drink] water, and not wine."

380. An old man used to say, "True obedience is like a chaste woman who is betrothed, and is not drawn aside after strange voices. The ear which turns away, even so little from the truth, is like an adulterous woman who turns away from her husband. The mind which is led by every doctrine of error like a harlot, who obeys everyone who calls her. Let us then rebuke the wandering mind which is corrupted by strange voices, and loves the voice of its seducer instead of the voice of the true bridegroom, for it has accepted to be called by the name of a stranger, and not by that of Christ."

381. An old man used to say, "If you have prayed for your companion you have also prayed for yourself. If you have prayed for yourself only you have impoverished your petition. If you have shown that your brother has offended you, you have also shown that you have offended yourself. Those prayers which have not taken their mind with them when they have ascended and gone up, stand outside the door. It is love which opens the door before them. The prayer which does not possess the wings of the spirit to [mount up] on high stands before the mouth of him that prays it, and thinking that it has flown away, he does not perceive that it remains [near him]. Offer with your offering salt, as it is written 'And every oblation of your meat offering shall you season with salt; neither shall you suffer the salt of the covenant of your God to be lacking from your meat offering: with all your offerings you shall offer salt.'" (Leviticus 2:13)

382. One of the holy men used to say thus, "I have passed the whole period of twenty years in striving so that a strange thought might not enter into my heart. I have seen Satan, until the ninth hour, with his bow stretched ready to shoot an arrow into my heart. When he could not find an opportunity, he was filled with disgust, and would depart each day, ashamed."

383. An old man said, "If you are a [true] penitent you have nothing whatever to do with these who are in the world."

384. There was a certain holy man in Egypt who dwelt in the desert. A little way beyond him was a Manichean elder. This Manichean was obliged to make a journey and to go to one of the same faith as himself. As he was going along the road, he arrived at eventide at the place where the holy man lived. The Manichean was distressed, for he had no place near at hand to enter. He was afraid to go to the holy man, for he thought that he would recognize him, and would not allow him to enter [his cell]. Being sore pressed, and not knowing where [else] to go, he knocked at the door of that holy man who opened the door. The Manichean went in, and the holy man received him with gladness, knowing who he was, urged him to pray, and he relieved all his wants. The Manichean slept, and was refreshed. It came to pass during the night that the Manichean came to himself, and said, "What is it that there is nothing this blessed man could do for me and he has not done? Truly this is a man of God." The Manichean rose up, fell down at the holy man's feet, saying, "From this day onwards I shall believe as you believe." He turned to the truth, became a friend of the holy man and lived with him always.

385. I have heard that Abba Isaac said concerning Abba Muthues his Abba, now they both arrived at the dignity of the episcopacy. First of all Abba Muthues built his monastery in the country of the Harbelaye (Herakleans). Being much troubled by the multitudes who came to him, he left that place, departed, and went to another spot in order that he might find quietness. There he built a monastery for himself there. By the work of Satan, he found there a certain brother with whom he was at enmity and afflicted him greatly. The old man saw [this], rose up and departed to his village, so that the man might not be vexed through him. There he built a monastery, and shut himself in. After a time, the fathers of that place wherefrom Abba Muthues had departed gathered together, and took that brother who was aggrieved, and went to him in order to entreat him to bring him to his monastery. When they had arrived at the place where Abba Sorion used to dwell, they left their cloaks there, and the aggrieved brother was with them. When the fathers had knocked, the old man brought forward a ladder, recognized them, and said to them, "Where are your cloaks?" They said, "They are here with us, with such and such a brother." When the old man heard the name of that brother, in sheer joy he took an axe and opened the door. He ran to the place where that brother was. The holy man fell at the feet of the saint, made entreaty to him, kissed him, and saluted him. He brought him and the fathers to his cell. He refreshed (hosted) all for three days. He made a meal, which he was not in the habit of doing, rose up and went with them with great joy. Afterwards he was called to the office of Bishop. He became a worker of signs and miracles. He also made his disciple Abba Isaac a Bishop. He continued to lead a life of spiritual excellence until the end of his life.

386. They used to say of Abba Serapion, the Bishop, that whenever a man came to him to receive the monastic garb, he said to him, "When you pray say, 'Lord, teach me to do Your will.'"

387. Abba Paphnutius was living in a remote desert. It happened that a certain brother came to him and found him sick. The brother took him, washed him, and brought him food to eat. When he saw [this] he answered saying, "In very truth it had passed from my mind that this gratification for the children of men existed." He brought him a cup of cream. When the old man saw him, he wept, and said, "I never expected that, even to the day of my death, I should drink wine."

388. One of the fathers told a story, saying: "Two brethren according to the body came to the desert to a certain monk. They conducted themselves in an excellent manner. They were praised by the whole brotherhood. It came to pass that one of them fell into a sickness which lasted not a few years. His brother ministered to him. Certain fathers came to visit him, and began to praise the brother who ministered the sick, saying, 'Your willingness and abstinence profit the whole brotherhood.' He answered them with great humility, saying, 'Forgive me, O my fathers, for I have not as yet begun to lead a life of rule, but it is my brother who does the works of excellence, and that you may indeed learn that such is the case, come after me and see.' Then he took them in to where his brother is lay, and he said to him, 'Father, where is the axe which I gave you yesterday?' He began to search for it. He said to him, 'See, O my brother, do an act of grace and search with me.' The sick brother took it upon himself to be asked for that which he had not taken. Having profited [by his example] the fathers departed from that place."

389. An old man used to say, "Flee from that love which subsists by means of the things which are corrupt, for by that a man passes away and is destroyed."

390. Abba Elijah used to say, "The love which a man possesses for his neighbor, and which is caused by some temporal matter is, in the process of time, turned into fierce enmity."

391. He also said, "Whatever has its being for God's sake, this endures and abides forever with those who are true."

392. On one occasion the priest of Pilision heard that certain of the brethren were idle and lazy. They were constantly in the city, swam in the baths, and neglected the works of excellence, which belong to the life of the monk. When they came to the congregation he took their garbs. Having done [this] he was sad at heart, repented, went to Abba Poemen and informed him about them. The old man said to him, "Have you nothing of the old man in you? And he said "Yes." And the old man said to him, "Therefore you yourself are like to them, and you are near to sin." The priest went on, expressed his sorrow to them, and he put on them the garbs of monks [once more]. They were twelve in all.

393. Once tribulation came upon the monks in a certain place where they were living, and wished to forsake it to go to Abba Ammon. Abba Ammon was traveling in a boat, and saw them going along by the side of the river. He ordered the boatmen to bring [the boat] close to land. Then he called these brethren and said, "I am Ammon to whom you wish to go." And he entreated them to go back to their place." He comforted them, and told them to endure patiently, for there was in the matter no loss to the soul, but only human vexation.

394. Once, an old man went up from Scete to the brethren in the mountain. When they saw that he was a man of great ascetic labors, and that he practised stern self denial, they entreated him to let them make a meal for him. They brought him a little wine to drink. The people of the country heard about him, and brought him a man who was afflicted with a devil that he might heal him. When the devil saw him, he began to revile him, saying, "Have you brought this winebibber to me?" The old man did not wish to cast him out because of the praise of men. Because the devil had reviled him, he said to him, "I believe in Christ, and I shall not have drunk [this] cup of wine until you have gone out." As he began to drink that devil cried out, and said, "You are consuming me." Before the old man could drink that cup [of wine] the devil went away by the grace of Christ.

395. They used to say that a certain recluse father had a brother, according to the body, who lived in another cell. That brother fell ill, sent to him a message to come and see him before he died. His brother said, "I am unable to go out for the sake of my brother in the flesh." His brother sent him another message, saying, "Come, if it is only in the night, that I may see you." The recluse said, "I cannot do so, for if I did, my heart would not be pure before God." So the brother died, and they did not see each other.

396. They once wanted to make Abba Isaac a priest in Scete. When he heard [this] he fled to Egypt, and went into a field, hiding himself among the crop. The fathers were pursuing him. When they came to that field they began to weary a little and they turned the ass which they had with them out to feed. He left the whole field, went and stood up in that place where Abba Isaac was hidden. In the morning they went out to look for the ass, and they found the ass and the old man [together]. They marveled. When they wished to make Abba Isaac take an oath [not to run away] he would not allow them [to do so]. He said to them, "I shall not flee again, for it is the will of God, and wherever I flee I shall come to this thing, for this is a consecration by God."

397. Abba Macarius asked Abba Arsenius, saying, "Is it good for a man not to have any pleasure at all in his cell? I know a brother who used to have a few garden herbs in his cell, and to prevent himself from having any gratification from these, he pulled them up by the roots." Abba Arsenius said to him, "This is good, but every man [must do] as he is able, and if he does not have the strength to persist in this perhaps he should plant others."

398. The old men who were in Egypt told Abba Elijah that Abba Agathon was a great man. The old man said to them, "Considering his youth he was a great man in his generation. He was very far removed from the old men. I saw in Scete an old man who was able to hold back the sun in his course in the heavens like Joshua, the son of Nun." And when they heard [this] they marveled and praised God.

399. A certain brother asked Abba Poemen about fornication. The Abba, answered and said, "[It comes upon a man] because our eyes will not allow us to see the help of God which surrounds a man, for a man is constrained to humility and to the fear of God at all times, even as he is constrained [to draw] the breath which goes out from his mouth."

400. An old man used to say, "If you wish to learn to know [your] neighbor praise him more than you rebuke him."

401. They used to say that whenever one of the fathers wished to sleep a little, he would sit down in his cell at some distance from the wall, so that whenever he nodded his head he became wide awake.

402. They used to say that whenever another old man lay down he used to hold up a book above him, and when he dropped off to sleep the book would fall down and wake him."

403. Abba Besarion said, "I stood up for forty nights and did not sleep." Abba Anthony said, "I do not fear God, on the contrary I love Him."

404. One of the old men while exhorting the brethren to work of spiritual excellence used to say, "Troubles are hard for those who are not accustomed to them. Troubles are like dogs, for as dogs bite those who are not familiar with them and wag their tails at those who are, so are labors, because they give pain to those who have no experience of them, and they are pleasing to those who are trained in bearing them. This exception must, however, be made: lusts are needed to produce troubles and adversities, but troubles are the cause of pleasure and delights."

405. On one occasion Abba Ammon came to cross the river, and found that they were making a boat ready to take [some] men over. He sat down in the boat. There was another boat which was going to take over some women, and they cried out to him, "Come here, father, and cross over with us." He answered them saying, "If I had not been going to cross over in the public boat I could not cross [with you]." He had with him a bundle of palm leaves. He sat down and plaited mats until that boat was ready. He crossed over the river [in it]. The brethren expressed their regrets, saying, "Why have you done thus?" The old man said to them, "Because I do not travel in great haste always, and because my thoughts are not always in turmoil. Now this is a proof that a man should travel on the path of God with a well ordered mind."

406. One of the old men came to one of the fathers [and asked him] to go and visit Abba Joseph. He said to him, "Tell your disciple to go with us." The father said, "Call him, and whatever you command him, he will do." The old man said to him, "What is his name?" The Abba of the disciple said, "I do not know." The old man said to him, "How long has he been with you? Do not you know his name?" The father said, "Behold, he has been with me for two years." The old man answered and said, "If he has been with you for two years, and you have not learnt his name, how can I learn it in one day?"

407. A brother asked Abba Poemen, saying, "Once, I was distressed. I begged one of the holy men to lend me a certain thing. He gave it to me as a free gift. If God prospers me, shall I give it to another man, or shall I return it to him who gave it to me in the time of my tribulation?" The old man said, "The gift was most certainly from God. It is necessary for you to return it to him, for it belongs to him." That brother said to him, "Supposing that I carry it to him, and he refuses to take it, and says to me, 'Go and give it as a free gift to anyone at your pleasure, what am I to do?'" The old man said, "The thing still belongs to him. For if a man brings you something of his own accord and you have no knowledge about it, in this manner the thing is his. If you have borrowed something, either from a monk or from a man in the world, and he refuses to take it back, it belongs to you and you may do what you please with it."

408. Abba Joseph related that Abba Isaac said, "I was once sitting with Abba Poemen, and I saw that he was in a state of great stupefaction. Because I possessed some influence over him, I offered entreaty to him, saying, "Father, where is your mind?" After I had pressed him greatly, he answered and said, "My mind was in the place of the Crucifixion, where the holy woman Mary, the God-bearer, was standing and weeping by the Cross of our Redeemer. I was wishing that I might feel thus endlessly."

409. They used to say that Abba Sisoes the Theban wanted to dwell among the reeds of Arsania, where there was, at some distance from him, an old man who was sick. When he heard [of it] he was distressed, for he fasted two days at a time, and that day was the day on which he ought not to eat. He said in his mind, "What shall I do? For perhaps the brethren will compel me to eat, and if I wait [to go to the old man] until tomorrow perhaps he will be dead. I can only do this. I will go, but will not break the law and eat." So he went, and did not eat. Thus he did not break the rule of life which [he observed] for God's sake.

410. They used to say that Abba Netira, a disciple of Abba Sylvanus who dwelt in his cell in Mount Sinai, trained his body, and exercised it in ascetic labors with moderation. When he was called by force to the episcopacy, he afflicted himself with stern and laborious works. His disciple said to him, "Abba, when we lived in the desert you did not lead such a life of abstinence and self-denial as you now do." The old man said to him, "There I had the desert, silence, and poverty. I only had to direct my body in moderation so that it might not become ill but here I have the world. I must vex my body so that it may not be caught by whatever lust and that I may not lose my labors."

411. They used to relate that Abba Poemen and the brethren were once working with their hands, but he could not sell their work. They were distressed because they had no one to buy their work. One of the brethren, who was a friend of theirs, went to a certain believing merchant and informed him of the matter. Abba Poemen [always] refused to accept anything from any man, so that he might not be entreated [for alms] by the multitude. When the merchant heard [about their need], because he wished to do something for the old man, he made the excuse that he was in need of [the kind] of work [which they did]. He bought a camel and carried away the work as if he had been in need of

Questions & Answers on the Ascetic Rule

the same. The brother who had told the merchant came to Abba Poemen. Hearing that the merchant had come and carried away what they had to sell, he said to Abba Poemen, "Truly, O father, the merchant has taken [the work] away, although he did not want it." Then Abba Poemen said to Abba Job, his brother, "Arise, stop the camel, and bring him back, for if you do not do so Poemen will not dwell here with you. For I do not wish to wrong any man by making him unnecessarily to suffer loss on my account, and to take my profit." The brother departed and brought the camel back with great difficulty. Then Abba Poemen was persuaded to stay with them, and when he saw [the camel] he rejoiced as one who had found a great treasure.

412. A certain stranger came to Scete, and brought much gold. He entreated the priest that it might be given to the brethren. The priest said to him, "It is useless to them." Having entreated him many times, and the priest not consenting [to this], the man laid the gold down openly at the door of the church. The priest said, "My brethren, if any man has a need let him take [some]." They refused to touch it. Some of them would not even look at it. The priest said to him, "God has accepted your gift, go, and give it to the poor." Having been greatly helped he departed.

413. A steward of Scete went up to Constantinople. There, the Emperor asked him how the fathers in Egypt were. The steward did homage, and answered the Emperor saying, "Behold, they eat each other, and live." When the Emperor heard this, he marveled, and asked him, "What is the meaning of 'They eat each other?'" The steward said, "The meaning of 'They eat each other' is this, 'When it happens that one of them is going to die, he commands that whatever he has shall be given to various men according to their needs. Similarly, when a man works he brings [the results of] his labor, refreshes all the brethren with these, and in this way they live.'" The Emperor said to him, "Truly blessed are you, for you are saved and freed from the cares of the world. You are freed also from the judgment of Gehenna. We, on the other hand, are troubled by the cares of the world, and Gehenna is prepared for us because of our sins."

414. They used to say of Abba Betimius that, when [the brethren] were coming down from the harvest to Scete, they brought down as a gift a jar of oil for the brethren who were there. The jar contained the measure of a kesta, and was sealed with plaster. At the return of the period the year following when they were going to the harvest, they brought everything which was of benefit to the church. Abba Betimius had made a small hole with a needle in the vessel of oil, and had poured out a little for himself. He thought that he had done some great thing in not having consumed the whole of the oil which was in the vessel. When the brethren brought their vessels with the intact plaster coverings and the vessels themselves unopened, while his vessel had been perforated, he stood there full of shame, just like a man who thinks that he has been found [committing] fornication.

415. There was a great holy man who used to dwell in the inner desert. He was of a state of glorious ascetic excellence, gifts of casting out devils, and the healing of the sick had been given to him by God. He used to work great miracles in the Name of Christ, and the beasts made themselves subject to him at his command. Once it happened when he was journeying in the desert he saw a herd of wild asses feeding, and he said to them, "In the Name of our Lord Jesus Christ, let one of you come here." One of them came, and crouched before him very gently. The blessed man mounted him, sat upon him, and the animal carried him where he wished to go.

416. One day the blessed Anthony was sitting in the desert with the brethren. Suddenly there fell upon him a state of stupor, and he became exceedingly sad and sorry. He bent his knees and prayed. When, after a long time, he stood up, he wept and groaned. The old man began to pluck out his hair, and to throw it away. When the brethren saw him weeping they entreated him to tell them what he had seen. He answered, saying, "A great pillar has fallen this day from the church." He spoke concerning that holy man who had fallen from his rule of life. He sent to him straightaway two brethren to see what had happened and to comfort him. When the holy man saw them, he wailed, cried, took dust and cast it upon his head. He fell down before them, saying, "Go and say to Abba Anthony, 'Pray for me that ten days may be given me to live, and I believe that I shall repent.' But he died before five days had passed, and did not remain long enough to offer up repentance for his sin."

417. There was a certain man of noble rank who sold everything which he had. He divided [the money] among the poor and the strangers, shaved his head, went and dwelt in a monastery. There he left to him a remnant of his possessions sufficient for his wants. After a little time, when he had obtained freedom of speech, he began to be proud and to exalt himself above the other brethren, saying, "They lack education, and the knowledge of learning." The blessed Saint Basil, the Bishop, sent him a message in a letter, saying, "You have lost the great name which you had in the world, for you were called a nobleman, and you have not become a monk."

418. Abba Gregory made an answer regarding the thoughts. He said to the brethren, "My brethren, in as much as we have passed the measure of children, let us cease from the mind of children, that is to say, let us free ourselves from the careless habits of filthy lusts for it would be a shameful thing for us if, since childhood has passed from us, and old age has come upon us, the things of shame had not also passed away from us."

419. They used to say that once when Abba Macarius was walking in the desert, he found a beautiful spot which was like the Paradise of God. There were fountains of water in it, numerous palm trees, and trees of various kinds which bore fruit. When he had come and told the brethren about it, they begged and entreated him to go and settle them there. The old men, and the aged members of the congregation, who led lives of stern labor, entreated them not to leave their place. They said, "If pleasure and delight can be found in that spot, and if a man may live there without vexation and labor, what pleasure and delight do you expect to receive from God? No, it is right for us to endure the hardness of this place where we dwell, and to suffer tribulations so that we may enjoy pleasure in the world to come." When they had said these things the brethren were restrained and did not depart.

420. There was a certain holy man who used to see visions, and he told the following story, saying, "Once when I was standing up in prayer, I heard a devil complaining in the presence of his companion, saying, 'I am [suffering] great labor and trouble.' When the other devil asked him so that he might learn from him the cause of his trouble, he said to him, 'This is the work which has been handed over to me. When I have carried these monks, who are in Jerusalem and its neighborhood to Mount Sinai, I have to bring those who are in Mount Sinai to Jerusalem, and I have no rest whatever.'"

421. There was a monk who lived in a cell, far away in the desert. This monk had a brother who lived in the world, and whose end was near, for he had to die. He sent a message to the monk, saying, "For God's sake do an act of grace, and come that I may see you before I die." When the monk heard [this], he shut the door of his cell, and set out to go to him. As he was traveling through the desert, he saw an old man sitting on the wayside mending nets. This old man was the calumniator, who was making ready his snares to catch in them those who were journeying on the road of spiritual excellence. He was exceedingly anxious to overthrow that brother, and to trip him up by his snares, for he not only had never allowed his foot to become entangled in the meshes of his nets, but also he had slit in pieces and destroyed his pitfalls through the remembrance of God. The monk did not know that the man who was sitting by the roadside mending his nets was Satan. He said to him, "Why are you sitting here in this parched desert? What are you doing here?" The calumniator said to him, "I am mending my nets with which I wish to catch the gazelle which are in the desert." The monk said to him, "Make me a net also, for I want to catch with it the gazelle which go to my garden and lay it waste." That devil said to him, "Go on with your journey, and I will make a net for you which shall be better than that you now see." When the monk had gone to his brother, saw him, and remained with him for two days. On the third day his brother died, he wrapped him up in his grave clothes, and buried him with the honor which is due to believing men. As he was lying there in his brother's house, his brother's wife rose up by night, came and laid down by his side through the agency of the Calumniator, and began to say to him, "God has sent you here to provide for your brother's children, to bring them up. Take me as a wife, and take care of your brother's house and of his children. Stay here in peace in your own house." When the monk heard what she said to him, he was moved to wrath against her, and said, "Fie upon you, O woman! Get behind me, Satan!" He rose up straightaway, took his staff, and set out to go through the desert to his cell. As he was journeying along the way, he saw that old man sitting in his place and mending his nets. The monk said to him, "Are you still sitting here, O old man? Have you prepared for me that net concerning which I spoke to you?" Satan became furious, and looked at him in fierce anger and said, "Get away from my presence. Yes, you have indeed broken the net which I made for you. Did not you know that you were breaking and slitting in pieces during the past night that other net which was better than the first one? I am not able to make a net which [will catch] you." As he was speaking he changed himself into a great serpent. When the monk saw this he understood that it was Satan who had appeared to him, he fled from the place in fear, and went to his cell. He gave thanks to God Who had delivered him from the snare of Satan, who had wished to snare him and to drag him down into his net through his brother's wife.

422. A certain brother had recently received the garb of a monk. He went shut himself up in a cell, and said, "I am a desert monk." When the fathers heard [this], they came, took him out of his place, made him to go about to the cells of the brethren, and to make apologies to them, saying, "I am not a desert monk, and I have only just begun to be a disciple."

423. Once Abba Abraham went to Abba Area. While they were sitting talking, a certain brother also came to the Abba, and said the following, "There was a certain rich man in Jerusalem who had become rich by means of fraud, avarice, oppression, and wicked acts of various kinds. When this man came to himself, and understood that there was judgment to come, he drew near to a certain teacher, and said to him, 'I beseech you [to hearken to me]. My mind is led captive by worldly care, and anxieties which are of the earth make me whole then, so that I may not perish.' The teacher gave him to read the Book of the Wisdom of Solomon. As he was reading [it], he found a verse which said, 'He who has compassion upon the poor, lends to God.' Then he shut the Book, and gave it to the teacher, saying, 'Who is there that is more sure and more to be trusted than God, Who if I show compassion upon the poor, will give me back both principal and interest?' Then he went immediately, sold everything he possessed and divided it among the poor. He left nothing to himself except four dinars, which were to be [spent] in burying him. He fell into need, became exceedingly poor, and he went about begging. No man either showed compassion upon him or gave him food. Finally he meditated within himself, and said, 'I will go to the Lord my God, and will enter into judgment with Him because He led me astray and made me scatter all my possessions.' As he was returning to Jerusalem, he saw two men fighting with each other, and each was striving to take from his companion a certain stone of great excellence, which had fallen from the ephod which was on Aaron, the high priest. The men did not know what the stone was. Then the man said to them, 'Why are you fighting and contending with each other?' They answered saying, 'We have found a stone, and we do not know what is its value.' He said to them, 'Give it to me, and take four dinars.' They gave him the stone gladly. The man went into Jerusalem and showed the stone to a goldsmith, who, as soon as he saw the stone, said to him, 'Where did you find this? For behold, because [of the loss] all Jerusalem has been in an uproar for the last three days. But go, and give it to the high priest, and he will make you a rich man.' When he had gone into the temple, the angel of the Lord appeared to the high priest, and said to him, 'Behold, a man has come to you, and has with him the stone which was lost give him, then, gold and silver, and precious stones according to his desire, and rebuke him and say to him, "Have no doubt whatever in your mind, and do not restrain yourself from lending to God as if you were not a believer and a true man, for, behold, I have given to you twofold in this world [for what you did lend Me], and in the world to come life everlasting."'"

424. The fathers also said, "There was a rich philosopher in a certain city and he never gave anything to any man. The Bishop of the city said to him, 'Do you know, O my beloved brother, that when we came into this world we brought nothing in with us, and that we shall not be able to carry anything

out with us? But from that which Christ has given to you, you should lend in this world, and in the next He will reward you several times over.' The philosopher said to the Bishop, 'Will you assure me that if I lend [money] to him, he will reward me?' The Bishop answered and said, 'Yes, I will assure you.' The Bishop having become surety to him, straightaway the rich man began to scatter his possessions. Whenever he gave alms to any man he used to write thus, 'Behold, I have lent to Christ such and such things, Bishop So-and-so being security for the same.' And he did thus until he had scattered all the riches which he possessed. When the day arrived for him to go forth from the world, he commanded his household, saying, 'I make you to take an oath by Christ, in Whom I have trusted, that this paper shall be laid with me in the grave and they took the oath even as he made them to do.' After many days the Bishop came to the city, went to the kinsfolk of the philosopher, comforted them and said, 'Did not he give you any commands? Did not he make a will?' They said to him, 'When he was dying he made us swear that the paper of indebtedness should be laid with him [in the grave], and we did even as he said.' The Bishop said to them, 'Come you and show me his grave.' When he had gone and entered into the grave, he saw the paper laid on the breast of the philosopher. He took it, opened it, and found that there was written in it thus, 'I, the philosopher so-and-so, have gone to Christ, and everything which I lent to Him He has returned to me many times over and henceforward I have no claim Whatever upon Him, except for tranquility and peace.' Everyone who saw and heard [this] praised God, to Whom all things are easy.

425. There was a certain rich man in Alexandria whose name was Dymyanos. He fell sick of a grievous disease. Being afraid that he was going to die he divided thirty pounds weight of gold among the poor. It happened that he recovered, so he repented of what he had done. He had a rich friend, who was a chaste and excellent man. He revealed to him everything about which he repented, and the friend answered and said, "Do not be sad, O my brother, for it is important that you should rejoice, because you have made an offering to God of your gold." The rich man did not agree with him. He said to him, "I will give you thirty pounds weight of gold, and you must not be vexed, but come with me to the temple of Mar Mina the martyr, and said thus, 'It is not I who have given these alms, but this man, and take that which is yours and go.'" Having done this, he took thirty pounds weight of gold, and went out the door of the church. The angel of the Lord hit him. He fell down straightaway, and died. The priests who were in the temple of Mar Mina gathered themselves together, and they said to the friend, "Take your gold, and go." He said to them, "God forbids that I should take anything from Christ, for I have offered

Questions & Answers on the Ascetic Rule   265

it to Him, and it is His, but if it seem [fit] to you let it be divided among the poor." It was divided according to his command. Everyone who heard feared and glorified God. My brethren, let us admire the excellence of that friend, and let us not be sad when we offer alms and oblations to God, for we [only] offer to Him what is His. He Himself has written that He is the debtor and the borrower. He has promised a reward even for a cup of cold water, saying, "Whatever you do to one of these little ones, you do it to Me." (Matt. 10:42, 45:40) May He make us worthy to do His will. Amen. Follow the counsels which belong in order to the old man who spoke against the thoughts of fornication, saying, "Be like to a man who passes through a street of taverns..." (See Book I, 593).

426. O man, for your sake Christ was born, and the Son of God came that He might make you to live. He became a babe, He became a child, and He became a man, being [at the same time] God in His Nature, and the Son of God.

427. He Who was the Lawgiver became a reader. He took the Book in the synagogue, and read, saying, "The Spirit of the Lord is upon me, because he has anointed me to preach the gospel to the poor; he has sent me to heal the brokenhearted, to preach deliverance to the captives, and recovering of sight to the blind, to set at liberty them that are bruised.'" (Luke 4:18)

428. Like a subdeacon He made a whip of cord, and drove out from the temple all those who sold oxen, rams, doves, etc.

429. Like a servant He girded a napkin about His loins, and washed the feet of His disciples He commanded them to wash the feet of their brethren.

430. Like a priest He sat among the priests and taught the people.

431. Like a Bishop He took bread, and blessed [it], and broke, and gave to His disciples. He was beaten for your sake, He was crucified for your sake, and He died for your sake, yet for His sake you will not even bear disgrace! He rose as God, and He ascended as God. He wrought all things for us, fittingly and in order, that He might redeem us. Let us, then, be watchful, zealous, and constant in prayer. Let us do all things which are pleasing to Him, and which gratify those who love Him, so that we may be redeemed and live. Was not Joseph sold into Egypt, and was not he in a strange land? And the three Holy Children in Babylon, perhaps they acquired knowledge with man and stood in front of them [of themselves]? No, it was because they feared God that He helped them, and made them glorious.

432. An old man, who delivered himself to God, used to say, "The monk has no will of his own. He who abides in ministering to the will of God never wearies. If you perform your own, you will become weary and exhausted, because God does not support you."

433. The old man said, "When a soldier enters the battle he takes care for himself only. So also is it with the huntsmen. Let us then be like to these, for riches, kinsfolk, and wisdom are dung without a correct rule of life and conduct."

434. The old man said, "God dwells in the man who works with God, for He said, 'I will dwell in them, and I will walk in them, and they shall be to Me a people, and I will be to them a God.'"

435. The old man said, "God says to you thus, 'If you love Me, O monk do that I wish you to do, and do not do what I do not desire.' The life of a monk consists of good works, obedience, training, not to blame his neighbor, not to calumniate any man, and not to complain, for it is written, 'The mercy of the Lord hates evil things.'"

436. The same old man used to say, "The life and conduct of a monk are these, he must not act iniquitously, must not look upon evil things with his eyes, must not hearken with his ears to things which are alien to the fear of God, must not utter calumnies with his mouth, and he must not seize things with his hands. A monk must give especially to those who are in need, he must neither be exalted in his mind nor meditate with wicked thoughts, and he must not fill his belly. All these things he must perform with intelligence, for by them a monk is known."

437. A certain brother vexed an old man several times by saying to him, "What shall I do in respect of the wicked and filthy thoughts of all sorts and kinds which go through me?" The old man answered and said to him, "You are like to a stagnant pool which is at one time filled with water, and which when water has been drawn up from it, runs dry. Why can't you rather be like the spring which never fails? Patient persistence is victory. Victory is constancy. Constancy is life. Life is kingdom, and kingdom is God."

438. Abba Epiphanius used to say, "Whatever food you wish to eat with pleasure, do not desire to give to your body, especially when you are not sick. The food for which you lust, you shall not eat. When, you are eating the things which are sent to you by God, give thanks to Him at all times. Be grateful to Him. We have received pleasures and delights because of the name of monastic life. But we do not perform the works of monks. It shall be that you are not a monk. What then? Will not you play the man that, perhaps, you may be clothed in the apparel which is alien to you? Tell me, O brother, how can a man possess the seal of service unless he possesses humility? For the humble man who sees another sinning weeps bitterly, saying, "This man may perhaps sin today, but how many times shall I sin tomorrow? But, if any man sins before you, no matter who he may be, do not condemn him. Consider yourself to be a greater sinner than he is, even though he is a child of this world, and he makes people to sin against God."

439. Abba Epiphanius used to say, "Know yourself and you shall never fall. Give work to your soul, namely, constant prayer, the love which is in God, before another can give it evil thoughts and pray that the spirit of error may be remote from you."

440. Abba Epiphanius used to say, "Whatever you do successfully, and make a boast of, that destroy. It is not right for a monk to boast about his good deeds. If he boasts he will fall."

441. When you pray say with a hidden voice to God, "Lord, how am I to acquire You? You, even You know that I am a beast, and that I know nothing. You have brought me to the highest point of this life. O redeem me for Your mercy's sake. I am Your servant and the son of Your handmaiden. O Lord, by Your wish make me to live."

442. The old man is falsehood, and the new man is truth. Truth is the root of good works, and falsehood is death. If the liar, the thief, and the calumniator knew that they were to be exposed and made known to all at a subsequent period they would have never committed their offences. It is as such with those who commit adultery.

443. The sons of Eli, Hophni and Phinehas, were priests of the Lord, but they did not fear God. They and their house perished.

444. He who lays hold upon, and binds, and who takes to himself the remembrance of evil things, is like the men who bury fire within chopped straw.

445. If you would talk to a man concerning life, and if you would say a word to him with suffering, with repentance, and with weeping, speak to him who hears. If you do not [do this], do not speak at all, lest you die. Depart without profit from the words with which you wished to vivify others. God says to the sinner, "What are the Books of My commandments to you, for you have taken My covenant in your mouth?"

446. Abba Epiphanius said, "When the thought comes to fill your bosom, or your heart, with vainglory or pride, say to it, 'Old man, behold your fornication.'"

447. Abba Epiphanius said, "If we do evil things God will be unmindful of His longsuffering. If we do good things, these things will not help us greatly. For in order to increase the profit of freedom, and that the merchandise of the will may not be spoiled, a man must rejoice in contending."

448. The brethren entreated Abba Epiphanius, saying, "Speak to us, father, something whereby we may live, even though you speak and we do not keep the seed of your word because our ground is a salted thing." The old man answered, saying, "He who does not receive all brethren, or who makes distinctions between them, he who does these, I say, cannot be perfect."

449. If a man reviles you, bless him. If he accepts the blessing it shall be good for both of you. If he does not, he shall receive the reward of his reviling, and you that of the blessing.

450. It is right for a monk to live even as Abba Arsenius had lived. Take care each day to stand before God without sin. Draw near to Him with tears as did the sinful woman. Pray to the Lord God as if He were standing before you, for He is near and looks at you carefully.

451. He who wishes to dwell in the desert must be a teacher by his own knowledge. He must not be in need of being taught, lest, perhaps, he is harmed by devils, lest he scrutinizes his understanding too closely, and lest, in some form or other, he becomes a laughing stock to the beings who are above, and to those who are below.

452. The correct rule of conduct for him who loves God is to be without blame.

453. A certain old man said to the brethren concerning fighting evil thoughts, "Now I beseech you, O my brethren, if we cease from the ascetic life and its labors. And if we also desist from the anxieties of evil thoughts, what are we for? A sound which comes from the fine dust, or a sound which comes from the dust of the ground. Joseph of Rama, having asked to [be allowed to] take away the body of Jesus, removed it, swathed it with swathing of fine linen, and laid it in a new grave. Now the pure heart is the new grave of the new man."

454. The devils said to one of the old men, wishing to lead him astray, "Do you wish to see Christ?" He said to them, "My curse upon you, and to what you say. For I believe in Christ Who said, 'Then if any man shall say unto you, Lo, here [is] Christ, or there; believe [it] not.'" (Matt. 24:23) The devils immediately disappeared.

455. "What is [the meaning of] the word which the Apostle spoke, 'Unto the pure all things [are] pure: but unto them that are defiled and unbelieving [is] nothing pure; but even their mind and conscience is defiled.'" (Titus 1:15) The old man said to him, "If a man comes to this word, and arrives at this measure, he will see that he himself has more shortcomings than any other creature, and that he is inferior to every being." The brother said to him, "How is it possible for me to consider myself more imperfect and inferior to a murderer? Is it possible for me to consider the murderer and the fornicator, whose actions are abominable, better than myself?" The old man answered saying, "If a man attains this word, and he sees his neighbor committing a murder, or doing something else which is not good, he will think within himself, saying, 'This is [only] one sin, and this man has only committed this one sin, but I am at all times a murderer through hatred and a wicked will.'"

456. A brother asked Abba Job, the brother of Abba Poemen, concerning a word which the Apostle spoke, saying, "Let each esteem the other better than themselves." (Phil. 2:3) The old man answered and said, "If a man has arrived at this measure, and he sees the offence of his brother, he will conceal it as if it had never happened."

457. An old man used to say, "I never take a step without first learning where I am about to put my foot. I stand up, and look about me carefully. I am not careless, and I do not let [my foot go] until God guides me, and leads me on the path to the place which pleases Him."

458. An old man used to say, "God gives a man the opportunity to repent as long as he wishes to do so, and in proportion as he wishes, for it is written, 'Speak first your sins, and you shall be justified.'"

459. An old man used to say, "Silence is filled with all life, but in the speech which is abundant, death is hidden."

460. The old man also said, "Lying and sin are wanting to lie in ambush in the words which are long and broad."

461. An old man used to say, "Humility never becomes angry, and never provokes a man to wrath."

462. Abba Joseph said to Abba Lot, "You are unable to become a monk, but you may become wholly like a flame which burns and blazes fiercely."

463. An old man was asked, "What is humility?" He answered saying, "If your brother offend you, and you forgive him before he can repent and entreat you, [that is humility]."

464. An old man said, "Keep your conscience with your brother, and you shall find rest."

465. Abba Paphnutius used to say, "He who esteems himself as nothing, wherever he goes, or dwells, he shall find rest."

466. The same old man said, "During all the days of the life of the old men I used to go and visit them twice each month. My cell was distant from them about twelve miles. In respect of every thought about which I asked them, they never said to me anything except, 'Wherever you go consider yourself as nothing, and you shall find rest.'"

467. One of the old men used to say, "Love does not know how to keep a storehouse [full] of possessions."

468. The same old man also said, "I do not know the actual thing whereby, on two occasions, the enemies led me into error, and into the committing of sin, and into the transgression [of the Law]."

469. Certain old men asked John the Less, saying, "When you were in Crete with the fathers, how did you see them conducting themselves?" He said to them, "By day and night they were performing with all their might the work of God. [They were reciting] the service, they prayed, read, and were anxious with divine solicitude. Instead of being idle they worked with their hands."

470. Once Abba Ammon came to the brethren, and they, while expressing regret [for troubling him, asked him] to say some words of excellence to them. The old man answered and said to them, "It is right that we all should travel the path of God with well-ordered [minds]."

471. Abba Anthony used to say, "When we rise up in the morning each day let us think that we shall not abide until the evening. When we come to lie down also let us think that we shall not abide until the morning for we do not know the days of our life, but they are known to God. If we do this each day we shall not sin, we shall do nothing wicked before God, we shall not lust eagerly for anything of this world, and we shall not be angry with anyone, but in everything we shall be regarding our souls, even as men who await death."

472. He also said, "As fish die when they are drawn out of the water, even so do monks, who have forsaken the world, become sluggish. When they remain with the children of this world or dwell with them it is then meet for us to hasten to the mountain even as fish haste to the water."

473. They used to say that Abba Anthony was wholly [illumined] by the appearance of the light of the spirit. He could see what was happening from a distance. On one occasion he saw the soul of the blessed Ammon being taken up into heaven by the hands of angels, although he was distant from him ten stages.

474. One of the brethren asked him once about the thoughts. The old man answered and said, "Do not carry them into effect, but let them settle down and down until they breed worms and perish."

475. Abba Poemen used to say, "If a man passes a hundred years in the cell he will not understand his departure from this world and become a monk, unless he attributes sin to himself at all times, and makes himself to be remote, both in his mind and in his actions, from those things which he knows will separate him from God, and he must make supplication to God at all times through suffering and tears."

476. A brother asked Abba Poemen, saying, "What is the repentance of sins?" He said to him, "The repentance of sins is where a man does not commit the same sin again from the moment he repented of it. On account of this the righteousness were called spotless, because they had forsaken sins and cleansed themselves from them."

477. And another brother also asked him, saying, "Give me a word whereby I may live." The old man said to him, "The first thing of all which the fathers have given us [to do] is to mourn."

478. Abba Poemen used to say, "The passions are four heads." A brother said to him, "What are they?" The old man said to him, "Worldly grief that comes because of many things. The love of money. Vainglory. Fornication. It is necessary that we watch against these before all other passions."

479. He said also, "If a monk hates two things, the gratifications of the body, and vainglory he is able to free himself from the world."

480. The same old man also said, "Wrath is a natural thing in the man. It is his nature, but it must be used to cut off evil passions. Hunger is natural in the man, but it must be employed [in satisfying] the need of the body, and not [to gratify] the feeling of eager lust [to eat], as the blessed David said, 'Lord, my heart is not haughty, nor mine eyes lofty: neither do I exercise myself in great matters, or in things too high for me.' (Ps. 131:1) Sleep, too, is natural in the man, but [it must not be indulged] to satiety."

481. A brother asked Abba Poemen, saying, "Tell me, why it is that when I offer repentance to a brother who is angry with me I do not see him pleased with me?" The old man said to him, "Tell me truly: when you offer repentance to him, do you believe you are repenting because you have sinned against him, or because of the commandment?" The brother said to him, "It is so, because of the commandment." The old man said to him, "Because of this God does not permit him to be pleased with you. You are not offering repentance to him in fulfillment of your own desire. In other words, you are not repenting because you had sinned against him, but because he had sinned against you."

482. They used to say that when the disciples of Abba Agathon were building a cell he remained with them for a period of four months. When they finished it, on the first Sabbath on which they dwelt in it, the old man saw in it something which he did not like. He said to his disciples, "Arise, let us go away from here." When they heard [this], they were greatly troubled, and they said to him, "If you had this thought to depart, why have we done all this work and built the cell? Moreover, men will be offended, and will say, 'They have left this place because they can abide nowhere.'" When the old man saw that their souls were grieved, he said to them, "If some men are offended by us, there are others who will be edified by us, and they will say, 'These blessed men departed for God's sake, and they considered nothing [else].' However, he who wishes to come with me, may come. I shall certainly depart." They threw themselves on the ground, and entreated him to let them go with him.

483. Abba Agathon also used to say, "The monk's cloak is a sign of the absence of wickedness." He also said, "God asks those who begin the service of the works of the fear of God nothing except that they shall order their bodies by obedience to the commandments against the passions of the lusts."

484. Abba Agathon also said, "He who removes accusations, disgrace, and belittlement far away from his eyes, is able to live."

485. A brother said to Abba Agathon, "Father, I had the order to dwell in a certain place, and I have war there. I want to depart so I would fulfill the command, but I am afraid of the war." The old man said to him, "If it were Agathon, he would keep the command, and overcome the war."

486. The same old man also said, "If the inner man is watchful, he will be able to guard the outer man. But if he is not, let us guard the tongue by every means in our power."

487. The old man Benjamin was asked by a brother, "What does the life of a monk consist of?" Benjamin replied, "A mouth of truth, a holy body, and a pure heart."

488. They used to say concerning a certain old man that, on account of the great humility which he possessed, God gave him the gift of becoming a seer of visions. He could see beforehand when anyone was coming to him, and it was revealed to him concerning it. Now the old man was sorry and did not wish for this thing. He made supplication to God that it might be taken away from him. He went to an old Abba, entreated him, saying, "My brother, labor for me, so that this gift may be removed from me." Each of them sat down in his cell and made entreaty to God concerning this matter. A voice was heard by that old man, saying, "Behold, I remove the gift from you, but whenever you wish, it is yours." He went straightaway to the old Abba and showed him what had been said to him. When he heard [it] he gave thanks to God.

489. The fathers once asked Abba Sylvanus, saying, "What work of ascetic excellence have you performed that you did receive the wisdom which you do possess, and the gift with which your face is endowed?" The old man answered and said to them with great humility, "[I received these things] because I never left in my heart a thought which could provoke God to wrath." They used to say that the face of Abba Sylvanus shone so brightly, even as did the face of Moses, with the glorious splendor which he had received from God, and that no man was able to look at it with wide open eyes.

490. Zeno, the disciple of Abba Sylvanus, said, "Do not dwell in a place which is famous. Do no not abide with a man of a great name in asceticism."

491. One of the brethren asked an old Abba, saying, "Abba, what shall I do? For whenever I see the face of a woman the war of fornication is stirred up against me." The Abba answered and said, "My son, guard your eyes against looking on a woman, and behold, henceforth you will have no fear." The brother said to him, "Behold, how very often does a man meet women by chance, without expecting to do so!" The old man said to him, "As far as it is possible for you to do so keep watching carefully, both within and without yourself. As concerning that which happens by chance, where a man meets women without thinking about it, [in that case] passion will have no power to bestir itself. Take good heed to yourself that such a thing does not happen to you by your own will. It is this what the Holy Book condemns, saying, 'Every man who looks upon a woman to lust after her has already committed adultery with her in his heart.' When you are not thinking about women, so if you meet a woman and the passion stirs against you, lift up your mind immediately to God, and He will help you. Then wishing especially to strengthen then that brother, he answered and said to him, "Behold, my son, know that you have been with me for two years, and that I have not as yet seen what manner of face you have, whether it is good, or bad. It was this [fact] which urged me to tell you to guard your eyes from the sight of women." Afterwards the Abba made a prayer over him, and sent him away to depart to the coenobium, for that brother used to dwell in the church.

492. They used to say about one of the old men that when the church was dismissed, he fled straightaway and departed to his cell, and [they said] that he had a devil, but the holy man was [only] fulfilling the work of God.

493. An old man used to say, "Do not do anything without prayer, and thus you will not be sorry."

494. A brother asked an old man, saying, "If I am in a clean place, and the time for service has arrived am I to return?" The old man said to him, "Who, when he remembers riches, will return to poverty?"

495. The old man Theodotus used to say, "Constant hunger makes monks to be emaciated and drives them mad."

496. Abba Daniel used to say, "Constant vigil especially dries up and makes the body to diminish."

497. Abba Ammon asked Abba Sisoes, saying, "When I read in the Book, my mind wishes to arrange the words so that there may be an answer to [my] question." The old man said to him, "This is unnecessary, for only purity of heart [is required]. From this it arises that a man should speak without too much care."

498. Abba Theona used to say, "Because we put ourselves out of the sight of God we are led captive by the passions of the body."

499. Abba Poemen used to say, "Temptations are a sure sign whereby a monk may be known."

500. Abba Agathon once fell sick, and one of the old men was with him. As they both were lying in the cell, a brother read the Book of Genesis to them. When he reached to where Jacob said to his sons, 'Joseph is not, and Simeon is not, and you would take Benjamin away that you may bring down my grey hairs with sorrow to Sheol,' the old man answered and said, 'Were not the other ten sons sufficient for you, O Jacob?' Abba Agathon said, 'Hold your peace, old man. If God holds a man to be innocent, who shall condemn him?'"

501. One of the fathers came to Abba Theodore of Pirme, and said to him, "O father, behold, brother so-and-so has gone back to the world." The old man said to him, "Do you marvel at this? Do not wonder at this. Be surprised when you hear that a man has been able to flee wholly from the world."

502. "If a man thinks filthy thoughts, does he himself become defiled?" Some of the old men said, "Yes, he is defiled," and others said, "He is not defiled, for if he does it is impossible for simple folk like ourselves to live at all but [the truth] is that a man must not carry his filthy thoughts into deeds."

503. A certain brother went to a strenuous and tired old man. He asked him about this matter. The old man said to him, "Every man is required [to do] according to his ability." Then a brother entreated the old man, saying, "For our Lord's sake explain these words to me." The old man said to him, "Behold! Supposing that some very desirable things were placed here. Two brethren came in, one being of great stature and the other of little stature. If the mind of him that is of full strength were to say, 'I wish to possess that thing,' and he did not carry his soul's desire into effect, but straightaway cut it short, the man would not be denied. If then the man of lesser strength were to desire the thing, being incited by his thoughts, and he did not take it, he also would not be defiled. But, if he desired to take it, he would be defiled."

504. The old man said, "If you see a young man going up to heaven of his own will, lay hold upon his leg, and sweep him away there from for thus will a man help him."

505. The same old man used to say, "If you cry to God in prayer with a pure heart, your prayer shall not return to you fruitless."

506. The same old man used to say, "As two words cannot be uttered [at the same time] by one voice, and be recognized and understood, so is it with the mixed prayer which is uttered by a man before God."

507. He also said, "If you see the wings of ravens stretched out in flight, even so is the foolish prayer of the mind which is lifted up."

508. He also said, "If you are earnest in asking God for things, but will not pay back as far as you are able, you must hear the words, "You shall ask and shall not receive, because you did accept a loan and did not pay it back."

509. He also said, "The words of his mouth that prays purely before God are a chains with which he shall be able [to bind] the devils beneath his feet like a sparrow. As prisoners tremble before their master, even so will they quake at the words of his prayer."

510. He also said, "As the rain when it falls upon the earth takes the place of a key in the lock, and opens [it] and brings out to sight the growth of the seeds and roots which are in it, so are the soul and the mind of him who receives and tastes the heavenly raindrops. For by the words of his lips shall be made known to man his hidden conduct before God, I mean to say, that when a man's request and entreaty about everything are made within the words of his pure prayer, he opens the door of the treasury of the Trinity, Who is the Lord of treasures, and brings out there from the treasures which are hidden for those who are worthy of them."

511. Concerning Abba Anthony they used to say, "There was a man with an unclean spirit which sought to cast him into the water, and the monks who were with Abba Anthony came and entreated him to pray over the man who was thus troubled, but he excused himself [from doing so]. And when the demoniac had remained with him for a long time, he hit the blessed man on his cheek, upon which the old man made ready the other cheek and having done this that evil spirit took to flight."

512. A brother asked Abba Muthues, saying, "What shall I do? For my tongue vexes me. Whenever I sit among the brethren I am unable to restrain myself, but I condemn them in every good work, and treat them with contempt. What shall I do, then?" The old man answered and said, "If you are not able to restrain yourself, get away, and stay by yourself, for this is a disease. He who sits among the brethren must not possess four corners, but he must be altogether round, so that he may move smoothly in respect of every man." The old man said to him also, "I myself do not dwell alone as an example of spiritual excellence, but as an emblem of feebleness, for mighty men are those who are among the brethren."

513. When the brethren were talking to an old man about the thoughts they said to him, "Our hearts are hard, and we do not fear God. What are we to do so that we may come to fear God?" The old man said to them, "I think that if a man will lay hold in his heart upon that which rebukes him, it will bring to him the fear of God." They said to him, "What is the rebuke?" The old man said to him, "In every act a man should rebuke his soul, and say to it, 'Remember that you have to go out to meet God.' And let him say also, 'What do I seek with man?' I think that if a man maintains these things the fear of God will come to him."

514. Abba Timothy said to a certain brother, "How are you?" The brother said to him, "I destroy my days, O father." The old man said to him, "My son, my days also are destroyed, and I give thanks."

515. An old man used to say, "The Shunammite woman received Elisha because she had no human promise with man and they spoke of the Shunammite woman [as] a person of the soul, and of Elijah [as] a person of the Spirit of God when the soul makes itself remote from commotion and trouble, the Spirit of God abides on it, and then it is able to bring out, though until now it has been barren."

516. Abba Ammon used to say, "I said to Abba Poemen, 'If I go to my neighbor's cell, or he comes to mine concerning whatever matter, are both of us be ashamed to speak, lest some alien subject of discourse appear between us?' The old man said to him, 'You will do well, for youth has need of care and watchfulness.' I said to him, 'What do the old men do?' He said to me, 'The old men have been skilled, have had experience, and have arrived at the measure for speech, for in them there is nothing alien which they can speak with the mouth.' I said to him, 'Supposing that I have the necessity to talk with a neighbor, would you prefer that I should speak with the words of the Scriptures, or with the words of the old men?' He said to me, 'If you are not able to hold your peace it is better for you to use the speech of the old men rather than that of the Scriptures, for there is danger in a man employing the speech of the Scriptures.'"

517. Abba Daniel used to say that a man of business once came to Abba Arsenius, and brought him a testament of a certain kinsman who had left him a very large inheritance. Having received the deed he wished to tear it to pieces. The man of business fell down at his feet, and said, "I beseech you, do not tear it up, for if you do I shall die." Abba Arsenius said to him, "I died before he did, though he has only now died, but shall I live?" He sent the man of affairs away without having taken anything.

518. A monk went to a nunnery to visit his sister who was sick. She was a woman who was great with God, a firm believer, and never allowed herself to see the face of a man, not even that of her brother, lest through her he might go in among the women. She sent him a message, saying, "Go, my brother, and pray for me, that Christ, by His grace, may make me worthy to see you in that world of the kingdom of heaven."

519. A brother asked an old man and said to him, "What is the best thing for me to do, so that I may do it and thus live?" The old man said to him, "God [alone] knows which is best but listen: One of the old men said that the mind which rebuked a man was his [best] adversary, for it resisted a man who sought to carry out his desires in the flesh, to rebel against God, not to be obedient to Him, and it would also deliver a man over to his enemies."

520. An old man also said, "It is right that the soul should be occupied in the service [of God] by day and night, even like Huldah, the prophetess, who used to sit in the house of the Lord with supplication and ministration and also like Hannah, who never ceased in her ministrations during a period of eighty years."

521. A brother asked an old man, saying, "What shall I do, father? For my belly vexes me, and I am unable to restrain it, and therefore I am leading a life of luxury." The old man said to him, "If you do not throw on it the fear of fasting you will never be able to straighten the path. Place before it the following parable: A certain man had an ass. As he was sitting upon it and journeying along, the animal would not go straight, but went first to this side of the road and then to that and he took a stick and hit it. The ass said, 'Do not beat me, and I will go straight.' When he had gone a little further on, the man alighted from the ass, and placed the stick in [his] cloak-bag which was on it. The ass did not know that the stick was on his back. When the ass saw that its master was not carrying the stick, the ass began to hold him in contempt, and walked among the crops after which his master ran after him. The master took the stick and beat him with it until he went straight. The belly of the body is like this ass."

522. A brother said to Theodore of Parme, "Speak a word to me, for behold, I am about to perish." With great labor the old man said to him, "I stand in danger myself, and what have I to say to you?"

523. Abba Kerion used to say, "I have performed more bodily labors than my son Zechariah, but I have not reached his measure of humility and silence."

524. Abba Macarius used to say, "Guard yourself against freedom of word and deed, for it is right for a monk not to permit his thought to be his judge in anything whatever."

525. Mother Sarah used to say to her brethren, "It is I who am a man, and you who are women."

526. A brother asked Abba Poemen, "How can it be right for me to take good heed to my ways when I am sitting in my cell?" The old man said to him, "For a season I was a man who had fallen into the mire up to my shoulders, a basketful of gall hung from my neck, and I was crying out to God, 'Have mercy upon me.'"

527. They used to say of the men who were in the cells that their rules were so strict that during the night they slept four hours, assembled for service four hours, worked for four hours that during the day, and worked with their hands until the ninth hour. After that they prepared the small quantity of food which they ate, and if any man had anything to do in his cell he then did it. In this way they filled up their day.

528. A brother asked Abba Sisoes, saying, "Why do not the passions depart from me?" The old man said to him, "Because their possessions are in you. Give them their pledge, and they will depart."

529. The fathers were summoned by the Archbishop Theophilus. They went to Alexandria to meet him so that he might make a prayer and cleanse a house of idols. As they were eating with him, a flesh of a calf was set before them, and they ate it in simplicity, doubting nothing. The Archbishop took a piece of meat and gave it to an old man who was near him, saying, "Behold, this piece of meat is very good, father." They all answered and said to him, "Behold, up to now, we have been eating herbs. If it is flesh, we do not eat flesh." And none of them ate anything more.

530. They used to tell a story of a brother who was the neighbor of an old Abba. The brother said that he would go into the cell of the old man, and steal whatever he found there. Although the old man saw him, he never rebuked him, but worked with his hands and wearied himself the more, saying, "Perhaps that brother is in need." The old man suffered much tribulation at the thought, and ate his food in sadness. When the old man was about to die, the brethren sat around him. When he saw in their midst the brother who used to steal from him, he said to him, "My son, come near me." When he had drawn near him, he kissed his hands, saying, "My brother, I am grateful to these hands, for through them I shall enter the kingdom of heaven." When that brother heard these things he was sorry, and repented. He became a well tried monk through the things which he had seen in that old man.

531. When Abba Agathon was traveling, with some young men, one of them found a small bag on the road, and said to him, "Father, do you wish me to take this little bag?" The old man looked at him in wonder, saying, "My son, did you place it there?" The young man said, "No." Then the old man said to him, "If you did not place it there, how can you desire to take it?"

532. Abba Joseph, the priest of Ascalon, told us the following story. There was a certain merchant in Ascalon who borrowed from people much money. He hired a ship for himself and sailed. A fierce storm arose up against him, and he lost everything which he had with him. He himself was saved. When he returned to the city those to whom he owed money seized him, and they took everything which he had in his house, sold it, and shut him up in prison. They left him his wife as an act of charity, so that she might beg for him and feed him. The woman went about from door to door, and begged for bread for her husband. One day as she was sitting and eating bread with her husband, one of the chief men of the city went in to give alms to the prisoners who were there. He saw the woman and lusted for her, for she was beautiful. He sent his servant to call her, and she came thinking that he wished to give her alms. He took her aside, and said to her, "Why have you come here?" She related to him the whole matter. Then he said to her, "If I pay one-third of your husband's debt will you lie with me this night?" That chaste, free woman said to him, "I have heard that the holy Apostle said, 'A woman has no power over her body, but her husband.' I will first ask my husband, and whatever he commands me that will I do." Having come she told her husband, and he was grieved and wept. The husband said to her, "Go, and say to him, I have told my husband, and it has not pleased him. I have hope in God that He will not forsake us." There was in the prison a certain thief who had been a highway robber, and was shut up [in a room] inside beyond them. At that moment he happened to be sitting at a window which faced them, and heard everything which they were saying. With tears he said to himself, "Woe is me! For although these people are in such great trouble, they are not willing to deliver over their freedom, and accept money, and go forth from this place, but they hold their chastity to be more valuable than riches. What then shall I, the wretched one, do? For the thought that there is a God has never entered my mind, and I never remember that my evil deeds will be judged, and I have committed many wickedness, and many awful murders. And I know that when the judge comes here he will kill me without asking a question, as is just." And the thief answered and said to the woman and her husband, "Because I see that you preserve the purity of your bodies for Christ's sake, and that you have chosen to remain in great tribulation and not to destroy your chastity, God has put it into my heart to do to you an act of grace which you deserve, and perhaps God will show me mercy through you on the day of judgement. Go you to the northern side of the city wall, and dig there in a certain place, and behold, you shall find there a large earthen pot, beneath which is a vessel full of gold. Take it, and pay your debt, and may a great blessing abide with you so that you may live upon it but I beseech you to pray for me continually, that I may find mercy before God in the day of judgment." After three days the judge came to the city, and ordered them to cut off the head of that thief without [asking any] questions. After he had been slain, that noble woman said to her husband, "Will you command me to go and see if that which the thief said is true?" He said to her, "Go." She went at the time of evening, and by the indications which the thief had given her, she found the place. She had dug a little, then she found the money, as he had told her. She took the money and went to her house, giving thanks to God. She brought it out little by little, and she gave it to the creditors, who thought that she brought it to them as the result of her begging. A little from here and a little from there then when she had paid her husband's debt, he came out from the prison, thanking and glorifying God. Abba Joseph said to us, "Behold these men, O my brethren! Because they chose to live in affliction, and refused to despise the command of God, God multiplied His grace to them without delay. For even if the woman had hearkened to that lascivious man he might not, perhaps, have given her what he promised her but because they preserved their chastity which is pleasing to God, God rewarded her with the whole amount of their debts, and brought them to a greater state of prosperity than [that which they enjoyed] at first. And, my beloved, I think thus concerning Adam when he was in Paradise. Had he kept that little command, honor greater than that which he had at first would have come to him but when he transgressed the command of his Lord, he fell from and was driven out of the delight and pleasure where he lived. May our Lord make us worthy to keep His commandments! Amen."

533. When Abba John and the brethren who were with him were going up from Scete, he who was guiding them lost the way. The brethren said to Abba John, "What shall we do, father? For this brother has lost the way, and perhaps we shall die in wandering about." Abba John said to them, "If you tell him he will be grieved and feel ashamed. But behold I will feign to be sick, and will say that I am not able to go on any further." The brethren said, "Father, you have well said." They acted thus, and decided that they would stay where they were until the morning, rather than rebuke the brother who was guiding them.

534. Abba Serenus used to say, "I have passed the whole period of my life in cutting and twisting and sewing palm leaves, and in spite of it all, had not the hand of the Lord fed me I should not have had enough to eat."

535. Those who are in despair, and who have delivered themselves over to the filthy work of their abominable lusts, and who make loose their ways at all times, and who love the lusts which harm them, are like the sterile land, and the arid desert, and a house laid waste, and a vineyard without grapes, and an empty vessel, and a body without a soul, and eyes without light, and a dead body without a voice, and hands which are cut off, and knees which are bowed, and a paralytic lying on a bed, and a vessel filled with foul odor.

536. AGAINST THOSE WHO LOVE VAINGLORY, AND THOSE WHO BOAST OF THEIR ALMS. Those who love vainglory, and those who boast of their fair works and life, are like a broken cistern, a bag with a hole in it, a tree without fruit, a naked man, a moth-eaten garment, a worm-eaten beam of wood, and to other things which are consumed by their [false] glory.

537. AGAINST HIM THAT IS NOT WATCHFUL IN RESPECT OF HIS TONGUE. He who is not watchful in respect of his tongue is like him whose house's door is open, and whose riches are plundered by every man. He is like an uncovered vessel (or unrolled garment), and like that which is unsealed.

538. AGAINST THOSE OVER WHOM EVIL THOUGHTS HAVE DOMINION, AND IN WHOSE MIND WICKED THOUGHTS RISE UP. Those who through their sluggishness give a hand to the thoughts which make a mock of them, and by their negligence help filthy devils to have dominion over them, are like an abode which is full of snakes, a house which is full of evil-smelling things, a ship which is tossed by the waves, a poor piece of land which is full of briars and brambles, and the thorns that choke it, the end of which is burning.

539. AGAINST HIM WHO DOESN'T SUPPRESS IN HIMSELF WRATH AND ANGER, AND WHO KEEPS HIS HATRED AGAINST HIS BROTHER. He who does not suppress in himself wrath and anger, who keeps his hatred against his neighbor, is like a savage animal which cannot be tamed, which goes along every road, and wanders about in an imperfect manner. He is like the man who buries fire in chopped straw, puts in his bosom the spawn of serpents, a den which is full of enraged serpents, a cleft in the rock which is full of reptiles which shoot out venom, a mad dog that barks at every man, a wild boar that gnashes his teeth as soon as he sees a man, the evening wolf which goes about with his mouth wide open to destroy the simple lambs, the panther which leaps upon the gazelle in the desert, the ship which sails on the sea with an evil spirit for her steersman, and the savage beast which cannot be subdued which walks on every road and wanders about in error without discernment. These [words] are [directed] to those who are not humble, so that they may correct themselves and their savage habits, and to those who are lifted up against their brethren in their pride, and who do not wish to travel in the path of the humility of Christ.

540. AGAINST THE CHANGE OF THE EVIL WILL OF THOSE MEN WHO DENY THE GRACE WHICH IS PERFORMED TOWARDS THEM. One of the teachers said, "If you have made yourself humble, they despise you without discernment. If you have made yourself angry, they hate you without understanding. If you have made yourself pleasant, they swallow you, and you disappear. If you have made yourself bitter (or cruel), they reject you, and you are reviled. If you have mingled with folk they hold you to be a liar, fair [-spoken], and wandering. If they have fallen ill, they command you, and if they are despised, they judge you; if they are visited, they abuse you; and if you are whole, they leave you; and if they are reclining, they drive you away; and if aught is required from them, they curse you; and if mercy be shown to them, they oppress you. Neither grace (or goodness), nor justice will ever please those who belong to every evil of every kind."

CHAPTER SIXTEEN

Conversation between a Brother and an Old Man

B*ROTHER*: "How is love (or charity) acquired by men of understanding?"
O*LD* M*AN*: "True and pure love is the way of life, and the haven of promises, and the treasure of faith, and the interpreter of the kingdom, and the herald of that which is hidden."

542. B*ROTHER*: I do not know the power of the word.
O*LD* M*AN*: "If a man does not love God, he cannot believe in Him, and His promises are not true [to him], and he fears not His judgment, and he follows Him not. Now because love is not in him [he cannot] be free from iniquity, and await the life which is promised, but he performs at all times the plans of sin; and this [happens] because the judgment of God is [too] exalted in his sight. Therefore let us run after love, with which the holy fathers have enriched themselves, for it is able to pay back [what is due] to its nature and its God. This then is praise."

543. B*ROTHER*: How does wisdom dwell in man?
O*LD* M*AN*: "Now when a man has gone forth to follow after God with a lowly mind, grace bestows itself upon him, and his conduct becomes strengthened in the spirit, and when he hates the world he becomes sensible of the new conduct of the new man, which is more exalted than the impurity of the

human abode; and he meditates in his mind the humility of the rule of the life which is to come, and he becomes a man of greater spiritual excellence."

544. BROTHER: How is love made known?
OLD MAN: "By the fulfillment of works, and by spiritual care, and by the knowledge of faith."

545. BROTHER: What are the works?
OLD MAN: "The keeping of the commandments of the Lord with the purity of the inner man, together with the labor of the outer man."

546. BROTHER: Is he who is destitute of work also destitute of love?
OLD MAN: "It is impossible that he who is of God should not love, and it is impossible for him that loves not to work, and it is impossible to believe that he who teaches but works not is a true believer, for his tongue is the enemy of his action, and though he speaks life he is in subjection to death."

547. BROTHER: And is he who is in this state free from retribution?
OLD MAN: "Such a man who speaks the things of the spirit, and performs the things of the body, and supplies his own wants, is not deprived of reward, but he is deprived of the crown of light, because the guidance of the spirit refuses to rule him."

548. BROTHER: What are fasting and prayer?
OLD MAN: "Fasting is the subjugation of the body, prayer is converse with God, vigil is a war against Satan, abstinence is being weaned from meats, humility is the state of the first man, kneeling is the inclining of the body before the Judge, tears are the remembrance of sins, nakedness is our captivity which is caused by the transgression of the command, and service is constant supplication to and praise of God."

549. BROTHER: Are these able to redeem the soul?
OLD MAN: "When internal things agree with external, and manifest humility appears in the hidden works which are from within, truly, a man shall be redeemed from the weight of the body."

550. BROTHER: And what is internal humility?
OLD MAN: "The humility of love, peace, friendship, purity, restfulness, tranquility, subjection, faith, remoteness from envy, and a soul which is free from the heat of anger, and is far from the grade of arrogance, and is redeemed

from the love of vainglory, and is full of patient endurance like the great deep, and whose motion is drawn after the knowledge of the spirit, and before whose eyes are depicted the fall of the body, and the greatness of the marvel of the Resurrection, and the demand for judgment which shall come after the revivification, and its standing before the awful throne of God. [If the soul has these things] redemption shall be to it."

551. BROTHER: Is there any man who fasts that shall not be redeemed?
OLD MAN: "There is one [kind of] fasting which is from habit, and another from desire, and another from compulsion, and another from sight, and another from the love of vainglory, and another from affliction, and another from repentance, and another from spiritual affection; for although each of these seems to be the same as the other in the mind externally, yet in the word of knowledge they are distinct. Now the way in which each is performed by the body is the same, and the way in which each is to be undertaken is wholly the same by him who travels straightly on the path of love, and who bears his burden with patient endurance spiritually, and who does not rejoice in his honor."

552. BROTHER: Who is the true [monk]?
OLD MAN: "He who makes his word manifests in deeds, and bears his passion with patient endurance; with such a man life is found, and the knowledge of the spirit dwells in him."

553. BROTHER: Who is the pure habitation?
OLD MAN: "He who is destitute of the good things of the body, and who rejoices in the love of his neighbors in the love of God; for spiritual relaxation is produced in proportion as need rules over the soul."

554. BROTHER: How can a man overcome lust?
OLD MAN: "With spiritual remembrance. If the desire for the delights which are to come does not obliterate that of the things which are here, a man cannot conquer; for if the ship of the merchant did not arrive over and over again by means of hope, he could not endure the storms, and he would go on his way of tribulation."

555. BROTHER: How does a man go out from the world?
OLD MAN: "By forsaking entirely the gratification of desire, and by running to the utmost of his power in the fulfillment of the commandments; for he who does not act in this way falls."

556. *Brother*: How had the old men triumphed?
Old Man: "Through the fervor of their supernatural love, and through the death of the corruptible man, and through the contempt for pride, and through the abatement of the belly, and through the fear of the judgment, and through the promise of certainty; through the desire for these glorious things the fathers have acquired in the soul the spiritual body."

557. *Brother*: How can I conquer the passions, which trouble me when they are fixed in me by nature?
Old Man: "By your death to this world; for if you do not bury your soul in the grave of persistent endurance the spiritual Adam can never be quickened in you. When a dying man departs from this temporary life he has no consciousness of this world, and all his perceptions are at rest and are abated. Now if you forsake that which is of nature naturally, and you do not perform it voluntarily in your person, you are dead but if you desire to die in repentance, the whole of [your] nature ceases from this temporary life by the death of the spirit just as do the motions of the body at the natural end of time."

558. *Brother*: To what extent is a man held capable of revelation?
Old Man: "To the same extent as a man is capable of stripping off sin, both internally and externally. For when a man dies by spiritual sacrifice, [he dies] to all the words and deeds of this habitation of time, and when he has committed his life to the life which is after the revivification, Divine grace bestows itself upon him, and he becomes capable of divine revelations. For the impurity of the world is a dark covering before the face of the soul, and it prevents it from discerning spiritual wisdom."

559. *Brother*: Can a man who loves money be able to believe the promises?
Old Man: "No. If he believes, why does he possess [riches]? Perhaps our hope is [set] upon gold, or perhaps the hand of the Lord is too small to redeem [us]? The body of our Lord is given to us for [our] happiness, and His blood is the drink of our redemption. He withholds from us the loaves of bread and the apparel which grows old. He who loves money is divided in his mind concerning God, and prepares pleasures for himself before God gives them to him. Though he rejoices in the promises in [his] word, he makes them to be a lie by his deed. True indeed is the word of our Lord which He spoke, 'It is as difficult for the rich man to enter the kingdom of heaven as it is for a camel to go through the hole of the needle; it is impossible to possess in one dwelling both God and mammon.' Monks should not, then, belong to the things which

are seen."

560. BROTHER: Who is the man of excellence?
OLD MAN: "He who cries out always that he is a sinner, and asks mercy from the High, whose word is laden with the feeling of discernment, his senses with the watchfulness of deeds. It is he who, being silent, yet speaks, and who, though speaking, holds his peace, and whose actions are wholly good fruits for the life of time, and the revelation of Christ."

561. BROTHER: What is the way of life?
OLD MAN: "The going out of a man from this world on his entrance into another. If a man forsakes his childhood of humility and comes to the old age of this world in his love, he reveals the way of life. To go out truly from this world is to be remote from it."

562. BROTHER: What shall I do in respect of the world, which troubles me?
OLD MAN: "This world troubles you because its care is in your mind, its love is in your body, and its pleasures are in your heart. Forsake the world and it will depart from you. Root up from yourself all its branches. Behold, the war will then die down in you. For if body seeks its gratifications, and its lust is of this world, you are not capable of life."

563. BROTHER: What is a pure prayer?
OLD MAN: "A pure prayer is little in speech and great in deeds, for if it were not so, work would be more excellent than supplication . . . For if it is not so why do we ask and yet not receive, seeing that the mercy of God abounds? The method of penitents is, however, something different, as is also the labor of the humble, for the penitents are hirelings, and the humble are sons."

564. BROTHER: What produces the love of money?
OLD MAN: "From desire, for unless a man desires it he does not possess it. When a man desires he possesses. When he possesses he has fulfilled his desire. When he has fulfilled his desire, he becomes greedy. When he has become greedy he commits fraud. When he has committed fraud his possessions have become many. When his possessions are many, his love diminishes. When his love has diminished the remembrance of God is removed from his heart. When the remembrance of God been removed from his heart, the mind becomes darkened, and his understanding is blinded. When his understanding has become blinded the power of discernment is darkened, and when the power of discernment has become dark, the soul loses its sight. When the soul has

lost its good sight, it is rooted out from within, wickedness enters in, and sin takes up its rule. When sin has taken up its rule the thought of God is blotted out, and the passions of the body are stirred up, and they seek to satisfy their needs. Having taken that which they sought for, it is necessary for much money to be collected. When money is multiplied, the gratification of the body is fulfilled, it eats, drinks, commits adultery and fornication. It lies and works fraud and oppression. It transgresses the covenant, destroys the Law, and treats the promises with contempt, and the lust for the things which are seen is fulfilled. Let money be an abominable thing in our sight. Let us not love money. If we perform the lust of the flesh it is an absolute necessity to love money; for money belongs to the flesh and not to the spirit, even as said the Apostle, 'The flesh hurts the spirit, and the spirit the flesh, and both are opponents each of the other [Gal. 5:17].'"

565. BROTHER: What kind of prayer is not acceptable before God?
OLD MAN: "The destruction of enemies, and asking for evil things [to come upon] those who do harm to us, the health of the body, a multitude of possessions, and abundance of offspring. Prayers for these things are not acceptable before God. If God bears with us while we are sinners and commit offences against Him, how much more is it right that we should bear with each other? It is not right for us to ask for the things which belong to the body, for the wisdom of God provides for all things."

566. BROTHER: What is the purity of the soul?
OLD MAN: "Remoteness from anger and from the error of the remembrance of evil things, and being weaned from the bitter nature, and reconciliation with our enemies, and peace which is beyond troubling, and simplicity of love which is above this world; with these things is the inner man cleansed, and he puts on Christ and is redeemed."

567. BROTHER: What is envy?
OLD MAN: "Hatred towards the virtues of other folk, wickedness towards the good, a bitter mind towards the innocent, anger against those who are prosperous in this world, the cloaking of the upright conduct of those who repent, and vexation with the peace of the lovers of God."

568. BROTHER: How should we pray before God?
OLD MAN: "For the return of sinners, and the finding of the lost, and the bringing near of those who are afar off, and friendliness towards those who wrong us, and love towards those who persecute us, and a sorrowful care

for those who provoke to wrath; if a man does these things, truly there is repentance in his mind, and sinners will often live, and their soul[s] will be redeemed in life. For the prayer which our Lord delivered to us for the need of the body is a word which covers the whole community, and was not uttered solely for those who are strangers to the world, and who hold in contempt the pleasures of the body. For he in whose dwelling the kingdom of God and it's righteousness are found lacks nothing, even when he asks [not]."

569. BROTHER: What is remoteness from the world?
OLD MAN: "The thought which overcomes the love of the body; for if the body be not trampled upon by the feeling of patient endurance a man cannot conquer in his strife."

570. BROTHER: Is the soul of a man, which is held fast in the lust of the things which are seen, fair in the sight of God?
OLD MAN: "Who is able to live chastely when the body is making demands upon him? Or, in what soul is found the love of our Lord which bestows itself upon the things which are seen and which are corruptible? A servant cannot serve two masters, and the soul cannot please God with spiritual excellence so long as the memories of the things which are corruptible are in its mind, for the mind of the flesh cannot please our Lord; and except the world die in the heart humility cannot dwell there, and except the body be deprived of its lusts, the soul cannot be cleansed from thoughts."

571. BROTHER: Why does a mind get disturbed when meeting women?
OLD MAN: "Because they make use of the lust of nature. For, when the sight has fallen upon the construction for the production of children and the gratification of the body, that old poison lays hold upon it, and the law of the desire is confounded; now desire conquers nature, not by the stirring up of the passions, but by the will, [and] by the fulfilling of works of humility, which, by the might of our Lord, conquer everything by their love, and by the patient endurance of the merit of Christ."

572. BROTHER: Who is the mighty man, he who is remote from the world, or he who dwells in the world?
OLD MAN: "The mighty man conquers in every place, whether he is in the world or without. Nevertheless, the fathers departed to the wilderness, the place which is preserved from the uproar of those who are afraid that as long as they dwell in the body the passions which give trouble will cleave to them. Now, for those who have ended the great strife of their conflict in the world

Divine grace has worked with its power, and it still works for the remembrance and benefit of the community, and truly great is the crown of those whose spiritual ship has not sunk to the bottom of the tossed and troubled sea of this world, and has not ceased its course heavenwards by the straight road which is full of fear."

573. BROTHER: Is it helpful to the soul to make oneself a stranger?
OLD MAN: "With perfect thanksgiving it does help, provided that the soul bears chastely afflictions, and rejoices in our Lord who gives pleasure; but if it does not, its good seed is made of no effect because it does not give fruit beloved of God, and if it endures and utters blessing it has a reward, but if it lack these things it becomes a mere wandering of the mind, and a sight which is without profit. The best thing of all is the quietness of the mind which is akin to God."

574. BROTHER: Since all the creatures of God are holy, why do the fathers make the sign of the Cross over what they eat?
OLD MAN: "It is true that all the creatures of God were pure [when they came from] Him that created them, but because sin gained dominion everything became polluted; but the advent of our Lord came, and sin was abrogated and righteousness had its rule, and everything was made holy, whether it was in the heavens or on the earth. But because the blessed fathers knew the wiles of Satan, and that they would certainly bring upon them that which would do them harm by means of such things as are employed as food, they signed what they ate with the holy sign of the Great Cross so that they might slay all the craftiness of the Calumniator."

575. One of the fathers said, "Once, I was lying down at night. I thirsted for water to drink. There was near me one of the holy men who lived in a holy manner. He saw that I took up the vessel to drink without having made over it the [sign of] Cross. He said to me, 'Wait, master, wait.' He made the sign of the Cross over it, and straightaway the Calumniator fell from the vessel in the form of a flash of fire, and we both saw it. We wondered at the great might of our Redeemer, and at the marvelous symbol of His merit. A variant [reads]: One of the fathers said, 'I was lying down one night, and I thirsted for water to drink. There was with me a certain widow who lived a chaste life when she was with her husband. Afterwards, she said to me, "Wait, master, wait," and she made the sign of the holy Cross over the vessel of water, and straightaway there fell from it the Calumniator in the form of a flash of fire. We both saw him. We wondered at the might of the Redeemer, and at the marvelous symbol of His merit.' These things were indeed told to us by the blessed mouth, which is remote from falsehood. It is required of us necessarily to do this [i.e., make the sign of the Cross] for the protection of our life. The Enemy used to wage war openly against that widow who did these things, even as I have learned from the chosen ones of our Lord, and one of the holy men who heard [this] from her own mouth spoke thus, 'The blessed woman said as follows, "One day I went to the house of God, and Satan drew near, and said to me, 'Why do you pray like a man, saying, "Glory be to the Father, and to the Son, and to the Holy Spirit?"' I said to him, "How then shall I pray?" Satan said to me, "You should pray in this wise way, saying, 'Glory be to you, Mary, mother of Christ.'" I answered and said to him, "there is dust in your eyes, Satan. Why should I forsake the Lord and worship a handmaiden?"' He disappeared from me.'"

576. The blessed man said to me also, "The same old woman said in my presence. 'I again went to the church according to [my] custom, I entered in, and prayed. The Enemy came and made my eyes blind, and I could not see. I called one of the women, and she took me to my house. After three days he departed from before my eyes, and began to go in front of me. Then I said to him, "There is a thing which you must do for me. Go to where you did first seize me." We went to the church, me and him. I left him where he had seized me, and went away a short distance. Turning around I looked for him, and I saw him standing like a shadow. I went a little further, I turned around again, and I [still] saw him. I shut the door of the church, went out, and then opened it again and went in. I saw him still standing there. He ceased to practice his wiles upon me.' These were the great things which happened to the blessed old woman. For the monk must not boast himself over the man who is in the world, for mighty men are in the world. If such things are to be found in Eve, how much more should they be found in Adam, which has been redeemed by [the second] Adam?"

577. One of the fathers said, "While I was sleeping one night, the enemy came and hit me. The enemy said to me, 'Go to the world and work righteousness; why do you shut yourself up like a beast in a cave?' Knowing the wickedness of the enemy, who regarded me with an evil eye, I made the sign of the Cross, and he fled from me. Then, having waited a few days, he came and hit me on the neck in a bantering fashion, saying, 'Now that you have become a righteous man, go to the world that I may not destroy you.' When I prayed and made the sign of the Cross over my face he departed from me. After a short time he came again, and took up a seat upon my neck. I bade my soul to be of good cheer, stood up, made the sign of the Cross, the symbol of merit, before him, and he disappeared again, for he was not able to stand before me. These things happened in this wise in very truth, and we may therefore know and understand the conduct by which God rejoices. There is, even as this [story shows], no reason for fearing the devils and all the evil spirits. Whoever holds in contempt the humility, the penitence of the mind, the subjugation of the body, and remoteness from the interest in the things which are seen, falls into the inclination of the world, and despises the good riches of the fear of God, and his hope for the inheritance of holy men is cut off. For the delights of heaven which neither pass away nor are dissolved. May we, through the grace and mercy of Christ, be held to be worthy of these things! Amen."

CHAPTER SEVENTEEN

Questions & Answers on the Vision of the Mind

A BROTHER ASKED AN OLD MAN, SAYING, "In what manner ought a monk to dwell in silent contemplation in his cell?"
THE OLD MAN said, "He should have no remembrance of man whatsoever while he is dwelling in the cell."

579. BROTHER: What kind of labor should the heart perform?
OLD MAN: "The perfect labor of monks is for a man to have his gaze directed towards God firmly and continually."

580. BROTHER: How can the mind persecute abominable thoughts?
OLD MAN: "The mind is unable to do this of itself, and it has not the power [to do it], nevertheless whenever a thought [of evil] comes against the soul, it is required of it to flee immediately from the performance of it, and to take refuge in supplication [to God], and that shall dissolve the thoughts even as wax [is dissolved] before the fire, for our God is a consuming fire."

581. BROTHER: How did the fathers who dwelt in Scete give answers to their enemies?
OLD MAN: "That service also was great and excellent, but there was labor there, and not every man was able to stand firm there, and there was in it, moreover, wandering of the understanding."

582. *Brother*: How?

Old Man: "When a thought has come against the soul, and the soul has, with great difficulty, been able to drive it out, another thought makes ready to come, and in this manner the soul is occupied the whole day long in a war against the thoughts, and it is unable to occupy itself with the sight of God, and [to enjoy it] continually."

583. *Brother*: With what intent, then, should the mind flee towards God?

Old Man: "If the thought of fornication rushes upon you, seize your mind, carry it to God immediately, and raise it upwards with strenuous effort. Do not delay, for to delay is to be on the limit of being brought low."

584. *Brother*: If a thought of vainglory rises up in my mind, and it makes me think that I can be free from the evil passions, is it not necessary that I should contend against it?

Old Man: "Whenever you contend against it, it will become exceedingly strong against you, and will act cruelly and sharply. You will not, as you imagine, be strengthened by the Spirit of God, as it is better to be able to contend against you than you are able to contend against it. You will [not] find yourself, apparently, sufficient of yourself to resist the passions of the thoughts. For as it is with the man who has a spiritual father, that gives to him his every desire, and who is without any care whatsoever, and who has, therefore, no judgment with God, so also is it with him that have committed his soul to God. It is, hence forward, unnecessary for him in anyway to fall into care concerning the thoughts, or to allow a thought to enter into his heart. If it should happen that a thought has entered, lift it up strenuously towards your Father, and say, 'I myself know nothing; behold, my Father knows.' While you are raising up your mind, the thought itself will leave it and take to flight half way. The thought cannot ascend upwards with you, and it does not dare stand with you there. There is no service which is superior to this, for it belongs to confidence, and it has no care in all the Church."

585. *Brother*: How could the fathers of the Scete make use of answers against their enemies, and please God?

Old Man: "Because they worked in simplicity and in the fear of God. Because of this God helped them. Afterwards the service of the vision of God rose upon them, with His help, because of their works of excellence, and because of the mercy of God, and that old man who taught in this wise said, 'Once I went to Scete to visit an old man there who had become aged in ascetic labors. Having saluted each other we sat down in silence. That old man made [me] no answer at all. Then, while I was sitting down, my mind became occupied with a vision of God. That old man continued to sit there, making baskets of palm leaves. He neither lifted up his gaze to me, nor did he tell me to eat. For six whole days I ate nothing. That old man was occupied with basket-making the whole daylong. When the evening came he soaked some palm leaves in water, and worked the whole night through. On the following day, after the ninth hour, he answered and said to me, 'Brother, when have you the power to perform this work of the spiritual vision?' I answered, saying, 'Yes, father, and where do you have the power [to work thus]? We have accustomed ourselves to learn this from our youth.' The old man said to me, 'I have never received teaching of this kind from my fathers. But as you see me now, even so have I been all [my] days. A little work, a little meditation, a little singing of the Psalms, and a little prayer; I have cleansed my thoughts according to my power, and resist [as far as I can] the thoughts which rush upon me. In this manner, afterwards, there dawned upon me the spirit of visions, as I learned this [faculty]. I did not know that any man possessed this gift.' I answered and said to him, 'I have learned this from my youth up.'"

586. BROTHER: How can a man see the order of the divine vision?
OLD MAN: "The Scriptures have shown us how."

587. BROTHER: How?
OLD MAN: "Daniel saw Him as the Ancient of Days. Ezekiel saw Him on the chariot of the Cherubim. Isaiah saw Him upon a lofty and glorious throne. Moses persisted in being with Him Who cannot be seen, as if he saw Him."

588. BROTHER: How could the mind see what cannot be seen?
OLD MAN: "A King cannot be seen, as far as his exact image is concerned, when He is sitting on the throne."

589. BROTHER: Is it right for a man to depict God in this manner?
OLD MAN: "What is better, for a man to depict God in his mind in this manner, or to bow himself down to many abominable thoughts?"

590. BROTHER: Then is this accounted as sin?
OLD MAN: "No. Only you must hold according to what the Scriptures have shown [you], and the fulfillment of the matter will come of itself, even as the Apostle said, 'Now, as in a miracle, we see in parable, but then face to face, the meaning of which is as if a man were to say, when the mind has been made

perfect, then it will be able to see with ease and freedom.'"

591. *Brother*: Is there any confusion in the mind in respect of this?
Old Man: "If a man performs his strife in truth there will be no confusion in the mind. I have passed a whole week of days without a remembrance of any human thing having entered my heart. Another old man said, 'I was once journeying along the road, and behold, I saw two angels close to me, one on this side, and one on the other, and they walked along with me, and I did not look at them.'"

592. *Brother*: Why?
Old Man: "Because it is written, neither angels nor powers shall be able to separate me from the love of God, which is in our Lord Jesus Christ" [Rom. 8:39].

593. *Brother*: Can the mind be occupied with, and stay with the divine vision continually?
Old Man: "Although the mind cannot be occupied with or stay with the divine vision continually, still when it is pressed by the thoughts it can fly to God, and it shall not be deprived of the divine vision. I say to you that if the mind is perfect in this respect, it shall be easier for you to move mountains than to bring it down from above. For as the blind man who is enclosed in darkness, if his eyes are opened and he goes out into the light, will be unwilling for the darkness to overtake him again, so is the mind having begun to see the light of its own person, hates the darkness, and is unwilling to remember it again. One of the fathers said, 'I wished to look upon my mind, saying, "Perhaps if I allow my mind to do so it will go and wander about in the world" but when I set it free it stood still, and was silent, and did not know where to go. Again, I lifted it up on high, for it knew that if it departed and wandered about I had to admonish it; quietness and prayer make strong this class of service.' The same old man said, 'If a man prays continually it will bring correction to the mind immediately.'"

594. *Brother*: How can man pray continually, as the body becomes ill through constant prayer?
Old Man: "The standing up of a man in his prayer [once] is not said to be prayer, but [he must do so] continually."

595. *Brother*: How is [prayer to be made] continually?
Old Man: "Whether you are eating, or drinking, or even traveling on the road,

or if you are doing some piece of work, you shall not let prayer be remote from your heart."

596. BROTHER: But suppose I am talking with someone, how can I fulfill the command, and be praying continually?
OLD MAN: "Now concerning this the Apostle spoke, in [all your] prayers, and in [all your] supplications, pray at all times in the spirit; and when it would be unseemly for you to pray, because you are speaking with another man, pray through supplication."

597. BROTHER: What manner of prayer is it necessary for a man to pray?
OLD MAN: "The prayer in the Gospel which our Lord taught His disciples."

598. BROTHER: What limit ought there to be to prayer?
OLD MAN: "No measure has been laid down to prayer; because He said, 'Pray at all times, and continually.' He did not lay down any measure to prayer. For if the monk only really prays when he stands up in prayer, he who is thus does not pray with the heart but with the mouth only. The old man said, 'It is necessary for the man who is thus to look upon all [men] in the same way, and he must be remote from all calumny for the love of Christ; to Whom be glory forever!' Amen."

599. In another manuscript I have found the following [story]. A certain monk who was a foreigner, and was chaste in his conduct, and who came from the city of Antioch, from the monastery which is called Kawsyan, went once to pray in Jerusalem, and to see the holy places where our Lord Jesus Christ went about, and after he had lived there for a long time, and had worked a way which was full of every excellence, he wished to return to his country in peace. Now he lacked food for the journey and the money which was necessary for his wants, and he knew not what to do; and when he had gone in to pray in the great temple of the Resurrection of our Lord, he prayed, and sat down in sorrow, and he was troubled about his departure, and the lack of that which he needed. And having sat down, he dropped into slumber, and slept, and he saw in his dream our Lord Jesus Christ, Who told him to be of good cheer, saying, "Arise, be not sorrowful, but go in to the steward of My house of the Resurrection, and say to him, 'Jesus has sent me to you so that you may give me the one dinar of which I am in need, and when He comes He will give it [back] to you for me.'" When the monk had awoke from his sleep, he arose, and prayed first and believed the vision which had appeared to him, and he rose up and went to the steward [of the Church] of the Resurrection, as he had been commanded to do, and he spoke to the steward, as he had been told in the vision. The steward said to him, When will Jesus come and repay me? The monk said to him, "I have told you what I have heard from Him, and as for you, you must do what you wish" The steward said to the monk, give me a paper in your own handwriting for the dinar, and take [it] and go; and the monk sat down and wrote thus: I, John the monk, the stranger, from Antioch, a city of Syria, and from the holy monastery of Kawsyan hereby testify that I have received from the steward one dinar for food by the way, and I have, of my own free will, set my handwriting here saying that when Jesus comes He will pay him for me. After the monk had taken the dinar and departed, the steward saw that same night in a vision of the night, that a man of splendid appearance came and said to him, "Take the dinar which you gave to that monk, and give me the written paper which he gave you." The steward said in the vision, "My Lord, the monk said to me, Jesus will come and repay me, and will take from you the paper which I have written." The man said to the steward, "I, even I, am Jesus; take your dinar, and give Me the writing which the monk gave you. Or, would you take anything more from him?" Then the steward took the dinar from Him, and he laid it in his hand, and gave Him the written paper, and He tore it up. When the steward awoke from his slumber he found the dinar in his hand, but the written paper had disappeared; and he marveled, wondered, and praised God. He sent some of his people to bring back the monk wherever he might be found, and having gone they found him praying, and they said to him, come with us; behold, the steward of the Church of the Resurrection seeks you. When the monk heard [this], he feared greatly, and said in his heart, "Perhaps he wishes to take back the dinar." He went with them being troubled and sorrowful. When the steward saw him, he said to him, "For the love of Christ I entreat you to eat with me this day." While they were eating, the steward said to him, "What have you done with the dinar?" The monk said, "Behold, it is still with me." The steward said to him, "Abba, take as many dinars as you wish, only give me the paper which you did write [saying] that Jesus would come and repay me." The monk said to him, "My lord, forgive me, but I have received nothing else from you, for that which I did take was sufficient for me." The steward related to him that which had appeared to him, saying, "The dinar has been paid back to me, and the paper which you did write has been taken by our Lord Jesus Christ from me." The steward entreated the monk, saying, "Take from me, if you wish, ten pounds of gold, only write me [a paper, saying], Jesus will come and pay you for me, and do, my lord depart in peace." The monk said to him, "Master, truly I say to you, you shall not receive from me another jot, and I will not take anything else from you. And all those who heard [this story] praised God Who does not neglect those who call upon Him in truth."

600. AN ADMONITION OF THE HOLY FATHERS. Be an enemy to all folly and sin. Dejection drives away the fear of God, captivity [to sin] drives away the virtues from the soul. There are three excellences which illumine the mind always; a man must not see the vices of his neighbors, and he must do good to those who do evil to him, and he must bear with gladness all the trials which come upon him. These produce three other excellences, namely, a man must not look upon the vices of his brother, and this excellence produces love; and he must bear the trials that come upon him, and this excellence produces self-denial. There are three excellences of which the mind has need, and a man should observe them always, He should lean away from follies, and he should not be lax in his service, and he should make strong his heart. There are three excellences, the which if a man see them with him he knows within himself that he is delivered from devils, namely, knowledge whereby he will be able to understand and to discern between thoughts, and the sight of everything before it comes to pass, and the power of not becoming entangled with evil thoughts of any kind. There are three things which gain dominion over the soul until it arrives at great weakness, captivity [to sin], and dejection, and sickness, and these contend against every man's soul, and from them are produced evil thoughts, and when a man builds up they overthrow [what he has built]. There are three excellences which benefit and strengthen the soul: mercy, the absence of lust and long-suffering, and besides these three excellences the mind has need to pray without ceasing continually, and a man must fall down and cry out before God, and hate all evil passions.

601. He also said, "The fear of God drives away all evil things, but dejection drives away the fear of God from a man; the wandering of the thoughts drives away good works from the soul. There are four things, which are good: silence, the keeping of the commandments, humility, and tribulations. There are four good things, which protect the soul: love towards everyman, absence of lust, long-suffering, and a man severing from himself wickedness. The soul has need of the four following virtues at all seasons. A man must pray without ceasing, he should pour himself out before God continually, he should declare his own defects in his heart, and he should judge no man, and his own mind should be tranquil. The following four things help a young monk: doctrine, the repetition of the Psalms at every moment, and he should not be lax in obedience to fasting, and he should esteem himself to be of no account. Through four things the soul is corrupted. For a man to walk about through the city without guarding his eyes, for a man to have anything to do with women, for a man to have friendship with the rich men of the world, and for a man to love empty talk. Of four things fornication is begotten; by eating, drinking, sleeping excessively, idleness, laughter and silly words, and the arrangement of the apparel. By four things the mind is darkened; by a man hating his neighbor, by hating his brother, by crying out evil things, and by uttering them. By four things is the soul laid waste: by a man not keeping silent, by loving the works of the world, by trafficking in material things, and by the evilness of the eye. Through four things anger comes: By a man giving and taking (i.e., buying and selling) in the world, by doing his own will, by loving to teach, and by thinking in himself that he is a wise man. There are three virtues, which a man acquires by weariness (or exhaustion): by mourning always, by observing his sins, and by having his death before his eyes every day. He who takes care to keep these virtues shall be able to be saved by the mercy of God and, to speak briefly, these are necessary for the man who seeks to live: Faith, and hope, and love, and love of God, and obedience, and humility, and patient endurance, and self-denial, and fasting, and constant prayer, and vigil, and service, and going into exile, and voluntary poverty, and absence of evil passions, and the silence of discretion, and deprivation of various meats. For if a man does not believe, he can neither hope nor love, nor have affection, nor be obedient; and if he be not obedient, he cannot either be humble, or endure patiently; and if he cannot endure patiently, he cannot practice self denial, and if he cannot practice self denial, he cannot draw near to fasting. And if he cannot fast, he cannot pray continually, and if he has no prayer, he cannot keep vigils; and if he keeps not vigil, service will not be found in him, for he will say and sing the service in a hurried manner. He who possesses these things only in a little degree cannot go into exile and become voluntarily poor, and without the love of these things he cannot deprive himself of meats; and a man cannot acquire the silence of discretion when all these things are remote from him. Let us, then, take care to perfect all these things in ourselves with all our might, through the help of God, to Whom be glory forever and ever! Amen.

602. AN EXHORTATION. Therefore I have written down for you all these things so that your soul may not become sluggish, and so that you may not become the cause of [others] being like to you. Because of this I counsel you to take the yoke of pleasantness upon your neck, for it will help you to sit by yourself in silence, and to withdraw yourself from human intercourse, and from cares about the things of this world which will hinder you. Make yourself as the dust in [your] humility towards every man, knowing [at the same time] that there is hope [for you]. Do not cease weeping from your eyes, for there is the occasion of tears. Make your cell a hall of judgment of yourself, and a place for striving against devils and evil passions, and let there be depicted there the kingdom [of heaven], and Gehenna, and death and life, and sinners and the righteous, and the fire which never is quenched, and the glory of the righteous, and the outer darkness, and the gnashing of the teeth, and the light of the righteous, and their joy in the Holy Spirit, and the Passion of our Lord, and the memorial of His Resurrection, and the redemption of creation. Let your habitation be free from superfluous things, for one of two things will happen to you; either through thinking of them you will suffer injury, or in withdrawing yourself from them your war will be added to and become fiercer. Take heed lest, through [holding in] honor and sparing other folk, you bring yourself to evil case in the war; whatever belongs to lust and is of the eyes you shall not possess, for the wars of your passions are sufficient for you. Heal and make whole in your habitation those in whom God has pleasure; it is He Who knows your sitting down, and your coming in, and your going away. In all your conduct; be constant in prayer, especially in the night seasons, for [night] is the acceptable time for prayer, as it is written, 'Be like your Lord, Who prayed to God continually throughout the night until the rising up of the sun.' When all voices are quiet, fill your mouth with praise, and your tongue with glorifying. While others are lying like dead men on their biers, depict in yourself the waking of the Resurrection. The night which is darkness to other folk shall be bright to you as the day. Instead of filling yourself with wine as other men do, fill yourself with the love of God; and in the night season, when silver and gold are stolen, steal the kingdom [of heaven] like a thief. In the night season, when sinners perform their evil deeds to their own injury, you labor for the benefit of your own soul, and take care, continually of all excellences. Then He Who is merciful in His gifts, and rich to everyone who upon Him, will come to you quickly and will help you, and you shall smite the Evil One, and shall bring to nothing his crafty acts. You shall make your mind to shine, and the Lord of All shall place in you the innocent thoughts of uprightness, and He shall comfort your mind; then shall the rugged ground become smooth before you, and the difficult ground shall be as a plain, and your ship shall anchor in [its] haven. You shall lead beforehand the life which is to come, and you shall fulfill the Will of God, according to His Will, both in heaven and on earth; and your knowledge shall grow and your joy increase in proportion to your spiritual conduct, and you shall be held to be worthy of the sight of the righteous by the grace and mercy of Christ our Lord, to Whom, with His Father, and the Holy Ghost, be glory now, and always, and for ever and ever! Amen.

603. An admonition of Abba John. "You will not be able to find a more excellent way than this: He who would repent to Christ of his sins and follies must fall on his face many, many times, [and be sorry for] the sins which he has committed. He must make supplication and entreaty to the mercy of God. Moreover, our other fathers have incited [us] to kneel down, and he who continually kneels down and prays rejoices in God. Woe to me, me the man of negligence! Now he who sighs, weeps, and sheds tears in prayer, possesses all excellences together; for if we do not keep watch on and remember always our feebleness, while despising ourselves, and holding ourselves in contempt, the devils will lead us astray. Wake yourself up, O my beloved one, and keep in your remembrance always three moments, and forget them not; the first is the moment of death, with its sorrow, and grief, and trouble, which is immeasurable, that overtakes every man, when [a man shall stand] before the awful throne of Christ; the second moment is the moment of fear and quaking when men and angels shall rise up, when a man does not know what command shall come forth concerning him, whether it shall be for life everlasting or for torment everlasting; and the third moment is that when the penalty (or decree of doom) shall come forth upon us, with its repentance of soul which shall last for ever, and shall be with us afterwards in the years which shall have no end. At the [remembrance of] three moments all men fear and quake; may God in His compassion save us from Gehenna and its endless torments! Amen. I am an apostle, and I cast out devils, and I perform mighty deeds, but how am I to know that the end of Judas may not be mine, and how am I to know that I shall [not] inherit hanging, and be called by our Lord Satan and son of perdition? If you see, moreover, a man who is a murderer, and a thief, and an adulterer, and a shedder of blood, you may think that I shall know [this]; for if this murderer at the end confesses Christ, he will precede me in the kingdom of heaven, and you shall think thus concerning every man. If you, O man of God, wherever you go, think these and suchlike things continually, and if your humility be in proportion to the greatness of your power, you shall never fall. But if a man be neglectful, even for the twinkling of an eye, of his humility, and if pride be mingled in his negligence, he shall be cut off quickly from the height of the love of God, and he shall fall, even as quickly as a glass vessel full of water, which is suspended by a thread of a spider's web, would fall if that thread were to be severed. Now the conduct of humility is thus. If at the beginning, or in the middle, or at the end, or wherever it may be, a man first of all lays hold upon perfect humility, and upon complete contempt of himself, the devils will be unable to approach him, on the contrary, they will flee before him, like flies before smoke, both they and their thoughts; but if a man [does not] acquire humility, either at the beginning, or in the middle, or at the end of his career, there is nothing which [can stand up] against the strife and contest. As the holy man Evagrius said, "After the vanquishing of [all] the other passions, there still remain two which will wage war against the perfect man until death, namely, vainglory and pride." John, the seer of Thebes, used to say, "He against whom the devil of vainglory still fights, wanders without measure, and is divided [in his mind] to a boundless degree." The Teacher used to say, "Humility possesses two characteristics which are superior to the other excellences of the spirit, for it sees to what degree it can abase itself to the lowest depth, and grace also exalts to God, [and] to the height which is above; and because grace exalts it continually towards God, it acquires faith at all times, and strengthened confidence. And the second characteristic of humility is that it fears not that which oppose it, that is to say, it fears neither devils, nor wild animals, nor evil men, even as the holy man Evagrius said, 'The man who is proud and wrathful is a timid man, but the humble man is without fear.'" He said, "Humility by itself vanquishes both passions and devils, and the labors of the body, and the contests of the mind only serve to strengthen humility the more. Therefore there is never a time when the monk has not need of humility. Now it is right for him that dwells in silence wishing to arrive speedily at purity of heart, and to take care of [his spiritual] splendor, to guard the three following things: he must guard his hearing against listening to any word which may strike him and may rouse him up to anger; and he must guard his tongue, not only against rebuking and chiding any man, even though he be a man of no account whatsoever and a man of ignorance, and he must not [attempt] to teach or to admonish. But if a man ask him for a prayer, he must esteem himself to be the servant of him that asks him, and he must kneel down before the cross and say, O Lord, provide for my brethren according to Your Will, and according to Your design, and according as it may be beneficial for them before You, and make me, a sinner, worthy of Your mercy through my prayers; let him pray after this example, and it shall suffice. Do not think in your mind, which may lead you astray, that you will be able to acquire spiritual excellence, no matter which it may be, without afflictions and troubles, whether with or without the desire; for no man who feeds his body daintily on lusts is able to enter through the door, even as the camel cannot go through the narrow hole of the needle. The pleasures of the body come into being because of unbelief, because the wretched body does not believe in those good things which are promised to the hungry, and in the woes which are prepared for those who are filled with food and who live delicately. Therefore he, who believes in promises and threats, goes hungry, and he denies himself, and he watches in prayer, and he humbles himself, and he lays hold upon abstinence, and restrains himself from the gratification of his pleasures, and he inherits the purity which is promised to those who are blessed. But if he leads a life of sluggishness and pleasure, from it he shall inherit the impurities and the punishments, which are prepared for him in Gehenna. The desire of the Holy Spirit is thus: Remoteness from the habitation of men, continual quiet, weeping and sorrowful cries, joyful hymns, the singing of the Psalms, and praises, fasting, and abstinence, and vigil, poor apparel, a humble gait, the cloaking of the thoughts of the passions, the hidden prayer of the mind; know then that such are the things in which those who are in the desire of the Spirit wish to walk, and they never wish to perform the lusts of the flesh. To speak briefly to you, O my brethren, fasting, and service, and standing up, and vigil, and abstinence from meats, are the constituent parts of a fair rule of life and conduct, and those who perform them will receive a reward from the true God if they perform them in truth, and if there be no alien pretence in their service. But listen, O my brethren, for this is the true work of the monastic life, the binding of the understanding which is in God, and the suppression of the alien thoughts which enter his heart; and whosoever has his heart [set] upon God acquires for his soul pleasure, and the life which is everlasting. Amen.

Here ends the history and the narratives of the triumphant acts of the holy fathers and the monks which were composed by the holy and excellent Palladius, Bishop of the city of Helenopolis, and which he wrote to Lausus the prefect. To God be glory and honor and adorations and worship and exaltations, for ever and ever, Amen.

APPENDIX

Questions of the Brethren

THE BRETHREN SAID THAT THERE WERE TWO BRETHREN who were the sons of a merchant, and their father died, and they divided their inheritance between themselves, and to each one there came five thousand dinars. One of the brethren divided his inheritance among the churches, and the monasteries, and the poor, and he himself became a monk, and he chose for himself a life of continual silence, and fasting, and prayer. The other brother built a monastery for himself, and gathered brethren to him, and he took care of the strangers, and the poor, and the sick, whom he received and relieved. When the two brothers were dead there was questioning among the brethren about them, and they went to Abba Pambo and asked him, which manner of life and conduct was the more excellent and exalted? Having learned from God, he said to them, "They are both perfect, and in my view they appear to be of equal merit." Explain to us now the old man's words, for how can the man who is destitute and the man who has possessions be equal [in merit]? The old man said, "Since the whole conduct of these brethren was to God, and since whatever they did they did it for God, with an upright aim, and since the aim of each was the same, they appeared to be in the old man's opinion of equal merit before God."

605. The brethren asked Abba Nastir, "What rule of life and conduct should a man follow?" The old man said, "All rules of conduct are not alike. Abraham was a lover of strangers, David was a humble man, Elijah loved silence, and God accepted the work of all of them. Whatever work is of God, if your soul desires it, do it, and God be with you" The brethren said, "Abba Pambo said, "If there be three monks in one place, and one of them lives in silence [it is] well, and if another is sick and gives thanks in his weakness, and if another ministers to men and relieves them, all three of them are in the same service." Reveal to us now the mind of this holy man. Abba Pambo said, "If a man dwells in silence for God's sake, and not for the sake of vainglory, or any other human thing; and if another, who is sick, gives thanks to God for his sickness, and he endures him that ministers to him with longsuffering, he becomes like him that is in silence; and if he who ministers to men does it not for a reward of this world, but for God's sake, and if he constrains himself in everything, and does the will of those who are ministered to by him in love and gladness, he thus becomes like him who shuts himself up in silence, and like him that is sick. In this way the work of all three is of equal merit. For Abba Joseph and Abba Poemen divided he perfect ascetic life into three classes, and therefore Abba Nastir said to that brother, "If you conduct yourself according to any one of the three you shall be perfect. And this is well known from that which Abba Anthony said, 'Many have afflicted themselves with labors and tribulations, and because they had not in them the power of discernment, they did not know the way of truth.' Again he said, 'One man might live in a cell for a hundred years, and yet not know how to dwell there [rightly] for one day, because he humbles not himself, and accounts not himself a sinner, and a feeble man, and ignorant, but he justifies himself, and blames others; nevertheless it is right that we should know that, even though some are sick, and others relieve the wants of men and minister to them with an upright aim, those who lead a life of silence lead a superior life, and follow a line of conduct which is more excellent than all the rules of life which are followed among brethren.' And this life is superior in the same way that the Spirit of God is more exalted than the holy angels, according to what we have learned from the history of the holy men Abba Arsenius and Abba Moses the Ethiopian. For when one of the brethren went to the blessed Arsenius [to enquire of him] concerning the love of a silent life of contemplation, he neither set a table for him nor gave him refreshment; then he went to the blessed Abba Moses and he both welcomed him and gave him refreshment. And when one of the great fathers heard [this], he entreated our Lord to reveal to him this matter, saying, "How is it that one flees for Your Name's sake, and another welcome and gives refreshment for Your Name's sake?" There appeared to him on the river two ships, in one of which was Abba Arsenius, and the Spirit of God

Who was traveling along in silence, and in the other was Abba Moses, who was traveling with holy angels that were feeding him with honey, with the comb. And by this the fathers understood that the life of silent contemplation was as greatly exalted above alms and ministrations as was the conduct of Matthew the Evangelist above that of Zacchaeus the tax-collector.

607. The brethren said, "The brethren asked Abba Pambo, saying, 'Supposing that a man who lives in the world has a wife and children, and supposing that he gives much alms, and sets free slaves, and redeem those in captivity, and visits the sick, and relieves those who are afflicted, and fulfills all the things which are proper for him [to fulfill], is not such a man equal in labor to one of the three classes of monks, that is, to the man that dwells in silence, or him that is sick, or him that ministers to the poor?' The old man said, 'Not altogether.' The brethren said, 'Why?' The old man said, 'Because, although the man who is in the world leads a life of righteousness, his whole conduct is outside the body, but all the labor of the monks is inside the body, that is, fasting, prayer, vigil, hunger, thirst, the constraint of the will at every moment, and wars, both secret and manifest.' It is well known and manifest that the men, who are in the world and who are exceedingly excellent in their conduct, are not equal to the monks in their labors; for our Lord Jesus Christ surnamed the monks 'sons of light,' and those who are in the world 'sons of the world.' The monks with their members, and their thoughts, their bodies, and with their conduct serve God perfectly with stern labors and afflictions, and they offer themselves up to God as a living, and rational, and holy sacrifice, with rational and spiritual service, and they are crucified to the world, and the world is crucified to them, according to the word of our Lord, Who said, "Whosoever wishes to come after Me, let him take up his cross, and follow Me," that is to say, Let him not fulfill his own will, but let him do My will only, and bear tribulations of all kinds. And monks shall leave father, and mother, and brothers, and sisters, and kinsfolk, and country, and in return for these they shall receive a hundredfold, and shall inherit everlasting life. To the men who are in the world, He said, "Acquire for yourselves friends of the mammon of unrighteousness, so that when it has come to an end they may receive you into their everlasting habitations." For as men who are in the world receive monks into their houses, so shall the monks receive those who have lived in the world into the kingdom of heaven; and by this our Lord showed that all the good things of God and His kingdom belong to the monks who, from their youth even to their old age, have labored to God in the excellent works of the ascetic and monastic life. But it is right that we should know to what degree the soul is superior to the body. The life which is led by the monks in silent contemplation, and their works, are as much superior to the life which is led by righteous men in the world, as the life and conduct of the angels are superior to those of men. The life and conduct of the monks are superior to those of men who are in the world, because the latter please God because of their love for men, while the monks do so because of their love for God."

608. The brethren said, "Into how many orders have the fathers arranged the monastic life?" The old man said, "Into three orders."

609. The brethren said, "What are they?" The old man said, "The perfect, those who are half-perfect, and the beginners."

610. The brethren said, "Where can you prove to us that this is so?" The old man said, "From the words of our Lord in the Gospel. For he said, The sower went out to sow. Some [seeds] fell on the roadside, and others fell on the rock, and others among thorns [Matthew 9:3-5] These three [kinds of] seed are those who are in the world. And as concerning the other seed of which He spoke, saying that it fell on good ground, and gave fruit, some thirty fold, and some sixty fold, and some a hundredfold. These are the grades of monks, for the seed which yielded fruit thirty fold is the beginners, and that which yielded sixty fold is the half-perfect, and that which yielded one hundredfold is the perfect."

611. The brethren said, "And supposing a man in the world conducts himself in a wholly perfect manner, and according to what is right, is not his labor equal to that of a beginner?" The old man said, "No."

612. The brethren said, "Why [not]?" The old man said, "Although the monk is little and is a beginner, he is still more excellent than the man in the world who keeps every just [demand] of righteousness."

613. Why did Abba Anthony say to Paula, his disciple, "Go and dwell in silence that you may receive the temptations of devils?" The old man said, "Because the perfection of the monk arises from spiritual conduct, and spiritual conduct is acquired by the conduct of the heart, and purity of heart arises from the conduct of the mind, and the conduct of the mind from prayer which is unceasing, and from strife with devils; but unceasing prayer, and the contending with devils, both in the thoughts and in visions, have no opportunity for existence without silence and solitariness."

614. The brethren said, "What is the meaning of that which Paphnutius and James the Lame said to Saint Evagrius, 'Every lapse which takes place through the tongue, or through lust, or through an action, or through the whole body, is in proportion to the measure of pride which a man possesses?' Now what is the lapse which comes through lust? What is the lapse which comes through an action? What is the lapse which comes through the whole body? Enlighten us about these [various] kinds of lapses." The old man said, "The lapse through lust is the fall which takes place inwardly through pride, even as the blessed Macarius said, 'You shall not be lifted up in your heart and in your mind through the knowledge of the Scriptures, lest you fall into a spirit of blasphemy in your mind.' The lapse through the tongue resembles that into which one of the monks once fell through his pride, and he reviled the holy man Evagrius and the fathers who were in the desert of Scete. The lapse through an action resembles that into which another monk fell when he became lascivious and abominable; and the lapse through the whole body resembles that when, through his pride, one of the brethren was abandoned to the hands of thieves, and they burned him with fire."

615. The brethren said, "Palladius said that once the blessed man Diodes said, 'The mind which falls from God is either delivered over to the devil of wrath, or to the devil of fornication.' I said to him, 'How is it possible for the human mind to be with God uninterruptedly?' He said, 'In whatever work of the fear of God, the soul [is engaged], provided that the soul has due care, its mind is with God.' 'What is the meaning of the action of which the old man spoke?' The old man said, 'He calls [a man's] care concerning God's promises, action of the fear of God, wishing to say thus, "If you are unable to bind your thought continually in various ways to God, though you think about His Majesty, and His power, and His grace, and you pray to Him without ceasing and without wandering prayers, then your mind cannot be with Him; but if you reduce your understanding by means of the constant labor of prayer and by the thought which is on God, and more particularly through the war with devils that [accompanies] this work, bring down your mind by degrees from the thought which is about God, and from prayer, and chain it with the thought which is lower than this, and meditate on the promises of God, and think about His commandments and the correction of yourself. Do not set your mind free from spiritual care, and do not make it wander and think the thought of passibility, but chain your mind to some thought of excellence, which will make it gain profit. And when it has rested somewhat, then raise it up on high, and make it to labor in the thought which is of God, and in pure prayer which has no wandering. For as the growth of the capacity of those who are as yet in the grade of bodily prayer and the reading [of the Scriptures] still exists, even when they are exhausted by standing up, and by the singing of the Psalms, and they rest their bodies for a little by sitting down and by meditation upon the reading, and when they have rested their bodies and their mind has become enlightened through the reading, they stand up for service and prayer, so also it is right for those who have arrived at a correct conduct of the mind, and who think continually about God, and who pray to Him without wandering, when they are exhausted by this severe labor, to bring down their minds from time to time, and to relieve it by means of thought concerning some profitable subject which is less exalted than the thought about God. And this thought must take the place to them of reading, and they must meditate upon God's promises and commandments, and upon their straightness which is in God; and if some abominable thought knock [at the door of their minds] they must quickly make their minds to enter into prayer and into the thought which is upon God. And if there stir in their heart a thought of passion, as soon as they have refreshed themselves by means of thinking about some profitable subject, they must make their mind to enter into the height of prayer, and they must pray without ceasing, and meditate upon God. And from this we know that when the soul meditates with understanding upon some profitable subject, or upon some profitable action, its mind is with God, even as the blessed man Diocles said. Similarly, whenever a monk thinks about the passions of sin, or about deeds connected with the world, his mind is with Satan.""

616. The brethren said, "Why is it that the Divine Light did not shine in the hearts of all the monks until a long time after they had been cleansed by labors and contests? And why is it that the light of grace did shine upon some men before they went forth from the world and came to the ascetic life, as it did in the heart of Abraham Kindondya through the Divine revelation on the day of his feast, and immediately he left his feast, and went forth from the world?" The old man said, "Whenever this light rises in its order in the hearts of men, according to what the fathers say, it comes in this wise. First of all Divine Grace makes a man hot with the love of God, and he hates all the glories and honors of this world; and next he comes in a state of poverty to this rule of life, and Divine Grace itself first gives him the love of labors, and it makes the things which are hard easy to him. And it protects him from the fierce attacks of the war of devils, so that they may not, whenever they wish and will, assault him, but only according to his strength, and his capacity, and as is convenient for his growth. Thus after many labors and contests, his heart is purified with abundant humility, and he shines with the light of grace, and he is held to be worthy to see Christ in a revelation of light. The fathers also said, that in proportion as the monk himself travels along the path of ascetic excellences to meet our Lord by means of labors and contests, so does our Lord advance to meet him with light until they meet each other, and then the monk remains in our Lord by means of labors, and our Lord remains in him by means of his light, even as Abba Isaiah said in his interpretation of that which our Lord said, 'Remain in Me and I in you.' Thus you see, O my brother, that He wishes us to remain in him first of all by the labors of righteousness, and then He will remain Himself in us in purity and in light. And the words, 'The monk travels along the path of ascetic excellences until he sees Him and is illumined by Him, explain the verse, My soul thirsts for You, the Living God...'"

617. The brethren said, "Why is it that though the holy fathers incite us continually to the labors of excellence, and to the contending against passions and devils, Abba Isidore restrained Abba Moses the Ethiopian from works, and from contests with devils, saying, 'Rest you, Moses, and do not quarrel with the devils, and do not seek to make attacks upon them, for there is a measure [i.e., moderation] in everything'; does this apply also to works and to the labors of the ascetic life?" The old man said, "Because at the beginning Abba Moses was ignorant of the rule of the ascetic life, and because he was healthy of body, he worked too much, and he thought that he would be able to prevail mightily against devils by the multitude of his works alone, and that he would be able to vanquish them. Therefore, because the devils perceived his object, they attacked him more severely with frequent wars, both secretly and openly, but Abba Isidore, wishing to teach him the truth, and to make him to acquire humility, said to him, 'Without the power of the Spirit which our Lord gave us in baptism for the fulfilling of His commandments, which is confirmed in us each day by the taking of His Body and Blood, we cannot be purified from the passions, and we cannot vanquish devils, and we cannot perform the works of spiritual excellence.' So Abba Moses learned these things, and his thoughts were humbled, and he partook of the Holy Mysteries, and the devils were conquered, and they reduced their war against him, and from that time forward he lived in rest, and knowledge, and peace. Many monks have imagined that their passions would be healed, and that they would acquire soundness of soul merely by their labors and strenuousness, and therefore they were abandoned by grace, and fell from the truth. For as he who is sick in his body cannot be healed without the physician and medicines, however much he may watch and fast during the time he is taking the medicine, so he who is sick in his soul through the passions of sin, without Christ, the Physician of souls, and without the partaking of His Body and Blood, and the power which is hidden in His commandments, and the humility which is like to His, cannot be healed of his passions, and cannot receive a perfect cure. Therefore, whoever fights against the passions and the devils by the commandments of our Lord is healed of the sickness of the passions, and acquires health of soul, and is delivered from the crafts of the devils."

618. The brethren said, "With what object did those two monks say to Abba Macarius, 'If you are not able to become a monk like us, sit in your cell, and weep for your sins, and thus you shall be like us?" The old man said, "Because they knew that, if a man was able to be a solitary in his body, and a dweller in silent contemplation, and a worker both in his soul and in his body, who made himself humble and who wept each day for his sins, and who cut off from himself all memories of every kind of passion and anxious thought, and who meditated only upon God and upon his own correct behaviour, such a man was a monk (or solitary) in very truth, even as the blessed Evagrius said, 'The monk who is remote from the world is he who has cut off from himself all the motions of his passions, and has fastened to God all the mind of his soul.'"

619. The brethren said, "Why is it that certain of the Fathers were called Meshannayane [i.e., men who transferred themselves from one place to another], since they were recluses, and never departed from their cells?" The old man said, "Because after much silent contemplation, and unceasing prayer, and watching of the mind, they were worthy to depart from the earth in their minds, and to ascend to heaven to Christ the King. They did not do this on occasions only, but continually, for whenever they wished, or whenever they sang the Psalms, or prayed, or meditated upon God, straightaway their mind was exalted to heaven, and stood before our Lord. But there were other [kinds of] Meshannayane, that is to say, those who lived with wild beasts in the deserts, such as Abba Bessarion, and others who were like him."

620. The brethren said, "What is [the meaning] of the fact that when one of the monks saw a brother in the mountain he fled from him, and was unable to bear the smell of the children of men?" The old man said, "The monk fled because he saw that the brother was carrying silver. When the brother saw that the monk fled, he cast off his garments and pursued him. When the monk saw that he had cast off his garments, he waited for him, and welcomed him gladly, saying, 'Since you have cast off the matter which is of this world I have waited for you. I was not able to bear [the sight of you] because I myself am naked.' I looked beyond my rule of life and saw that he was carrying a burden upon his shoulder like a man who was in the world."

621. The brethren said, "Why did the monk not permit that brother who came to him to dwell in the cave by his side, but did say to him, 'You are not able to bear up against the attack of devils?'" The old man said, "Because he knew his manner of life and works, and also that he possessed not the labors and the strenuousness which were sufficient to make him strong to resist the fierce assault of the savage nature of the devils which make war against the monks. For according to the labor of every man, and according to his striving, and his rule of life and strenuousness, and according as he is able to bear, so much the greater are the ferocity, and the wickedness, and the bitterness, and the craftyness of the devils who make war against him. Similarly, when one of the brethren entreated Abba Apellen to allow him to live with him in the desert, he said to him, 'You are not able to bear the temptation of the devils.' Finally, when the brother urged him [to let him do so], he commanded him to dwell in a cave by his side. The devils came against him in the night and sought to strangle him, until Abba Apellen came, and surrounded the cave with the sign of the Cross, after which the brother was able to live in the cave. For not all monks are able to fight against the devils, but only such as are perfect and humble."

622. "Why is it that the two Romans who went to Abba Macarius, did not, during the whole period of three years which they lived [near him] come to him and ask him, or any other aged man, questions about the thoughts?" The old man said, "Because the elder brother was exceedingly wise, and perfect and humble. Had he gone to Abba Macarius, or to one of the other old men, his perfection would have been revealed, and he would have [received] praise throughout Scete from the Fathers, who would have wondered, saying, 'How is it that a young man has become perfect in three years?' It is, however, not right for us to make ourselves like to these two brethren, and to neglect the doctrine of the old men. As for the two brethren, the elder was perfect, and the younger was humble, and learned from him."

623. The brethren said, "The history of the triumphs of Bessarion said that during all the days of his life he dwelt in waste places, and in the desert and in the mountains, and among the rocks. Once having come to a certain monastery, he stood up by the door like a wandering beggar, and then sat down weeping and crying out, even as one who had been rescued from a storm. When the brethren entreated him to go in and rest with them, he said, 'Before I find the possessions of my house which I have lost I cannot endure being under a roof; for thieves fell upon me on the sea, and a storm reared itself up against me, and I have been robbed of the riches which I once possessed, and from being a man of high estate I am become of no account.' Now what were the riches which [he inherited] from his parents and lost? And what does this [story] mean? Who are parents? What does he refer to by the word 'sea,' and storms, and waves? Who were the thieves? Are these words spoken of himself or of the other persons?" The old man said, "These things are said of all the monks who are still striving and contending against passions and devils, and who are lacking at the present time purity of heart, and fruits of the spirit, and visions of our Lord, and they are not spoken of men who are perfect as he was. The word sea he applies to the sea of the mind upon which the monk sails with works of spiritual excellence, and enters the haven of impassibility, even as the blessed Macarius said, 'He who wishes to cleave the sea of the mind, makes himself longsuffering.' And he call temptations storms, and the passions waves, and the thieves are devils, and his parents are the Father, and the Son, and the Holy Ghost, One God, in Whose image and likeness we are made, even as our Creator said, 'Come, let us make man in our image and likeness,' and also as our Lord said, 'Be like your Father, Who is in heaven.' And He call the spiritual excellences, which contain likenesses of the similitude of our Father, Who is in heaven, and which make us heirs of God, and sons of the inheritance of Jesus Christ, by the name of riches and possessions of his parents, and these are faith, and hope, and the love of God and man, and joy, and rest, and peace, and graciousness, and pleasantness, and lowliness, and humility, and longsuffering, and patient endurance, and integrity, and simplicity, and purity, and mercy, and cleanness of heart, and the holy light of the mind, and pure prayer, and the divine light which rises on the heart at the hour of prayer, and spiritual prayer, and Divine knowledge, and the visions and revelations of our Lord. These are the possessions of the soul, some of which it acquires naturally, and some by Divine Grace; now those which it acquires naturally are they which the Creator sowed in its nature at the beginning of its creation, and those which it acquires by Divine Grace are they which are bestowed upon it by the baptism in Christ. And these possessions are lost to a man through pleasures, and honors, and lusts, and benefits, but they are found and acquired, and the soul waxes rich in them, through tribulations, and reviling, and oppression, and hardships. Now although Abba Bessarion, and men who were as perfect as he was, possessed these things, other men lack them and are strangers to them. [And as regards the words] He once came to a certain monastery, and sat down outside the door like a wandering beggar, [they mean that] he saw clearly with the secret eye of the mind that the greater number of the monks were destitute of this spiritual possession, and of the spiritual excellences and gifts which have been already mentioned. And being incited there by the law of affection and of brotherly love, he cried out and wept on

Questions of the Brethren

their behalf, as if it had been on his own, and he made supplication to the loving kindness of God that He would make them worthy of the riches of His love, and of the possession of His Grace.

624. The brethren said, "What are the nine spiritual excellences which that holy man possessed, and what did he lack?" The old man said, "Although they are not written down I think that they were as follows:
1. Voluntary poverty;
2. Abstinence;
3. Constant evening fasting;
4. Vigil;
5. The recital of the whole Book of the Psalms seven times during the night and day;
6. The reading of the Holy Books between times;
7. Lowliness;
8. Humility; and
9. Love of man.

These are the nine spiritual excellences which he possessed, and by means of them he vanquished all passions. By poverty he overcame the love of money. By abstinence he conquered unbridled appetite and gluttony. By fasting he overcame the passion of the love of the belly. By vigil he vanquished sleep. By the recital of the Psalms he did away idleness. By reading he kept away the converse of evil. By lowliness he dispelled wrath and anger. By humility he overcame vainglory and pride. By love of man he conquered hatred, and spite, and enmity. Now the spiritual excellence which he lacked, and which is the tenth, was the constant fervor of the love of God, which is in our Lord Jesus Christ, and this can [only] be gathered together, and established and acquired by the secret prayer of the mind, which is unceasing and wanders not, and by the strict and constant suppression of the thoughts of the passions, and the incitements of devils, when they first begin to stir themselves in the heart. And because among all the works of ascetic excellence there is none more difficult [to do] than this, for, even as the blessed Macarius said, 'All the fighting and fierce, and crafty, and evil temptations of the devils are set in array against it, the holy man is not able easily to become perfection in the love of Christ, which is acquired by the concentration of the mind and by deep thought about God.' Therefore the blessed Evagrius said, 'If you can overcome the wandering of the thoughts, it is the end of all ends; and if you can make deep thought about God have dominion in you, you can overcome all passions, and you shall be worthy of the perfection of the love of Christ.' By the love of man and by the other virtues a monk may, by the help of God, vanquish all the passions; but by the love of Christ he shall conquer the evil passion of the love of the soul, which is the first of all the passions, and which embraces them all. Even as Saint Evagrius said, 'The first of all the passions is the thought of the love of the soul, and after it come the following eight.' And again he said, 'Conquer the strife of the love of the soul which is in your bosom, by that which is towards God.' For until the monk is worthy of this love, he is unable to acquire exact consolation from the remainder of the labors of the other spiritual excellences, even though it be that he obtains assistance from them. As Abba Isaiah said, 'Although the children of Leah were a help to Jacob, yet he loved Joseph most of all, and when Joseph was born, he wished to leave Laban and go to his parents,' that is to say, when a monk has become worthy, and has acquired the perfect love of Christ, which is established by silent contemplation, and the power to pray without ceasing, and his soul is at all times rejoicing and exulting with gladness, he will not be content to remain in this life; but each and every day he will be desiring eagerly and longing to depart from the body, and to be with our Lord in Paradise, which is the habitation of the spirits of just men who have become perfect, and the holy country which is exalted above the passions, and devils, and the striving of those who cultivate the virtues until the revelation of our Lord Jesus, Who loves to make perfect a man with the never ending happiness of His love in a glorious kingdom."

625. The brethren said, "Explain to us the course of life and labor of the old man [who made] baskets, [and dropped] small stones in them." The old man said, "The course of life of that old man was one which was of the mind, and it was stern, and excellent, and it swiftly brought the monk to purity of heart. And as concerning that which he said, 'I set two baskets, one on my right hand and one on my left...' It does not [mean] that he sat the whole day with his baskets round him, but that his two baskets were set in two places. And he himself was occupied with service and prayer, and with his toil, and for every thought, good or bad, which entered his mind he cast a pebble [into the baskets], that is to say, the labor is very severe for the man for a certain time at the beginning, because the devils are envious at the purity of heart which is acquired by him, and therefore they afflicted this old man also for a longtime with the multitude of evil thoughts which were stirring in him, even as he said, 'Many days I have eaten nothing, because the good thoughts did not outnumber the bad ones.' He used to afflict his body with the labor of much fasting, so that he might do away the evil thoughts, because it is not the soul only which feels the labors of the body, its counterpart through its union with it, but also those devils which wage war against the soul, and they feel the labors of the body more than does the soul. For immediately the devils see the monk afflicting his body with labors, they become afraid, and stagger about, because they are more tormented by the labors than is the man who is engaged in them. Therefore the blessed Evagrius, when the demon of fornication assailed him, stripped off his tunic and stood the whole night long, in the season of winter, under the open sky, and by these means he made the demon to suffer pain, and he fled from him. Again, when the demon of blasphemy attacked him, he stood naked under the open sky, in the season of winter, for forty days. And because the thought of gluttony stirred in the heart of Abba Zeno, and made him to eat a cucumber by stealth, he crucified his soul in the sun, during the season of summer for five days. In this wise the holy men were afflicting themselves with labors and tribulations, and when the devils were stirring up in them the thoughts of sin, the demons were afflicted and tortured far more than they. The demons were afflicted and tormented by the labors of the patient endurance of the monks not only in their minds but in their persons, through the operation of the holy angels, and by the command of God, even as, on one occasion, one of the devils was tortured the whole night in the cell of those two brethren who were brothers naturally, when he wished to separate them from each other. For when the younger brother lighted a lamp the devil threw down the candle stick, and extinguished the light, whereupon the [elder] brother struck him [on] the cheek; and the other brother expressed his contrition, and said, 'My brother, have patience, and I will light the lamp [again].' And when God saw the patient endurance and humility of the young man, He commanded His angel, and he fettered the devil the whole night long in their cell; and the devil was tormented there until the morning because of that [blow on] the cheek which he made the one brother to suffer from the other through his wicked agency; and that wicked devil was fettered and tortured the whole night long. And the devils are tortured not only when we afflict our bodies with labors, in order that we may not consent to the will of devils, but also when they stir up in us evil thoughts; if we constrain ourselves a little, and cast them from us, at the same time calling our Lord to our assistance, immediately the holy angels which cleave to us will constrain the demons, and will drive them away from us, and we shall be full of light, and of fervor, and of gladness. Even as one of the demons said to Abba Pachomius, 'A certain monk, against whom I wage war, is very strenuous, and whenever I draw near to him to sow evil thoughts in him, he betakes himself to prayer, and I, though burning with fire, have to depart from his presence blazing even like iron which has been thoroughly well [heated] in the fire.' Now monks are, at the beginning [of their career] afflicted for a long time, not only by the stirring up of the evil thoughts themselves, but also by their tarrying in the heart; but after a known time a man receives strength from our Lord, through their tarrying, and also after a known time their motion is restrained, and then the monk also has rest from strivings, and he is held to be worthy of purity of heart. For at the beginning of the strivings the devils stir up evil thoughts in the heart mightily; sometimes, however, these are destroyed through prayer at the very beginning of their movement, and sometimes they remain. And afterwards the mind becomes strong against them, and does not permit them to tarry altogether in the heart, but it is as yet unable to restrain their violent movement, and the [tribulation which they cause], even as one of the old men said, 'I carried on a strife for twenty years in order that an evil thought might not enter my heart, and until the ninth hour I used to see Satan with his bow drawn to shoot an arrow into my heart. And when he found no opportunity of doing this, he would become dejected and go away ashamed each day.' Now the old man [of whom we first spoke] held fast to his rule in respect of the baskets, and though he was afflicted for a long time by the motion of evil thoughts, and sometimes even by their tarrying in his heart, finally he received power over their tarrying only, for their rising up remained for a considerable time. And having labored in striving for twenty years against the motion of the thoughts, finally he became strong [enough to resist them], and he overcame them. And the devils fled from him, and he arrived at a state of purity, and at the haven of impassibility, and he was held to be worthy of revelations."

626. The brethren said, "If the holy men themselves afflict themselves with labors of tribulation because of the tarrying of the evil thoughts which stir themselves in them, and if they sin against God though not consenting to them, why should we toil against the motion of the devils? For behold, even as the blessed Evagrius said, 'Whether they fight against us or not the matter is not in our hands.'" The old man said, "The perfection of the monks arises from a spiritual rule of life, and a spiritual rule of life comes from purity of heart, and purity of heart from divine vision: 'Blessed are those who are pure in heart, for they shall see God.' When, therefore, a monk labors, and afflicts himself because of the motion of evil thoughts, in order to prevent their remaining for a long time in his heart, and when after a considerable time his heart becomes pure, there remains disgust only, and it vexes the mind of the monk, and prevents his ascent to God, and cuts off his journeying to Him, and does not allow him to enjoy the vision of glory. Now when a monk works for a considerable time because of the motion of evil thoughts [in him], God has compassion upon his trouble, and not only does his heart become cleansed, and his soul pure from every thought of evil, but he is also held to be worthy of the sight of our Lord in a revelation of light, and henceforth, the devils never again dare to stir up evil thoughts in the heart of him that has been esteemed worthy of this great thing. Should it happen that they dare so to do, they suffer pain and burn even as he suffers who is hot, and who kicks away with his feet the piercing goads of iron which glow with heat in the fire. During the interval between the beginning of the strife against evil thoughts and [the attainment of] purity of heart, the devils sometimes vex the monk, and sometimes are vexed by him, even as the blessed Evagrius said, 'If those go down to afflict [others], they are themselves afflicted; so the devils afflict us, and they are also afflicted by us. They afflict us when we receive their evil thoughts, and they are afflicted by us when we, by means of prayer and wrath, suppress their thoughts. When, then, we labor and afflict ourselves for a considerable time in order that their thoughts may not tarry in us, we also afflict ourselves with labors and prayer so that they may not vex and hinder us by [their] violent motion, and afterwards power is given to us by our Lord to lift ourselves up upon the necks of our enemies, and thenceforward our heart rests and is at peace, not only from the perception of their thoughts, but from all the violence of their motion. And the peace and rest of God rule over our souls, and we see that there remains only the war which is manifest of the visions of devils until the time of death merely to terrify us, so that we may not be exalted [unduly] and destroy ourselves. Should it happen that the devils stir up thoughts in the heart of him that has been made perfect, straightaway they become extinguished, even as fire is extinguished when water falls on it."

627. The brethren said, "Why do the devils fear the labors of the monks, even as the Fathers say, 'If you wish the devils to be afraid of you, despise lusts?'" The old man said, "They are afraid because of three things. First, because our Lord treated with contempt three kinds of passions, which included and contained all the various classes of passions, and they are: The love of the belly, the love of money, and vainglory. By means of these the Calumniator fought against our Redeemer, and through His constancy in the wilderness, and silent contemplation, and fasting, and prayer, He overcame Satan; therefore all the monks who travel in His footsteps, and who by means of fasting, and prayer, and silent contemplation, hide away all the thoughts of sin, and who perform their labors in righteousness, our Lord makes to conquer by His strength, and He vanquished the devils who are their enemies. And as the demons fear and tremble, not only by reason of the Crucifixion of Christ, but even at the sign of the Cross, wherever it be made apparent, whether it be depicted upon a garment, or whether it be made in the air, so also do the devils fear and tremble, not only by reason of the labors of our Lord and His constancy in the wilderness, but also at the existence of the monks in the wilderness, and at their silent contemplation, and their fasting, and their prayers, and their patient persistence in the performance of difficult labors, which take place for Christ's sake. Therefore on one occasion Abba Macarius said to Palladius, 'Speak to the devils which war against you with disgust, and sluggishness, and despair: "If I had no labors of spiritual excellence, nevertheless for the sake of Christ I would guard these walls and His Name would be sufficient for the redemption of my life."' Secondly, the war and contest which the devils [wage] against the monks possess both rule and system, and they are neither irregular nor unsystematic. And as when the devils stir up the monks by means of evil thoughts of sin, and the monks accept them, and consent to them, and let themselves be incited to commit sin thereby, immediately their souls become dark, and remote from God, and sorely afflicted, and ashamed, and guilty, and weak and miserable, so when their souls accept not these thoughts, and they do not consent to them, and do not allow themselves to be incited to sin, but drive them away and cast them out as soon as they begin to have motion [in them], and call upon our Lord to help them, immediately all the former things which come against the monks, inasmuch as they do not comply in their inciting, are hurled upon the demons with greatly intensified force, and they become ashamed, and tremble, and are destroyed. Even as the blessed Mark said, 'As he who breaks into a house which is not his own takes to flight with fear and trembling as soon as he hears the voice of the master of the house, so also does Satan...' Thirdly, because without labors and humility we who are rational beings are unable to please God, and because without them neither men nor angels can enjoy His love and His blessings, therefore also the demons and devils, which live wholly in a state of pride and laxity, [can not enjoy them].

628. The brethren said, "Why is it that although the Fathers gave the admonition, 'Whenever a demon appears to a man in any form whatsoever, let that man make the sign of the Cross, and pray, and that similitude will disappear,' we see that on several occasions the devils still remain, and not in appearance only, but also in terrors, which remain for a long time, and in many cases in blows and stripes?" The old man said, "The holy Fathers gave the admonition because it would apply in the majority of cases. For since our Redeemer was crucified for us, and since He exposed to disgrace the Rulers and Dominions, which are evil demons, and put them to shame openly by His Person, even as it is written, from that time onwards, whenever they have made themselves visible to the adorers of Christ in diverse form [to do them] harm, as soon as a man has made mention of the Name of Christ, and has signed himself with the sign of the Cross, the devils have fled immediately, and their forms have disappeared. This happens not only in the case of holy men, and perfect men, but also in respect of ordinary men who possess shortcomings."

629. The brothers said, "Why was the blessed Martinyana, after all the great ascetic practices which he had acquired, and the gifts of the Spirit which he had received, and after he had burned his fingers for the sake of the harlot, still afraid of the war of fornication, and why, having gone and dwelt in the island in the sea for thirty years, did he not stay [for] a season with that woman whom he had brought up from the sea, but cast himself in the sea being afraid of the contest?" The old man said, "Because the whole strength of the demon of fornication was discharged upon him, and he was, therefore, properly afraid. For those who have not with them this war in all its fierceness imagine that they have overcome it, but let them not boast themselves, and let them know the truth, that is to say, they have not vanquished the demon of fornication, and it is only that he has not waged war against them with all his strength, because he has not been permitted so to do, and he has not been permitted to do so because of their feebleness and laxity. For the war of fornication which comes upon a man only attacks him in the degree which he is able to bear. For, behold, the great and famous fathers who endured this war in all its severity for a long time were always in a state of fear and trepidation, as was also Abba Arsenius, who was a man eighty years old; and when the noble lady came to him and said, 'Remember me in your prayers,' he did not hesitate to say, 'I will pray to God that He may blot the remembrance of you out of my heart.' And by means of this which he spoke, he put to shame the demon of fornication, and showed how great was the hatred for this unclean passion that wars against the holy men which he possessed."

THE STORY OF MARTINYANA AND THE HARLOT IS AS FOLLOWS: There was a certain monk who dwelt in the desert, and whose name was Martinyana, and he labored in great works, and God wrought by his hands many mighty deeds, and he was applauded by all men. Now when Satan, the Evil One, saw that he was greatly applauded he became bitterly angry, and he wished to distract and to withdraw him from his rule of life and ascetic labors. One day Satan saw that many folk were glorifying him, and he went and dwelt in a certain harlot, and he sent her to the blessed man in order to make him fall. So the harlot took her attire, and placed it in a bag, and went to the holy man, and when she arrived at his abode it was evening; and she knocked at the door and said, O Saint Martinyna, open the door to me, so that the wild beasts may not eat me. Now the holy man thought that she was a phantom, and he rose up and prayed, and since meanwhile she ceased not to cry out, he rose up from his prayer, and opened the door to her, and said to her, "From where do you come to me, O devil?" And she said, "[My] companions have forsaken me on the road, and I wandered about in the desert, and have arrived here." And he left her [there], and went into the inner cell, and shut the door between himself and her. And after the old man had laid down to sleep the harlot arrayed herself in her attire, and put on her ornaments, and then sat down; and when the morning had come, the old man went forth from his cell, and seeing her dressed he said to her, "Who are you? What is your business?" And she said, "I am a daughter of people of high degree, and my parents are dead, and they have left me great wealth. I heard that you were a great man, and I have come to you, and I beg you to come to my house and take me as a wife, and we will live on your excellence." Then the old man said to her, "How can I forsake my labor, my rule of life, to take a wife, and fall from my covenant?" She said to him, "What sin is in there? Did not Adam, all the Fathers, Noah, and Abraham, take wives from whose seed Christ has risen?" Now by repeating these and suchlike things, she well near succeeded in leading the holy man away captive, and he said to her, "O woman, tarry a little so that I may see, lest perhaps some one may come and see us." Having gone up to the roof to look, he woke up in his mind, and he made a flame of fire and stood up in it, and stayed in the fire until he burnt his toes; and when the harlot saw this, she fell down at his feet and wept, saying, "I have sinned against God and you." She revealed to him the whole truth, [saying], "I repent." The holy man sent her to a nunnery, and he remained in his cell until his feet were healed of the burning of the fire. After he was healed of his sickness, he rose up and went and dwelt in an island in the sea, where there were neither women nor men.

630. The brethren said, "What is the meaning of what one of the old men said, "If you see the wings of ravens flying about you will also see the prayer of him that is oppressed in mind being exalted?" The old man said, "As the ravens do not in the course of their flight mount upwards to the height of heaven like the eagle, but fly close to the surface of the ground and fly about [seeking] their unclean food, so is the mind of the man who is not fervent in the love of God, and who is continually in a state of sluggishness and dejection, for when he stands up for service or for prayer, his thought will not be exalted to the height of the love of Christ, but his mind will wander after evil passions."

631. The brethren said, "An old man said, 'If you see a young man who, in his desire, ascends to heaven, take hold of his foot and bring him back, for in this way you will help him.' What is the meaning of the words, 'who in his desire ascends to heaven?'" The old man said, "This resembles what Isaiah spoke about. If the mind seeks to ascend to the Cross before the feelings cease from feebleness, the wrath of God shall come upon him because he has begun to do something which is beyond his capacity, without having first of all cured his feelings. Some beginners in the ascetic life are so silly and bold as to dare to undertake things, which are far above their capacity and their strength. They do not wish to learn, and will not be persuaded by the commands of their Fathers. They, without having lived the proper period of time in the coenobium, dare to enter the cell, even as it is written concerning one of the brethren in the Book of Paradise, for immediately as he had received the garb of the monk, he went and shut himself up as a solitary recluse, saying, 'I am a monk of the desert.' The fathers went and brought him out into the monastery [again]. There are others, too, who seek to shut themselves up for a week at a time, and this does not help them. There are others, the children of this world, who at the beginning of their careers imitate the exalted rule of life of the Fathers, and imagine that they can imitate the rule of the mind, that is to say, of the spirit, when as yet they have not fulfilled the rule of the body. Therefore their lives and works are not open to the Fathers. They will not receive correction, but they live according to their own desire. They are delivered over into the hands of the devils who make a mock of them."

632. The brethren said, "One of the brethren asked Abba Poemen, saying, 'My body is feeble, and I cannot lead an ascetic life.' Abba Poemen said to him, 'Can you lead the ascetic life in your thought, and do not permit it to go with deceit to your neighbor?'" The brethren asked him, "Tell us how the feeble man was able to lead the ascetic life in his thoughts." The old man said, "This question belongs closely, both in order and meaning, to what a certain brother asked Abba Poemen, saying, 'My body is feeble, but my thoughts are not.' In the former case he spoke having regard to those who were afraid that through pains and sickness they would become negligent of the labors of spiritual excellence, and, in a different manner, that they might fall into pains and sickness by way of punishment. In the latter case he spoke having regard to those who had toiled for a very long time in the labors of self-denial, and who had finally become enfeebled, either through old age, or through pains and sicknesses, and who were ceasing from ascetic labors.' Now this is what Abba Poemen [meant] when he said, 'If you are not now able, by reason of your weakness, to toil in the labors of the body as you did formerly, toil in the labors of the soul.' That is to say, the ruling of the thoughts, which is the ruling of the mind. If you are unable to fast from meats, fast from evil thoughts. If you are no longer able, through the weakness of the body, to stand up and to recite as many Psalms as formerly, make your mind to stand up before our Lord, and pray before Him vigilantly with the prayer which is secret and pure, be tranquil, humble, pleasant, good, forgiving, merciful; and endure your sickness and weakness with praise. Make no man be sorry by your tongue. Do not judge, or blame, or condemn your brother in your heart. These excellences may be cultivated in the soul with the labors of the mind, and not those of the body. They are not impeded by the weakness of the body."

633. The brethren said, "Why is it that the monks are obliged to go round about begging for the meat and raiment of which they have need, like those who are in the world, although our Lord promised them, saying, 'Seek first the kingdom of God and its righteousness, and that of which you have need shall be given to you (Matt. 6:33).'" The old man said, "This [saying] is a proof of the wisdom and grace of God towards those who are in the world, for, in the majority of cases, the righteousness of the children of this world consists of alms and compassion; but the children of light are righteous men and monks who, in their persons, and in their members, and in their thoughts, serve our Lord. God has made the monks to have need of the children of this world because of His love, so that they may care each for the other, and may pray each for the other, that is to say, the children of the world must care for the monks, and the monks must pray in love for them. As the children of the world make the monks associates with them in the corporeal things of the world, the monks must make the children of the world to be associates with them in the things of heaven, for our Lord spoke to the children of the world, saying, 'And I say to you, make friends for yourselves by unrighteous mammon, that when you fail, they may receive you into an everlasting home (Luke 16:9).'"

634. The brethren said, "What is the difference between [the words], I will dwell in you, and I will walk in you, which God spoke concerning the righteous? And what is the meaning of dwelling, and walking?" The old man said, "God dwells in the saints through the constant remembrance with which they remember Him, as they marvel at Him, and His works; but He walks in them by means of His visions and revelations [which He sends] upon them as they marvel at His majesty, and rejoice continually in His love."

635. The brethren said, "With how many, and with what names is the meditation upon God called?" The old man said, "Its names are six, and they are as follows:
1. Hope in God;
2. The state of being bound to our Lord;
3. The continuance with God;
4. Persistence in all the good works of God;

Questions of the Brethren

5. Holding fast to God; and
6. The dependence upon God.

Hope in God [means], fix your gaze upon Him, and hope in Him. Meditate upon Him. Being tied to our Lord [means] that we should be bound to our Lord. Fast and pray, until the old man comes to an end, both without and within. Continuance with God is the state of being gratified through Him. Persistence [means] that we should possess persistence in the Lord in all the good works of God. Holding fast to God [means], cut off from yourself all cares which are not of Him, and let your mind fasten its gaze upon God only. Dependence upon God [means], hang yourself on God, to whom is the glory! Amen."

636. The brethren said, "An old man was asked a question by one of the brethren, who spoke thus, 'If I am in a state of admiration of God, and in purity of soul, and the time of prayer arrives, ought I to come to prayer or not?'" The old man said, 'Will a man who possesses riches make himself poor?'" "Explain to us the meaning of the words of the holy man." The old man said, "The holy man calls admiration of God and purity [of soul] that to which the blessed Mark gave the name meditation upon God and atmosphere of freedom. There are some brethren whose hearts become pure after labors and great strivings, they become worthy of pure prayer, their hearts also become illumined from time to time by the light of Divine Grace, they attain to the meditation which is on God, and to the spiritual understandings which are superior to custom. The Fathers would not permit the men who attained to this capacity, when they were standing in the purity of soul of this nature, and in the atmosphere which was free from trouble, and when the beater struck the board, and the season for prayer arrived, to leave this enjoyable meditation, and to stand up and sing the Psalms, but they [allowed] them to remain there until it had come to an end. For a man to sing the Psalms and to perform the service could always be found, but such meditation and such purity of the understanding, and the atmosphere of freedom could not at all times be acquired, and a man is neither able nor has the power to attain to this state whenever he pleases, for it is a gift from heaven which is given by our Lord from time to time to him that is worthy. For this reason one of the Fathers gave the following commandment: 'If a man enjoys such meditation while he is standing up at the service, let him not interrupt it until it comes to an end, for such meditation fills the place of the service of the Psalms.' See then that you do not drive away from you the gift of God, and let your subservience to the same stand firm; but it is right to know that certain brethren have not as yet attained to meditation of this kind. They have thought that these words were spoken for every man and for men of every kind of capacity, and although their minds have been illumined somewhat by the Psalms and prayers, they have relaxed the fulfillment of the canon of their service, where are placed their consolation, and their wages, and their profit, and have occupied themselves [with the meditation], but on several occasions they have been interrupted in the meditation which has come to them by the devils. It is, therefore, not right for the brethren who are beginners in the ascetic life to do this, but they should commit their life and works and meditation wholly to God, and if it should happen that this meditation comes to them, let them reveal the matter to one of the old men who is acquainted with such things, so that the demons may not lead them astray and work their destruction."

637. The brethren said, "By what means did the Fathers sing the Psalms of the Holy Spirit without wandering [of mind]?" The old man said, "First of all they accustomed themselves whenever they stood up to sing the service in their cells to labor with great care to collect their minds from wandering, and to understand the meaning of the Psalms, and they took care never to let one word (or verse) escape them without their knowing its meaning, not as a mere matter of history, like the interpreters, and not after the manner of the translator, like Basil and John [Chrysostom], but spiritually, according to the interpretation of the Fathers, that is to say, they applied all the Psalms to their own lives and works, and to their passions, and to their spiritual life, and to the wars which the devils waged against them. Each man did thus according to his capacity, whether he was engaged in a rule of life for the training of the body, or of the soul, or of the spirit, even as it is written, 'Blessed are the people who know your praises, O Lord.' That is to say, blessed is the monk who, while glorifying You with praise, collects his mind from wandering, and understands clearly the knowledge and meaning of the Psalms of the spirit, even as it is written, 'Sing to God with praise, sing to our King.' When then a man sings the service in this manner, and pays attention to the meaning of the verse, he acquires daily the faculty of singing a song mingled with the meditation of God and with the gaze [which is fixed] upon Him. After the time in which he has arrived at the spiritual rule of life, immediately a monk has begun to sing the Psalms, though one or two sections of them become too great for him, he is permitted to sing them with understanding and with the meditation which is on God, and he refrains from the customary Psalms, and he sings a song which is superior [to that of] body and flesh, and which is like that of angels, even as the Fathers say.

638. The brethren said, "By means of what thoughts of excellence may the

Questions of the Brethren

children of this world not be offended by the monks, when they see or hear concerning the stumbling which come upon the monks through the frailty or [their] nature, and from the wars of the devils?" The old man said, "When they consider and look upon the monks as frail men, who are clothed with a body which is full of passions, and who although they are monks are striving to imitate the life and deeds of angels, yet owing to the weakness of their bodies, and the inclination of their souls, and the need which cleaves to them, and the strivings of the devils against them, the children of the world will see that it is quite impossible that the monks should not be snared, involuntarily, by certain weaknesses. For behold, some of the people mentioned in the Old and New Testaments were caught in snares against their will, through the frailty of their nature and the war of the devils, as, for example, the blessed and perfect men Moses, Aaron, David, Samson, Hezekiah, Peter, and Paul."

639. The brethren said, "Why do the monks who have led a life of hard labor become in their old age silly, and simple, and act in a foolish way like children and drunken men?" The old man said, "Because all the ascetic excellences which God has placed in the nature of their souls, and which appear in them from their youth up, perish through the relaxing of the will, and through the love of the body, and the war of the devils, and finally through labors and contending. Sometimes they receive them from our Lord as gifts, even as it is written, 'Except you turn, and become as little children, you shall not enter the kingdom of God, even as our Lord said.'"

640. The brethren said, "What should be the beginning of the fight against sin, of the man who has cast all impediments out of his soul, and who has entered the arena, and where should he begin the contest?" The old man said, "It is well known to every man that in all the contests against sin and its lusts the labor of fasting is the first thing [to undertake], and it is so especially in the case of him that fights against the sin which is within him; and the sign of the enmity against sin and its lusts becomes apparent in those who go down to this invisible conflict when they begin to fast. Next comes the rising up in the night and whoever loves the occupation of fasting all the days of his life is a friend of chastity. For as the pleasure of the belly, and the laxity caused by the sleep which incites to a polluted bed, are the head and chief of all the sins which are in the world, and all the abominations of them; so fasting, and strict vigil in the fear of God, with the crucifying of the body throughout the night against the pleasures of sleep, are the foundation of the holy path of God, and of all the spiritual excellences. For fasting strengthens all spiritual excellences. It is the beginning and end of the strife. It is the foremost of all virtues; and as the enjoyment of the light cleaves closely to the eyes which are healthy, so does the desire for prayer cleave closely to the fasting [which is observed] with discernment. For as soon as a man has begun to fast, he desires greatly to converse with God in his mind. The body which is fasting cannot continue to lie on [its] bed the whole night, for fasting naturally incites to wakefulness towards God, not only by day, but also by night; for the empty body is not fatigued so much by its conflict with sleep, even though it be weak in the senses, for its mind is towards God in supplication, and it is better for it to cease from labor through weakness than from the weights of meats. As long as the seals of fasting lie upon the mouth of man, his thoughts meditate upon repentance, and his heart makes prayers to arise; and mildness lies upon his countenance, and abominable motions are remote from him, and rejoicing never, in the smallest degree, appears in his forehead, for he is a foe of lusts and of unprofitable converse. The man who fasted regularly and with understanding his abominable lust brought into subjection has never been seen, for fasting is the abode of all spiritual excellences, and he who holds it in contempt disturbs them all. The first commandment which God laid down for our nature at the beginning gave [Adam] warning concerning the eating of food, and the head of our race fell through eating, therefore, at the point where the first corruption took place [in asceticism], must begin the building of the fear of God, when they lay down the first course for the observance of the law. Moreover when our Lord showed Himself at the Jordan He also began at this point, for after He was baptized the Spirit took Him out into the wilderness, and He fasted for forty days and forty nights; and all those who travel in His footsteps lay the beginning of their strife on this foundation. For who shall treat with contempt, or hold lightly the armor which has been forged by God? If He Who laid down the law fasted, who is there among those who would keep the law that has not need? Immediately as this armor appears on a man, terror falls upon the thoughts of the chief of the rebellion, that is, Satan; and his power is shattered at the sight of the arms which our Captain of the host has placed in our hands, for as soon as he sees the might of this armor on a man he knows at once that he is ready for the contest. What armor is there which is as strong or which gives such boldness in the fight against evil spirits as hunger for the sake of Christ? For in proportion as a man is brought low in his body, at the time when the phalanx of Satan surrounds him, does his heart support itself with confidence, and he who treats this with contempt is lax and is a coward in respect of other spiritual triumphs, because he has not worn the armor whereby the divine athletes have gained the victory. At the very beginning the sign of weakness appears in him, and he himself gives the opportunity of defeat to his adversary, and since he goes naked into the strife it is evident that he will emerge from there without victory, because he has cast away from him the strength which would stir up in him the divine zeal; for his members are not clothed with the flame of hunger, that is to say, fasting. As merchants cannot without labor and trouble save up riches, so the righteous man without anguish and labor for the sake of righteousness cannot expect the crown and the reward."

641. The brethren said, "If a man attains to purity of heart what is the sign of it? How will he know if the heart is coming to purity?" The old man said, "When he sees that all men are fair, and when no man appears to him to be unclean or polluted; whoever is thus indeed stands in purity. If this be not the case, how can he fulfill the word of the Apostle which said, 'When a man stands wholly in purity, he will think that every man is better than he in heart and in truth,' until he attains to the state of him of whom it is said, 'He whose eyes are pure sees not wickedness.'"

642. The brethren said, "What is purity? To what length does its limit extend?" The old man said, "In my opinion purity consists in oblivion of the various kinds of knowledge which are beyond nature, and which nature has discovered in the world; and its limit is that a man should be wholly free from them, so that he may arrive at the state of natural simplicity and integrity which he possessed at first, and which somewhat resembles that of a child, except in the case of small matters."

643. The brethren said, "Is it possible for a man to attain to this state?" The old man said, "Yes. Behold, one of the old men attained to this state to such a degree that he was in the habit of asking his disciple continually if he had eaten or not. On one occasion one of the saints, who was a very old man, became too innocent and simple, and attained to such a state of simplicity and purity that he did not even know how to keep watch upon himself so that he might partake of the Mysteries, or whether he had done so or not, until at length his disciples kept him in his cell, and took him that he might partake of the Mysteries, just as if he had been a child. Now although he was in this state as regards the things of this world, he was perfect in his soul."

644. The brethren said, "What are the [subjects of] meditation and conversation which it is necessary for a man to have while he is living the life of the recluse and passing his time in silent contemplation, so that his understanding may not occupy itself with casual thoughts?" The old man said, "Do you ask concerning meditation, what shall a man have with him to put to death the world in his cell? Has the man whose soul is strenuous and watchful any need [to ask] the question as to what labor he shall occupy himself with when he is alone? What is there for the monk to occupy himself with except weeping? If, then, the monk be unoccupied with weeping, and he is able to pay attention to [any] other thought, what is the meditation which has died out of him? If we come to silent meditation, we can also be constant in weeping, and therefore let us beseech our Lord most earnestly with the mind that He may grant this to us."

645. The brethren said, "Since, then, a man is not sufficient for the constant exercise of this faculty, because of the frailty of his bodily nature, it is right that he should have something else besides this which shall be useful for the consolation of his mind, so that the passions may not attack him through the idleness of the understanding." The old man said, "The passions cannot attack the soul of the monk, whose heart has been cut off from the world by living a solitary ascetic life, unless he has been negligent of the things which it is proper for him to do; and this is so especially if he has, besides the employment [of reading] the Scriptures, the helpful thoughts of the man who is occupied with spiritual excellence. Living alone and in silence will help this [result] greatly, and he will receive in his mind the hope of the world which is to come, and the glory which is laid up for the saints."

646. The brethren said, "One of the old men said, 'I have toiled for twenty years that I might see all men equally. How can a man attain to this measure, and when, and by what means? Give us a demonstration concerning this matter." The old man said, "It is only the perfect men who attain to this measure, and according to what the Fathers say, without contemplation in silence, prayer, great conflicts, and humility, no man can attain this. There is a similarity to this demonstration in the case of natural parents, for as they regard all their children in the same way, and as they love them all equally, and pity and spare all of them alike, even though there be among the great and small, and healthy and sick, and righteous and sinners, and good looking and bad looking, so the strenuous Fathers after the labors and the contests which they have passed through during long periods of time spent in silent and solitary retirement, regard all men, both the righteous and the sinners, in the same way, and they love them all alike and without distinction. As God makes the shadow to fall upon all men, both upon the righteous and upon sinners, even though he loves the righteous for their righteousness, yet He shows most compassion upon the sinners. The coming of our Lord was for the sake of sinners, for [He said], 'I did not come to call the righteous…'"

647. The brethren said, "Why was it, when the brother, according to the body, of one of the Fathers who was living the life of a recluse, sent to him, when he was about to die, to come and see him, that he would not do so, and that the one brother died without seeing the other? And what is the meaning of the words which he spoke, 'If I go out and see him my heart will not be pure before God?'" The old man said, "The holy man was living secluded in a cell, in a habitation of the brethren, and his brother according to the body was also living, like the other brethren in another cell, and when the latter became sick to death, he wished to see his brother before he died. Now to the holy man, since he was keeping silence in respect of all the other brethren, it did not appear to be right to go out to his brother according to the body, and not to go out afterwards to his spiritual brethren, that is to say, to those who dwelt in the monastery with him. Had he gone out to his brother according to the body at the season of his death, and had not gone out to his brethren in the spirit, he would not have found freedom of speech with God at the season of prayer, but his mind would have passed judgment upon him, and his mind would have been darkened, as if he had held in contempt and treated his brethren in the spirit in a dishonorable fashion, and had done more honor to his brother according to the body than to them. This is the meaning of what he said, 'I cannot go out, for if I do, my heart will not be pure before God.'"

648. The brethren said, "The sage said, 'Whoever does not possess the art of laboring, that is, either the things which belong to the labor of the spirit, whereby he may find consolation from God in his inner man in the spirit, or the things which belong to the art of human labor, cannot tarry long in his cell; whoever does not possess one or other of these cannot tarry long in his cell.' Explain to us the words of the old man." The old man said, "The things which belong to the art of human labor are well known to every man; but things which belong to labor of the spirit he call the following: fasting, vigil, the singing of psalms and hymns, the prayers which are said kneeling down, anguish, weeping, tears, and other labors which are like to these. Together with these [there must be the recital of] the offices for the seven hours of the day and night, and the reading of the Holy Scriptures and of the [books of] doctrine of the old men, and these make the monk to acquire patient endurance, and the ability to live the ascetic life alone in a cell, and they produce for him joy and spiritual comfort. If he be a beginner in the ascetic life and strong, and he toils in labors, he will acquire consolation; and if he is a feeble old man, or sick, he will labor in the labors of the mind, and will find joy. For as all the objects which are of gold are wrought by means of anvil, and a hammer, and a pair of tongs, so by means of the labor of the body in a place of silence and seclusion, and the striving of the mind, are wrought all the fruits of the spirit, which the Apostle said were love, joy, peace, faith, humility, graciousness, pleasantness, longsuffering and patient endurance."

649. The brethren said, "On one occasion, when the brethren were sitting down and asking questions about the thoughts, one of them said, 'It is not a great matter if a man sees thoughts afar off.' What did he want to say? Explain to us the words of the old men." The old man said, "When the brethren drew near to the Fathers and asked them questions [wishing] to learn concerning the mode of action and thought in respect of the wars of the devils, the Fathers did not persuade those among them who appeared to possess subtlety of thought, and intelligence, and understanding, and to hate the passions, and to be fervent in the spirit, to cast out from themselves immediately the thoughts of the passions whenever they stirred in them, and to make them to depart foolishly, but they ordered them to tarry with them, and to examine carefully how they arose, and then to contend against them; for in proportion as they were trained in the knowledge of strivings and contending against the passions and against devils they would benefit not themselves only, but many other people also. In this way acted also Evagrius, that man of understanding, and Abba Poemen, and others who were like them. Therefore Abba Joseph said to Abba Poemen, 'When the passions rise up in you, give to and receive from them, and understand carefully their crafty nature, and train yourself to contend against them.' There are certain weak and foolish brethren whom in no way whatsoever does it benefit to dally with the rise of the thoughts of the passions which are in the heart, on the contrary, it is far better for them to immediately as they perceive the motions of the passions, to cast them out from them by prayer, and with anger and hatred. Therefore, when several of the Fathers were gathered together and were discussing the conflicts of the thoughts, and whether it was right to dally with them because of knowledge [concerning them], or to suppress them by means of prayer through fear [of them], one of the Fathers said, 'Even to understand the thoughts afar off is a great and excellent work, but it is a far greater work, and one which makes a man to acquire practice, for him to understand the thoughts, and to wage war against them.' When he has gained experience of their crafty character, then he will suppress them and make them to disappear by the power of prayer and humility. The meaning of this question is this: When a man has labored in conflict and contest against the passions for a long time in seclusion, by the grace of our Lord his heart becomes purified, and rest and peace reign in his soul, and he has relief from tribulation, and he rejoices in God at all seasons, and the devils have no power henceforth to stir up evil thoughts in his soul, because his heart is filled with divine thoughts, and the understanding of spiritual things, and he is never without the mind which is in God, and the remembrance of His fear and mercy. Should the demons dare to stir up thoughts in him, they will not [succeed] in rousing those which cause anguish and which bring to naught spiritual excellences, but only those which are of an ordinary nature, and which impede the vision, even as Evagrius said."

650. The brethren said, "How is it possible for a man to live in such a way as to be pleasing to God?" The old man said, "It is impossible for a monk to rise to the height of the love of God, unless he first of all regard with affection and love man, the image of God; for this is the end of all the commandments of our Lord Jesus Christ, even as He Himself said, 'If you love Me, keep My commandments.'"

651. The brethren said, "An old man said, 'If there rise up in your mind a thought about the need of the body, and you cast it out once, and it comes to you a second time, and you cast it out, should it come a third time, pay no regard to it, for it appertain to war.' Explain to us these words." The old man said, "If while you are in seclusion, and are engaged in spiritual labor, Satan, being envious of you, and wishing to drive you out of the cell, or to impede your spiritual progress, stirs up in you one of the thoughts which goad a man into sin, either to eat before the proper time, or to lie down and sleep, or to visit some one, or to do something else; and if he shows you your power of discretion [saying], 'It is unseemly for you to do this thing'; or again, should some evil devil constrain you, and hinder you, and wishing to make you to cease from your labor, should mock and scoff at you; then stand up quickly, and stir yourself boldly, and bow your knee before our Lord, and pray, and ask, and entreat for help, and mercy, and protection. For that brother who soaked palm fibres in water, and who sat down to plait ropes and mats, was engaged in a similar war, and a demon roused up in him the thought to go and visit one of the brethren; and he cast the thought from him twice, and thrice. Finally, because he did not understand that the war was of the Evil One, who sought to stop [his work] and drive him out of his cell, he was overcome by the war, and he left the palm leaves soaking in the water, and ran and hurried out in great haste. At length the matter was revealed to one of the holy men who was a neighbor of his, and he cried out to him, saying, 'Captive, Captive,' and made him to come back to his cell, and afterwards the devils cried out with a loud voice, saying, 'You have overcome us, O monks.' For the demons are so wicked, and they are so envious of the monks when they remain constantly in seclusion for our Lord's sake, that on several occasions they have, in an irregular manner, driven them out of their cells, as if for a good object, but their object was not a good one."

652. The brethren said, "Why was it that Abba Ammon was not able to overcome the passion of wrath for fourteen years, although he said to us, that he had entreated God, with anguish and tears, by day and night unceasingly, to give him the victory over it?" The old man said, "That passion probably overcame him to an excessive degree through the natural constitution of his body, but it is quite certain that the passions and the devils waged war against him like a mighty man and a warrior. For the devils made war upon the Fathers with intense fierceness and violence, upon each man according to his capacity, and in proportion to their power to triumph, through long suffering, that is to say, through patient and persistent endurance, the battle against them was protracted."

653. The brethren said, "Abba Dorotheus said, 'Our lack of ability to distinguish between matters will not permit us to acquire great excellence in the virtues.' Explain to us what the old man [intended] to say." The old man said, "He wished to say as following. Because of our lack of ability to distinguish between matters we do not make progress in the virtues, and our heart is not quickly purified, and we do not ascend to perfection, because we do not labor with the knowledge and power of discernment which it is right [for us to have]; but [we progress] painfully, and [only] for the sake of vainglory, and as the result of chance circumstances, and without discretion. As it comes, this resembles that which the blessed Evagrius spoke, saying, 'As it is not the material foods themselves which nourish the body, but the power which is in them, so it is not matters themselves which make the soul to grow, but the power of discernment which [comes] from them.' He also said, 'As the feeding, and health, and growth of the body do not come through the actual materials of our foods, for these are cast out of the body in the draught, but from the hidden power which is in them, so also the nourishment and the growth of the soul take place through the fear of God.' The healthy state which arises through impassibility, and the perfection which is in righteousness, do not exist through the labors of the body only, but from the deeds and acts which [are performed] with knowledge, that is to say, with a straight object, and from the action of the mind which hates passions, and from the prayer which is joined to humility, and from the mind which is in God."

654. The brethren said, "Abba Arsenius said to one of the brethren, 'Lead the ascetic life with all the strength that you have, and the hidden labor which is within, and which is performed for God's sake, shall vanquish your external passions.' To what does he give the name of passions?" The old man said, "In his case Arsenius calls the labors of the body, passions. For labors are also called by the name of passions, because they constrain those who toil, and make them feel pain, even as Abba Macarius said, 'Constrain your soul with pains and labors of every kind in ascetic excellence.' This is what Abba Arsenius said to that brother, 'Labor with all your might in the work of righteousness, and toil with the labors of the mind more than with all the various kinds of work of the body.' For the labors of the body only incite and gratify the passions of the body, but the labors of the mind, that is to say, the thought which is in God, and prayer without ceasing, and the suppression of the thought[s] with humility, liberate [a man] from all the passions, and they vanquish devils, and purify the heart, and make perfect love, and make him worthy of the revelations of the spirit."

655. The brethren said, "What is the meaning of that which Abba Benjamin said, 'Had not Moses been gathering the sheep into the fold he would not have seen Him that was in the bush?'" The old man said, "What he said was this. As the blessed Moses, who was held worthy of the vision in the bush, first gathered together the sheep which he was tending into one company lest, when going to see that wonderful sight, his mind should be perturbed through anxiety about the sheep which were [wandering] in the desert, so also is it with the monk, for if he wishes and desires the purity of heart which looks upon God in the revelation of light, it is right that first of all he should abandon every earthly possession, and his feelings, and his passions, and he should live in seclusion always, and should collect his mind and free it from all wandering and straying, and should have one object only to gaze upon, that is God. In this manner he will become worthy of purity of heart, and he will enjoy visions and revelations concerning Him."

656. The brethren said, "Hieronymus said that the blessed Evagrius commanded the brethren who were with him not to drink from where they fill water, and said, 'There are always demons in the places where there is water; what opinion is this?'" The old man said, "The blessed Evagrius interpreted these words spiritually, as being suitable to our mode of life, and he said what our Lord said, 'The demon goes round about in the places where there is no water, that he may seek for rest, and he does not find it.' This saying makes us to understand that when the unclean devil of fornication wages war against the monk, if the monk afflicts himself by eating food sparingly, and especially by drinking water sparingly, Satan will never be able to injure him by means of this passion. The devil will never be gratified at the fulfillment of this passion by him, for there is nothing which will dry up the arteries, prevent the accident of the night, and make a monk to possess chaste and quiet thoughts by day, so much as the restraining of the belly by thirst. Some fast the whole day until the evening, and some fast for [several] nights at a time, yet when they break their fast and eat a little food, because they drink much water, they benefit in no wise by their fasting and by the sparing use of food which they practice because of the war of lust. For the drinking of much water fills the arteries [of the monk] with [excessive] moisture, and Satan finds an occasion for exciting him by means of thoughts in the daytime, and he trips him up by means of dreams by night, and he deprives him of the light of purity. Therefore, in another place, Abba Evagrius admonishes the monk, saying, 'If you wish for chastity make your food little, and restrain yourself in the drinking of water, and then impassibility of heart shall rise upon you, and you shall see in your prayer a mind which emits light like a star.'"

657. The brethren said, "In how many ways does Divine Grace call the brethren to the life of the solitary ascetic?" The old man said, "In very many and different ways. Sometimes, Divine Grace moves a man suddenly, even as it moved Abba Moses, the Ethiopian, and sometimes by the hearing of the Scriptures, as in the cases of the blessed Mar Anthony and Saint Simon the Stylite, and at others by the doctrine of the word, as in the cases of Serapion, and Abba Bessarion, and others who were like to them. Concerning these three ways whereby Divine Grace call to those who would repent, I would say that Divine Grace moves the conscience of a monk in the manner which is pleasing to God, and that through these even evil-doers have repented and pleased God. And there is, moreover, the departure from this world by the hands of angels, by terrors, and sicknesses, and afflictions, even as that which took place in respect of the blessed Evagrius; and sometimes God Himself calls from heaven and takes a man out of the world, as in the cases of Paul, and Abba Arsenius."

658. The brethren said, "Why is it that the beginning of the doctrine of the old men is laid down in the books from the choice of Abba Arsenius, and on [his] coming forth from the world into a monastery, and from a monastery of the brethren into the seclusion which is in a cell?" The old man said, "Because he was called by God to the monastery, and from the monastery to the cell, and because it is certain that these two calls were according to the Will of God, well was it that the beginning of the doctrine of the old men [was derived]

Questions of the Brethren

from the history of this holy man."

659. The brethren said, "Explain to us these two calls of Abba Arsenius. What is the meaning of what was said in the first call, 'Flee from the children of men and you shall live,' and what is the significance of that which was said at the second call, 'Flee, keep silence and live a life of contemplation in silence, for these are the principal things which keep a man from sinning?'" The old man said, "The meaning of 'flee from the children of men, and you shall live,' is thus. If you wish to be delivered from the death which is in sin, and to live the perfect life which is in righteousness, leave your possessions, family, country, and depart into exile, as the desert and mountains to the holy men. There cultivate with them My commandments, and you shall live a life of grace. The meaning of 'flee, keep silence, and live a life of contemplation in silence' is thus. Since when you were in the world you were drawn towards anxieties about its affairs, I have made you to come out from the world, and I have sent you to the habitation of monks, so that after a short time of dwelling in the coenobium you may be drawn, first to the cultivation of My commandments openly, and secondly to contemplation in silence. Now that you are trained in the former sufficiently, you may flee, that is to say, get out from the monastery of the brethren, and enter into your cell, just as you did go out from the world, and did enter into the monastery. The meaning of 'keep silence, and lead a life of contemplation in silence,' is this. Having entered into your cell to contemplate in silence, you shall not give the multitude an opportunity of coming in to you, and talking to you unnecessarily, except on matters which relate to spiritual excellence; if you do not do this you will benefit by sitting in silent contemplation. For through the sight, the hearing, and the converse of the multitude who shall come in to you, the captivity of wandering thoughts will carry you off, and your silence and your contemplation will be disturbed. Do not imagine that the mere fact of having left the brethren in the monastery, or not bringing other men into your cell to be disturbed by them will be sufficient to make your mind to be composed, or to enable you to meditate upon God, and to correct yourself, unless you do take good heed not to occupy your mind with them in anyway whatever when they are remote from you. For until a man arrives at a state of impassibility, and overcomes by striving both the passions and the devils, whenever a monk remembers any man in his cell, he remembers him in connection with some passion, that is to say, with desire, or with anger, or with vainglory. And if it should happen that the mind wanders in respect of ordinary things, unless he cuts them off from him, his wandering inclines through absolute necessity towards a remembrance, which is allied to some passion. It is also thus in the case of a novice, for whenever during his contemplation in silence he remembered women he falls into the lust of fornication; and whenever he remembers men, he is either wroth with them in his thoughts, and he makes accusations against them, blames them, condemns them, or he demands from them vainglory, and he inclines to passibility. Therefore when Abba Macarius was asked, 'What is the right way for a novice to live in his cell?' He said, 'Let no monk when he is in his cell have any remembrance of any man, for he cannot profit in any way in restraining his feelings from the conversation of men, except he take care to withhold his thoughts from secret intercourse with them.' This is the meaning of the words, 'Flee, keep silence, and contemplate in silence.'"

660. The brethren said, "What is the meaning of the words which one of the old men spoke, saying, 'He who dwells with men, because of the commotion of worldly affairs is unable to see his sins; but if he dwells in the silent repose of the desert he will be able to see God in a pure manner?'" The old man said, "The excellences which are cultivated in the world, and to which our Lord, speaking in the Gospel, ascribed blessing, are loving kindness, peacemaking and the other commandments which are like them, and it is quite possible for such virtues to be cultivated in the world by certain strenuous persons. But the purity of heart which sees God, and to which our Lord ascribed blessing, saying, 'Blessed are the pure in heart, for they shall see God,' cannot be acquired without dwelling in the desert, with solitary and silent contemplation. The monk must acquire it in the following way. First of all a man must go out from the world, and dwell in a monastery. After his training in a monastery and having gone into his cell, he must die through contemplation in silence, through the other labors of his body, through striving against the passions, and through conflict with devils. Then through the tranquility of mind [which he will acquire] in silent contemplation, he will remember his sins. When he hates his passions, has petitioned for the remission of his sins, has suppressed his thoughts, has become constant in pure prayer, and has cleansed his heart from odious thoughts, then he shall be worthy to see in his heart, even as in a polished mirror, the light of the revelation of our Lord [shine] upon it, even as the Fathers say. Well, did that holy man say to those brethren, 'Visit the sick, reconcile the men of wrath, for he who cultivates spiritual excellences in the world cannot, by reason of the commotion of the affairs, see his sins.' If he continues in silent contemplation and prayer, he shall see God."

661. The brethren said, "What is [the meaning of] what Abba Sisoes said to Abba Ammon, 'Freedom of my thoughts in the desert is sufficient for me?'" The old man said, "Sisoes was a great and a perfect old man. He dwelt all the days of his

Questions of the Brethren

life in the remote desert. After he had become old, and was exceedingly feeble, the Fathers brought him to the monastery of the brethren, who used to go in and visit him each day, for the sake of some profitable discourse and helpful prayer. Because he was unaccustomed to feel comfortable in the presence of many folks, his mind began to wander about in remembering the brethren, and to meditate upon many things. He was unable to find that dominant freedom for the continuous, secret prayer of the mind, which is superior to every influence that would make it decline, and is free from every [other] attraction. He was, therefore, rightly grieved. One day, Abba Ammon went to visit him, and saw that he was sorry about his coming from the desert, and said to him, 'Father, it is not right for you to be sorrowful because you have drawn near to the place where the brethren dwell, for your body has become feeble, and you are unable to perform those works where you were used to labor in the desert.' When Abba Sisoes heard these things, he looked at Abba Ammon sternly, and answered him with indignation, saying, 'What do you say to me, Ammon?' Was not the freedom of the thoughts which I had in the desert sufficient to take the place for me of all labors? As regards to yourself, O Ammon, who are conscious of the life and acts of the freedom of the mind, and who are not subject to the constraint of wandering and disturbance of the mind, and who are not impeded by old age and infirmity, tell me what you are able to do in the desert at your great age? Even if I am unequal to the labors of the body, because I have become infirm through old age, I am better able to perform the labors of the mind than I was in the time of my early manhood. Or, perhaps in your opinion the clear shining of the mind, are these which a monk acquires by a life of contemplation in silence, the constant intercourse with God, the prayer which is without ceasing, the remembrance of Christ, the constant gazing upon Him, the exultation of the soul in Him, the favor of His love, the affection for His commandments, the desire for His good things, the meditation upon His glory, the thought about His excellence and His majesty, and the admiration of His humility, small and contemptible matters? All these labors of the mind, and many others which are like to them, neither old age nor infirmity impedes, but they are prevented, and brought low, and, by degrees, are destroyed, by converse with the children of men, and by seeing many people, and by care about worldly affairs.'"

662. The brethren said, "They used to say that when the service in the church was over, Abba Macarius used to flee to his cell. The brethren said, 'He has a devil, but he does the work of God.' Now who were those who said that he had a devil? What was the work of God which he used to do?" The old man said, "Those who said that he had a devil were the lazy brethren. Whenever Satan sees the monks who are leading a life of spiritual excellence in the monastery, the devils stir up the lazy brethren to wage war against them, by means of abuse, reviling, backbiting, calumny, and by means of the trials which they bring upon them. The work of God which Abba Sisoes did when he fled [to his cell] was: prayer accompanied by weeping and tears, according to the exhortation of Abba Isaiah, who said, 'When the congregation is dismissed, or when you rise up after eating, do not sit down to talk with any man, either concerning the affairs of the world, or concerning matters of spiritual excellence. Go into your cell, and weep for your sins.' As Abba Macarius the Alexandrian said to the brethren who were with him, 'Brethren, flee.' The brethren said, 'Father, how can we flee more than [in coming] to the desert?' He laid his hand upon his mouth, and said to them, 'Flee in this manner.' Immediately every man fled to his cell and held his peace.

663. The brethren said, "Abba Anthony said, 'As a fish dies when it is lifted out of the water, so does the monk [dies] if he remains long outside his cell.' Explain these words to us." The old man said, "Because the remembrance of God is, in our Lord Jesus Christ, the life of the soul, which the Fathers call the repository of life, and the breath of the life of the soul and of the mind, when the monk tarries in the cities, and in the sight and converse of the children of men, he dies in respect of the breath of life which is in God, that is to say, he forgets God, and the love of Christ grows cold in his heart, the love which he has acquired by many labors, and he forgets his virtues, and he becomes lax in respect of [his] liking for tribulations, and he loves pleasures, and has an affection for lusts, and the sincerity of his heart is troubled through the disturbance which enters into his senses, that is, seeing, and speaking, and hearing, which are indeed the strength of the soul. And it happens also that he falls into great passions, where from may Christ, God, save us! Amen."

664. The brethren said, "The excellent man Hieronymus said in the history of the triumphs of the blessed Isidore, the archimandrite, that he had in his monastery one thousand monks. They all lived within the gate of his habitation, and none of them ever went outside it until the day of his death, except two brethren who only set out from there to sell their handiwork, and who brought in only such things as were required for their absolute needs. How is it that in an assembly of our early Fathers, that is, a congregation containing one thousand brethren, two men only were sufficient [to provide for] their ministrations? In our generation if there was a congregation of fifty-five monks, only five would lead a life of ascetic excellence in seclusion. The [other] fifty would be going out and coming in ceaselessly and without rest to supply them with what they needed." The old man said, "Concerning the love for labors, and the watch which the early Fathers kept [on themselves], and concerning the love of pleasure, and the laxity of ourselves who belong to a later time, if it be right to tell the truth, we ought to speak most concerning the laxity and ignorance of the governors of monasteries. In former times the brethren who lived lives of contemplation and seclusion and loved spiritual repose were many, and those who went out on to the high roads, and entered the cities, and performed outside labors were few; but in our days, in a congregation which, as you have said, contains fifty-five monks, five will lead a life of spiritual repose inside the monastery, and the other fifty will toil ceaselessly in the works which are outside it. During the whole time they will complain and blame the five who are inside, because they do not go out and serve as do they. Through the words of these foolish and insolent men all the spiritual excellences which are cultivated in the monastery will perish and come to an end. According to what I say, if the Fathers set the life of contemplation in silence against the whole of the labor of the ascetic life, and if it be more excellent than it all, who would blame him that loves spiritual contemplation and repose, and the quiet of the cell?"

665. The brethren said, "Once a congregation of monks assembled on the great festival of the Resurrection. There were gathered in the monastery all the Fathers, and all the recluses, and other monks, and all the old men in the congregation were asked, 'What is the mightiest and most severe war which can come upon monks?' They all agreed that no war is harder or crueler than one that makes a man leave his cell and depart. When that war is fought down, all other contests may be easily reduced. Explain to us the meaning of these words." The old man said, "Constant spiritual repose in a cell has hope closely bound up in it, but going out there from is united to despair. As long as a man lives in spiritual repose, and loves the tranquility of the cell, little by little he goes forward, one step at a time, according to the order of succession; and he has hope that our Lord will vanquish each of the passions, and that through his repose and labors he will acquire spiritual excellences and the grace of Christ. If the life becomes tedious to him, and he goes out, leaves his cell, and wanders about, he will neither vanquish the passions, nor acquire spiritual virtues. But he will incline to despair, and to utter destruction. Therefore the Fathers have well said that no war is crueler than the war of wandering."

666. The brethren said, "Abba Theodore and Abba Luka passed fifty years in being harassed by their thoughts which urged them ferociously to change [their] place [of living]. They said, 'When the winter comes we will change.'

When the winter had come, they said, 'We will change in the summer.' Thus they continued to do till the end of their lives. Reveal to us if it were the devils who were urging these famous Fathers to go out from their cells for a period of fifty years, that is, until their death." The old man said, 'The devils urged the great Fathers to wander and to go out from their spiritual repose because they well knew the benefit which accrued to them in their cells. These holy Fathers were urged by the devils also, but did not leave their cells. Today, in this generation, the same devils harass the monks, drive them out of their cells by this war of departure, and therefore the great Fathers who have felt this war of wandering and of departure have said, 'There is no war which is more cruel to the monk than this.' May Christ help us and deliver us from it."

667. The brethren said, "Abba Anthony used to say, 'He who dwells in the desert is free from three wars; speaking, hearing, and seeing.' Explain these words to us." The old man said, "The old man did not speak [thus] because the strife of him that dwelt in spiritual repose in the desert was less fierce than that of him that wandered about and mingled with men, but that he might show how much more hard and laborious was the war of devils which takes place in the heart of those who dwell in spiritual repose than that which comes in the heart of those who dwell with brethren. Because of this the fathers pursued after a life of contemplation in silence, lest when the wars of speaking and seeing and hearing were added to that which was already in their heart, they would fall by reason of their severity, even as actually happened on one occasion. A woman came to the monks who were living a life of silent contemplation, and there was added to the war which was already in their hearts the wars of seeing, hearing, and speaking. They would have been vanquished by the severity of the war had it not been that the grace of our Lord supported them. That the war which takes place in the senses of the soul against the monks who live a life of silent contemplation is mightier and fiercer than that which takes place in the senses of the body, is well known from the words which the blessed Evagrius spoke, saying, 'Against the monks who lead a life of silent contemplation the devils in person wage war. But against those who lead a life of spiritual excellence in a general assembly of brethren, the devils only stir up and incite the lazy brethren. The war which arises from the sight, the hearing, and the speech is much less fierce that that which is waged against the monks who dwell in silent solitude."

668. The brethren said, "What is the meaning of that which Abba Anthony said, 'A monk's cell is the furnace of Babylon, and it is also a pillar of light?'" The old man said, "There are two things peculiar to the cell, firstly the warmth

Questions of the Brethren 345

and fire, and secondly the light and rejoicing. To novices it is oppressive and troublesome, by reason of the many wars and the dejection which are in there, but it rejoices the perfect and makes them glad, with purity of heart, impassibility, and revelations of light. It is even thus with those who begin to live in silent contemplation, for although at the beginning they are for a considerable time afflicted by the wars of the passions, and by devils, they are never forsaken by the help of Divine Grace. For our Lord Himself, the Son of God, Jesus Christ, comes to them secretly, and becomes as a helper and a companion. After they have overcome both passions and devils, according to systematic order, He makes them worthy of the happiness which is in His perfect love, and the revelation of His glorious light."

669. The brethren said that Abba Moses the Ethiopian was on one occasion reviled by certain men, and the brethren asked him, saying, "Were you not troubled in your heart, O father, when you were reviled?" He said to them, "Although I was troubled, yet I said nothing." "What is the meaning of the words, 'Although I was troubled I did not speak?'" The old man said, "The perfection of monks consists of two parts, firstly the impassibility of the senses of the body, and secondly the impassibility of the senses of the soul. Impassibility of the body takes place when a man who is reviled restrains himself for God's sake and does not speak, even though he is troubled. The impassibility of the soul takes place when a man is abused and reviled, and yet he is not angry in his heart when he is abused, even like John Colobos. For on one occasion, when the brethren were sitting with him, a man passed by and upbraided him. He was not angry, and his countenance did not change. The brethren asked him, saying, 'Are not you secretly troubled in your heart, O father, being reviled in this fashion?' He answered and said to them, 'I am not troubled inwardly, for inwardly I am just as tranquil as you see that I am outwardly; and this is perfect impassibility.' At that time Abba Moses had not arrived at this state of perfection, and confessed that although outwardly he was undisturbed, yet he was waging a contest in his heart, maintained silence and was not angry outwardly. Even this was a spiritual excellence, although it would have been a more perfect thing had he not been angry either inwardly or outwardly. The blessed Nilus made a comparison of these two measures of excellence in the cases of the blessed men Moses and Aaron. The act of covering the breast and heart with the priestly tunic, which Aaron performed when he went into the Holy of Holies represented the state of a man who, though angry in his heart, suppresses his wrath by striving and prayer. While the state of a man not being angry at all in the heart, because he has been exalted to perfection by [his] victory over the passions and the devils. Nilus compared to that which is said of the blessed Moses, saying, 'Moses took the breast for an offering, because the soul dwells in the heart, and the heart dwells in the breast.' Solomon said, 'Remove anger from you heart.' Concerning Aaron, the Book said, 'He was covering his breast with the ephod and tunic,' this teaches us monks that it is important for us to cover the wrath which is in the heart with gentle, humble, and tranquil thoughts, We should not allow it to ascend to the opening of our throat, otherwise, the odiousness and abomination of it shall be revealed by the tongue."

670. The brethren said, "Why is it that, although all the fathers used to admonish the brethren to ask the old men questions continually, and to learn from them, to reveal to them their thoughts, to live according to their directions, one of the old men said to one of the brethren, 'Go, sit in your cell, and your cell shall teach you everything?'" The old man said, "There is no contradiction in these words of the Fathers. What the old man has said, has an object, the meaning of which is well known. The old man who admonished the brother that he should learn like a beginner was great and famous. To that brother who asked him the question he said thus: In the early days when you go to your cell lay hold upon the habits of the novices, live according to them for a considerable period, that is to say, with fasting, vigil, reading, reciting the offices, and all the other things, until at length, after the lapse of time, the life of contemplation in silence shall give you the order which befits your seclusion, will add those things which are seemly, and will diminish those which are not. This is the meaning of that which was said by the holy man, 'Sit in your cell, and it shall teach you everything.'"

671. The brethren said, "One of the old men used to say, a man shall have no care, shall contemplate in silence, and shall cover up himself. Three meditations shall teach purity. What is the meaning of these three words?" The old man said, "A man shall have no care means that he shall not care concerning the shortcomings of others. All his anxiety shall be concerning his own shortcomings. He shall contemplate in silence means that he shall not speak even concerning matters of spiritual excellence if it will trouble any man or condemn him. He shall cover up himself means that he shall not reveal his life and deeds, but as far as possible, he shall be unknown and unhonored. By these things, purity of the heart is established, which sees God in a revelation of light."

672. The brethren said, "How can a monk die everyday for the love of Christ, even as the blessed Paul said, 'I swear by your boasting, my brethren, that, in our Lord Jesus Christ, I die daily, and the world is dead into me, and I am crucified to the world, and the world is crucified to me, and I live, yet not I, but Christ live in me?'" The old man said, "A man [can do this] if he contemplates in silence at all seasons, performs the other works of the body, I mean fasting, vigil, the recital of the books of the Psalms, prayers, genuflections, groanings, pain, weeping, tears, sighs, and the reading of the Holy Scriptures. He must take care concerning the works of the mind, which is the constant remembrance of God, and meditation upon Him, His blessings, His commandments and His threatening. And his gaze must always be on our Lord, and his prayer must be without ceasing and without wandering. The odiousness of the passions must be away from the heart, and he must suppress with zeal the thoughts of the devils which arise at their prompting. He must possess the excellence, which is the first and most important of all the spiritual virtues, and labors of the ascetic life of the mind, that is to say, death in respect of all the anxieties and cares of this world. A monk must have no care, no anxiety, and must not think about anything, or seek anything, or desire anything, or lust for anything, except for the time when he will attain the perfect love of God in our Lord Jesus Christ. He must fulfill at all times the command of the blessed Paul, and his admonition to us where he said, 'Love your Lord, rejoice in your hope, pray without ceasing, be fervent in spirit, endure your tribulations, be not anxious about anything, cast all your care upon the Lord.' And let all your prayers, and all your requests, and all your petitions be made known to God, to Whom be glory for ever and ever! Amen."

673. The brethren said, "How can love be acquired by men of understanding?" The old man said, "True and pure love is the way of life, the haven of promises, and the treasure of faith. Understanding shows [the way of] the kingdom. Understanding is the expositor of the judgment, and the preacher concerning what is hidden."

674. The brethren said, "We do not know the power of the word." The old man said, "If a man does not love God he will not believe in Him, His promises are not certain to him, he does not fear His judgment, he does not go after Him. But because love is not in him, so that he may flee from iniquity, and wait for the life which has been promised, he is always performing the work of sin. He does this because His judgment is raised too far above his eyes. Therefore let us run after love, where the holy fathers were rich, for it is able to reward its nature and it's God, and this is its praise."

675. The brethren said, "How does the wisdom live in a man?" The old man said, "When a man has gone out to follow God with a sincere mind, grace takes its abode in him, and his life and deeds are strengthened in the Spirit, and he has taken a hatred to the world, for he perceives that new spiritual life which is in the new man, and which is exalted above the impurity of human life, and in his mind he thinks of the humility of the life and works which are to come, and which are [more] excellent than those here."

676. The brethren said, "By what is love made known?" The old man said, "By the fulfillment of work, and by spiritual meditation and by the knowledge of faith."

677. The brethren said, "What are works?" The old man said, "The keeping of the commandments of God in the purity of the inner man, together with the [performance of] labors by the outer man."

678. The brethren said, "Is every man who is destitute of works also destitute of love?" The old man said, "It is impossible for the man who is in God not to love. It is impossible that he who loves does not work; and it is incredible that he who teaches and does not work is indeed a believer, for his tongue is the enemy of his actions. Although he speaks life, he is in subjection to death."

679 The brethren said, "Is he who is in this state destitute of reward?" The old man said, "The man who speaks the things of the spirit, and performs the things of the body is not destitute of reward, and what he needs is fulfilled for him, he is deprived of the crown of light, because he does not desire that the rule of the spirit shall have dominion over him."

680. The brethren said, "What are fasting and prayer?" The old man said, "Fasting is the subjugation of the body, prayer is converse with God, vigil is the war with Satan, abstinence is being weaned from meats, standing up is the humility of the primitive man, genuflection is the bowing down before the Judge, tears are the remembrance of sins, nakedness is our captivity through transgression, and [reciting the] service is the constant supplication and the praising of God."

681. The brethren said, "Are these things able to redeem the soul?" The old man said, "When the things which are within agree with the things which are without, when the humility which is manifest appears in the hidden works which are within, in very truth a man is redeemed from the heaviness of the body."

682. The brethren said, "What is internal humility?" The old man said, "It is humility of love, peace, concord, purity, restfulness, gentleness, subjection, faith, and the remoteness from envy. [And it is] where the soul lacks the fervor of anger, is remote from the lust of arrogance, is separated from vainglory, is filled with patient endurance like the great deep, and whose motion is drawn after the knowledge of the spirit, and before whose eyes is depicted the departure from the body, the great marvel of the Resurrection, the call to judgment which [shall come] after the quickening, its standing before the awful throne of God, and the being redeemed."

683. The brethren said, "Is it possible for a man to fast and not to be redeemed?" The old man said, "There is a fasting which is a matter of habit, another which is of desire, another which is of constraint, another which is of the sight, another which is of vainglory, another of tribulation, another of repentance, and another of spiritual love. Although each one of them is the same outside the mind, yet in the word of knowledge they are distinct. Although the manner of each in respect of the body is the same, yet each should be undertaken with its thorough purpose, and a man should journey straightly along the way of love, and should bear his burden with spiritual patience, and should not rejoice in his honor."

684. The brethren said, "Who is the true [monk]?" The old man said, "He who makes his word manifest indeed, and endures his pain patiently. With such a man, a new life is found, and the knowledge of the spirit dwells in him."

685. The brethren said, "Who is he who lives purely?" The old man said, "It is He who is free from the delights of the body, and who rejoices in the love of his neighbors in the love of God; for in proportion as need has a rule over the soul is spiritual repose produced."

686. The brethren said, "How can we vanquish lust?" The old man said, "With the remembrance of the good things of the Spirit; for, if the desire for the good things which are to come does not abrogate the lust for the delights of this world, a man cannot overcome at all. Except the merchant's ship is laden with manifold hope it will not be able to endure the storms, and will sail on the path of tribulation."

687. The brethren said, "In what way does a man go forth from the world?" The old man said, "He does this when he forsakes the gratification of all his lust, and when, so far as it lies in his power, he runs to fulfill the commandments; the man who does not do this will fall."

688. The brethren said, "Through what did the men of old triumph over nature?" The old man said, "Through the fervor of their love which was above nature, through the death of the man which is corruptible, through contempt of arrogance, through abatement of the belly, through the fear of the judgment, through the sure and certain promise; and through the desire of these glorious things the Fathers acquired in the soul a spiritual body."

689. The brethren said, "How can we vanquish the passions which afflict us, since they are placed in our nature?" The old man said, "You can vanquish these passions through your death to the world. Unless a man buries himself in the grave of continence the spiritual Adam can never be quickened in him. For when a dead man departs this temporary life, he has no perception of the world, where all his senses are at rest and are useless. If he who appertains to your natural body you forsake naturally and you do not do the same voluntarily in respect of your own person, you will die. If your desire dies through repentance, [your] nature will cease from this temporary life in the death of the spirit, even as the natural emotions of the body ceased through its natural end."

690. The brethren said, "To what extent is a man held to be worthy of revelations?" The old man said, "To the same extent as he is held to be worthy to cast off sin inwardly and outwardly. For when a man dies through spiritual slaughter to all the conversation of this temporary life, and when he has committed his life to the life which is after the quickening, Divine Grace alights upon him, and he is held to be worthy of divine revelations. For the impurity of the world is a dark covering to the soul. It prevents it from discerning spiritual meanings." The brethren said, "Can the man who loves money be faithful to the promises?" The old man said, "If he believes why does he possess [anything]? Is our hope fixed upon gold? Or is the hand of the Lord too short to redeem? He gave us the Body of our Lord for happiness, and His holy Blood as a drink for our redemption. He has kept back from us the loaf of bread and the apparel, which grow old. He who loves money has a doubt in his mind concerning God, and prepares [the means of] life before God gives them to him. Although in his words he rejoices in the promises, he makes them to be a lie by his deeds. True is the word of our Lord, Who said, 'It is easier for a camel to go through the eye of a needle than for a rich man to enter the kingdom of God (Matt. 19:24).' To possess both God and mammon in one abode is impossible. Now those who follow the ascetic life do not belong to the things which are seen."

692. The brethren said, "Who is truly the man of ascetic excellence?" The old man said, "He who at all times cries out that he is a sinner, and asks mercy from the Lord, whose speech bears the sense of discretion, whose feelings bear the excellence of works, who though silent yet speaks, and who though speaking yet holds his peace, and whose acts and deeds bear good fruit to his temporary life and the manifestation of Christ."

693. The brethren said, "Where is the way of life?" The old man said, "It is the one whereby a man goes out from this world in his entrance into the other. If a man forsakes his childhood of humility, and comes to the old age of this world in his love, he reveals the way of life. The true departure from this world is remoteness from this world."

694. A brother said, "What shall I do to this world when it troubles me?" The old man said, "The world troubles you because its worries are in your mind, its love is in your body, and its delights are in your heart. Let the world depart from you, tear out all its roots from you. Then the war against it will cease. For as long as your body seeks [its] worldly pleasures and lusts, it is impossible for you to live."

695. The brethren said, "What is the pure prayer?" The old man said, "[It is a prayer] which is of few words and is of abundant deeds. For if [your] actions are not more than your petition, your prayers are mere words where the seed of the hands is not. If it is not thus, why do we ask and not receive, since the mercy of Grace abounds. The manner of the penitent is one thing, and the labor of the humble is another. The penitent manners are hirelings, but the humble are sons."

696. The brethren said, "How is the love of money produced?" The old man said, "From lust, for unless a man lusts he will not possess [money]. If he does not possess [money] he will not lust. When a man lusts, he possesses [money]. Having acquired money he fulfills his lust. Having fulfilled his lust, he becomes greedy. Becoming greedy he commits fraud. Having committed fraud, his possessions will increase. When his possessions increase, love becomes little in him. When love has diminished the remembrance of God is wanting in the heart. The intelligence becomes darkened; his power of discernment becomes blinded. When the power of discernment becomes blinded, the power of distinguishing is darkened. When the power of distinguishing become darkened, the soul goes blind. When the soul has become blind goodness is rooted out from the soul, and wickedness replaces goodness. Sin has then the dominion. When the sin obtains a dominion, thought of God is blotted out, the passions of the body are roused up, and they seek for the means for working out their needs. When they have obtained that which they seek it becomes necessary for much money to be gathered together. When money is multiplied, the pleasure of the body is fulfilled; a man eats, drinks, commits adultery, fornication, speaks fraudulently, transgresses the covenant, destroys the Law, and despises the promises. Lust is thus fulfilled, and God is wroth. For if the lust for the things which are seen be hated in our sight, we shall not love money. But if we perform the lust of the flesh it is necessary to love money, because it belongs to the flesh and not to the spirit. As the apostle said, 'For the flesh lusts against the spirit, and the spirit against the flesh; and these are contrary to one another, so that you do not do the things that you wish (Galatians 5:17).'"

697. The brethren said, "What kind of prayer is that which is not acceptable before God?" The old man said, "[The prayer for the] destruction of enemies. When we ask that evil things [may come] upon those who do harm to us, for bodily health, abundance of possessions, and fertility in respect of children, these requests are not acceptable before God. If God bears with us, the sinners who offend Him, how much more is it right that we should bear each with the other? It is, then, not necessary that we should ask for the things which concern the body. The wisdom of God provides everything [necessary]."

698. The brethren said, "What is purity of soul?" The old man said, "It is the remoteness from anger, from the error of remembrance of evil things, being weaned from a bitter disposition, friendliness towards our enemies, peace which is superior to troubling, and sincere love which is above the world; by means of these the hidden man is purified and he puts on Christ, and is redeemed."

699. The brethren said, "What is envy?" The old man said, "It is the hatred towards the virtues of others, wickedness towards the good, a bitter disposition towards the innocent, anger against those who are prosperous in this world, the concealment of the upright penitent deeds, and vexation at the peace of the friends of God."

700. The brethren said, "In what way should we to pray before God?" The old man said, "For the repentance of sinners, the finding of the lost, the drawing near of those who are afar off, the friendliness towards those who harm us, the love towards those who persecute us, and the sorrowful care for those who provoke God to wrath. If a man does these things truly with a penitent mind, the sinners will often gain life, and the living soul will be redeemed. The prayer, which our Lord delivered to us as to the needs of the body, is one which applies to the whole community. It was not uttered for the sake of those who are strangers to the world. But for those who hold the pleasures of the body in contempt. He in whose habitation the Kingdom of God and His righteousness are found lacks nothing, even when he asks not."

701. The brethren said, "What is remoteness from the world?" The old man said, "The thought which vanquishes the love of the body. If the body is not trodden down by the lust of patient endurance, a man cannot conquer in the fight."

702. The brethren said, "Can the soul of a man who is held fast in the love of the things which are seen be pleasing to God?" The old man said, "Who is able to live in chastity when the body is making demands upon him? Or, how can be found the love of our Lord in the soul which has its abode with the things which are seen and are corruptible? No man can serve two masters. The soul cannot please God with spiritual excellence as long as the remembrances of corruptible things are in its mind. The mind of the flesh is not able to please God. Unless the world dies out of the heart, humility cannot live in the heart. Unless the body is deprived of its lusts, the soul cannot be purified from thoughts."

703. The brethren said, "Why is the mind disturbed at the meeting with females?" The old man said, "Because they are employed in the fulfillment of the lust of nature. When seeing the body which [is intended for] the production of children, and for the pleasures of the body, the poison of the past time seizes the man. The law of his will becomes confused. The will conquers nature, not by the stirring up of the passions, but by the fulfillment of works. The humble, by the power of our Lord, conquers everything by his love and through the patient endurance of the merit of our Lord."

704. The brethren said, "Who is mightier, he who is remote from the world, or he who dwells in it?" The old man said, "The mighty man, wherever he dwells, conquers whether he is in the world or out of it. The fathers departed to a quiet place, free from noise and tumult, because they were afraid that so long as they abode in the body the passions which afflicted them would cleave to them. Those who have completed the great strife of their contest in the world [have performed] an act of grace the power of which has been and still working, for the help and benefit of the community. Truly, their crown shall be a great one, because into the disturbed and troubled sea of the world their spiritual ship has not gone down, for it was on its way to heaven along the straight path which was full of fear."

705. The brethren said, "If a man makes himself a stranger to the world, is it helpful to his soul?" The old man said, "If it fulfills with praise it is helpful. If it endures tribulation in chastity, and rejoices in our Lord, it is beneficial. It is not beneficial if it removes away the good seed and prevents it from producing beloved fruit to God. If it is blessed, it has a reward. If it lacks these things, it becomes a wandering to the mind, and a sight which is profitless. The best of all these things is the tranquility of the mind, which is near to God."

706. The brethren said, "Since all the creatures which God has made are holy, why were the Fathers in the habit of making the sign of the blessed Cross over such of them as they ate as food?" The old man said, "Truly, all God's creatures are pure, through the Grace of Him that created them. Yet, because sin obtained dominion, every one of them became polluted. Then came the advent of our Lord and abrogated sin, the righteousness obtained dominion, and everything became sanctified, whether it was in the heaven or on the earth. But because the blessed Fathers knew the harmful disposition of Satan, who even by means of such things as are used as food carries on a war to our injury, they sealed their foods with the holy sign of the Great Cross, that they might bring to naught all the crafts of the Calumniator. For one of the old men said, 'On one occasion, when I was lying down at night, I thirsted for water to drink. And there was near me a holy man who lived chastely, and he saw me take up a vessel of water to drink without having made over it the sign of the Cross.' He said to me, 'Wait, master, wait.' He made the sign of the Cross over it, and immediately the Calumniator in the form of a flash of fire fell from the vessel. Both he and I saw this, marveled at the great power of the Redeemer, and at the wonderful sign of His merit. Another version of the story reads, 'One of the Fathers said, "On one occasion I was lying down at night, and I thirsted for water to drink. There was near me a certain widow, who led a chaste life, both when she was with her husband, and afterwards, and she said to me, 'Wait, master, wait.' She made the sign of the Holy Cross over the vessel of water. Immediately the Calumniator fell from the vessel in the form a flash of fire. Both she and I saw it, marveled at the great power of our Redeemer, and at the wonderful sign of His merit." These things were indeed spoken by that holy mouth which was remote from falsehood. Therefore we must necessarily do this (i.e., make the sign of the Cross over our food) for the protection of our life. For against this holy woman who did these things, the enemy waged war openly, according to what I have learned from a chosen man of God, who heard the matter from her own mouth. He spoke thus, 'The blessed woman spoke to me, saying, "One day I went to the house of God, and Satan drew near, and said to me, "Why do you pray like a man, saying, 'Glory be to the Father, and to the Son, and to the Holy Spirit?" I said to him, "If I am not to pray thus, how shall I pray?" The blessed woman said, "Satan said to me, 'Pray saying, "Glory be to you, O Mary, the mother of Christ."' Then I answered and said to him, "[There are] ashes in your eyes, O Satan. Why should you forsake the Lord and adore the mother?" Satan disappeared. The blessed man also said to me, 'This same old woman said to me, "On another occasion I went to church according to custom. I knelt down and prayed. Then the enemy came and made my eyes blind. Hence I could not see, I called to one of the women, and she led me to my house. After three days Satan departed from before my eyes, and began to go before me. Then I said to him, 'There is something which I must make you do. Go to the place where you seized on me.' We went to the church, both he and I, and I left him where he seized me. Then I went away a short distance. When I turned and looked at him I saw that he was standing like a shadow. I went on again, turned, and still I saw him. I shut the door of the temple and went out. I then opened it again, went in, and I saw him still standing [there]. At that time his wiles ceased from me." Such were the great things, which happened to that blessed old woman.' The monk must not boast himself over the man who lives in the world, for there are mighty men in the world. If such qualities are found in Eve, how much greater ones should be found in the Adam, which is redeemed by Adam? One of the Fathers said to me, 'One night while I was sleeping, the enemy came, hit me, and said to me, "Get into the world and cultivate righteousness, for why do you shut yourself up like a beast in caves?" Knowing the wickedness of the enemy, who was looking at me with an evil eye, I made the sign of the Cross in his face, and he fled from me. He waited for a few days, came back and hit me on the neck. He said to me mockingly, "Now you are a righteous man, rise up, and go into the world, that I may not destroy you." Having prayed, and made the sign of the Cross over my face, he departed from me. A little while afterwards he came again, and sat upon my neck. I made myself bold, stood up, and made the sign of the Cross, the emblem of merit, before him. Again he disappeared, for he was unable to resist me.' All these things took place in very truth, that we may therefore know and understand that there is no rule of life in which

God so much rejoices, or which is so terrible to the devils, and to all evil spirits, as the rule of humility, penitence of mind, the subjection of the body, and remoteness from the things which are seen. Whoever despises these things will fall into the mire of the world. Whoever holds disrespects to the good riches of the fear of God, shall have his hope of the saintly inheritance and the delights of heaven, which never pass away and never end, destroyed."

May you all be held worthy of these through the grace and mercy of our Lord Jesus Christ, the True God, to Whom with His Father, and the Holy Spirit, be glory, now, and always, and forever and ever! Amen.

www.ingramcontent.com/pod-product-compliance
Lightning Source LLC
Chambersburg PA
CBHW072003150426
43194CB00008B/976